CASES IN

INTERNATIONAL RELATIONS

PRINCIPLES

AND APPLICATIONS

SEVENTH EDITION

DONALD M. SNUW

THE UNIVERSITY OF ALABAMA

ROWMAN &
LITTLEFIELD

Lanham · Boulder · New York · London

Executive Editor: Traci Crowell
Assistant Editor: Mary Malley
Senior Marketing Manager: Kim Lyons
Interior Designer: Ilze Lemesis
Cover Designer: Sally Rinehart

Published by Rowman & Littlefield
A wholly owned subsidiary of The Rowman & Littlefield Publishing Group, Inc.
4501 Forbes Boulevard, Suite 200, Lanham, Maryland 20706
www.rowman.com

Unit A, Whitacre Mews, 26-34 Stannary Street, London SE11 4AB, United Kingdom

British Library Cataloguing in Publication Information Available

Library of Congress Cataloging-in-Publication Data

Names: Snow, Donald M., 1943– author.
Title: Cases in international relations : principles and applications / Donald M. Snow, The University of Alabama.
Description: Seventh edition. | Lanham : Rowman & Littlefield, [2018] | Includes bibliographical references and index.
Identifiers: LCCN 2017045318 (print) | LCCN 2017056345 (ebook) | ISBN 9781538107294 (electronic) | ISBN 9781538107270 (cloth : alk. paper) | ISBN 9781538107287 (pbk. : alk. paper)
Subjects: LCSH: International relations.
Classification: LCC JZ1242 (ebook) | LCC JZ1242 .S658 2018 (print) | DDC 327—dc23
LC record available at https://lccn.loc.gov/2017045318

♾️™ The paper used in this publication meets the minimum requirements of American National Standard for Information Sciences—Permanence of Paper for Printed Library Materials, ANSI/NISO Z39.48-1992.

Printed in the United States of America

Contents

Preface

This book is, and always has been through its various editions, about explaining basic concepts, forces, and dynamics in international relations and how these principles help shape and guide applications to contemporary situations. It has always had two basic missions: providing basic instruction in important dynamics of how international relations work (hopefully in a lively and engaging manner) and providing updated and relevant information and interpretation of major events helping to shape the world. These have been the goals since the first edition appeared in 2002; they remain for this, the seventh edition.

The issues dominating international relations at any point in time change. New events and forces appear on the stage of world affairs, providing new perspectives and applications of underlying principles. Since the last edition of this book appeared in 2014, the most seismic new forces have surrounded the Islamic State (IS) as a major terrorism factor and force in the Middle East, and the election in the United States of a president with highly unorthodox and sometimes erratic views of international affairs that have impacts on both the international system and on the American view of and position within the international system. Both these changes are reflected in the pages that follow. Chapters 1 (on sovereignty) and 14 (on terrorism) explicitly address the impact of IS; three chapters (2, 11, and 12) reflect the impact of the Trump presidency. Other chapters include discussions and analyses of other pressing and topical international concerns.

One of the difficult parts of writing a supplementary casebook is trying to make it coherent; it is a problem with which I have struggled since the first edition. A "reader" should, in my view, be more than a cobbling together of a collection of papers, articles, and the like that are on interesting topics but have little beyond that about them. It is impossible to repackage previously published materials into a common format, and particularly to give the product a flow and continuity that makes it possible to read the parts as contributions to a coherent whole. Finding supplements that were real books has always frustrated me, and it was one of the reasons this book is and always has been a collection of original chapters written in a format that is consistent across topics. I believe, and always have, that students appreciate this continuity, particularly in contrast to compilations of articles that have hardly anything in common other than being between the same book jacket.

The contents of this volume reflect my progress to date in trying to produce a coherent casebook reader. Its basic theme, captured in the subtitle of the volume, is principles of international relations and their applications to contemporary events. This two-pronged theme is reflected both in the organization of the table of contents and in the structure of individual chapters. The volume is divided into two basic parts. Part I, Principles and Dynamics, lays out seven basic principles of international relations largely from a realist perspective. Part II, Continuing Issues and Problems, offers an examination of contemporary international difficulties, largely framed within the context of the principles in Part I.

Each chapter reflects the same concerns. They all begin with the discussion of an underlying theoretical concern or principle, followed by the application to a contemporary situation. In Part I, the principles tend to be theoretical concerns and their impact on a current policy area. Thus, chapter 1 has the question of state sovereignty as its principle, and the perverse effects of this principle on the Islamic State's stated desire for statehood (as a precursor to establishing its imperial caliphate) as the application. In Part II, the principles tend to represent policy areas, updated by the application. In chapter 13, for instance, the general problem of resource scarcity is exemplified by the problems associated with secure access to potable water and energy resources. I hope that the result is a volume that is interesting, informative, and readable for students and instructors alike.

New to this Edition

Each edition of *Cases in International Relations* has been different from its predecessor in at least three distinct ways. First, to accommodate dynamics that have appeared or been accentuated since the last edition, I have added more contemporary cases and concepts. To keep the book manageable in length, each addition has been matched by scrapping or amending cases from the previous edition. In this edition, the total number of cases has been reduced from sixteen to fourteen to make the volume somewhat shorter and more affordable. Second, each edition has seen updating, modifying, and even replacing of the case applications from the previous edition. Third, there has been substantial reordering and restructuring of the order of cases within and between sections of the book.

The result is a thoroughly new book designed to emphasize the most current ideas and events. There is one entirely new chapter, "National Interests and Conflict: Russian Oil and U.S.-Russian Relations," which illustrates the depth of change in the text. It introduces a concept not highlighted in previous edition, national interests, and then applies it to U.S.-Russian relations, primarily regarding American help in Russian exploitation of its vast petroleum reserves (a process in which Secretary of State Rex Tillerson was involved as CEO of ExxonMobil). Additionally, five chapters (1, 3, 7, 10, and 11) have undergone major revisions that leave them substantially new efforts, and four more (4, 8, 12, and 13) have had important revisions. The focus of chapter 8, for instance, has been broadened to include a discussion of NAFTA and continued U.S. participation in it, and chapter 13 now features water as a scarce resource. Four chapters have had less extensive but meaningful updates (5, 6, 9, and 14). Two chapters from the last editions, on pivotal states and the Arab Spring, have been eliminated. The net result is a very new, fresh volume.

Although it runs the risk of some oversimplification, the most important of the changes in this edition can be summarized as follows:

- an explicit set of definitions and applications of key international relations concepts such as sovereignty, national interests, and power;
- an expansion of the discussion of the nature of territorial disputes to include both Palestine and Kurdistan;
- a specific application of the norms of war crimes to the use of chemical weapons against its citizens by the Syrian government;
- inclusion of a detailed discussion of peaceful attempts to deal with human conflict, misery, and humanitarian disasters;
- an extended examination of the interrelated problems of climate change and the need for scarce energy resources;
- a discussion of the problem of international population migration from the vantage points of security, humanitarian concerns, and the economic need for immigrants in the developed world;
- an examination of trends in international economics, including a discussion of free trade in the context of the controversy over NAFTA and the impact of Brexit on the European Union and globalization; and
- an updated examination of contemporary terrorism with special attention to the problems posed by lone-wolf terrorists and Islamic State/Al Qaeda type groups (including an assessment of the possible fate of IS).

The structural arrangement of the book has changed. Rather than the four parts in previous editions, it is now divided into two parts, as already noted. Part I—Principles and Dynamics—consists of seven chapters, dealing with sovereignty and its impact on the Islamic State (chapter 1), national interests and their effects on U.S.-Russian relations (chapter 2), power as it applies to China (chapter 3), territorial disputes among peoples, emphasizing the Palestinians and the Kurds (chapter 4), asymmetrical warfare and the "never-ending" war in Afghanistan (chapter 5), nuclear proliferation, with special emphasis on North Korea and Iran (chapter 6), and war crimes, emphasizing Syria (chapter 7).

Part II—Continuing Issues and Problems—also has seven chapters. Their foci are globalization and trade, emphasizing WTO and NAFTA (chapter 8), regional economic integration, especially in light of Brexit (chapter 9), efforts at promoting international well-being and development, with emphasis on South Sudan (chapter 10), international population migration from American and European perspectives (chapter 11), climate change in light of the Paris Agreement (chapter 12), resource scarcity involving water and energy (chapter 13), and the evolution of terrorism, featuring lone wolves and IS-type organizations (chapter 14).

Features

What distinguishes this effort from other supplementary texts in the field? One answer is that all the chapters included in the volume are original papers written specifically for this volume. The reason for doing so was to allow for more timely coverage of ongoing situations than is possible with the publication lag time of scholarly journals and their availability to readers and other compendia. It also allows casting the cases in a common format that makes it easier to compare the contents of the various cases without wading through disparate styles and formats of various authors and publications. In addition, journal articles are written for academic peers rather than more-or-less lay students, meaning they are generally rendered in language and theoretical trappings that are less than accessible to student readers. Finally, writing original articles facilitates updating and modifying materials as events and dynamics change, which hopefully adds to the freshness, accuracy, and timeliness of the materials contained in these pages. Presenting the most contemporary set of portraits possible has certainly been a major purpose of this and earlier editions.

A word about what this book is—and is not—is appropriate at this point. It is a casebook, presenting a series of individual instances of dynamics and trends within the international arena. The effort is neither inclusive nor encyclopedic; it covers selected concepts and events, not the universe of international concerns. A series of fourteen important, underlying concepts and principles of the international system have been chosen and discussed, and the discussion of these principles has been applied to contemporary, important, and interesting real-life examples. The result is not a systematic overview of the international system or its history, which is the province of core textbooks in the field. Likewise, it does not offer a unifying theoretical explanatory framework of international politics, a task that more specialized books purporting grand "theories" of international relations propound. Rather, the intent is to introduce and apply some basic concepts about international relations and how they apply in real situations.

Acknowledgments

This book, as were the previous editions, is dedicated to my good friend and colleague, the late D. Eugene Brown. Gene and I met in 1989 at the U.S. Army War College, where we both served as visiting professors and shared an office for two years before he returned to his permanent home at Lebanon Valley College in Annville, Pennsylvania, and I returned to the University of Alabama in Tuscaloosa. In the ensuing decade, we were collaborators on several book projects; *Cases in International Relations*, which was mostly Gene's idea, was to be a continuation, even culmination, of those efforts. Unfortunately, Gene left us before the original project was complete. His shadow remains, I hope with a smile on his face.

I would like to thank the following reviewers for their useful feedback: Lynda K. Barrow, John W. Dietrich, Binnur Ozkececi-Taner, Rita Peters, George Poluse, Marius Ratolojanahary, Matthew Wahlert, and John Allen ("Jay") Williams. I have also received generous and very helpful assistance from the team at Rowman & Littlefield. In particular, I would like to thank three members of the R&L team. My editor, Traci Crowell (a fellow University of Colorado alum—Go Buffs), encouraged and helped from the outset getting the reversion of rights to me so I could do this edition, and encouraged me throughout the writing process. Alden Perkins did a thoroughly professional job turning the manuscript into a book. Special thanks go to Mary Malley, who cheerfully and efficiently came to my aid when my lack of knowledge and empathy with the dynamics of electronic infernal machines left me in a bewildered panic (a recurrent burden on her). Thanks for everything, guys!

DONALD M. SNOW
PROFESSOR EMERITUS
UNIVERSITY OF ALABAMA

PART I
Principles and Dynamics

1

Sovereignty

Dealing with the Caliphate

Sovereignty—supreme authority—has been the capstone concept and operational principle of the international order since the Peace of Westphalia
ended the Thirty Years' War in 1648. Since that time, sovereignty has been
defined territorially; operationally, this has meant that state sovereignty is the
principle on which world political order is grounded. Within sovereign states,
there can be no authority greater than that of the state. In principle, that sovereignty is absolute in scope. In practice, there are infringements on the total control of the state. There is some philosophical and political debate about where
sovereignty resides within states (e.g., is its seat the people or the government?).
Sovereignty is a controversial concept, in that its logical extension justifies armed
violence and can be a shield behind which atrocity is sometimes committed.
Established sovereignty does, however, endow its possessor with international
legitimacy, making it a valued commodity among political actors.

In 2015, the terrorist organization known variously as ISIS, ISIL, or more
simply the Islamic State (IS) declared it was establishing a religiously based
sovereign state in parts of Iran and Syria under its control and that it planned
to expand this territorial entity to form a new Caliphate that would ultimately
encompass all Muslim parts of the world. Therefore, it was a major physical and
conceptual assault on the established international order. No other government
recognizes the Islamic State's sovereignty, and its boundaries are physically contracting. Nonetheless, its existence and persistence is a notable challenge to the
Peace of Westphalia order established over 350 years ago.

Principle: The Concept of Sovereignty

Any discussion of the underlying philosophy, structure, or operation of international relations must begin with the concept of sovereignty. Defined as "supreme
authority," it is the operational base of both international and domestic political
life, although with quite opposite effects on the two realms. Ever since it emerged
as the bedrock organizational principle of world politics as part of the Peace of
Westphalia that concluded the Thirty Years' War in 1648, it has been a somewhat
controversial foundation for world affairs. Controversy has surrounded matters
such as the location of sovereignty (who has it?) and the extent of power that it
conveys to its possessors (what can the sovereign do—and not do?), and concepts
have changed over time. Disagreements about sovereignty are prominent parts
of some of the debates about the evolving international order, and the assault on

its basic function is part of international dialogue. Despite all this, sovereignty is an attribute that all governments cherish and guard jealously.

Sovereignty has a long history and has evolved over time. It emerged as a concept in the period leading up to the Thirty Years' War, a time when modern political states had not emerged except in limited places such as France and England. During this period, questions of political authority still revolved around whether people owed their ultimate loyalty and even existence to sectarian authority represented most prominently by the Catholic Church or to secular monarchs in the locales where they resided. One of the most important elements of the Peace of Westphalia (the collective name given to the series of treaties that ended the conflict) was to wrest political control from the Church and to transfer that power to secular authorities. This transfer was accompanied by the effective installation of sovereignty as the basis of relations among secular political communities. A primary outcome of this "marriage" was to associate sovereignty with territorial political jurisdictions. Since those territories were essentially all ruled by absolute monarchs, the conjunction effectively created the precedent that the power of the sovereign was absolute. This association is symbolized by the fact that the monarchs of the time were also known as sovereigns.

This association has changed over time. Reflecting the political period in which sovereignty became the bellwether concept of an evolving secular state-based system, it began as a principle that legitimized and promoted authoritarian rule, since sovereignty was possessed by absolute rulers. That principle was challenged with the rise of democratic thought in more modern times, suggesting that sovereignty was a characteristic of not only the ruler but the ruled as well. From this challenge arose the modern notion of popular sovereignty.

Understanding why sovereignty is such an important concept in contemporary political life requires examining it and how it has evolved in some more reasonable detail. The discussion thus moves to the origins and evolution of the idea, the major characteristics and implications of those characteristics for the operation of contemporary politics, and the most basic challenges to sovereignty in the international system of today. All of these factors feed into understanding the phenomenon of the Islamic State (IS) as a pretender and aspirant for sovereign status.

Origins and Evolution

Understanding how and why sovereignty came to be the major organizing principle of international relations begins with an enigma of sorts. The heart of sovereignty (discussed more fully in the next section) is territorial supremacy—whoever has sovereignty has ultimate authority in the physical territory where it is claimed and enforced. This means that in the domestic affairs of sovereign entities, sovereignty provides the basis for political *order* by endowing its possessors with the ability to develop and enforce rules and laws that provide some form of political system. It does not predetermine *who* within the jurisdiction has sovereignty or the *extent* to which it can be exercised, and these are matters on which there have been evolutionary disagreements. It does, however, provide the basis for order.

The impact of sovereignty on the relations *between* sovereign territories (in modern terms, the world's states or countries) is quite the opposite. The supreme authority that sovereignty creates means that no other entity can claim to exercise any form of authority over another state. A common way of expressing this relationship in the nineteenth century was in terms of the "billiard ball" analogy, which depicted individual states as impermeable billiard balls that periodically encountered and bumped into one another but could not penetrate one another's authority, which was protected by their possession of sovereignty. Although the analogy was never taken quite literally, the result was that international relations (the interactions between states) was effectively a state of *anarchy* (the absence of government) where no state could legally be impelled to do things it did not want or that might offend others within their sovereign domains. The only recourse that a political authority aggrieved by the actions of another sovereign state was through *self-help*, which often effectively meant the recourse to arms.

The fact that sovereignty created the justification both for order and disorder was not a concern of its early chroniclers and enthusiasts. The concept was first introduced by the French philosopher Jean Bodin in his 1576 book *De Republica*. Bodin's major concern was the promotion of the consolidation of the authority of the king of France over his realm. The problem that he sought to alleviate was the practice by lower feudal lords within France of effectively claiming sovereignty over their realms by charging tolls to cross their territories, a practice that interfered with the monarchy's overarching control over its territory.

To deal with this situation, Bodin countered with the concept of sovereignty, which he defined as "supreme authority over citizens and subjects, *unrestrained by law*" (emphasis added). Bodin, who was a staunch monarchist, felt the italicized element was necessary to keep the monarch from being hamstrung by parochial laws in his quest to establish the power of the monarchy and to spread its sway over the entire country. This part of the definition has fallen from common conceptions of sovereignty, but its implications remain and are part of ongoing disagreements on the meaning and controversies surrounding the concept. If the sovereign is indeed above the law, then nothing he or she does can possibly be illegal, at least when committed within the sovereign jurisdiction over which the sovereign reigns. Taken literally, acceptance of this principle absolves tyrants of things such as war crimes and would have undercut the legal justification for prosecuting Nazi executioners after World War II.

When Bodin enunciated the principle of sovereignty, he was not concerned about its extension to forming the basis of international relations. The period in which sovereignty was gestated, after all, was when European monarchs were consolidating their political control and in which all countries had similar governmental types. These monarchies did not come into the fundamental disagreements that countries in the modern, ideologically driven world find themselves. The result was to promote the notion that sovereignty and absolute monarchism were related as an alternative to anarchy. This position was widely associated with political philosophers such as Thomas Hobbes.

The extension of the implications of sovereignty to international affairs occurred as the state system evolved and the structure of the modern state emerged and was solidified in an increasing number of European states. The major publicist of this extension was the Dutch scholar Hugo Grotius, who is generally acknowledged as the father of the idea of international law. He first proclaimed state sovereignty as a fundamental principle of international relations in his 1625 book *On the Law of War and Peace*, and by the eighteenth century it was accepted as a principle of both domestic and international relations despite its contradictory effects (order and disorder) in the two settings.

By the nineteenth century, the modern state system was taking form, and the changes entailed in that evolution had implications for both questions raised earlier: with whom does sovereignty exist within sovereign jurisdictions? and how extensive are the legitimate powers that reside in the holder of sovereignty? Both remain basic questions.

The question of the locus of sovereignty was a product of greater citizen participation in the political process within evolving countries, and especially with democratization. When monarchism was universal and accompanied by the belief that the monarch was supreme over his or her realm, it was natural to assume monarchical control over the state—the sovereign had authority over his or her realm, and others gained rights and claims only at the pleasure of the monarch. When political philosophers such as the Englishman John Locke and his French counterpart Jean-Jacques Rousseau made the counterclaim that the sovereign's powers were limited and could be abridged by the people, the question of the locus of sovereignty was joined. The premise of both the American and French Revolutions was that the people were the source of fundamental political legitimacy, which translated into the idea of popular sovereignty. The premise of this notion, which gradually took hold as the state system matured in Europe, was that the people were sovereign, and that that they voluntarily bestowed parts of that sovereignty to the state to legitimize state power and to ensure domestic order. Even in states where power is concentrated in one or a few individuals in the contemporary world, it is rare for that condition to be justified on any notion of the absolute sovereignty that underpinned the early emergence of the Westphalian system.

A sovereign "unrestrained by law" could, in essence, do whatever he or she wanted (or was capable of doing), but the idea of popular restraint suggested that there were limits on the extent of the freedom of states to act as they might want to. Within democratizing states, the major limit (or restraint) on sovereign authority was what the people would tolerate. This expression was asserted gradually: after a republican form of government was established in the United States, other states, notably France (which alternated between democratic and authoritarian rule before 1870) and Great Britain (which gradually expanded political rights), began to democratize during the nineteenth century, in the process accepting, explicitly or implicitly, the doctrine of popular (or limited) sovereignty. The symbolic acts of embracing this notion in domestic politics were the United Nations Charter and various declarations after World War II, although full implementation of the concept has not yet occurred.

Changing Conceptions of Sovereignty

Applying changing conceptions of sovereignty to the relations *among* sovereign states has been a more difficult proposition. In a technical sense, sovereignty as the basic principle of international relations remains largely conceptually intact. Some countries are more jealous of the protections from outside interference that their sovereignty bestows upon them, and the United States and China are among the most jealous guardians of their sovereign status and the most resistant to any international attempts to infringe upon them. Most of the attempts to do so come from international efforts to limit the degree of control and even perse-cution to which states can subject their citizens (extensions of the idea of popular sovereignty) such as the UN Declaration on Human Rights and the Conven-tion on Genocide, neither of which the United States ratified until the 1990s (they were first drafted in the 1940s). The nature and implications of sovereignty remain controversial in contemporary international politics for different reasons. Three of them are worth noting as examples.

The first is the connection between sovereignty and war. The most com-monly stated objection to sovereignty in this regard is that the concept justifies and even glorifies war as a means to settle differences between states. In a system of sovereign states, after all, there is no authority to enforce international norms on states or to enforce judgments resolving disputes that arise between them. In domestic societies, there are normally prescribed methods, judicial in nature, both to resolve differences and to enforce whatever judgments may arise from adjudication: there are, in colloquial terms, judges, courts, and police to deter-mine and enforce the law. These mechanisms are conspicuously (and purposely) missing in the relations among states. Since there can be no superior authority to that of the sovereign, no one can enforce anything against a sovereign (at least in principle). The reason is simple: states have what are generally referred to as *vital interests*, conditions on which they will not voluntarily compromise, and are thus unwilling to empower any authority that could dilute that power (the concept of national interest is the basis of the next chapter).

Lacking enforceable methods to resolve differences between states, the alter-native is based in the principle of self-help, the physical ability to bring about favorable outcomes to differences, often at the expense of other states. This means that when sovereigns interact, their means of conflict resolution is the application of *power* (the ability to get someone to do something he or she would not otherwise do). One form that power can take, presumably in extreme cases, is the threat or use of military force to gain compliance. This formulation is fun-damental to the operation of the *realist paradigm*, which is described in detail in Snow, *National Security*. The effect of the paradigm is to make the use of force legitimate in some cases. A fairly large number of scholars and others decry this situation, because it makes it more difficult to move international relations in a more peaceful direction where conflict resolution is achieved by nonviolent means more resembling how differences are resolved within states.

The second objection to sovereignty in some quarters is the degree of control it gives states over their citizens, including the right to suppress and even murder individuals and groups. The assertion of this objection is largely contemporary, a postwar phenomenon reflecting global outrage in the aftermath of the genocide during the Holocaust. The notion of absolute sovereignty implies that the sovereign has total control over the realm, including those who reside within its legal boundaries. Taken literally, this means the sovereign can do anything he or she wants or can do to those citizens—including killing all or parts of the population—with no outside legal sanction or basis for interference in any atrocities arising from that treatment.

That scenario, of course, describes the Holocaust carried out by Nazi Germany against the Jewish and Gypsy population of Germany and other countries it occupied. The anomaly this created is captured in the opinion of one American Supreme Court justice assigned to the post–World War II war crimes tribunal, which argued that German officials could be prosecuted for the slaughter of *non-German* Jews and Gypsies, but that they could not be tried for the extermination of people who were German citizens, since sovereignty gave the German government total control over them. Reaction to this kind of reasoning has formed the basis for much of the postwar movement to limit the ability of states to commit atrocities against their own populations.

This assault represents, at least implicitly, an attack on absolute—and an advocacy of popular—sovereignty. It has also been the subject of attacks that argue the assertion that government control over its citizenry is fundamental to the conceptual underpinning of the state system, and that, despite the merits of protecting people from atrocity, it should be opposed on the basis that it erodes and undermines the basic conceptual underpinning of the state system.

The third, and somewhat mitigating, factor is that sovereignty in practice has never been as sacrosanct as it is in theory. The billiard balls of the nineteenth century were not actually impermeable, and they are less so today. Countries can and do regularly penetrate and interfere with the affairs of other countries. The attempts by Russia to influence the 2016 American presidential election were presented as something unusual and extreme, but they were not. During the Cold War, the Soviet Union regularly attempted to influence American elections by manipulating relations to make different candidates they favored or opposed look good or bad, and the United States also has a long history of interfering with elections through the use of clandestine intelligence operations to do things such as financing campaigns to either elect or defeat candidates and, in the most extreme cases, to carry out "wet operations" to eliminate disfavored politicians from some countries, notably in the Western Hemisphere.

The United States is by no means the only country that engages in these kinds of violations of the state sovereignty of other countries. It is a kind of general rule of thumb that large states—those with considerable and extensive interests and the means to realize them—are more likely to cross the sovereign rights line in other countries than weaker and smaller states that lack those levels of interests and those means. To paraphrase an old saw, with regards to the maintenance of sovereignty, the powerful states do what they can and the weak states suffer what they must.

The gap between sovereignty in theory and practice is growing in the contemporary world for a variety of reasons. As one example, global electronic communications provide access to almost everyone across national boundaries to information, including material that states would just as soon withhold as part of their attempt to maintain control over their citizens. At the same time, economic globalization means an increasingly unfettered flow of economic activity across state boundaries that states have very little, if any, ability to stanch meaningfully. Like the old gray mare, sovereignty "ain't what it used to be."

The U.S. Position

The United States has been one of the chief proponents of the retention of maximum sovereign rights for the government. Most of the assault has focused on human rights abuses—from genocide to torture—in the form of international conventions and treaties, mostly sponsored and sanctioned under the United Nations. In general, these treaties specify things governments cannot do and prescribe penalties, up to and including criminal penalties for the leaders of countries breaking the international agreements. They also specify that acceptance includes incorporation of prohibitions within domestic laws, a clear infringement on the "right" of countries to do anything they please within their sovereign jurisdictions. As an example, the Convention against Terrorism (CAT) makes the suborning or commission of torture a war crime, and its acceptance by the United States has meant that torture is a crime under American law as well.

All the existing international accords in essence codify American practices and the beliefs of Americans, but their implementation and acceptance is opposed by large political segments within the American political system. The result is that the United States has either delayed or refused to ratify some of these accords—the United States is one of the few countries, for instance, that has not accepted the jurisdiction of the International Criminal Court (ICC), which is the venue for prosecuting international crimes. Why?

There are two basic reasons generally cited. One is the fear that acceptance of some international restrictions on sovereignty would encourage groups *within* the United States to prosecute claims against the United States. Groups alleging suppression of rights, such as civil rights protesters during the 1950s and 1960s and American Indian tribes who were mistreated by the United States in the nineteenth century are often-cited examples. The other reason is more principled and is based on the precedent set by sovereignty-restraining actions on the overall notion and basis of state sovereignty.

These examples may seem abstract, but they are nonetheless fundamental to understanding the role and difficulties surrounding sovereignty as the prime standard for international relations. In contemporary international relations, the terms *sovereignty* and *state sovereignty* are basically synonymous. States (or countries) and their governments possess sovereignty, and possession of the requisites for state sovereignty forms the basic requirement for full participation in the international order. That status and challenges to it form the heart of understanding sovereignty in the modern world.

The Bases of State Sovereignty

In order to be a fully participating member of the international community, a country must possess sovereignty. Entities that are not sovereign may have a more limited form of recognition for particular purposes. International governmental organizations (IGOs) such as the United Nations and its affiliated agencies have some power and the ability to act in some situations, but their legitimate ability to do so derives from authority granted to them by sovereign states; in the case of the United Nations, the members of the UN, all of which are sovereign states, grant that ability. To be a full-fledged operating member requires being a sovereign state; sovereign status is the "gold seal" of international status. Any individual or group that does not possess sovereignty is a lesser influence on world politics.

Characteristics of Sovereignty

Given the importance of sovereignty, it is vital to understand what the accepted properties of sovereign entities—states—possess that no other organizations have. Although lists of these properties vary slightly in terms of arrangement, a sovereign state possesses (and must possess) four characteristics: a recognized territory and population; recognized jurisdiction and legitimate authority over the territory and its inhabitants; autonomy from external control; and recognition by other states. The requirements are cumulative and related. A state can be considered sovereign only if it possesses all these characteristics. If any of these characteristics is lost or falls under question, the sovereignty of the entity is compromised and can be questioned. Each characteristic is sufficiently important to warrant some examination.

Territory and Population

States are inherently physical places, the delineation of which is based on political boundaries on a map. For sovereignty to be established feasibly, there must be a recognized place over which that sovereignty can be claimed, and a population that resides in that area. For this reason, for instance, it has always been controversial whether claims of sovereignty can be made for Antarctica, which has no permanent human population. One way that sovereignty in an unpopulated area can be asserted is to colonize that area with people who become permanent residents of the area, for which there is no accepted process.

Accepted Jurisdiction and Legitimate Authority

In addition to simple possession of a territory with a population, claiming sovereignty requires that whoever does so has a legitimate claim to that possession that supersedes the claims of any other body and that the claimant is able to exercise control politically: legitimacy and authority. These characteristics are most often called into question when a particular group physically seizes another territory and attempts to rule as a sovereign in its name. Seizures, normally the result of invasion, are illegal under international law and undermine the legitimate claim that a claimant may make. Countries that are experiencing civil conflicts between internal factions for physical control of government create controversy when they claim sovereignty while control is still being contested, and the sovereign status of areas that have been infiltrated by and fall under the effective control of terrorist groups and the like are also controversial in sovereign terms.

Autonomy from Outside Control

This characteristic is often subsumed under other requirements, but it refers specifically to the independence of whoever claims sovereignty from outside forces. This situation describes the condition when a country is invaded and conquered, and the invader puts a puppet regime in nominal charge of governance. In this circumstance, the puppet regime may claim that it is sovereign, but its claims are unlikely to be accepted by other sovereign states. The German-installed Vichy regime in France during World War II, which consisted of French Nazi collaborators, claimed to be the sovereign regime of the country, but that claim was universally rejected by countries not controlled by the Axis.

Recognition by Other States

The acceptance that a physical territory and its rulers possess the other characteristics leads to the bestowal by other states of the claimant's status as a sovereign state. The symbols of that acceptance include such things as formal states of recognition, the exchange of diplomatic personnel and establishment of embassies, and regular interaction between the sovereign state and its counterparts. In the contemporary world, membership in the United Nations is a prime indicator that the member possesses sovereignty.

Contemporary Relevance

Although the content and meaning of sovereignty is in a state of flux or adjustment, the concept retains considerable force as conditioning parameters about how countries deal with one another and even *if* they interact. Almost all the situations derive from questions about whether different states possess all the elements of sovereignty or whether they can successfully protect their sovereignty from outside intrusion. A few examples will illustrate this continuing relevance of the concept in contemporary international affairs.

Some of the more extreme cases exist in the Middle East and parts of Africa. Yemen, for instance, has not had a functioning national government for several years, due to the chaos created by internal violence between Sunni and Shiite elements of the population, some of which is created or made worse by sponsorship by outside states—the Shiites supported by Iran and the Sunnis by Saudi Arabia. To exacerbate the situation, Al Qaeda in the Arabian Peninsula (AQAP, which is also Sunni) occupies areas of the bleak Yemeni hinterlands, from which it launches operations many would like to see suppressed. The difficulty in dealing with these problems is that there is literally no government with which anyone can interact to aid in calming the situation. Yemen is widely regarded as a "failed state," which is another way of saying that it is not a fully sovereign entity. The same dynamics plagued Somalia from the early 1990s until the early 2010s, a period in which, for example, there was no authority to expel Al Qaeda (AQ)—which eventually left on its own because, ironically, the situation was too chaotic and lawless for the terrorists—or to control pirates menacing shipping off its coastline.

A second kind of anomaly occurs when countries resolve and there are differences about the resulting repository of sovereignty. In 2011, for instance, the Republic of South Sudan successfully seceded and created a separate sovereign state with its capital in Juba. There remained, however, differences over the status of the Darfur Province in the remaining Republic of Sudan, which was occupied by UN-deputized peacekeeping forces. At the same time, increasingly bitter and bloody intertribal fighting between the Dinka and the Nuer in South Sudan had created a massive humanitarian disaster that by 2017 the country was incapable of resolving. The result was that the entire area of Sudan granted independence in 1956 as a sovereign state was dissolving into a chaos in which *nobody* could meet the criterion of control over population and territory.

Issues of where sovereign control resides exacerbates politics in other ways. One extreme example is the tribal regions along the border between Afghanistan and Pakistan. The nineteenth-century British-imposed border (the Durand Line) is not recognized as legitimate by the people living on either side of it (the Pashtun), who regularly ignore it, leaving the border porous to transit by Al Qaeda and the Taliban, both parts of the Afghan situation in which the United States has a stake. The United States would like Pakistani assistance in suppressing movement across the border and the provision of effective sanctuary for its foes in the areas, but Pakistan refuses to allow American operation on the basis of violation of its sovereignty. The United States continues anti-AQ and anti-Taliban actions from the air, which involves flying over and violating Pakistani sovereign air space. The most spectacular case (which also involved American ground forces) was the raid into Abbottabad, Pakistan, that resulted in the killing of Osama bin Laden. The issue of sovereign intrusion remains a serious source of difficulty between the two historically close allies.

Application: The Islamic State

The Islamic State (IS) is arguably the most vexing, troubling, and challenging phenomenon of the early twenty-first century. The millennium began, and has its signature dynamic, with the terrorist attack of September 11, 2001, which ushered Islamic religious terror onto the center stage of global concern. As will be discussed in more detail in chapter 14, terrorism per se is not a new occurrence in world history, although its frequency and the degree to which it upsets world affairs has been steadily on the rise for a century or more. Religion has been one of the banners that terrorists unfurled as rationale and promotional purpose for their actions as well, if not in as widespread a manner as is possible in the contemporary environment. Yet, modern terror has achieved a pervasiveness and publicity that the phenomenon has seldom if ever achieved before. It has changed, mutated, and grown in the years since 9/11; IS and its pervasive "war" is the current culmination, the current mutant.

What makes IS a subject appropriate as the case application of a study on the concept of state sovereignty is that the Islamic State, in its declaration and dream of establishing a modern Caliphate, is more than a terrorist organization with "conventional" terrorist goals and methods. IS also has pretensions of establishing a sovereign state under its aegis, a unique aspiration among those who have professed "terrorism in the name of God," to borrow the title from Jessica Stern's 2003 book. This ambition distinguishes IS from other terrorism-based organizations in terms of the grandiosity of its goal. It also creates a physical and conceptual Achilles' heel that may bring about its eventual demise.

Recognizing that an examination of the methods and activities of IS will be covered in chapter 14, the discussion will proceed sequentially through four steps. The first will be a brief history of the organization, notably its terrorist roots and how they have been inflated. The second will be a sketch of the goals of the most ambitious conceptualization of the Caliphate, and why that concept changes and distinguishes IS from more "normal" terrorist organizations. That will lead to the collision between IS pretensions and their implication in a world of sovereign states: the "Sovereignty Wall." The discussion concludes by examining how the Caliphate's ambitions and reality have collided to form a "shriveling" Islamic State.

The Unconventional History of the Islamic State

During his abortive campaign for the 2016 Republican presidential nomination, former Florida governor Jeb Bush was confronted by a detractor who yelled, "Your brother created ISIS!" The charge, of course, was more metaphorical than literal, but it contained a hint of plausibility. President George W. Bush played no physical part in the emergence of the Iraqi terrorist organization that would morph into the Islamic State, but the organization did come into being as a direct reaction to the American conquest and occupation of Iraq, and especially its disadvantaging of the Sunni portion of the population that had previously ruled and was displaced by the American action, both of which occurred under Bush's terms as president.

What the world now knows as IS came into existence in 2003 in the Sunni area of Iraq, notably Anbar Province, which has a heavy Sunni Muslim majority population. It was formed by a fanatic Jordanian expatriate who had been a marginal part of the resistance to the Soviet intervention in Afghanistan in the 1980s but who had had been less than welcomed back to his native country after the war. Abu Musab al-Zarqawi formed what became known as Al Qaeda in Iraq (AQI) in that year, mainly to resist the American occupation that followed the invasion and conquest of that country. Its initial—and continuing—support base came largely from Iraqi Sunnis displaced by the occupation, notably military officers and civil servants who had been members of the Iraqi Baath Party and thus implicated in the regime of Saddam Hussein, all vestiges of which the Americans sought to purge. AQI and its Islamic State successor would eventually broaden their support and membership base to Muslims from other places, but the heart of many of its operations came from Iraqi Sunnis, an important recognition when assessing the IS future.

AQI faded from view largely because of two events that occurred in 2006. The first was the death of al-Zarqawi, who was killed in an American air attack in Anbar. The result was to leave AQI temporarily headless and to create a power succession that would eventuate in a new, more fanatic leadership that would declare the Caliphate. The second event was an American initiative known as the Anbar Awakening, in which the United States created an effective alliance with many Sunni tribal leaders to help drive out Sunni resistance, including that provided by AQI. As a viable force, AQI was forced to retreat, not resurfacing until the second decade of the century.

During the interim between its squelching in 2006 and its return to the public eye in 2013, AQI experienced a fundamental transformation in both leadership and mission. From the ashes of the old AQI, a new leader, Abu Bakr al-Baghdadi, arose to take the reins of power within the organization. The new leader possesses a much more ascetic, fundamentalist view of the Koran and the proper role of a radical reformist movement than had the previous leadership, which had been primarily obsessed with the more temporal problem of getting the Americans out of Sunni territory and reinstating some Sunni influence and power in the country. The new leadership sought to reframe the Islamic world.

The "coming out" party for the new organization was the Syrian civil war. Resistance to the rule of Shiite, Alawite rule by the al-Assad family had grown steadily since Hafiz al-Assad (the original Alawite ruler) died and was replaced by his son Bashar, the current ruler. Civil war broke out in 2011 between the regime and a host of Sunni-based resistance groups. Sunnis constitute over 70 percent of the Syrian population, but they were splintered into multiple competing factions, none of which rose to the top as a coherent alternative to the Assad regime. From among those fractious elements rose the Islamic State in 2013.

When it first burst upon the scene, the new and reformed AQI was an enigma. Its roots were clearly in Al Qaeda (although al-Zarqawi had split from the bin Laden organization before his death), which meant they were considered a terrorist group by outsiders such as the United States, which did not recognize or support it. Because it did have a history and some organizational infrastructure, however, it was more effective than other resistance groups, and it emerged as the most effective (or least ineffective) alternative to the Syrian government in a military, if not a political, sense.

The activities of IS since 2014 have framed the problem the organization poses for the West and also for itself. In 2014, al-Baghdadi declared the existence of the Islamic State, a designation that implies a territorial entity ruled under the principles of *sharia* religious law as it was practiced when the Prophet Muhammad ruled in what became modern Saudi Arabia during the seventh century.

It marked the manifestation of the Caliphate designation (which included al-Baghdadi's naming of himself as the Caliph or successor to the prophet). It also was the beginning of the concerted campaign to go out and establish and maintain a physical territory in Syria and Iraq, thus triggering the sovereignty conundrum central to thinking about and understanding the Islamic State.

Goals and Aspirations of the Caliphate

The declaration of the Islamic State (or Caliphate) fundamentally altered the nature of the movement and placed it in a unique position among the various terrorist-based organizations facing the West. The result has been a double-edged sword, one side of the blade of which creates problems for containing or suppressing IS not posed by non-territorial claimants, while the other cutting edge creates opportunities and challenges for the Caliphate and its leadership.

What does the Caliphate want to accomplish? At the most elemental level, its aspiration is the establishment of a pure sectarian state based on an extremely ascetic view of morality found in the Koran and accepted as a valid, if non-orthodox, interpretation of the Prophet's teachings widely within Islam. It is viewed by most Muslims as a very extreme vision and set of dictates that is not embraced by the vast majority. In terms of sectarian views within Islam, it is doctrinally closest to the beliefs of Wahhabism, which is also the state religion of Saudi Arabia. For this reason, much of the financial support for and leadership in the movement is among Saudis and citizens of other conservative kingdoms in the Persian Gulf region. (Precise statistics are impossible to attain, because they are either not kept or are held in secret.)

The heart of the appeal of the Caliphate is the commitment to purification of the faith and the conversion or elimination of those who do not share its tenets. The basic organizational framework is found in *sharia*, the religiously based legal code that organizes relations within society (the basis of civil and criminal law in secular societies) and religious beliefs and conformity. The interpretation of the faith on which the law is based dates to the formation of Islam and reflects the fact that Mohammad was both the recipient of the word of Allah and the political administrator of Medina.

The belief structure is evangelical and retributive. Because its practitioners believe their interpretation of God's will is the only correct path to moral life, everyone who disagrees with them is essentially apostate and must either accept conversion or be subject to swift and summary elimination. The often savage (at least to Western sensibilities) manner by which *sharia* justice is dispensed (e.g., public beheadings of Western journalists) is the result of a literal application of the fate of non-Muslims, and it is not entirely reserved for non-Muslim disbelievers. Its beliefs are based in Sunni Islam, meaning Shiites are among the apostate, but so are other Sunnis whose beliefs are not deemed sufficiently pious. Those who refuse to embrace Caliphate visions are also vulnerable to the fate of non-Muslim apostates. The summary immolation of a Jordanian Air Force pilot in 2016 is testimony to the harshness of Caliphate justice toward more moderate Muslims and helps explain why the appeal of IS doctrine is no greater within Islam than it is.

The Caliphate hopes to go beyond the status of a mere territorial state to that of an empire that encompasses all of Islam. As such, its model is a kind of return to the Arab Empire that spread across the Middle East and into the Mediterranean and southern Europe after the birth of the religion. To achieve this end, IS has sent acolytes and recruiters into other areas where there are significant Muslim populations, particularly in northern and central Africa. It has received a mixed reaction in these efforts, at least partially because citizens came to realize the harshness of its codes and their own vulnerability under them. It is interesting to note that it has become more externally evangelical as its hold on core territory in Iraq and Syria has become increasingly tenuous.

The "Sovereignty Wall"

The declaration of the Caliphate as the goal of IS distinguishes it from other organizations that are lumped together broadly as terrorist. Until it announced this aspiration, IS was not conceptually different from other terrorist organizations: its goals appeared, like those of its rival Al Qaeda, to influence the behavior of states in directions compatible with its demands. Al Qaeda's former leader bin Laden, for instance, consistently maintained that his organization's goal was to remove Western presence and influence from the holy lands of Islam. He viewed Western intrusion as an unwelcome form of physical and cultural/religious intrusion to be resisted and repelled.

The declaration of the Caliphate is a qualitatively different matter. A caliphate is, by definition, a physical place ruled by the caliph. If it pretends to be a place that it rules exclusively, it is, implicitly or explicitly, claiming to possess the basic characteristics of a sovereign state, notably including the possession of territory and the authority and ability to govern that territory. The Caliphate may claim that its status as a religious construct makes it a different (it would maintain, morally superior) form of state, but within the relations among states, it is nonetheless akin to and subject to the same requirements as any other state.

The Caliphate currently lacks one of the characteristics of sovereign states: recognition by other states. No other state recognizes the legitimacy of the Caliphate, as symbolized by the fact that the Caliphate does not exchange diplomatic personnel with any other state, has not had foreign embassies in its capital (Raqqa in Syria), and is not accorded membership in any international intergovernmental organization such as the UN. If the Caliphate is a state, it is a rogue rather than an accepted sovereign state. Particularly as long as it attempts to spread its religious tentacles more widely into other states through terrorist and other affiliations and actions, it is unlikely that this condition will change.

The declaration of itself as the Caliphate, however, endows it with some unavoidable consequences of statehood. The Caliphate is a physical place, and it must be capable of defending, holding, and governing the territory that it claims as its realm. That dictate is simply unavoidable. As Wood described the dictate in a 2015 *Atlantic* article, the Caliphate must maintain the physical characteristics of a state to continue to exist as an independent entity. "If it loses its grip on territory in Syria and Iraq," he argues, "It will cease to be a caliphate. Caliphates cannot exist as underground movements, because territorial authority is a requirement of statehood, one of the vulnerabilities of a state."

This is where the Islamic State slams into the "sovereignty wall." If the Caliphate aspires to be a leader among Islamic states that can spread its "gospel" without having its base under constant attack and its legitimacy unaccepted, it must reform its actions so that it can gain the acceptance of other states and thus achieve recognition as a sovereign state. It must, in some sense, at least become like Saudi Arabia, which is recognized as a legitimate state actor and as a religious state that exports Wahhabism informally by not forcing its citizens to either finance or physically join Wahhabist organizations, including the Caliphate. If it can do these things, it might be, if not embraced, at least accepted as an entity that is something more than a terrorist organization that has temporarily usurped the territory of other states.

The wall, however, is that doing what it would take to gain acceptance as a state would require the Islamic State to reform itself to the point that it would no longer resemble what it set out to be (a caliphate) to the point of potentially destroying itself and its mission. The Caliphate is territorially expansionist, after all. Its territorial footprint has been carved out of territory that is formally accepted on maps as parts of the sovereign states of Iraq and Syria. To gain acceptance as a state, it presumably would have to give back some of that territory and negotiate an accepted territorial base for itself either from part of that territory or elsewhere. If it remains expansionist and evangelical, however, it will remain at odds with others, who will likely view it as a threat to *their* sovereignty. Particularly as it attempts to spread its gospel (to expand the Caliphate), it will continue to be resisted and opposed by those over whom it seeks sway. There is, for instance, some evidence that Boko Haram and the Caliphate have come at odds in their alliance because of Islamic State acquisitive ambitions in parts of Nigeria occupied by Boko Haram.

The result is a dilemma for the Caliphate not shared by more conventional Islamic terrorist organizations, and it is one of the Islamic State's own making. Having physically established and defended a piece of territory it declares to be the vital core of the Caliphate, it has set itself up to be judged based on criteria relevant to comparison with accepted sovereign states. It cannot, like terrorist or asymmetrical, guerrilla-style movements, simply fade into the background and wait for another day to resume its activities. As Wood so eloquently put it, the Caliphate is a place, and there is no Caliphate if that place ceases to exist. If it has no effective "state," what happens to the Caliphate? Does it lose its base? Is its relevance undermined? These are questions that its supporters do not want to answer, but they are concerns that will certainly affect its ability, for instance, to attract recruits and other forms of assistance. What happens if the Islamic State ceases to be a physical state?

The Shrinking Islamic State

When it burst upon the scene in 2015 and seemed to be racing inexorably across parts of Iraq and Syria, there were very ominous cries about the challenge the

Caliphate posed to regional and international order. The regional map seemed to change daily as IS territorial gains spread across the regional like spilling black ink (based on the color of its flag, these gains have generally been depicted in black). At its zenith, its advance seemed to threaten the Iraqi capital of Baghdad. The rise and spread of the Caliphate seemed ominous and virtually inexorable.

Initial Islamic State successes were exaggerated and geopolitically overblown. The Caliphate did sweep across much of eastern Syria and well into Iraq, and even at the time, there were some doubts expressed as to how it could do so with an armed force that was generally considered to be in the range of 10–20,000 active fighters. As IS raced toward the outskirts of Baghdad, there was near panic over the danger posed by this seemingly inexorable force. Commentators in the West panicked and did not look closely enough at these "successes."

IS did make important advances, including the capture of key towns and cities such as Mosul. Most of the territory conquered by the Caliphate, however, was not so valuable either to IS or to the sovereign states from which it was captured. Indeed, most of the territory was virtually unpopulated desert, and the few people ISIS forces encountered were mostly discontented Sunnis looking for liberation from Shiite-dominated Baghdad. As Von Drehle explains, "Al-Baghdadi's forces raced through northwest Iraq . . . not because they were an unstoppable force, but because no one wanted to stop them. In city after city, they met seething citizens eager for a champion. It was a cakewalk." The Caliphate was, in some important ways, less than it seemed to be.

It does not look so formidable anymore. IS was repelled from its advance on Baghdad, and the Iraqi Army, Kurdish *pesh merga* militias, local militias, and foreign countries have merged to push the Caliphate farther back toward Syria. The fall of Mosul, which had served as the Iraqi "capital" of the Caliphate, was a particularly punishing blow. This retreat was not unpredictable, as Wood pointed out in 2016: "Properly contained, the Islamic State is likely to be its own undoing. No country is its ally, and its ideology guarantees that will remain the case." Brands and Feaver, writing in the March/April 2017 edition of *Foreign Affairs*, go a step further: "The international coalition fighting the Islamic State has driven the group out of much of the territory it once held, and, sooner or later, will militarily defeat it," they predict. "ISIS' defeat is now only a matter of time."

The unattractiveness of the Caliphate's appeal to most Muslims is certainly a major part of the reason for this turn of events: the majority of believers in Islam reject the ascetic, primitive Wahhabist beliefs and application of *sharia* by which they are enforced, including many in the "liberated" areas where they were initially viewed as liberators. These failings, however, also reflect the consequences of the transformation of IS from its AQI terrorist roots into its role as an aspiring sovereign state.

The other significant factor, however, is the collision between the Caliphate and sovereignty. The Islamic State's attempt to become a sovereign state may have been unintentional, but when it conquered and annexed territory that it claimed as its own, it was in fact asserting a claim of sovereignty the consequences of which it almost certainly had not completely thought through in advance. A consequence of being a sovereign state is that one must control and enforce some form of authority over that territory, a task very difficult for an organization with a limited membership also defending itself against outside assault. Sovereignty also includes an obligation to hold sovereign territory. Given its extremist ideology and its apparent disinterest in dealing with a hostile host of other sovereign states, IS could not expect any overt assistance from other states, and it did not receive any (its support from Saudi Arabia was limited to private and officially illegal transfers from private Saudi citizens). The Caliphate confronted the orthodox system of sovereign states as a rogue, and the system beat them. The Caliphate claimed to be a sovereign territory, and caliphates must be states to exist. IS thus bucked the system, and they are losing. According to Jones et al. in an April 2017 RAND study, "At its peak in late 2014, the group held more than 100,000 square kilometers of territory (an area about the size of South Carolina) with a population of nearly 12 million." By 2017, it had lost control of 83 percent of that population in Iraq and 56 percent in Syria. The loss of control over Mosul in Iraq and Raqqa in Syria are close to death knells for the physical caliphate.

The eventual dismantling of the Caliphate is not the same thing as the destruction of IS. Rather, it is likely to retreat to one of two possible forms, both still troublesome. Brands and Feaver, for instance, argue that "the group's defeat will not end the war on terrorism" or the IS role in it. Rather, it and its affiliates may "return to their insurgent roots." The goal of insurgencies ultimately is to replace governments with themselves (administer sovereign places), but that process is long and uncertain. At a minimum, it would provide the time for the insurgents to figure out how they might govern, but it would also mean they would face more concerted opposition than they have in the Iraqi and Syrian deserts. The other possibility is that it might retreat tactically to its AQI roots as a more conventional terrorist organization. Jones agrees: "It is evolving from an insurgent group to a clandestine group that directs and inspires wide-ranging terrorist attacks." Given its size and the skills it has demonstrated in areas such as electronic recruitment, this is an ominous prospect, as is discussed in chapter 14.

Conclusion

Joining the most basic concept of international order—sovereignty—with the most visible current source of disorder within that order—statist terrorism—may seem an odd combination, but it really is not. While the international order is formally anarchical, it is not chaotic, and sovereignty is a key method by which the international system regulates its members and thus the whole. Technically, sovereignty maintains that states can do domestically whatever they want, but practically, the existence of sovereignty makes punishable some acts that states commit. Committing acts of terror against other states is proscribed behavior, and states working in concert have devised conventions to deal with those who defy the accepted forms of behavior. Sovereignty thus cuts both ways in the order versus disorder dichotomy.

The Islamic State has clearly violated norms deriving from sovereignty in its terrorist activities in the Middle East and toward the West, and its de facto invasion and annexation of parts of Iraq and Syria as parts of the Caliphate clearly violated sovereignty-based norms and are thus punishable. The creation of the Caliphate, however, went a step further. States occasionally cede their sovereign control temporarily (the American occupation of Iraq) or as part of popular secession (the division of Sudan into two states), but since World War II, the only instances of involuntary, permanent accessions have involved the Ukraine and Russia, and the annexation of Crimea and parts of Eastern Ukraine remain highly controversial.

Sovereignty per se has not doomed the Islamic State as a temporal, physical state, but the obligations the Caliphate has been forced to accept have contributed to its likely self-destruction. A less territorially ambitious agenda—as an insurgency that can take and abandon territory as the situation dictates or as a more conventional terrorist organization—would not have created the need for a coercive and military capability that would overtax its assets. The Caliphate may have been and still may be more powerful than other terrorist organizations, but it has proven not to have the staffing resources both to enforce its authority within its boundaries *and* to defend itself from concerted outside efforts to roll it back physically and to extinguish its membership. Both of these are requirements for a territorial state, and they have proven to be "a bridge too far" for IS.

The result has been a conundrum for the Caliphate. If al-Baghdadi and his followers truly aspire to being the successor state to that created by the Prophet (as their declaration of the Caliphate suggests), then they must have a physical territory. Since their intent poses a threat to other sovereign states that are bound to oppose it, it must also be capable of defending its sovereignty successfully. It has not proven itself capable of this formidable task, and it will either try another way as a non-sovereign entity or it will fade away.

Study/Discussion Questions

1. Define sovereignty. When did the concept emerge as a central tenet of international relations? Who were Bodin, Grotius, Locke, and Rousseau and how did each contribute to the development of sovereignty?

2. Sovereignty has opposite effects on domestic and international relations. What are the differences? Explain the implications for international politics.

3. How has the concept of sovereignty evolved as a dictate in both domestic and international affairs? What is the U.S. position on sovereignty? Why?

4. What are the characteristics of a sovereign state? Apply these criteria to aberrations in the contemporary state system.

5. The Islamic State (IS) has been described as different from "normal" terrorist groups. How is it different? How do its differences make sovereignty an issue for it?

6. Trace the history of IS from its beginning as Al Qaeda in Iraq through the Caliphate and beyond.

7. What are the stated goals and aspirations of the Caliphate? How do these create a confrontation with the concept and dictates of sovereignty?

8. How does the "sovereignty wall" contribute to the problems of the Caliphate? How may these implications contribute to the demise of the Caliphate? What are the implications for IS if the Caliphate is destroyed?

Bibliography

Bodin, Jean. *Six Books on the Commonwealth.* Oxford, UK: Basil Blackwell, 1955.

Brands, Hal, and Peter Feaver. "Trump and Terrorism: U.S. Strategy after ISIS." *Foreign Affairs* 96, no. 2 (March/April 2017): 28–36.

Brierly, J. L. *The Law of Nations.* 6th ed. New York: Oxford University Press, 1963.

Brisard, Jean-Charles. *Zarqawi: The New Face of al-Qaeda.* New York: The Other Press, 2005.

Cockburn, Patrick. *The Rise of the Islamic State: ISIS and the New Sunni Revolution.* London: Verso, 2015.

Cronin, Audrey Kurth. "ISIS Is Not a Terrorist Group: Why Counterterrorism Won't Stop the Latest Jihadi Group." *Foreign Affairs* 94, no. 2 (March/April 2015): 87–98.

Cusimano, Mary Ann, ed. *Beyond Sovereignty.* Bedford, MA: Bedford St. Martin's Press, 1999.

Elshtain, Jean Bethke. *Sovereignty: God, State, and Self.* Reprint ed. New York: Basic, 2012.

Grimm, Dieter. *Sovereignty: The Origin and Future of a Political and Legal Concept.* Translated by Belinda Cooper. Columbia Studies in Political Thought/Political History. New York: Columbia University Press, 2015.

Grotius, Hugo. *On the Law of War and Peace.* New York: Cambridge University Press, 2012 (originally published 1625).

———. *The Rights of War and Peace: Including the Law of Nature and Nations.* New York: M. W. Dunne, 1981.

Hashami, Sohail, ed. *State Sovereignty and Persistence in International Relations.* University Park: Pennsylvania State University Press, 1997.

Hobbs, Thomas. *Leviathan.* Oxford, UK: Clarendon, 1989.

Jackson, Robert. *Sovereignty: The Evolution of an Idea.* New York: Polity, 2007.

Jones, Seth G., James Dobbins, Daniel Byman, Christopher S. Chivvis, Ben Connable, Jeffrey Martini, Eric Robinson, and Nathan Chandler. *Rolling Back the Islamic State.* Santa Monica, CA: RAND Corporation, 2017.

Krasner, Stephen D. *Sovereignty: Organized Hypocrisy.* Princeton, NJ: Princeton University Press, 1999.

Lester, Charles R., and Ahmed Rashid. *The Islamic State: A Brief Introduction.* Washington, DC: Brookings Institution Press, 2015.

Locke, John. *Two Treatises on Government.* New York: Cambridge University Press, 1988.

Lyons, Gene M., and Michael Mastanduno, eds. *Beyond Westphalia: State Sovereignty and International Relations.* Baltimore, MD: Johns Hopkins University Press, 1995.

McCants, William. *The ISIS Apocalypse: The History, Strategy and Doomsday Vision of the Islamic State.* New York: St. Martin's, 2015.

Morgan, Edmund S. *Inventing the People: The Rise of Popular Sovereignty in England and America.* Rev. ed. New York: Norton, 1989.

Rousseau, Jean-Jacques. *The Collected Works of Jean-Jacques Rousseau.* Hanover, NH: University Press of New England, 1990.

Sky, Emma. "Iraq, From Insurgency to Sovereignty." *Foreign Affairs* 90, no. 2 (March/April 2011): 117–27.

Snow, Donald M. *The Middle East, Oil, and the U.S. National Security Policy: Intractable Problems, Impossible Solutions.* Lanham, MD: Rowman & Littlefield, 2016.

———. *National Security.* 6th ed. London and New York: Routledge, 2017.

———. *Regional Cases in U.S. Foreign Policy.* 2nd ed. Lanham, MD: Rowman & Littlefield, 2018.

———. *What After Iraq?* New York: Pearson Longman, 2008.

Stern, Jessica. *Terrorism in the Name of God: Why Religious Militants Kill.* New York: Ecco, 2003.

Stern, Jessica, and J. M. Berger. *ISIS: The State of Terror.* New York: Ecco, 2015.

Von Drehle, David. "The War on ISIS." *Time,* March 8, 2015, 24–31.

Warrick, Joby. *Black Flags: The Rise of ISIS.* New York: Anchor, 2016.

Weiss, Michael, and Hassan Hassan. *ISIS: Inside the Army of Terror.* Updated ed. New York: Regan Arts, 2016.

Wood, Graeme. *The Way of the Strangers: Encounters with the Islamic State.* New York: Random House, 2016.

———. "What ISIS Really Wanted." *Atlantic* 321, no. 2 (March 2015): 78–90.

Wright, Lawrence. *The Terror Years: From Al Qaeda to the Islamic State.* New York: Knopf, 2016.

2

National Interests and Conflict

Russian Oil and U.S.-Russian Relations

Interests represent another premier concept of international relations, and sovereignty means that those interests are defined in national terms, given superior state authority over the territories in which people live. The basic term "interests" has multiple meanings in different contexts, but in the international system, they refer to values held by the state that must be secured, protected, and advanced for the state to remain secure or safe, which is its most important value. The base of the concept comes from the French term *raison d'etat* (reason of state), which establishes national interests (the values of the sovereign states) above those of other claimants. So stated, the idea is straightforward and easily comprehended. In practice, however, determining interests is not so easy, because people within and between states disagree fundamentally on the content and relative importance of interests as they affect themselves and other states. Interests come into conflict with those of other individuals and states, and the result can be conflicts that can, in the extreme, lead to violent resolution. Although the idea of national interest is a Holy Grail of sorts, the competitive pursuit of national interests by the world's sovereign states is highly controversial, ambiguous, and conflict producing.

The new Trump administration generated a potential conflict of interest in its early relations with Russia. The new president argued that closer, improved relations would be in the American national interest, an interpretation questioned by others who view the Russian government in a more adversarial light reinforced by accusations of attempted Russian meddling in the 2016 election. Lurking only slightly below the surface was a collision of Russian and American interests over Russia's place in the evolving order. Russia is heavily dependent on the production and sale of fossil fuels (both oil and gas), which provides most of its budgetary revenues and creates vulnerabilities to Russian pressure in recipient countries. Russia has some of the world's largest petroleum reserves in Arctic and Siberian locations that, if exploited, could enhance and perpetuate Russia's international status for a long time. Russia does not, however, possess the appropriate technology to exploit these reserves. American petroleum companies do, and the Russians have signed a huge contract with ExxonMobil (of which U.S. Secretary of State Tillerson is former CEO) to aid in their exploitation. This raises national and conflict of interest questions: is it in the national interest to aid Russia in maximizing its power? And does Secretary Tillerson have a conflict of interest when judging that question?

Principle: National Interest and Conflict

The term national interest commands a virtually sacrosanct position in political language, internally but especially in the relations between states where such interests can be incompatible and even come into significant conflict. These interests represent the hierarchical values that states have. The core of these interests, and thus their claim to premier status within sovereign states, is captured in the French description *raison d'etat*. The term translates "reasons of state," the ultimate of which is the survival and security of the state.

Preserving the state is the highest national priority and thus the supreme national interest. This attachment endows the concept of national interest with a virtually absolute importance and need for obeisance in even the most heated and contentious discussions. Defenders of different ideas and interpretations will invariably maintain fervently that the position they favor represents a necessary course to preserve the national interest, whereas the position favored by the opponent will degrade the country and lead to the weakening of its ability to preserve the national interest. Whoever can convince the audience that whatever they favor better serves the national interest has a strong leg up to seeing its conceptualization triumph.

National interests are controversial. It is easy to state the definition of what constitutes an interest, but applying that shell of meaning to the substance of actual situations is difficult. The idea that there *are* conditions that serve national values is virtually unassailable; *what* those conditions may be in general or in the context of often ambiguous situations is quite another matter, and is the basis for lively and spirited debates about national interest that are subjective in nature and thus difficult to resolve. What national interests are and how they can be arranged hierarchically is a matter of some importance and influences the heart of much of the debate in national security concerns. The key additional concept in these discussions is the idea of "vitality" of a particular interest to national interest realization.

Interests also come into conflict in two ways. One of these is when an individual holds incompatible interests in a particular case. This usage is most often associated with individuals and their transactions, but it can also occur in the relations between states, for instance when a particular action to enhance one value may cause harm to another value as a consequence. Interests have traditionally been described as national in nature in the Westphalian system introduced in the last chapter, but they may exist as challenges to national interests at other levels. Also, the concept of national interest is a linchpin of the international order as it emerged from World War II in the form of something called the realist paradigm, the validity of which is at least partly undermined in a system that does not promote the idea of national interest.

The Non-Intersubjective Nature of National Interest

Phrasing any issue as being in the national interest gives that position an aura of patriotism and virtue, because many people tend to equate national interest and national security, meaning the advocacy of something as being in the national interest suggests that it is contributing to that most vital of national interests, the country's security from harm. Sometimes that equation is valid and sustainable, but at other times it is not so clearly the case, for one or both of two reasons. One is that the issue may not really be important enough for this elevation, and the other is that the position the advocate has on the issue may or may not be the best way to attain the goal. The abstract idea of national interest may be rock solid, but the advocacies made in its name may not be.

There is a formalistic way to state this problem: *intersubjectivity*. The term is borrowed from the philosophy of science, and it refers to whether all observers can view the same phenomenon in the same way. A useful synonym for the term is objectivity, and it means that for something to be intersubjective, it must be viewable in the same way by all observers. The statement "President Donald Trump is a Republican" is intersubjective, because it is a fact with no embellishment or interpretation. The statement that Trump is a good (or bad) president is not intersubjective, because it requires a subjective interpretation that goes beyond objective fact to opinion, and people hold different opinions on things. If I assert that Trump is a good president, in other words, I am making an accurate (true) statement that he is the president; I am voicing a subjective opinion when I extrapolate the characteristic of good or bad to his presidency.

Questions of national interest are very much of this nature. The core of them begins from some generally objective observation (a statement of truth), to which two additional characteristics, neither of them objective, are made. One is whether the issue is in fact a matter of interest, and what degree of importance should be attached to doing something about it. The second characteristic consists of a prescription for appropriate action to alleviate whatever problem the situation creates. The first observation is generally objective: its truth or falsity can be demonstrated objectively. The other questions are subjective, because it is a matter of opinion what the nature and extent of the problem is and what needs to be done about it.

The ongoing national security issue of IS offers an example. It is objectively true that IS exists and that the American national interest would be served if the group ceased to exist or was weakened to the point that it offered no peril to the United States. Most Americans (as well as Europeans and others) would be happier with a world without IS (their preference is objective), but the importance of eradication or control (and the choice of which option to pursue) is not: different people can and do disagree on both issues.

The controversy over the intersubjectivity of the national interest is thus joined, and it becomes even murkier when one moves the discussion forward to solutions. The Trump administration, for instance, has depicted a variety of conditions in the world as posing basic threats to the United States as part of its rationale for a large increase in spending for military forces. There are indeed forces opposed to interests of the United States in the world: that China and the United States disagree about the Chinese claim to the South China Sea is an indisputable fact. What this disagreement *means* in terms of harm to American national interests is not objective, but a matter of disagreement based on the values and beliefs that different individuals hold. Such disagreements, in other words, are not intersubjective and can be matters of honest disagreement over which side is "right" depending on the subjective interpretation people place upon it.

One can make questions of what is and is not in the national interest look more chaotic and contentious than they in fact are. Determining interests is an ongoing exercise within governments and analysts where there is broad agreement on the general categories of those interests and at least in general about how to handle them. The content of what is in the national interest does not change so much as do challenges to that interest. The key concept is the idea of vital interests, the sole property of sovereign states.

Operationalizing the National Interest: The Key Role of Vital Interests

Scholars and policy makers alike have sought to make the determination and classification of national interests more concrete and objective. No one doubts that national interests exist and are supreme in a system of sovereign states. Likewise, everyone agrees that not all interests are equally important, that the consequences of their non-realization differ depending on their relative importance, and that different levels and kinds of national exertion are appropriate to attain or maintain them.

Within the realist interpretation of international relations, the most basic distinction is made between those interests that are *vital (VIs)* for the country to realize and those that are *less-than-vital (LTVs)*. VIs clearly are the most important interests, and are generally defined as conditions that are so important to the state that it will not willingly compromise on their attainment. Achieving those interests may not always be within the power of the state (which is the reason for the qualifier *willingly compromise*), but they are the baseline of a country's sense of security. This definition helps explain why states will not allow an authority superior to themselves to adjudicate their differences, because a verdict against them could affect their vital interests and would be unacceptable. LTVs, on the other hand, are matters of descending importance to the state that would cause varying but not basic discomfort or inconvenience to the state and whose non-realization might be discomforting but not entirely intolerable.

The VI-LTV distinction is critical because it is generally considered the effective boundary between those situations where the state will and will not consider the recourse to violence as a means to attain them. In simplest terms, vital interests are potentially worth going to war over to ensure; LTVs do not normally justify the recourse to force. Even this distinction is less sharp than the simple statement may suggest, because there will always be disagreement about the worthiness and appropriateness of force in a given situation. For this reason, it may be better to think of the boundary between VIs and LTVs as a "confidence interval" of differing interpretations rather than a sharp line.

These distinctions are important enough that they bear further elaboration both analytically and as a guide for political action. The late Donald Nuechter-

Table 2.1. The Nuechterlein Matrix

Basic Interest	Intensity of Interest			
	Survival	**Vital**	**Major**	**Peripheral**
Homeland Defense				
Economic Well-Being				
Favorable World Order				
Values Promotion				

lein, in a 1991 text, laid out a more elaborate way of distinguishing interests based on a four-by-four matrix reproduced as table 2.1.

The two dimensions are hierarchical in descending order of importance to the state. On the intensity dimension, the survival of the state is clearly its most intense interest, the inability of which to secure leaves other interests moot. Vital interests, as already suggested, may not entail challenges to national survival, but are important enough that states will engage in serious, including military, efforts to attain them. Border disputes often fall into this category, such as the conflict between the United States and Mexico over the Texas-Mexico border in the 1840s that resulted in the Mexican War. These two levels of intensity compose the VI level in the dichotomy between VIs and LTVs, which are represented in the other two levels of intensity. The differentiations are not precise or clearly intersubjective, but major interests are matters that would inconvenience and trouble a state (the terms of an international trade agreement might be an example) but whose non-realization would be tolerable. Peripheral interests attach to conditions the state might disfavor but with which it can fairly easily live: the outcome of winning or losing the right to host the Olympics might be an example.

These distinctions are arbitrary and subject to disagreement, particularly in the designation of vital versus major interests. To raise an example amplified in the next section, a border dispute between Russia and the United States over islands in the Bering Strait could entail a clash of vital interests, but what of Russian expansion into the Crimea, a territory that has been part of Ukraine since the dissolution of the Soviet Union in 1991? The Russians clearly believe its possession is vital to their interests, but the United States disagrees with the manner in which the Crimea was seized and generally supports the Ukrainian claim to the territory. How important is that American interest to the United States: vital, major, or peripheral?

The other dimension refers to categories of the content of interests. It is also hierarchically arranged. Clearly, matters of homeland security are of the most basic nature, and can be either survival or vital in intensity, depending on how extensive the threat is. Conquests of states clearly qualify as survival in intensity; the annexation of a small part of national territory may be vital but not survival threatening. Since the commodiousness of life within a state is related to its economic standing, economic well-being is also very important, and probably can take on the characteristic of vital or major importance depending on the situation.

Once again, the boundary between VIs and LTVs is probably between economic well-being and the next lower category, although it is certainly possible to argue that the resolution of most economic issues does not have intolerable consequences, making the boundary there somewhat ambiguous. As in major and peripheral interest intensity, the last two basic interests are of less intense concern. The United States would certainly find a world order composed of all market democracies highly desirable and might act to increase their number, but it clearly accommodates itself to a less ideal world. Similarly, the United States wants to promote its own political values, but this is of a lower order of priority than other policy matters.

The Nuechterlein matrix may help clarify some thinking about the relative priority of securing certain national interests, but it does not resolve all matters or provide ironclad guidance over what the country should do in all situations. All situations are to some degree idiosyncratic, meaning that past precedents are not perfect isomorphisms, that some judgments must be made in all cases, and that people will disagree about the nature and importance of given challenges to interests: into what pair of categories from the matrix does a particular situation fall? How important is it? Based on this assessment, what quality of actions is justifiable and acceptable to realize the interest, and which is not?

Clearly, the most important consequential differentiation involves the boundary between vital and LTV interests. As noted, this line is really a confidence interval (or band), because not everyone accepts the same frontier at which an interest passes from LTV to vital, and vice versa. Take the case of what to do about IS raised in the last chapter as an example. Does the destruction of IS represent a vital American interest? If so, what basic interest category is affected by accomplishing the interest? Those who have argued for a robust military response are at least implicitly arguing that a vital interest is involved, but is it a matter of homeland defense, and what is the basis of that claim? If it is a matter of economic well-being, does whatever happens to the Islamic State affect the economic status of Americans? The debate is important, because the designation of an interest as vital is the normal key to triggering the possibility of military action, an obviously important decision for a state. The interests of individuals and groups come into conflict where these kinds of matters are concerned.

Conflicts of Interest

The term *national interest* is misleading in one important sense: stated by itself and out of context, it implies that there is *a* national interest that is shared by all the citizens of any country, and that is not true in a comprehensive sense. All—or virtually all—citizens of any country generally agree on the most basic interests such as national survival, but even in such instances, their agreement is not complete. Different citizens will, for instance, disagree on how best to ensure interests that they agree are important. For instance, which threats to vital, survival-related national interests justify the threat or use of armed force to defend? If force is justified, what kind (American self-defense using nuclear weapons?)

and degree of force is appropriate, justifiable, and thus defensible? Even at the most basic levels, in other words, interests come into conflict. Resolving those conflicts of interest is the major burden of domestic political processes; figuring out how to resolve differences in international relations represents the same problem in a more difficult setting.

Sovereignty helps explain how conflicts of interest differ at the two levels. The resolution of conflicts within the state may be difficult, but it occurs within the context of a higher authority, that of the sovereign state. The state is the only entity that, by definition, has vital interests, such as those represented in the upper left-hand quadrant of the Nuechterlein framework. Different individuals and groups may quibble over the exact meaning of the national interest in a given situation, but they do accept that the content of that interest is overriding. The situation is more complex in international relations. In the relations between states, internal conflicts may be and often are present, but the interacting sovereign states also have differing and sometimes irresolvable national interests among them that cannot be resolved by reference to a higher authority. Moreover, the conflicts between states may themselves be contradictory, leaving the question of which conflicting interest should prevail in a given circumstance. The membership of the European Union, for instance, has an interest in good relations with Russia to ensure the flow of Russian natural gas to European furnaces during the winter. It also has an interest in Ukrainian independence, which recent Russian incursions have threatened. Which interest is more important?

There is another sense of conflict of interest that transcends domestic-international contexts. A classic use of the term surrounds the situation where an individual or organization (including a state) has a personal conflict of interest in differing outcomes of situations. The normal synonym for this situation is vested interest, where an official may have a personal interest in outcomes that contradict the positions that might flow from the definition of a national interest that individual is vested to protect. That potential situation has been recently associated with aspects of U.S.-Russian relations that are explored in the application section of this chapter.

National and Other Levels of Interest

The concepts of sovereignty and national interest are intertwined in another way that leads some to question the idea that national interest, like sovereignty, should be as supreme and overriding as it is. The objection that is raised suggests that state sovereignty has pernicious effects and has its parallel in the definition of the supremacy of national interest as opposed to the interests of individuals and the interests that go beyond those of states (international interests).

The objections arise from the inextricable conceptual link between the national interest and sovereignty. As noted, the supreme authority of the state means that the state has vital interests that are superior to those of any other entity. Reciprocally, the fact that there are asserted interests on which the state will not willingly compromise means that the state must have the supreme authority to ensure the maintenance of those rights: sovereignty implies vital interests and must be present to protect them. In this sense the relationship between the two dynamics forms an inextricable and crucial link in the reasoning that underlies realism and the realist paradigm, a construct discussed in greater detail in Snow, *National Security*, Sixth Edition.

The obvious implication of the elevation of national interest to conceptual supremacy is that as a result, interests at other levels occupy a lesser priority and importance, a consequence with which not everyone agrees, asserting that other levels of interest are of equal or arguably even greater importance than those of national interest.

Within international relations, objections come from both ends of a spectrum from interests that affect individual humans to those that affect the human condition. At one extreme are *individual* interests, the most important of which center on individual human rights and the conditions that maximize (or minimize) the survival and prospering of individuals. At the other end of the spectrum are *international* interests, those conditions and actions that contribute to or detract from maximum survivability and prosperity for everyone. The levels problem exists because the pursuit of one level may come at the expense of the others. More specifically, the pursuit of national interest as the supreme value may endanger or preclude the pursuit of individual or international interests.

Individual interests represent an extension of the arguments for popular sovereignty that can be endangered by an unfettered pursuit of national interests in several ways. Probably the most obvious is when national interests collide with those of another state, are sufficiently important to both that they cannot compromise on them, and thus result in a resort to armed violence. In that circumstance, individuals may well be involuntarily required to fight in the ensuing hostilities, a participation to which they may object and that certainly infringes on the pursuit of the individual right to survive.

Another example is a state that pursues a policy of economic expansion that requires it to industrialize, have to produce more energy to do so, and accomplish its goal by creating pollution levels that endanger the health of its own citizens, whose health and well-being is compromised in the name of national power. This example is not abstract, but fairly closely resembles the situation in China, where the government has moved to the burning of highly polluting coal (China burns 90 percent of the coal used in the world to produce energy), which has created enormous pollution and health-resultant respiratory difficulties for the mass of Chinese citizens. This problem, which the Chinese government has promised to address through the Paris Treaty on climate change of December 2015, also illustrates the challenge to international interests, since the effects of carbon emissions from Chinese coal-power energy generation affects other countries and the global ecosystem.

The other competing level is international interests, conditions that transcend national boundaries and that can be addressed only by international efforts, some of which are addressed in chapters 12 and 13. This level becomes a concern and source of international tension and disagreement, particularly when efforts to pursue national interests result in international effects that both make the disagreement over national interests greater and endanger the interests of humankind as a whole.

Possibly the most notable political science example of the clash of national and international interest levels is a construct called the *security dilemma*. John H. Herz first articulated this idea in a 1951 book; he referred to the situation where one state, feeling insecure in its security relationship with another state, takes actions to increase its sense of security. In the classic depiction, the threatened state builds up its military power to cancel a perceived inferiority, and this action creates a similar reaction by the other state (the dynamic is often referred as the action-reaction phenomenon) which, in the classic example, did not previously harbor animosity to the threatened state. It interprets the other's buildup as a hostile act, and increases its own armament, which, in turn, causes the other state to arm even more, and the situation spirals into an arms race in which both states end up being less secure than they were in the first place. This dynamic, as pointed out by scholars such as Jervis and Waltz, is most destabilizing when nuclear weapons are the currency of the arms race. Waltz's *Theory of International Politics*, reprinted in 2010 before his 2013 death, remains a classic statement. In the end, the point is that states acting to protect their own individual national interests can engage in behavior that makes the rest of the international system, including those states, less secure.

National Interests and the International System

The concept and pursuit of national interest are a natural and central element of realist academic theorizing and the actual practice of international relations. The supremacy of national over other levels of interest flows from a system in which the states have superior authority to all other political bodies. The major consequence of such a system is a formal state of anarchy in the political realm that both describes the pattern of interactions between the members and provides the contrast between domestic and international relations. By its nature, a system where the members' primary mission is the pursuit of their individual interests is one where conflict and self-help are natural vehicles for conflict resolution and where the ultimate retention of the option to use force remains central. A realist world is, in other words, a place where power is the major lingua franca.

Many theorists and some practitioners decry this situation, which is why there are calls to weaken sovereignty or to substitute other levels of interest for the interests of states as the primary focus. This reaction is stronger among theoreticians, at least partly because they tend to concentrate more on conflict—especially war—avoidance than the practitioners who may find the threat or use of force the optimal manner from time to time to dispatch their duties. The theoreticians seek to influence the efforts of the practitioners, and they have succeeded in some areas, which are discussed in subsequent chapters. At the applied level of international relations, however, the pursuit of national interests remains a central, and highly complex, part of international relations. Some of the complicated aspects and consequences of that pursuit are explored in the application section of this chapter.

Application: Russian Oil and U.S.-Russian Relations

For most of the period since 1945, the United States and Russia have been the primary protagonists of international politics. Their rivalry was at its zenith from the late 1940s until 1991, when the then Soviet Union collapsed and reverted to being Russia (technically the Russian Federation), an event that greatly reduced the centrality of Russia in international relations to depths it had not endured since World War II. Countering the spread of Soviet communist influence was the chief national security priority of the United States during the four decades of the Cold War, because the Soviet Union was the only country that, by virtue of its nuclear arsenal and the antagonism between the two countries and systems, posed a true survival threat to the United States. Russia retains a sizable portion of that arsenal but is generally not believed to be motivated to use it, and its power in other areas has drastically declined. The current Russian leadership is committed to reasserting Russia's Cold War status (or something like it) in the world, and it a popular aspiration because, as Lukyanov puts it, "Neither Russian elites nor ordinary Russians have ever accepted the image of their country as a mere regional power."

In terms of the interaction of the national interests of the two states, the major question is how the United States (and the West in general) should deal with a resurgent Russia that shows revanchist tendencies, such as those in Ukraine. Should the United States help the Russians to recover and assume what they view as their rightful place among the countries of the world, oppose that resurgence and work toward a supine, weak Russia, or aid the Russians while exacting concessions from the Russians in return for some help, knowing some of that assistance will go into military spending that could in some way threaten the United States? Which policy direction is most in the American national interest?

The question and appropriate answers are contentious. This contention has major sources in each country. Russian actions in Ukraine, including the annexation of the Crimea and effective occupation and influence over parts of eastern Ukraine, have raised serious questions in the West regarding Russian motives. At their most extreme, these questions surround Russian expansionism, a historic form of Russian behavior. In the United States, allegations of Russian meddling in the 2016 U.S. presidential election created a flurry of partisan disagreement about how to deal with the Russians as well. The Russian context for discussions is the trajectory of Russian power in the absence of virulent Russian behavior. Without outside help, Russia, very simply, is in geopolitical trouble. What, if anything, should the Americans do to influence that arc in Russia's standing in the world? The answer is a matter of subjective determination: what kind of Russia is in the American national interest?

Russia's Problem: Demographics and Beyond

Russia remains a country for which Winston Churchill's October 31, 1939, description of the Soviet Union still holds: "a riddle wrapped in a mystery inside an enigma." It is a place of enormous contrasts: as the Soviet Union, it spanned the Eurasian land mass from the Baltic Sea to the Pacific Ocean, and from the Arctic Ocean to the Black Sea, but its only warm-water port is on the Black Sea as part of the Crimea. Even after losing much of its territory as the Soviet Union disintegrated, it is still the physically largest country in the world, and has land borders totaling 12,650 miles with fifteen countries, most of which rightly view the Russians with apprehension or fear. Before the Soviet Union imploded, it was the third most populous country in the world; today it has a population of 142 million, tenth among the world's states. It has been a state in decline since its Cold War heyday, and most projections suggest that it will become less important over time unless it does something to reverse apparent trends.

Many of the trend lines are ominous. Despite its enormous land mass, its climate is so cold that only approximately 7 percent of its land is arable, and the result is that Russia cannot feed itself and must import food. Its largest outside supplier of foodstuffs has been Ukraine, which provides the Russians with necessary grains. National demographics are even more daunting. The population is in physical decline, with an overall population growth rate (PGR) of -0.3 percent, which is 200th in the world. As Eberstadt observed in 2010, "Since the end of the Soviet era, the population of the Russian Federation has fallen by nearly 7 million, [and] life expectancy at birth looks to be lower than it was four decades ago." English reports that this decline has been arrested in the last three years, but will it last? The Soviet/Russian economy was never able to compete with its Western counterparts during the Cold War, and post-Soviet industrial and other growth has been crippled by rampant corruption and mafia control, to say nothing of kleptocratic behavior by government officials—in some reports including Vladimir Putin. Since World War II, the major claim to great-power status was its military prowess, but its armed forces have declined as well, leaving the Russians vulnerable to the frequent charge against the Soviets of being "a frozen banana republic with nuclear weapons." This uninviting combination (discussed in some detail in Snow, *Regional Cases in U.S. Foreign Policy*) is not a formula for the reassertion of Russia as a great power, much less the lofty status of superpower it had during the Cold War.

The single bright spot in Russian prospects has been energy production. Russia possesses some of the world's largest deposits of major energy sources, including petroleum, natural gas, and even shale oil and gas, and it has acted aggressively to exploit them all as a way to increase its national wealth, to provide the basis for providing for its citizens, and as a lever for increasing its relative position in the world. Russia currently produces 10.44 million barrels a day (mbd) of petroleum, third most in the world, and it exports 4.72 mbd, second behind Saudi Arabia. Its geopolitical situation is enhanced because much of Europe is dependent on Russian natural gas to heat its homes during the winter, but that prominence comes with limits and drawbacks that cloud its future and that make its relationship with the United States critical to its future rise or fall among the world's powers.

The Russian Question: Expansionism and Meddling

The role the United States should play in Russian resurgence is a question of American interests in how Russian prosperity and return toward a more robust status will affect American interests. Is the United States a more secure place with a vibrant, assertive Russian Federation in the arena with it, or is the American national interest better served by a weaker and less assertive Russia? The answer is not crystalline and is a matter on which Americans disagree. Thus, whether American policies intend to and accomplish the possible goals of retarding or promoting Russian desires is a matter of difference among those charged with the national interest.

The Russian self-concept of their national interest is straightforward and historically based. Russia has for centuries been an ascendant state that aspires to full major-power recognition, a recognition that most European states never truly accorded the Russians. As the Soviet Union, Russia was recognized as one of the world's two superpowers, but the dissolution of the USSR in 1991 reduced its status drastically. This reduction has led President Putin to describe the breakup as the worst disaster of the twentieth century, a description that is certainly true for Russia. The 1990s saw a precipitous decline in Russia's situation and status, and it is the ongoing rationale of Russian foreign policy to return Russia to its "rightful" position as a great power.

Russia has acted to increase its position in the world order in historic Russian ways, and these raise questions about how the United States can and should respond to Russian actions that they feel promote their interests. They are important because they provide the fuel for assessing whether a more or less resurgent Russia is in the American interest. In recent years, two policy areas stand out.

The first Russian policy area has been expansionism. It is a recurrent theme of Russian history that whenever Russia feels threatened, its initial response is to protect itself by moving outward into troubling areas. The rationale for annexing the Baltic states on the eve of World War II, for instance, was to prevent Nazi Germany from occupying them, and the East European "empire" of communist states during the Cold War was, in geopolitical terms, a way to create a *cordon sanitaire* or buffer zone that ensured that another invasion from the West would be fought on East European rather than Soviet/Russian territory. The Soviet Union itself, composed of fifteen "socialist republics," was itself a largely conquered empire that dissolved in 1991, leaving only the Russian Federation under Russian control. The dissolution of empire has been the greatest physical symbol of Russian decline, and recouping some of that literally lost ground has been a major emphasis of Russian policy.

Russian actions to fulfill this aspect of its self-perceived national interest began in earnest in 2008, when the Russian government dispatched forces to come to the aid of alleged South Ossetian and Abkhazian separatists who claimed mistreatment by the Georgian government in Tbilisi. In the lopsided "war" that followed, the Russians prevailed, over the strenuous objection of the Bush administration, which had established close ties with the Georgian government. By terms of the agreement ending the conflict, the Russians withdrew, but only after establishing autonomy for the Abkhazian and South Ossetian regions.

The Georgian episode was less blatant than Russian interference into the Ukraine since 2014. It began when Russian forces moved into the Crimean Peninsula, which had been named part of the Ukraine by then Soviet leader Nikita Khrushchev in 1954 (it had been part of the Russian Empire/Soviet Union since 1783). During unrest in Ukraine, Russian forces moved into the Crimea and annexed the peninsula on March 18, 2014. For the Russians, the primary importance of the peninsula is strategic: its major port city in the Black Sea is at Sevastopol, which houses the Russian Black Sea fleet. The Ukrainians, most European states, and the United States have protested the annexation. To compound the problem, Russian "volunteers" have been active militarily in eastern Ukraine in support of ethnic Russians, who form a majority in some areas. This militancy has been countered by NATO (including U.S.) military maneuvers in places such as the Baltic countries and Poland, all to the chagrin of the Russians. It raises, however, questions about whether Russian-American relations should be improved given the prospects that doing so would increase both Russian power and expansionism elsewhere.

The other source of contemporary concern in U.S.-Russian relations surrounds the controversy over apparent Russian attempts to interfere in and influence the outcome of the 2016 presidential election in the United States. More specifically, this highly politicized, partisan issue has focused on the extent to which the Russians may have had contacts with officials in the campaign of President Trump in illegal ways that might have affected the election outcome.

There are basically two issues in this dispute. One of these is the factual determination of the extent and nature of Russian interactions with the Trump campaign and transition team before the new president entered office. These are essentially legal matters within the American system that go beyond the purview of this study: they are not direct matters of national interest in a strict sense, unless the intent and effect of Russian efforts succeeded in deflecting American policy away from the pursuit of its national interest. Whether that is the case, of course, depends on what national interest was affected and how.

The attempt by states to influence one another's politics is a simple part of international relations in which nearly all states engage. Sovereignty formally precludes such interference, but it is nonetheless true that interference occurs to a greater or lesser degree all the time as a part of operational intelligence operations. The U.S. government is certainly involved in such efforts, which includes minor actions such as taking policy actions that favor one political side in a country over another, financing different factions, and the like. In some cases, more active efforts such as those by the CIA against the Arbenz government in Guatemala in 1954 may lead to the overthrow of a regime (see Kinzer for an account), but such activities are normally shrouded so they can pass the litmus test of "plausible deniability" (the ability effectively to deny any part in a nefarious scheme).

There are unwritten rules about the extent to which outside interference beyond the clandestine collection of information is permissible. The allegations against the Russians in 2016 suggested that they had contacted officials within the Trump campaign and transition teams. This level of interference stands at the cusp of acceptability among major powers, and whether it represented an unacceptable form of meddling will depend on its extent and its effects, neither of which had been definitively established at this writing. If the Russians did cross the line regarding acceptable behavior and if their actions adversely affected American national interests, then the consequences could be substantial and affect the extent to which the United States is wise in cooperating with the Russians in the pursuit of *their* national interest.

Russian Resurgence: Oil and the Petrolist State

Russian ascent to great-power status has always been clouded by the performance of its economy. As the Russian Empire, the country was considered the least economically developed state in the European balance of power, and the infusion of Marxist economic theory and practices did not measurably improve the situation in economic terms. It is probably significant that it was the collapsing Soviet economy, aided by the Reagan administration's arms buildup that necessitated a Soviet response, that convinced Mikhail Gorbachev the only possible means of economic transformation was to join and emulate the West.

The chaos and emergence of a kleptocratic state during the 1990s only made matters worse. The fall of communism left a regulatory void that encompassed most aspects of life, including the economy. Russian "entrepreneurs" (often with Russian mafia ties) infiltrated the economic structure and took over activities formerly controlled by the state for personal gain. The rise of Putin and centralization of his authority may have moderated this situation somewhat, but the explosion of the energy sector also contributed to the continuation of corruption. Although not officially confirmed, it has been reported that Putin may be the wealthiest person in the world.

Energy production and sales have been a boon both to the Russian economy and the country's place in the world, but it may prove to be its bane as well. The exploitation of its fossil fuel wealth has fueled Russian prosperity across the board in the last decade, but it has done so at costs to Russia's place in the world and to how Russia operates. The Russian system became heavily dependent on energy production starting in the early 2000s, and while that marriage has produced prosperity and advancement, it has also left Russia heavily vulnerable to the vicissitudes of wild price fluctuations in the world energy sector.

For Putin and his associates, the expansion of oil sales worldwide helped lift Russia from the post-Soviet doldrums and its precipitous decline as a world power. It provided revenues that could be applied to solving discontent within the population and funding to rebuild a Russian military establishment that had both shrunk and deteriorated in the decade after the end of the Cold War. The 1990s were a period of ignominy and shame for the Russians; oil seemed to offer the vehicle for a return to greatness.

In the process, however, Russia has been transformed into a classic *petrolist state*, to borrow the term coined by Thomas L. Friedman in a 2006 article. The designation connotes a country where energy revenues are utilized to finance growing parts of the economy and provide prosperity to the population, in addition to filling government coffers to invest or, in some cases, to steal. Classic examples of petrolist states are found in the developing world—places such as Nigeria and Venezuela—and it is symbolic that Russia would find itself in the same category. From the turn of the millennium until the early 2010s, oil revenues provided Russia with wealth and standing, but that revenue was not, by and large, spent on development of other sectors of the economy that could sustain the economy without oil money. Instead, the revenues were used to support Putin's dream of returning Russia to a position of greatness, and the vehicle for that assertion has primarily been manifested in Russian assertiveness and expansionism.

The vulnerability of any state dependent on a commodity is the volatility of markets to fluctuations in demand and thus price for its commodity. Like all other countries heavily dependent on oil revenues, the Russians have been damaged greatly by the collapse of oil prices since 2013. As Kotkin described the situation in a 2016 article, "Russian dollar-denominated GDP peaked in 2013 at slightly over $2 trillion and has now dropped to about $1.2 trillion thanks to cratered oil prices and ruble exchange rates." That drop amounts to about a 40 percent fall in the GDP of a country whose national economy was not that robust anyway. Even before the collapse, Russia's GDP was only about one-eighth the size of the American economy (at $16.72 trillion). Contemporary estimates are not reliable, but on the eve of the collapse, per capita GDP in Russia was $18,000, seventy-seventh in the world and about one-third of American totals. That comparison has become more invidious since. The Putin regime has arguably dealt with this decline internally by its appeal to Russian xenophobia in places such as Ukraine.

The Russians are in a difficult bind. Dependent as they are on petroleum revenues, they cannot visibly cut back production without making matters worse in the short run. A longer-run strategy would suggest reducing production to drive down supply and cause a rise in prices, but the Russians cannot afford such a strategy and continue to pursue Putin's goals of geopolitical expansion. Ukraine is an example. Russian interests, according to Treisman, are to keep the Ukrainians dependent on their energy to keep Ukraine from flirting with NATO, to secure the naval base at Sevastopol, and to maintain access to Ukrainian grain. Only Russian energy maintains that leverage. Without it, only naked military action can enforce Russian preferences.

The other part of the bind is that Russia is depleting its exploitable energy reserves at an alarming rate, and unless the Russians can expand their access to their reserves, they will lose the ability to be anything like the world's second-largest exporter. There are vast reserves under Russian territories in the Arctic and in Siberia and huge shale deposits. The Russians, by and large, lack the technology to access those reserves without American help. The question is whether it is in the American national interest to provide it.

The U.S. Role: America and Russian Oil

Russian dependence on petroleum revenue as the "fuel" of its economic and national security efforts creates a strong Russian national interest in maximizing this segment of its economy. In 2013, for instance, the U.S. Energy Information Agency (EIA) reported that fully 68 percent of total Russian export revenues came from the sale of oil and natural gas. The oil reserves that the Russians can directly access are the world's tenth largest, and they are the world's second largest exporter. This combination points to future problems, because it means that at current rates of exploitation, the Russians will begin to see decreased capacity in the middle term—unless they can do something to change that situation.

Russia has the answer lying beneath its soil and under its adjacent waters. The problem is that much of this capacity lies beneath lands that are either locked by permafrost or are only accessible for short times of the year. If the Russians gain the ability to exploit all of their energy supplies, they will become at or near the top of energy sources worldwide. Their possession of traditionally mined oil and natural gas is among the largest in the world (reserve sizes change regularly, so figures are always subject to change), and they reportedly have the world's largest reserves of shale oil and gas as well. The problem is that Russian energy technology is inferior to that of the West, and especially the United States. Put simply, the Russians have enormous stores of energy resources that could underwrite their place in the world for the foreseeable future, but they cannot gain commercial access to it without substantial, meaning American, help.

This situation makes gaining access to exploiting foreign energy extraction capability a major, if not the major, foreign policy priority for the Putin regime. With invigorated and readily available access to their energy reserves, Russia can both satisfy many of the desires of its citizens and have enough left over to pursue traditional Russian geopolitical imperatives. The Putin regime understands the relationship between energy production and popular support for the regime. They also understand that they need help creating the situation where the energy can flow freely. That means they need access to Western—mostly American—energy extraction technology. The Americans (and Canadians) have experience in all the relevant areas: drilling for oil in the Arctic Ocean and on lands inside the Arctic Circle, and shale oil and gas extraction, to name the most obvious.

Actions in the Crimea and the Arctic are parallel. Although it received little publicity at the time, a benefit of the Crimean seizure was to give the Russians access to and potential control of sizable oil reserves under the Black Sea. This development also deprives the Ukrainians, who have very limited energy reserves otherwise, of access to this oil. The problem, once again, is that the Russians need help extracting these oil fields as well. In 2017, the Russians began building a military installation in the Arctic (Arctic Shamrock). The motivation for doing so was unclear, but reports suggest that one reason may have been to protect access to and control over Arctic oil in regions contiguous to Russia.

The sources of the technology the Russians lack are in the Western private sector, and specifically the American energy industry. Under the circumstances, it comes as no surprise that the Russians have courted those corporations that possess the needed technology with generous contracts and leases in return for the application of needed technologies to Russian reserves. In the United States, the primary company with whom the Russians have dealt has been ExxonMobil, with whom the Russians have negotiated very large contracts for both Russian and Crimean oil and natural gas. U.S. Secretary of State Rex Tillerson, of course, is the former chief executive officer of ExxonMobil and was active in negotiating deals with the Russians while in that capacity. In July 2017, the conflict became public. The U.S. government fined ExxonMobil for signing agreements with Russia in 2014 (while Tillerson was CEO) that violated sanctions imposed because of Russian actions in Ukraine.

Here is where the geopolitical rubber hits the road. Putin's Russia has clear perceived national interests in expanding its power and influence, and some of this expansion would come at the expense of Western Europe and even conceivably the United States.

Russian-American clash of national interests is by no means a new phenomenon. That two of the largest, most powerful and evangelical states in the world would be competitors with conflicting interests is not a surprise. It probably dates back at least to 1823, when one of the motivations of American proclamation of the Monroe Doctrine was to halt Russian fur trading activity in California that had reached as far south as San Francisco Bay. It certainly reached a climax during the Cold War, and has continued since. Although it is not widely considered in the United States, the Russians believe that their interference in the 2016 election was not unlike what the Clinton administration did in promoting a corrupt Boris Yeltsin reign in Russia during the 1990s. As English puts it, "Few Russians who endured this [American abetted] corruption and humiliation have much sympathy over Russian meddling in the 2016 election. And with any perspective on the 1990s, it is hard to fault them." When sovereignty-based norms and perceived national interest–based advantages come into conflict, often theoretical sovereignty suffers. That does not excuse Russian meddling, but it puts it into perspective. English argues that the Clinton administration in part supported Yeltsin because he was weak and corrupt; he also points out that Hillary Clinton as secretary of state advocated Ukrainian admission into NATO, an action Russia violently opposes.

Historical perspective notwithstanding, the question remains whether it is in the American national interest to help the Russians pursue accessing oil reserves they cannot currently reach. The Trump administration came to office with the hope of improved relations with the Russians, which lifting the oil sanctions would certainly promote. At the same time, once the Russians learn how to get to those inaccessible reserves themselves, will they have any further need for ExxonMobil and American technology? Will the oil wealth they reap be used to pursue traditional Russian ends and conflict with the interests of the United States? What indeed are American interests, where do they come into conflict with those of the Russians, and do some Americans have vested conflicts of interest that could compromise their objective pursuit of these questions?

Conclusion

Like sovereignty, the idea of national interests is a bedrock principle of international relations, and one way to look at the most fundamental dynamics of how international relations work is through the lens of the interaction of the national interests of the sovereign states of the world. That is not the only dynamic in the system, of course. The erosion of absolute sovereignty and the emergence of interests at other levels like that of the individual or humankind may attenuate that centrality and create a more complex reality in international life.

These limitations notwithstanding, the idea of national interests remains central to the practice and study of the subject. Studying national interest is made more complex by the elevated way in which people think about it. As noted, what is and is not in the national interest is a contentious question, and in any debate over whether particular actions are desirable will generally be presented by all sides as being in the national interest, whereas opposing views will be castigated as harming that interest. The national interest is a reality, but it is a controversial one.

The relations between the United States and Russia illustrate the dynamics and tensions that national interest–based interactions can manifest. The two countries are clearly rivals in many matters, and it is not clear how their relations can result in positive-sum as opposed to zero-sum outcomes some of the time. The current dispute over Russian interference in the 2016 election is part of that debate, as is the question of whether the United States should help the Russians unlock their vast energy resources.

Study/Discussion Questions

1. Define the terms interest and national and how they are combined as a basic principle of international relations. Why are they so important?

2. What does it mean to say national interests are non-intersubjective? How does this make them controversial in political discussions?

3. What is the distinction between vital interests (VIs) and less than vital interests (LTVs)? Use the Nuechterlein matrix to show how complex the difference is.

4. What is a conflict of interest? How do they apply to individuals and states? Also, what is the problem of levels of interest? What are the competing levels? How may they conflict with national interests?

5. Discuss the role of national interests in the operational international system, using U.S.-Russian relations as an example.

6. What is the heart of the Russian problem in the current system? How does it affect Russian pursuit of its national interests?

7. What national interests divide the United States and Russia, specifically in terms of Russian expansionism and interference in the 2016 U.S. election? Discuss.

8. What is the role of oil in Russia? How does it become an issue in U.S.-Russian relations? Is it in American interest to help the Russians solve their problem? Why or why not?

Bibliography

Art, Robert, and Kenneth A. Waltz, eds. *The Use of Force: Military Power and International Politics*. 7th ed. Lanham, MD: Rowman & Littlefield, 2009.

Cunningham, Nick. "Crimea Oil and Gas Will Not Come Easy to Russia." *Christian Science Monitor* (online), May 21, 2014.

DaVargo, Julie, and Clifford A. Grammich. *Dire Demographics: Population Trends in the Russian Federation*. Santa Monica, CA: RAND Corporation, 2007.

Dawisha, Karen. *Putin's Kleptocracy: Who Owns Russia?* Reprint ed. New York: Simon & Schuster, 2014.

De Ploeg, Chris Kaspar. *Ukraine in the Crossfire*. Atlanta, GA: Clarity, 2017.

Eberstadt, Nicholas. "The Enigma of Russian Mortality." *Current History* 109, no. 729 (October 2010): 288–94.

English, Robert Davis. "Russia, Trump, and a New Détente." *Foreign Affairs Snapshot* (online), March 10, 2017.

Friedman, Thomas L. "The First Law of Petropolitics." *Foreign Policy*, May/June 2006, 28–36.

Fromkin, David. *The Independence of Nations*. New York: Praeger Special Studies, 1981.

Gorbachev, Mikhail. *The New Russia*. New York: Polity, 2016.

Herz, John H. *Political Realism and Political Idealism*. Chicago: University of Chicago Press, 1951.

Jervis, Robert. *Perception and Misperception in International Politics*. Princeton, NJ: Princeton University Press, 1978.

Kaplan, Robert D. *The Coming Anarchy: Shattering Dreams of the Post Cold War*. New York: Random House, 2000.

Kinzer, Stephen. *The Brothers: John Foster Dulles, Allen Dulles, and Their Secret World War*. New York: Times Books (Henry Holt and Company), 2013.

Kotkin, Stephen. "Russia's Perpetual Geopolitics." *Foreign Affairs* 95, no. 3 (May/June 2016): 2–9.

Krasner, Stephen D. *Defending the National Interest: Raw Materials Investments and U.S. Foreign Policy*. Princeton, NJ: Princeton University Press, 1978.

Laruelle, Marlene. "Russian Nationalism and Ukraine." *Current History* 113, no. 765 (October 2014): 272–77.

Lukyanov, Fyodor. "Putin's Foreign Policy: The Quest to Restore Russia's Rightful Place." *Foreign Affairs* 95, no. 3 (May/June 2016): 30–37.

McDougal, Walter A. *The Tragedy of U.S. Foreign Policy: How America's Civil Religion Betrayed the National Interest*. New Haven, CT: Yale University Press, 2016.

Nalbandov, Robert. *Not By Bread Alone: Russian Foreign Policy under Putin*. Washington, DC: Potomac, 2016.

Nuechterlein, Donald. *America Recommitted: United States National Interests in a Reconstructed World*. Lexington: University of Kentucky Press, 1991.

"Oil and National Gas Production in Russia (2013)." Washington, DC: U.S. Energy Information Administration, September 19, 2014.

"Russia Eyes Crimea Oil and Gas Reserves." *Oilprice* (online), March 17, 2014.

Scott, Peter Dale. *The American Deep State: Wall Street, Big Oil, and the Attack on U.S. Democracy*. War and Peace Library. Lanham, MD: Rowman & Littlefield, 2014.

Snow, Donald M. *National Security*. 6th ed. New York and London: Routledge, 2017.

———. *National Security for a New Era: Globalization and Geopolitics*. New York: Pearson Longman, 2004.

———. *Regional Cases in U.S. Foreign Policy*. 2nd ed. Lanham, MD: Rowman & Littlefield, 2018.

————. *The Shape of the Future: World Politics in a New Century*. 3rd ed. Armonk, NY: M. E. Sharpe, 1999.

Toal, Berard. *Near Abroad: Putin, the West, and the Contest over Ukraine and the Caucasus*. Oxford, UK: Oxford University Press, 2017.

Treisman, Daniel. "Why Putin Took Crimea: The Gambler in the Kremlin." *Foreign Affairs* 95, no. 3 (May/June 2016): 47–54.

Trenin, Dmitri. "The Revival of the Russian Military: How Moscow Reloaded." *Foreign Affairs* 95, no. 3 (May/June 2016): 23–29.

Tsygankov, Andrei. *Russia's Foreign Policy: Change and Continuity in National Identity*. 4th ed. Lanham, MD: Rowman & Littlefield, 2016.

Waltz, Kenneth. *Theory of International Politics*. Rev. ed. Long Grove, IL: Wavelend, 2010.

Wilson, Andrew. *Ukraine Crisis: What It Means for the West*. New Haven, CT: Yale University Press, 2014.

3

Power and Rising Power

The Case of China

Power is one of the most ubiquitous and arguably overused concepts in international relations and its study. Generally defined, it refers to the ability of the possessor to cause the object of that power to do something it would not otherwise do. In an anarchical international system where sovereignty is the overriding operational principle and national interests the most basic value, power in its various guises represents the effective means by which differences between states are resolved. The result is to make power a pivotal commodity and to elevate its measurement and changes in it to a central concern. Among countries, a major exercise involves trying to determine whether a state's relative power is increasing or declining. A country that is becoming more powerful is often referred to as a rising power. In the past third of a century or more, the status of rising power is most often associated with the People's Republic of China. The application section of this chapter will examine the bases of claims of Chinese ascendancy as a rising power and beyond, and look at barriers and challenges to Chinese maintenance or expansion of that status.

One of the constants of international relations is the need and the ability of states to influence one another—in other words, to exercise power—to achieve their goals. The reason for this need arises from the basic nature of the international system as described in chapters 1 and 2. The international system is a state of literal anarchy, where there is no governance or authority over the member states in their relations with one another. This condition is not accidental, but flows from the bedrock status of sovereignty as the system's primary value as the way to ensure the ability of states to pursue those conditions most important to them—their vital national interests. Those interests are sacrosanct because they represent conditions so important to the state that it will not willing to cede the jurisdiction to adjudicate them—including rendering judgments denying those interests—to an authority that might rule against them, leaving them the devil's choices of accepting the unacceptable or becoming an outlaw by defying those judgments.

This dynamic creates the need for some way to promote and protect the state from its adversaries and adversarial situations. Lacking authoritative structures to resolve differences, the dynamic for self-protection and self-promotion is ultimately the principle of *self-help*, the ability to achieve the conditions it perceives as necessary on its own. Since adversarial situations inevitably are characterized by incompatible, and sometimes irreconcilable, differences, any outcome will force one or both sides to accept something less than what it considers necessary (or certainly desirable) in resolving the difference. Solutions, in other words, require that one or another of the adversaries must accept an outcome that requires them to make concessions or engage in compromises that they do not want to perform. A textbook definition of power is "the ability to get someone to do something they would not otherwise do." That means the operative element of self-help is the ability to cause opponents to do what they would not otherwise do voluntarily. Given that the things that may be required include those considered vitally important by one or all parties, the supreme need for power is clear.

Power is an elusive concept. Traditional realist interpretations of international relations use the term in various ways to include its defined dynamic and as a means to categorize both states and the likely outcome of interchanges between sovereign states in power-related situations. Power may take on numerous forms, one of which is military force (historically, military power and power per se have sometimes been used virtually synonymously), and many students of international relations find this connection unfortunate and the recourse to military force to solve differences undesirable, even unacceptable. As a result, there has been a tendency in many approaches to the subject to downplay the role of power and to promote other approaches to problem solving that are not so openly power based. Power, nonetheless, remains at the base of much international interchange, even if it may represent "the dark side of the force." Among the most basic realist historical writers are Thucydides and E. H. Carr. Morgenthau's text is the post–World War II classic, and a few modern examples include Art and Waltz, Brodie, Fromkin, Schelling, and Waltz, a list certainly incomplete and arguably not representative of the richness and pervasiveness of the approach.

Power is not immutable either. The forms of power change across time due to differing circumstances. Traditional military power, for instance, has declined as a primary measure of national power because it is not effective in many international situations (see the discussion of asymmetrical warfare in chapter 5) and because those who possess it also have nuclear weapons, making any military confrontation among major powers potentially unacceptable nuclear war. At the same time, other sources of power such as economic capacity may rise as elements in power calculations, a factor associated with China in contemporary discussions.

Because power is ubiquitous, power reputation is also important in practical international interchanges. It is self-evident that it is instrumentally better to be more rather than less powerful when one is in a situation with another country where relative power can influence or dictate the outcome. Because of this, states are often categorized by their relative ability to apply power, from superpowers to minor powers. Moreover, states may move upward or downward in power status. Powers that are less influential than they once were are sometimes described as "declining" or "descending" powers; states whose status is on the incline, by contrast, are sometimes referred to as rising powers.

There is certainly nothing that is new about the rising state phenomenon. If one looks back a century to the eve of World War I, the major powers were the countries of the old European Balance of Power (Britain, France, Germany/

Prussia, Russia, and the Austro-Hungarian Empire), and the major rising power was the United States. Prodded by World War II, the traditional powers declined, and from the rubble, the United States and the Soviet Union rose to primary status, a position both occupied until the Soviet Union imploded in 1991. During most of this period, military power was the major criterion by which power was measured.

With the demise of the Soviet Union, the United States was for a time the unchallenged world superpower, and the bases of its dominance were both military and economic. No other state has arisen to provide a serious challenge to American military strength, and the absence of deep politico-military division in the system has reduced the relevance of military strength as the major instrument of power. Economic competition has become the playing field on which power competition occurs most frequently.

The United States entered this redefined basis of power competition with a sizable advantage. Immediately after World War II, the United States sat astride an international economic system in ruin from the war. The American economy accounted for close to 40 percent of world activity (measured as gross domestic product, or GDP), but that proportion fell as other areas (notably the European Union and Japan) recovered. Still, the United States remained the world's economic giant. Rising powers thus ascend in comparison to the American economic system. China is the first country to challenge American dominance on this measure of power.

Principle: Power and Rising Power

Power is a term used in so many ways that it can be misleading and confusing. Almost all human interactions, from individual interchanges to the relations between states, have some power element some of the time. When interests collide, one or both parties must accept less than the outcome they prefer, whether it is where to go on a date or the location of the boundary between two countries. Sometimes situations can be solved amicably and without power-based menace, but sometimes they cannot. The less intense the conflict that must be resolved by one or more of the parties giving in to the other, the more likely it is to be resolved short of the use of some form of overt force. International relations normally revolve around the clash of vital interests, making the resort to force or some other overt manifestation of power more likely and the relative power reputations of different states more salient to solving conflicts.

Role and Nature of Power

Whole volumes have been devoted to the explication of power, its uses, and its ramifications, the details, subtleties, and ramifications of which go beyond present purposes. For the present, the discussion of power will be elaborated around three concerns. The first of these is the nature of power in application, focusing on power's relational nature and the specificity of its application. This leads to the second and related concern with what are normally called the instruments of political power, dealing with the mechanics and instrumentalities for applying power in specific situations. The third concern is with relative typologies of states in power terms and how and why these change across time.

Nature of Power

The problem of dealing with power is specifying exactly what power is in application, so that one can somehow measure it and observe it in operation. A basic ambiguity that has plagued political scientists and others studying power is the distinction between power as a concrete, observable attribute that can be measured and watched in action, and power as a relationship between parties where their relative possession of effective power helps decide outcomes. From an analytic perspective, treating power as a concrete attribute is appealing, because it allows the observer to compare the relative "amount" of power two parties possess so that can one can predict how a power confrontation will turn out in advance (e.g., "the more powerful state will prevail") and to explain outcomes after the fact ("the more powerful state prevailed"). When power is viewed this way, the approach to studying power tends to be to find indicators or measures of power (e.g., the size of military forces) and to compare how these indicators affect power situations.

Unfortunately, this approach does not always prove satisfactory in explaining apparent power situations. If, for instance, the most powerful state prevails in military confrontations, the United States must surely have defeated North Vietnam in the 1960s and 1970s, but it clearly did not. Why not? At least part of the reason is that power interactions are relationships at heart. One succeeds in getting someone to do something they would otherwise prefer not to do because of intangible, non-measurable factors such as comparative will and importance. Power is a relationship in which power commodities may play a part, but the heart of power is its relational character. In addition, the application of power also tends to be situation-specific. The effectiveness of power is specific to specific actors and situations. It is not enough, for instance, to say that the United States is the most powerful country in the world as an indicator of American ability to have things its way. The United States may possess great military and economic capability (power as an attribute), but those measures are applicable in some situations and not in others. The United States has a large arsenal of nuclear weapons while Malawi has none. This comparison is, however, entirely irrelevant in determining the outcome of a power-based situation between the two countries. At the same time, China has the world's largest army. Does this provide China with power over the United States, to which it could not possibly transport that force? North Vietnam prevailed over the United States because the outcome was clearly more important to them (a psychological factor that effectively trumped U.S. military capability) than it was to the Americans. How can one measure that comparison?

Instruments of National Power

Despite the difficulty of measuring power in any precise way, power is clearly a basic datum on which the resolution of international disputes occurs, and this naturally leads political leaders to try to maximize the attributes connected to positive outcomes in their interactions with others. The policy tools that states accumulate to maximize their ability to exercise power over others are known as the *instruments of national power.* They are the physical attributes that states incorporate in their "arsenals" of ways by which they persuade others to accept their positions when those interests come into conflict with the interests of others. In terms already used, they generally refer to attributes the state hopes will be relevant in tipping power relationships in their favor in specific situations.

Conventional analyses (see *National Security,* Sixth Edition, for a more detailed discussion) divide the instruments into three categories: diplomatic (or political), military, and economic. Indicators of diplomatic power include the quality and persuasiveness of a country's diplomatic corps, the attractiveness of its political profile and positions on important issues, and even the standing and respect others have for a country's leaders. To some extent, diplomatic power is enhanced or diminished by the ability or inability of a country to deploy the other instruments in support of its diplomatic and political efforts. Economic power refers to the availability and willingness to use economic rewards and deprivations to gain compliance with a country's demands, and it has become a much more frequently invoked capability in an increasingly interdependent, globalized world economy, as discussed in chapters 8 and 9. The final instrument, military power, involves the threat or actual use of military force to help achieve a country's goals.

The instruments are matters of perspective and are of differing relevance in diverse situations. Diplomatic efforts are most effective when dealing with basically like-minded powers, and depend on factors as idiosyncratic as whether the leaders of countries agree philosophically with one another and even "like" one another. Economic threats normally have negative or positive economic impacts on the country issuing the threat as well as the country at which they are directed, and some threats, such as those associated with economic sanctions, are of questionable effectiveness in some situations. Military power must pass the test of applicability (e.g., does American conventional force work well in developing world conflicts, a problem discussed in chapter 5) and the willingness of regimes and populations to support and sustain military actions in different circumstances.

Many analysts argue that this list is incomplete, and the content of any instrument is subject to substantive change. Cybersecurity and warfare represent a case in point of an instrument of power that does not conveniently fall into one of the traditional trilogy of instruments, but protecting and being able to control and manipulate cyberspace is clearly a capability that states desire, as numerous hacking episodes reveal. Cybersecurity was not a concern a decade ago, but it clearly is now, and there will be additional sources of new concern in the future.

The concept of instruments of power is slippery and imprecise in many applications, but the underlying need for something like the inventory of instruments is not. In an anarchical system, power and politics are intertwined inextricably, since self-help is the ultimate method by which states realize or fail to attain their most vital interests. Having power and being recognized for its possession are thus extremely important commodities: possession of the instruments to demonstrate capability, and status so that it has leverage. For this reason, states desire to be considered as powerful as possible.

Power Terms

One of the ambiguities about the power concept is that it is also used as a qualified noun to rank states against one another, and states seek to be ranked as high in the rankings as possible. Since the Cold War, the top ranking belongs to states that can be considered *superpowers*. The designation is a Cold War artifact and was invented originally to denote countries with large arsenals of nuclear weapons. Until 1991, the United States and the Soviet Union were the acknowledged superpowers, thus possessing power capabilities superior to those of other states. The collapse of the Soviet Union left the United States as the sole superpower, but the collapse of the Cold War took some of the prestige from nuclear possession and broadened the concept to include nonmilitary attributes, including economic power. Adding that criterion has elevated China to near-superpower status.

The *major powers* stand beneath the superpowers. They are generally states that are leaders in their region (Iran, for instance) and have interests beyond the geographical region in which they are located (e.g., Japan). Many are countries that were considered *great powers* before World War II (the major European powers, for instance). Below these countries are several overlapping designations such as *medium powers* and *minor* or *lesser powers*. Status as a power is also considered in terms of whether a state's relative power is on the decline or ascendancy. *Declining powers* are those countries whose status is on the wane, which is clearly an undesirable perception with which to be saddled, whereas being a *rising power* is clearly a desirable trait the attainment of which can become a major determinant of national politics. North Korea is a prime example of this aspiration taken to extremes.

Rising Powers

Comparative national power varies across time. One of the most certain things one can say about the dominant powers of any period of history is that eventually their dominance will be eclipsed by the emergence of some different country or countries. The contemporary situation is no exception. Although the United States has been *a* dominant power since World War II and *the* dominant power since the end of the Cold War, this observation is undoubtedly true for the United States as well. Others will rise, and the United States will, at least relatively, decline.

What does it mean to be a "rising power"? In the most general sense, a rising power refers to a country that, because of increased military, economic, or other power, is playing or has the potential to play an increasingly prominent role in the international system. The United States was such a rising power in the late nineteenth and early twentieth centuries, as was the Soviet Union during the middle of the twentieth century. Countries such as China and India are candidates for this status today.

The impact of rising powers is important. At the level of the international system, rising powers change the relative power balance between the major powers, with ripple effects throughout the system, often in ways that are controversial and difficult to predict. Will, for instance, a rising China eventually challenge American international predominance and lead to a transformation from an essentially unipolar to a bipolar or multipolar balance? Would such a restructuring be stabilizing or destabilizing? Is such a rise inevitable, and can the trajectory of ascent be affected?

The degree and extent to which rising powers challenge the given order depends to a great degree on the areas in which the rising powers seek to influence the existing order and establish their own places. Traditionally, for instance, world power comparisons have largely been at least implicitly military in content. "Power" and "military power" were used nearly synonymously, and the most certain way for a rising power to assert a challenge to the existing order was by building and flexing its military muscle.

Power status is not unidimensional in a globalized world. Economic capability has increasingly become a benchmark of global importance, and it is the primary claim China and several other countries have on rising power status. China, of course, is also a military power whose military might requires some concern, but Chinese history does not suggest it will be an outward-looking force in military terms beyond East Asia. As a power with global aspirations, the primary claim of China is currently concentrated in the economic realm.

The impact of rising states creates foreign policy questions for countries affected by the rising power. The basic question is whether the impact will help or hinder the realization of interests of the affected power. Will the rising power be a looming threat to those interests or a global partner assisting in their accomplishment? Or will it be both? These changes are never entirely clear in advance, leading to speculation and disagreement. Europe worried about the impact of an industrially gigantic United States, and the United States worried about the impact of a militarily powerful Soviet Union. The United States ended up a strategic partner of Europe, and the Soviets emerged primarily as a threat. Where do the current aspirants fit?

The contemporary period produces the same questions for at least two reasons. One is that judgments about rising states are based mostly upon economic projections, and these are inherently difficult and uncertain. As Sharma illustrates regarding current trends, "forecasts typically took the developing world's high growth rates from the middle of the last decade and extended them straight into the future. Later returns are throwing cold water on the extravagant projections." Despite what some economists would assert, economic prediction is much more art and much less science than its enthusiasts are prone to admit.

The second source of uncertainty is that the current crop of rising powers is drawn from the vast, heterogeneous developing world. There are multiple states in the developing world that can and do make a case for their emergence as more important powers. Many of these states are either of recent vintage, the results of European colonies breaking up, or are states that have no recent history in the global spotlight. As a result, how they will handle increased affluence internally and how they will project expanded status on the world stage is uncertain.

There are several countries in the contemporary system that may be thought of as rising powers. China is the most prominent of these for at least two reasons. One is the longevity of its conscious ascent, which can be dated to 1979 and the institution of the "Four Modernizations" reforms of the Chinese economy discussed in the next section. This initiative predates the efforts of other pretenders. The other reason is the sheer size and resulting potential of China. Of all the rising powers, China's power has the best chance to increase enough to achieve superpower status alongside the United States.

Application: The Case of China

The fact that China is considered a rising power is both ironic and illustrative of the observation that powers rise and fall in their relative global power standings. The irony, of course, arises because China was the first major world civilization. Hidden by self-isolation imposed because it viewed other civilizations as inferior and symbolized by the Great Wall, it was the first dominant power for literally millennia. It is illustrative because China's aloofness caused its civilization to stagnate and decline, to the point that by the nineteenth century it was a diminished power that could not sustain its sovereignty. It has only begun to rebound since 1979 to begin the process of reasserting something like its historical role. China was dominant, declined, and has risen again.

China's return to the world's center stage has been the most spectacular of any contemporary rising power. The world's oldest continuous civilization began to reemerge as a power after the country was taken over by the Communist Party in 1949, but its meteoric ascent to a world economic—and potentially military—giant began in the late 1970s. Since then, China has become the greatest challenger to American economic primacy, and many economic predictions suggest that China will pass the United States on important measures in the next decade or so. At the same time, China has some economic and other problems that may cloud the rosiest projections.

China has reached the global forefront against the backdrop of a difficult past. Forced out of its aloofness against its will, China endured a "century of humiliation" during the nineteenth and early twentieth centuries that reduced it to a semi-colony. The situation resulted from the loss of creativity; corruption and resistance to reform within the imperial court; the obsolescence of its emperor-based political system relying on a corps of bureaucrats chosen for their mastery of Confucian classics rather than their command of modern ideas; and the numerous unequal treaties imposed on it by foreign powers after its defeat in the Opium War with Great Britain in the 1840s. Westerners roamed throughout China. Merchants, adventurers, diplomats, and missionaries all enjoyed special privileges, placing them beyond Chinese authority, a situation that was humiliating to all Chinese.

Layered atop all of China's other discontents was a twentieth-century split between two centers of political and military power, each determined to unify, govern, and strengthen China. The United States generally supported the Kuomintang—or Nationalist—forces led by Chiang Kai-shek. In the 1920s, an initially small upstart group of communists led by Mao Zedong articulated its own vision to overthrow China's antiquated social order and restore unity to the country.

As the two forces battled for power, China endured yet another devastating blow, this time from Japan's exceptionally brutal aggression, first in its invasion of Manchuria in 1931 and then throughout its bloody drive through China proper from 1937 to 1945. The defeat of Japanese forces by the United States in 1945 renewed the violent conclusion of the internal battle to control China. By the autumn of 1949, China's communists emerged victorious and drove Chiang's forces to the island refuge of Taiwan. China was finally unified under a strong central authority, and foreign intervention in its internal affairs would no longer be tolerated. Beyond unification and the reclamation of China's sovereignty, it was Mao's abiding passion to create within China a radical, egalitarian society. To accomplish this goal, China remained largely outside the international community, and terribly repressive within, with its people mired in poverty throughout his rule from 1949 to 1976, when Mao died.

Mao's death created a scramble for power among China's ruling elites. Within a year, Deng Xiaoping had effectively consolidated governing authority within his own hands. After being purged three times during Mao's reign and standing less than five feet tall, Deng seemed a physically and politically unlikely ruler of the world's most populous state. Deng soon implemented his famous "Four Modernizations" campaign, a bold series of reforms designed to advance China beyond the revolutionary dogma of Maoism and to create instead a stronger, more modern country by loosening the reins of state authority; more fully embracing economic globalization in search of foreign markets, technology, and investment; and accepting income differentials in a society that had so recently been singularly animated by radical egalitarianism. Under Deng, China truly began to rise. It has not stopped yet.

Modern China in Context

Because of its physical and population size, China cannot avoid being a major power even if wants to do so. China's long self-imposed isolation from the world, premised on the belief that it was so much further advanced than any other society that it had nothing to learn from others and that contact could only pollute Chinese civilization, proved the folly of trying; isolation bred stagnation that allowed the rest of the world to pass it by in the nineteenth century. It is not a mistake the Chinese are likely to make again.

By any measure, China is bound to be a consequential power. In purely geographic terms, it is the fourth-largest country in the world with an area slightly smaller than that of the United States. It physically dominates East Asia and has land borders with fourteen other countries in the Eurasian land mass from Afghanistan in the west to North Korea and Russia in the east and touching on Southeast Asia and the Asia subcontinent, including the Himalayan Mountains.

This sweep means that it has borders with the other major Asian powers, notably India and Russia (including several former Soviet Republics), with which it has had occasional conflicts historically.

China's land mass has not been entirely beneficial for continuing Chinese growth and prosperity. The country is not well blessed with natural resources, especially in the energy area. China possesses the world's largest untapped reserves of shale oil and gas—the energy force that is underlying current American energy resurgence—but it is in remote parts of the country that are difficult to access or to transport the resources they might try to access. Moreover, the Chinese lack the hydraulic fracturing ("fracking") technology to mine these reserves, and it is not clear what country or countries will provide them with the help they would need (see Snow, *The Middle East, Oil, and the U.S. National Security Policy* for a discussion). China also lacks significant sizable traditional petroleum reserves. As a result, it is very active in Middle East energy politics and in provocative initiatives such as the construction of artificial islands in the South China Sea. China's only sizable energy resource is highly polluting coal, which both complicates its dealing with North Korea and makes Chinese participation in the Paris Climate Agreement so important (see chapter 12).

That territory is not all equally important to the Chinese. Most of the Chinese population lives in the eastern part of the country, which is also the most economically developed area of China. It is also the part of China that is the traditional home of the Han Chinese, who make up roughly 92 percent of the population. The other 8 percent of the population lives mostly in the less populated and less developed western part of the country, a drier and more severe landscape of which the Gobi Desert is a symbol. The non-Han minorities include Kazakhs, Koreans, Mongols, Tibetans, and Uighurs. The members of these groups generally do not consider themselves Chinese, some worship different religions (Buddhist Tibetans and Muslim Uighurs, for instance), and there are even separatist movements in parts of western China, of which the Tibetan movement symbolized by the Dalai Lama is the most famous. In terms of land area, these western lands constitute upwards of half the physical territory of China. They are also the part of the country most ignored by the regime, which adds to discontent.

The population of China is the largest in the world, although it is projected to lose that distinction in the upcoming years. According to the *CIA World Factbook*, the 2016 population of the country was 1.373 billion, slightly more than 100 million greater than India. Largely due to the draconian "one child" policy of the regime that began in the 1980s (which made it a punishable crime for couples to have more than one offspring), that population has leveled off. The population growth rate (PGR) for China is 0.45 percent, 164th in the world, compared to a PGR of 1.25 percent for India, 94th in the world. That population is also aging as life expectancy has extended to 73.5 years. These figures are consequential because, as argued later in the chapter, they are already having negative impacts on the size and nature of the labor force, trends that are certain to increase and that thus threaten to "rain on the parade" of the Chinese economic miracle of the last third of a century.

During the first quarter century after the triumph of the communist revolution, the country was so absorbed with its Maoist social experiment that it did not take full advantage of the considerable physical and demographic endowment that it had and has since exploited. Instead, China sought to reassert itself on the world stage as a regional military power, developing a huge People's Liberation Army (PLA) that it could not project from its soil and a large enough nuclear arsenal to join the circle of nuclear powers. It expelled the Americans and South Koreans from its border with North Korea (as discussed below) and fought turf-establishing skirmishes with India and the Soviet Union in the 1950s. At one point, Mao opined that China's size and population meant it was the only country that could survive a nuclear war—an observation that sent palpitations throughout the Western world.

That changed in the 1970s. Through secret channels facilitated by Pakistan, the Nixon administration opened secret talks with the Chinese government that culminated in Nixon's visit to China in 1972 and in the extension of full recognition to the PRC by President Carter in 1979. Mao died in 1976, succeeded by Deng Xiaoping. Deng had decidedly different ideas about how to guide the country to an ascending trajectory among world powers.

The Structural Impact: The Four Modernizations

The diminutive Deng believed that China's future lay not in military belligerency, but instead in economic reform and the transformation of the ruins of backwardness the communists inherited from the imperial past into the creation of an economically powerful state that could compete with the rest of the world on its own grounds. The utopian social and economic reforms of the Maoist era had proven a disaster for China, and Deng moved swiftly to replace the "great leap forward" by which Mao sought to create a communist "paradise" with an economic system that borrowed heavily from the capitalist West but retained some of the traditional trappings of the communist PRC.

The result was the Four Modernizations—agriculture, science and technology, industry, and military—in the country. It began in the countryside in the eastern part of the country, home to three-fourths of all Chinese. Gradually, socialist-style communal farming was phased out, and peasants could lease land individually from the state for private purposes such as growing and selling food. Without quite admitting it, Deng's regime injected market—that is, *capitalist*—incentives by allowing peasants whose production surpassed their obligatory quotas to the state at fixed prices to sell any surplus that they could produce for as much money as they could get for it. It set a communist world precedent that other countries, notably Cuba, have emulated. The older, Maoist norm of imposed egalitarianism was shelved quietly in the process. What the regime euphemistically called "Socialism with Chinese Characteristics" took its place. With the passage of time, this slogan became a way to describe capitalism with state supervision and some state participation, but with less direct central control. Gradually, the limited market system begun in the countryside spread to the cities. Individuals could open restaurants, shops, and factories. Workers could be hired and fired, something that had been utterly unthinkable under Mao's "people's" regime. The wheels of a more market-driven economy were thus set into motion.

The second and third modernizations—industry plus science and technology—inherently required China's leaders to turn outward to the most advanced industrial countries for investment capital, markets for Chinese goods, scientific know-how, and the most modern production technology and management skills. Four Special Economic Zones (SEZs) were established in southeastern China in which foreign corporations were encouraged to form joint ventures with Chinese partners and thus transfer their leading-edge technological, manufacturing process, and managerial expertise to initially quite limited enclaves of capitalist experimentation. Military modernization, the fourth element, remained under the strict control of the Chinese Communist Party and the Chinese military.

China's economic results have been the most dramatic. Riding a boom powered by foreign capital inflows and an aggressive export strategy, China's economy grew at an average annual rate of around 10 percent from the 1980s into the 2000s. Not all Chinese specialists accept these astounding government-promulgated growth statistics at face value, but there is no denying that China's economy grew dramatically after the Four Modernizations were adopted. In critical consumer sectors such as clothing, shoes, toys, and other low-technology products, China dominates world markets. As dramatic evidence of this rise, China became the world's leading producer of manufactured goods in 2008 with 17 percent of world production compared to 16 percent for the United States. The CIA *Factbook* reports the Chinese GDP for 2016 at 21.27 trillion, the largest in the world. China is the second-largest exporter in the world (after the EU) and third-largest importer (the United States is the third-largest exporter and second-largest importer). The Chinese growth rate is now down to 6.6 percent, sixteenth in the world but still formidable, given the base from which the percentage is calculated.

China's dramatic economic ascent is conditioned by a litany of domestic woes that, taken together, raise some concern and potential unrest. Its internal preoccupations include a mounting political crisis of regime legitimacy in what Minxin Pei describes as the "Chinese neo-Leninist state," severe environmental degradation, immense population pressures, official corruption, a growing gap in urban versus rural incomes, high unemployment, a steady loss of arable land, a diminished social safety net for the poor and displaced, scarcity of resources such as water and petroleum, and secessionist movements in Tibet and in the western-most province of Zinjiang. Gilboy and Read concur, stating that "Beijing faces serious challenges in maintaining sustainable growth and social stability, eliminating corruption, and improving government effectiveness in a one-party system."

China's rise as an economic power is thus paradoxical. China has made great strides as an industrial power, but it has done so within the confines of a political and social system that places serious constraints on the ability of China to expand, especially into a full-fledged world power, which is clearly its desire.

Thus, individually and collectively, what do these trends and problems mean, and how do they affect an assessment of China as a rising power?

Assessing China's Rise

Does China's economic and technological rise pose a threat to the world power balance? The sheer potential size of an economy energized by one-fifth of humankind raises concern: if China were to become competitive structurally with the world's most advanced economies, would that size not pose a danger of simply overwhelming the global economy and establishing itself as the "800-pound gorilla" that everyone else would have to treat with care and deference?

Opinions vary on this subject, based on differing assessments of the nature of the Chinese economy and the impact on the Chinese political system. Analysts critical of the notion that China poses a threat often point to factors in Chinese development that limit the threats China could pose. In a 2003 *Foreign Affairs* article, for instance, David Hale and Lyric Hughes Hale identified three of what they called the "dragon's ailments." The first is demographic and points to the extremely uneven character of Chinese development. There are, they point out, "great disparities between the integrated, largely urban coastal areas in the eastern part of the country and the fragmented, rural economies in the western part." In addition, there is a substantial unemployment problem, especially in western China, that results in considerable migration to the industrialized areas. China also faces the need "to find a way to support its rapidly aging population," a dilemma shared by many industrialized countries and that is becoming worse as Chinese live longer, retire, and place increasing demands on a retirement system questionably adequate for the challenge. The aging population also means a reduced workforce (particularly of young workers willing to toil for very low wages). Reports from 2016 suggest a loss of upwards of five million in the workforce, and it is not clear how they can be replaced given the demographic consequences of the one-child policy. One possibility is to import non-Han from the west or even additional North Koreans to fill jobs, but this solution is imperfect: the Chinese would be moving non-ethnic Chinese potential dissidents from the west, and there is enough simple racism in the country to make the influx of North Koreans (who are also racist) unappealing to the Han. The Chinese did, after all, build the Great Wall to keep the barbarians out, with barbarians basically defined as anyone who was not Han.

That is not all. China also has a politico-economic problem that raises serious questions about the future. These arise from a de facto bargain between the government/Communist Party (effectively the same thing) and the people. The bargain, simply stated, was that the party guaranteed prosperity and civil liberties to those in the SEZs if the people did not challenge the power and authority of the party. This was a generally good bargain for the majority, but it did not apply to non-Han Westerners, and exposure to the West by Chinese students and others going abroad has raised questions as well. How long the bargain will remain acceptable is uncertain.

The natural resource crisis is also part of the mix. A growing economy has an increasingly voracious appetite for energy, and most of the energy generated by China comes from the burning of highly polluting coal; this in turn makes the air pollution problem in the country severe and growing worse. China is highly dependent on overseas supplies of conventional petroleum and is the world's largest air polluter. It has pledged itself wholeheartedly to the Paris Climate Agreement, but with American withdrawal, the nature of its participation is problematical.

The other natural resource problem is water (discussed in chapter 13). China is a water-deficient country, and the problem is getting worse. The problem is greatest in the northern part of the country, where a large part of Chinese heavy industry is located. Water tables are dangerously low in many areas, and northern water problems are exacerbated by pollution of existing supplies, desertification partially caused by overuse, and the loss of productive agricultural land as the water table falls. About 20 percent of Chinese agricultural land has fallen out of use for lack of water since 1949. It is a further cautionary note that shale oil and natural gas exploitation involves the highly polluting use of extraordinarily large amounts of water.

All of these kinds of factors create a more mixed message about the Chinese economic challenge than is sometimes apocalyptically portrayed. China's economy has clearly expanded to the point of rivaling the economies of the world's major powers in sheer size, and this impact is growing. There are, however, limits to China's current growth. Most of that growth has resulted from manufacturing consumer goods that require little scientific contribution from China, and much of it is based on artificially controlled low labor costs used to achieve comparative advantage. The result has been large surpluses from foreign sales that allow further expansion, but it does not add to the vibrancy of China's innovative sector and thus its potential for future technologically based growth, which is critical for long-term economic health. At the same time, the huge Chinese labor pool will eventually have to be addressed in terms of things such as human services, and this will produce a significant burden, as suggested earlier.

How China will continue to evolve economically remains the major point of contention. Will China become a "normal" state whose economy and political system gradually become more and more like those of the rest of the world? Or will China use its growing muscle to challenge the current order? The answers are, of course, speculative. Positively, China has taken a place at the G-20 forum of world economic powers. There are, however, barriers to the continuation of the trends of the recent past. Sharma cites them as follows: "The even bigger story in the global economy . . . will be the three to four percent slowdown in China, which is already underway." He asserts that "China's population is simply too big and aging too quickly for its economy to continue to grow as rapidly as it has."

There is yet another leavening dimension, foreign policy. For China to rise to great power status, it must become a world political as well as economic power. To date, most of its noneconomic initiatives have been within the region, and their record achievement has been spotty. The two most obvious examples are its inability to date to rein in the bellicose and increasingly aggressive stance of the Democratic People's Republic of Korea (DPRK, or North Korea, as discussed in chapter 6) and its own controversial actions in the South China Sea.

The Chinese problem regarding the DPRK is admittedly difficult. China is essentially the only country with which the North Koreans have notable economic or political relations. The two countries, after all, border on one another and share at least a nominal continuing fealty to communism. China is the DPRK's major trading partner (principally coal), and North Korean temporary workers regularly cross the Yalu River frontier as low-paid workers in China, one of the DPRK's few sources of foreign exchange. Moreover, the Chinese did save the DPRK from absorption into South Korea by intervening in the Korean War.

North Korea and its mercurial leader Kim Jong Un are an embarrassment to the Chinese, who are under American and world pressure to rein him and especially his nuclear weapons program in. The Chinese have been reluctant to act decisively for fear that doing so would cause the DPRK regime to collapse. The likely consequence would be reunification of the Korean peninsula under South Korean rule, a prospect the Chinese oppose on two grounds. The first is that it would place a potentially adversarial regime on its borders, the avoidance of which is a cardinal Chinese foreign policy interest. The second is that it would likely create a massive flight of North Korean communists into China, a prospect the Chinese oppose on ethnic grounds.

The other problem is the South China Sea. It is consequential for two main reasons. First, it is a major segment of trade routes from East Asia to the Asian subcontinent and Middle East oil reserves. Control of the South China Sea and the Straits of Malacca strengthen Chinese claims on these routes and their bounty. The other source of importance is that there are very large oil reserves under the seabed, to which all the littoral states—including China—lay claim. Since China is currently the world's third largest importer of petroleum at 5.4 million barrels a day, the South China Sea is clearly important to them.

China's method of dealing with the problem has created enormous opposition in East Asia. The Chinese have claimed the entire sea as part of its territorial waters, a claim that no one else accepts. To bolster its physical presence, it has created a series of artificial island atolls in the sea and fortified them with a naval presence. The United States and other regional powers have denied the legitimacy of these efforts and have engaged in naval maneuvers and flights over Chinese facilities in the region.

The political side of Chinese efforts to move up the power "ladder" has been considerably less successful than have their economic achievements. There is little question that China is now a major economic power, even an economic "superpower" because of its position in the global economy. Its claim to an equivalent political and military status is less clear. Politically, it has yet to demonstrate its geopolitical clout within its region, as the ongoing impasse over the DPRK clearly demonstrates. Likewise, China has been building a large and impressive military machine, but it is not clear whether it can be projected very far from Chinese territory.

Conclusion

Power is and always has been an important—arguably the *most* determining—factor in the relations among political units. This importance has been chronicled since Thucydides wrote his epic *The History of the Peloponnesian Wars* between Athens and Sparta between 413 and 411 BC and has persisted since the calculations of political figures and as an organizational device for scholars trying to understand the nature and dynamics of international behavior. It is a controversial concept because it is often conflated with a preference for using military force to resolve differences. Since the essence of power is getting an adversary to do what it would rather not do, power will always have its detractors.

In an anarchical international system where self-help measured by the ability to apply power effectively is necessary for national success, power is also a characteristic and ability much valued and even envied. Among the most relevant aspects of power is whether a state's relative possession of power is increasing or declining—whether a state is rising or falling.

The exact nature and impact of rising powers is always somewhat difficult to project. It is always tempting to state the challenge posed by a rising state in dramatic, even apocalyptical terms, but these descriptions are likely to overshoot the mark. Menon argues that this is likely to be the case today especially regarding the relative position of the world's most powerful country, the United States. As he puts it, "those who expect a quick emergence of coequal partners to the United States are mistaken in their view. But so are those who see a future of unchallenged, open-ended American dominance."

To some extent, the existing powers generally have some role in the emergence of new challengers to their dominance, even if that contribution is unintentional. Capital from British banks in the nineteenth century, for instance, was critical in American expansion westward and the emergence of the United States as a rising global power in the twentieth century, and there is little evidence that the British either realized or nurtured that outcome consciously. As Menon further explains, the same is true today. "Dominant powers—by providing security, exporting capital, selling goods and services, and creating new technologies—unwittingly enable the rise of new centers of strength. They also stir envy and the desire to emulate. The United States has done all these things."

The question that remains is what does the rise of new powers mean for the United States and for the rest of the world? Certainly, their evolution will have a continuing impact on the structure and operation of the global economy, as Chinese growth since 1979 demonstrates. The question is how long and how far China can sustain its rise.

China is unquestionably a rising power, and it has already ascended to a position of world economic and possible military leadership. The consequences of this ascent, however, remain uncertain and subject to varying, even diametrically opposite, interpretations. No one can reliably predict the future and know how it will be: will China increasingly be a looming threat, a global partner, or some of each. No one knows for sure.

The Chinese case may or may not prove to be exemplary for other countries with rising state aspirations. China began its ascent with considerable advantages over others seeking to rise. No other aspirants can match China's sheer size, but that advantage is hedged by the fact that China also has problems, such as energy deficiencies and water availability and quality, that its size amplifies. The other major global pretenders to rising state status include a designation that includes India—the so-called BRIC states (Brazil, Russia, India, and China). Like China, they are all large countries with big potentials. How large their accompanying problems will prove to be will go a long way to determine the extent and trajectory of their rise.

Rising states are a natural and inevitable feature of global development. States decline in their relative power and importance within the international system, and other states arise to supplant them. The BRIC countries are the latest aspirants to rising power status, and they may continue their ascent—current trends and the sheer size of each country certainly point in that direction. At the same time, there are other aspiring states in the wings ready to mount their own challenges and become rising states themselves. In an anarchic world, that competition remains critical to national success.

Study/Discussion Questions

1. What is power? Why is it so important in a world of sovereign states? How does the concept fit into the conduct and study of international relations? Discuss the use of the term to compare the effectiveness of states in the international system.

2. What are the instruments of power? Describe each, including how they contribute to a country's effectiveness as an international actor. How does the concept of instruments of power relate to the comparative power rankings that states construct to describe one another? What are these rankings? Elaborate.

3. What is a rising power? What kinds of impact can they have on the operation of the international system? Why is the distinction important in the conduct of international relations, especially in the ability of states in influence one another? How does the status change?

4. Why is China's position as a rising power ironic? How does it show the relative nature of the rising state phenomenon? Explain, using examples from China's past.

5. What twentieth-century events set the stage for China's subsequent rise? Trace the discussion from the beginning of the century to 1979. Why was that year so critical?

6. What are the principal and human factors that empower and limit China's rise? Discuss, including in your answer the roles of energy, water resources, and demographics of the Chinese population.

7. What are the Four Modernizations? How has their adoption provided the basis for China's economic rise? What are the SEZs and why are they important to understanding both China's phenomenal economic expansion and the limits on it?

8. Is China's rise to great power/superpower status inexorable? What economic and foreign policy factors are parts of an assessment of that inevitability? Discuss.

Bibliography

Art, Robert A., and Kenneth N. Waltz, eds. *The Uses of Force: Military Power and International Politics.* 7th ed. Lanham, MD: Rowman & Littlefield, 2009.

Brodie, Bernard. *War and Politics.* New York: Macmillan, 1973.

Brown, Kerry. *CEO China: The Rise of Xi Jinping.* London: I. B. Tauris, 2016.

Bush, Richard C., and Michael O'Hanlon. *A War like No Other: The Truth About China's Challenge to America.* New York: Wiley, 2007.

Carr, E. H. *The Twenty Years' Crisis, 1919–1939.* London: Macmillan, 1939.

Chen, Gregory T. "China's Bold Economic Statecraft." *Current History* 114, no. 773 (September 2015): 217–23.

Christensen, Thomas J. *The China Challenge: Shaping the Choices of a Rising Power.* New York: Norton, 2016.

Cumings, Bruce. "Chinese Bullying No Match for US Pacific Power." *Current History* 113, no. 764 (September 2014): 245–51.

Dickerson, Bruce J., Bruce Gilley, and Dali L. Yang. "The Future of China's One-Party State." *Current History* 107, no. 701 (September 2007): 243–51.

Economy, Elizabeth, and Michael Levi. *By All Means Necessary: How China's Resource Quest Is Changing the World.* New York: Oxford University Press, 2014.

Fravel, M. Taylor. "China's Search for Military Power." *Washington Quarterly* 31, no. 3 (Summer 2008): 125–41.

French, Howard W. "China's Twilight Years: As Immigrants Replenish America, China's Population Is Shrinking and Aging." *Atlantic* 317, no. 5 (June 2016): 15–17.

Fromkin, David. *The Independence of Nations.* New York: Praeger Special Studies, 1981.

Garver, John W. *The History of the Foreign Relations of the People's Republic of China.* Oxford, UK: Oxford University Press, 2016.

Gifford, Rob. *China Road: A Journey into the Future of a Rising Power.* New York: Random House, 2007.

Gilboy, George J., and Benjamin J. Read. "Political and Social Reforms in China: Alive and Walking." *Washington Quarterly* 31, no. 3 (Summer 2008): 143–64.

Gill, Bates. *Rising Star: China's New Security Diplomacy.* Washington, DC: Brookings Institution Press, 2007.

Goldstein, Lyle G. *Meeting China Halfway: How to Defuse the Emerging US-China Rivalry.* Washington, DC: Georgetown University Press, 2015.

Hachigian, Nina, ed. *Debating China: The US-China Relationship in Ten Conversations.* New York: Oxford University Press, 2014.

Hale, David, and Lyric Hughes Hale. "China Takes Off." *Foreign Affairs* 82, no. 6 (November/December 2003): 36–53.

Klare, Michael. *Rising Powers, Shrinking Planet: The New Geopolitics of Energy.* New York: Metropolitan, 2008.

Kroeber, Arthur P. *China's Economy: What Everyone Needs to Know.* Oxford, UK: Oxford University Press, 2016.

Lanteigne, Marc. *Chinese Foreign Policy: An Introduction.* 3rd ed. New York: Routledge, 2015.

Lapton, David M. "The Faces of Chinese Power." *Foreign Affairs* 86, no. 1 (January/February 2007): 115–27.

Legro, Jeffrey W. "What China Will Want: The Future Implications of a Rising Power." *Perspectives on Politics* 5, no. 3 (September 2007): 515–33.

Mahbubani, Kishore. "Understanding China." *Foreign Affairs* 84, no. 5 (September/October 2005): 49–60.

Menon, Rajan. "Pax Americana and the Rising Powers." *Current History* 108, no. 721 (November 2009): 253–60.

Miller, Ken. "Coping with China's Financial Power: Beijing's Financial Foreign Policy." *Foreign Affairs* 89, no. 4 (July/August 2010): 96–109.

Morgenthau, Hans. *Politics among Nations.* 7th ed. Revised by Kenneth W. Thompson and W. David Clinton. New York: McGraw-Hill Education, 2005.

Paulson, Henry M. Jr. *Dealing with China: An Insider Unmasks the New Economic Superpower.* New York: Twelve Books, 2015.

Pei, Minxin. "The Dark Side of China's Rise." *Foreign Policy*, March/April 2006, 32–40.

Schelling, Thomas C. *Arms and Influence.* New Haven, CT: Yale University Press, 1966.

Shambaugh, David. *China's Future.* New York: Polity, 2016.

Sharma, Ruchir. "Broken BRICs." *Foreign Affairs* 91, no. 6 (November/December 2012): 2–7.

Snow, Donald M. *The Middle East, Oil, and the U.S. National Security Policy.* Lanham, MD: Rowman & Littlefield, 2016.

———. *National Security.* 6th ed. New York and London: Routledge, 2017.

———. *Regional Cases in U.S. Foreign Policy.* 2nd ed. Lanham, MD: Rowman & Littlefield, 2018.

Sutter, Robert. *Chinese Foreign Relations: Power and Policy Since the Cold War.* Lanham, MD: Rowman & Littlefield, 2016.

Thucydides. *The History of the Peloponnesian Wars.* New York: Penguin, 1954.

Tuttle, Gary. "China's Race Problem: How Beijing Suppresses Minorities." *Foreign Affairs* 94, no. 3 (May/June 2015): 39–47.

Waltz, Kenneth N. *Man, the State, and War: A Theoretical Analysis.* New York: Columbia University Press, 1959.

Wolf, Martin. "Why Is China Growing So Slowly?" *Foreign Policy*, January/February 2005, 49–52.

4

Territorial Disputes

This Land (Palestine and Kurdistan) Is *Whose* Land?

The discussion of sovereignty and national interest suggests an orderliness in international relations that is not always present in the real world. Numerous sources of international differences make world politics disorderly, conflicting, and occasionally violent. A major category of those imperfections arises over the question of rightful territorial possession both within and between states. States are the major actors in the international order, but the political map of the world does not always reflect the territorial jurisdictions that all people and groups feel are right. The result is disagreement about that map that can be both felt very deeply and the cause of considerable division and disagreement. Two major manifestations of the disagreement about territorial designations dominate the contemporary problem. One occurs when state boundaries arbitrarily divide members of a nationally defined state and where it is in the national interests of the states in which the group lives to enforce those boundaries. This is the situation where state boundaries divide a national group from exercising self-determination. The other exists when a group with national aspirations is housed within a disputed territory where those who exercise sovereignty preclude that national group from forming a state they view as representing their legitimate aspirations. Although the dynamics in the two situations are different, the effect in both is to create stateless nations where the aspiration to self-determination is denied.

The instances of these situations are not arithmetically great, but they represent a dynamic that often roils what might be more tranquil circumstances otherwise. The geographic area where they are most prevalent, predictably enough given its general instability, is the Middle East, and the two examples explored as applications both come from that region. Each is a classic case in its own way.

One example is the Israeli-Palestinian situation. It is fundamentally a question of which group—Israelis or Palestinians—has a superior sovereign claim over the West Bank of the Jordan River. Israel has occupied this space since 1967 and has established Israeli settlements in many parts of the region, an arguable de facto claim of sovereign authority. The Palestinian Arab population, many of whom were displaced during the establishment of the Israeli state, claims the territory as the basis of the Palestinian state. The other example is the Kurds. They are a distinct and ancient ethno/nationalist group that inhabits parts of four Middle Eastern states: Turkey, Iraq, Iran, and Syria. They form a majority in each of the areas where they live, but are in a minority in all four of the countries where those areas are located. Kurdish nationalism is very high, and there is virtually unanimous sentiment to carve a state of Kurdistan from the Kurdish regions of each country. They voted for independence from Iraq on October 2, 2017, an act that Iran and Turkey condemned. For differing reasons, each of those host states oppose Kurdish independence, and the result is that the Kurds are a classic stateless nation (a national group that lacks a state).

Principle: Territorial Disputes

An idealized vision of the international order begins from the premises of a series of sovereign states that are in essential harmony internally and with one another. In such a situation, the sovereign states would interact with one another in relative comity, with the only differences arising over the collision of national interests. This condition arguably describes the earliest years of the Westphalian system, when there were relatively few states, those states were similar (mostly absolute monarchies), and the rest of the world was struggling, in one way or another, with the consequences of the emergence of the state system. This tranquility gradually declined as the contours of the state system evolved, including the emergence of disputes about the size, shape, and boundaries of states and how they could or should govern themselves.

The effect of these differences, most prominently demonstrated since World War II, are in the form of territorial disputes—situations where multiple population groups claim rightful sovereign authority over the same territory. In the worst cases, the competing claims are very deeply held, mutually exclusive, zero-sum advocacies that are irreconcilable among the parties themselves and where outside parties either cannot or will not assert enough power to create and enforce outcomes that will be acceptable to some, and preferably all, of the affected parties.

The emergence of territorial disputes as a major systemic problem during the twentieth and into the twenty-first centuries is not coincidental. The heart of the problem—different, antagonistic groups of people living in proximity that sometimes becomes violently abrasive—is a large consequence of the breakup of colonial empires worldwide, first after World War I in Europe (the Austro-Hungarian Empire) and the Middle East (the Ottoman Empire). After World War II, decolonization spread to Asia and Africa. The result was to release animosities among people previously held coercively in check. The process of adjustment is ongoing. The major forms that territorial disputes take arise from multinationalism (where multiple national groups live together—unhappily—in the same state), and irredentism (where state boundaries separate national groups who wish to form a common state that brings the group into a common state). Instances of multinationalism are more common than are those of irredentism, but both can be deeply held and result in considerable instability and violence. It is a problem unlikely to disappear in a world where burgeoning global population is drawing people and groups into closer proximity.

These situations pose a fundamental challenge to the international order. Internal conflicts (what I have called developing world internal conflicts [DWICs] in several other places including *National Security*, Sixth Edition) have become the most common form of organized violence (war) in the contemporary international system, eclipsing and virtually eliminating traditional wars between states as sources of violent turmoil. Many of these DWICs arise either from multinationalist or irredentist roots and have arisen at least in part from the efforts of peoples in decolonized locales to come to grips with questions about the physical boundaries and appropriate holders of sovereign legitimacy in different areas.

The Role of Colonialism and Decolonization

Conquering and ruling areas and peoples is certainly not a byproduct of the modern age, and it is at least arguable that the modern manifestations and problems these actions create are not as primitive or savage as it has been in earlier times. With the exception of the Nazi genocide during World War II, there are relatively few cases of the depths of inhumanity practiced by Genghis Khan and his infamous horseshoe, where those being conquered were subjugated by a Mongol host that surrounded them in a horseshoe-like formation, which ended with the slaughter of all male adults and children. Still, when people conquer, suppress, and aggregate people in physical and political conditions with which they fundamentally disagree, the likely result is to activate what I have termed the three R's (resentment, rejection, and resistance) in *The Case against Military Intervention*. In real colonizing situations, the three-R process is likely to occur within multiple groups united in their opposition to the solution to that problem.

The most recent waves of colonization occurred by Europeans against Africans and Asians (although the Western Hemisphere was not exempted) and by the Ottoman Turks against other parts of what Westerners call the Middle East. The Ottoman Empire was long-standing, beginning in 1299 and lasting until 1923, when the last remnants of its dismantling after World War I was complete. It spread at its zenith to encompass large parts of Eastern Europe, northern Africa and most of the Middle East including parts of Persia (Iran), Kurdistan, and the Levant. It began to decline toward the end of the seventeenth century. By the time it joined the Central Powers in World War I, its core was Turkey and Levantine areas that included modern Iraq, Syria, Trans-Jordan, and what became Israel. The empire was formally dissolved as one of the terms of the Versailles Treaty, which created current states like Iraq and Syria in 1920 but denied the Kurds their own state. European expansion into Asia and Africa included the subjugation of virtually all of Africa and most of Asia (Japan and China were exceptions) between the sixteenth and nineteenth centuries. The European empires collapsed after World War II because the major European colonial powers could no longer afford to maintain control over restive areas.

From the current perspective, what is primarily important is the pattern and impact of colonization on those on whom it was imposed. The motivations of different colonizers were, of course, different, but the core was to benefit the colonizing party, not those on whom the imposition was placed. Traditional motives included the prestige and power of empire, sometimes including a religious element (certainly in the Ottoman case). European motives included the hope to profit from the "riches" of conquered areas (which often did not exist) and the prevailing notion that the distinguishing characteristic of great powers was their possession of empires.

A consideration of the population characteristics of those caught up in the colonizing experience was rarely present. In the case of European colonization of Africa in particular, the European powers generally simply claimed a stretch of coastline on the continent on which they were intruding and then extended their claim inland. This was usually accomplished by little if any understanding of habitation patterns, including ethno-linguistic or racial, religious, or other differentiations, and not much concern about the impact of putting together diverse, sometimes antagonistic peoples into common political units. Colonial maps were often physically flawed (the final dissection of Africa was accomplished with no accurate maps of much of the continent's interior). Moreover, it was conscious policy in most cases to make sure that diverse population elements in a given colony did not learn to cooperate with one another, since doing so might include cooperation to throw out the colonizer.

The result was new countries with deep divisions within the population that they were unequipped to accommodate. Many contained antagonistic groups who did not get along before colonization, and for whom the colonizing experience offered no more than an interruption in their conflicts among themselves, not a calming palliative wherein they learned to live together better. Indeed, the colonial experience even exacerbated rivalries and hatreds. In some cases, for instance, colonizers in Africa recruited coastal tribes to go inland and capture rivals from interior tribes, who were then sold to slave traders for transportation to slave-holding countries. In others, forced conversion of natives who were adherent to traditional religious belief systems exacerbated differences and antagonisms.

The other impact, however, was to give the colonized populations a glimpse of the greater affluence and standard of living of the colonial rulers (it was, of course, a major purpose of colonization to enhance that wealth) and, in the process, to make them envious and desirous of the same kinds of status. Most of the colonies had been traditional and thus very poor societies when the colonizers arose, and there were simply not enough resources available to uplift them on their own. The result was competition for available wealth that pitted natives against one another and created social maladjustments that continued after independence.

Irredentism, Multinationalism, and DWICs

The key element in understanding the maladies that plague parts of the international system begins with the dichotomy between the anthropological term "nation" and the political and legal term "state." The international system is sometimes said to be composed of "nation-states," suggesting a conjunction of the two concepts that would produce stable sovereign entities and result in minimal instability and violence. The problem is that, in a literal sense, there are very few actual nation-states, and where the connection breaks down, instability, often involving territorial boundaries, is most likely to occur.

The term nation refers to the identification people have with others. The nation, however its members define it, is the primary point of loyalty people have, and this identification extends to political loyalties to the state or some other entity. Although no list is comprehensive and not all nationally defined groups possess all the characteristics, common indicators of national identification include race, ethnicity, language, religion, common territorial habitation, and shared historical experience. The national identity that groups adopt is the basis for their loyalty to and support for—or opposition to—the state.

The ideal combination of state and nation is expressed in the idea of the nation-state. In this conceptualization, almost all the citizens share a common national identity—being French or British or American—that they equate with the state—France, Great Britain, or the United States. This does not preclude the incorporation of minorities with different national identities as long as they do not override loyalty to the overall territory defined as the state. It is acceptable, for instance, for a British citizen to self-identify as being a Welshman, as long as the individual's primary loyalty is to Great Britain, of which Wales is a part. Similarly, many Americans are self-pronounced nationally hyphenated individuals (so called because terms such as Italian Americans and so forth are often written with a hyphen), but these self-identifications do not override their common identification as Americans.

Problems exist when nation and state either do not coincide or when conflicts between the two develop. When the two concepts come into conflict within a territory, the designation "nation-state" is technically incorrect, and the prospect for instability exists. One or both of the conditions identified in the heading for this section may develop, and one consequence can be violence in the form of DWICs.

The most common form of discontinuity between the concepts of nation and state occur where at least two self-identified national groups live within a state, the basic definition of multinationalism. The terms multiethnic and multicultural nationalism, both of which convey much of the essence of nationality, are sometimes used to distinguish this political connotation of multinationalism from its other meaning, which centers on multinational corporations, their operation, and their impact on the international system.

This situation is common to almost all the countries of the developing world and, to a lesser degree, in the developed world as well. Writing in 1993, for instance, Welsh surveyed the world's countries and concluded that 160 of the then 180 recognized sovereign states were multinational in one way or another. It becomes a destabilizing source of territorial dispute when one or more of the groups decide they no longer want to be part of the state. The major reason for this decision tends to be domination of the state by one national group at the expense of other nationalities, which can result in internal violence to overthrow the offending national group or even to secede.

An example may illustrate this dynamic. The Sudan, a country in east Africa through which the Nile flows before entering Egypt, was granted independence as Africa's physically largest state in 1956. Unfortunately, Sudan was an almost totally artificial state whose various regions and peoples shared essentially none of the characteristics of a nation. The country was effectively divided into a Muslim north controlled by fundamentalist, essentially Wahhabist Arabs who sought to rule using fundamentalist precepts that were unacceptable to others. Those who disagreed with Khartoum included members of less strict Muslim sects and virtually the entire citizenry of the southern part of the country, whose people considered themselves African (with different tribal loyalties and identifications) and who were generally either Christians or animists. The Islamist government in Khartoum insisted on imposing *sharia* law during the country's first year of existence, triggering a civil war that lasted from 1956 to 1972. A period of passable tranquility existed until 1983, when another fundamentalist Islamic regime imposed Islamic laws countrywide, triggering another civil conflict between the northern Muslims and the southerners that ended in 2005. Simultaneously, less fundamentalist Muslims in the western region of Sudan went into rebellion in the province of Darfur, which the government suppressed through an alleged genocidal campaign. Part of the 2005 Comprehensive Peace Agreement was a negotiated secession of South Sudan, which occurred in 2011. Unfortunately, this did not solve all the problems of Sudan, as members of the two largest southern tribes (the Dinka and Nuer) fell out over which would dominate the south, and a vicious civil war has gripped South Sudan ever since.

The case of Sudan is an admittedly extreme example, but it does illustrate the depths that multinationalism can create within and between countries. It is a simple, if regrettable, fact that the depiction of international relations as an interaction between nation-states is a convenient fiction. If countries were indeed places where loyalty to nation and state were coterminous or where loyalty to the state's integrity outweighed national loyalty defined in terms other than the state, the depiction would be accurate and the relations among the world's states would be a great deal more tranquil than they are.

Multinationalist-inspired instability is the most common form of disconnection that underlies territorial disputes, but it is neither the only one or even, in some cases, the most difficult and intractable form that territorial disputes take. Another form, often associated with particularly difficult, intractable territorial situations, arises from instances of irredentism.

Irredentism is a term with an interesting genesis. The term itself, which derives from the Italian word that means "unredeemed," was first used to describe aspirations about Italian lands during the process of unification of Italy in 1870. It is now used more generically to describe what the *Free Dictionary* calls a movement or sentiment the purpose of which is "the recovery of territory culturally or historically related to one's nation but now subject to a foreign government." If the broad purpose of multinationalist efforts is to alter the state to make it more congenial to some or all of the national groups that reside in a particular sovereign territory, irredentists challenge the rightful possession and exercise of sovereignty by groups in territories they consider rightfully theirs.

The fundamental purpose and impact of these groups is to attack the problem of stateless nations. Groups making irredentist claims are basically arguing one of two pernicious conditions that prevent them from what they regard as their rightful national endowment. One of these is territorial occupation that prevents their assertion of sovereign authority over territory that would allow them to serve as a sovereign state. The other is the situation where territory they view as rightfully theirs is within the unjust sovereign jurisdiction of several states and where their intent and purpose is to unite those areas into a single state. These two situations are sufficiently important that they form the bases for the two applications in the next section.

When these kinds of situations cannot be resolved peacefully to the satisfaction of all or most national groups in a country, the result is often the resort to DWICs, which are the dominant form of violent conflict (along with terrorism) in the twenty-first-century environment. This category of violence is manifested in several different ways discussed in later chapters, but its most salient characteristics are that its causes are generally internal in nature, that it tends to be unconventional (or asymmetrical) in its conduct, and that it is almost entirely confined to the developing world.

Territorial Disputes and International Relations

As already suggested, the pattern of violence in the international system has changed markedly since World War II, which was a watershed event in the modern conduct of war. Even after that conflict ended, the dominant Cold War powers configured themselves militarily in a way that anticipated that a future conflict would be much like the wars of the first half of the century, featuring large, heavily configured armed forces engaging in massive military campaigns— essentially the European style of warfare. These encounters were largely traditionally territorial, as aggressors like the German Reich or the Japanese Empire sought to increase their sovereign control over expanding territories and peoples, and those who resisted acted out of protection of their most vital national interests. It was warfare that conformed to the Clausewitzian dictum that "war is politics by other means."

Nuclear weapons invalidated much of the underpinning logic of traditional warfare. The kinds of total wars (those fought for the total purpose of conquest) made most sense when conducted by all the military means available to both (or all) sides, but the enormous, civilization-threatening effects of nuclear weapons as the ultimate form of national military power raised the very real prospect that any war fought between nuclear weapons possessors could be an all-out nuclear conflict in which all would be destroyed and in which the territorial "prize" might be an irradiated wasteland. Both the superpowers came to recognize this possibility, and given its dire worst outcome, moved to reduce the problem by making the possibility of any war between nuclear possessors progressively less likely. One victim was the rationale for Cold War military preparations, which in turn undercut most of the underlying justification for the competition.

What was left in the wake of the decline in major interstate warfare and its potential nuclear consequences was internal warfare, or at least warfare in which there was a substantial internal catalyst. Conflicts that were primarily internal had been a staple of the decolonizing world—especially Africa and Asia, including the Middle East—since the 1940s, when the disintegration of European empires began. They were given less emphasis then because of the overwhelming geopolitical cloud cast over international relations by the Cold War and because what concern existed tended to be focused on the Cold War implications of these conflicts—how, for instance, could support for one side or another in an internal war by a superpower give it advantage in the central competition?

The end of the Cold War changed this emphasis in some ways but not in others. The most important change was to extinguish the Cold War spotlight on international relations, in the process allowing the other dominant form of conflict in the world, the DWICs, to be treated as a much more important element in the fabric of violence. The world's gaze, which had been averted from developing world dynamics and instabilities, pivoted to them. The pattern also changed to the extent that the Cold Warriors, with their confrontation cancelled by default, lost some of their Cold War–created interest in developing competitions and retreated from support, leaving the primary participants more on their own.

The result has been a process of change that is still ongoing and not entirely understood. Internal conflicts are still about traditional questions such as who has the right to exercise sovereign authority over territory, but outside interference in resolving these conflicts (where resolution is possible) is no longer as prominent a factor in violent dynamics.

There are two major physical differences in the pattern of post–Cold War DWICs. Both have implications for the developed world and are addressed in detail in subsequent chapters. The first is a change in the dominant form of warfare from traditional European-style engagement (sometimes called symmetrical) to asymmetrical warfare (the topic of chapter 5). Major differences include the nature and generally smaller composition of combatant forces, their style of fighting in greater conformance to ideas grounded in "light," non-conventional tactics and smaller, less sophisticated weaponry, and the methods of conflict termination. All of these run counter to traditional Western warfare as practiced in the twentieth century, and the extent to which asymmetrical warfare is becoming the more or less sole way in which war is fought raises questions about methods of preparation for military forces. The second is terror (the subject of chapter 14). Terror emanates from many of the same places, arises from the same kinds of concerns. The two dynamics are deeply intertwined: terrorist campaigns are a form of asymmetrical warfare, and asymmetrical warriors include terror in the operational "playbooks."

These changes are important to understand, because they represent problems that are the underlying precipitants of violence and instability in the world today and which are unlikely to abate in the foreseeable future. Territorial disputes are unlikely to disappear as a source of disagreement that sometimes turns violent, sometimes because they result from fundamental, irresolvable national interests among groups, and because the world is getting more, rather than less, crowded, and the result is that territory and jurisdiction will become more, rather than less, problematical in the future.

Application: This Land (Palestine and Kurdistan) Is *Whose* Land?

Territorial disputes are present in virtually all the developing world and in some limited parts of the developed world. The question of what group has the legitimate claim to exercising sovereignty has various roots and longer or shorter histories depending on the region and particular conflict. All share a commonality: the forced cohabitation of antagonistic groups in the same territorial space and the desire of one group or another to break away and seek its own separate state. The disputes tend to be irresolvable or close to it, because the contesting groups of people dislike or distrust one another to the point that they cannot amicably reach mutually acceptable outcomes.

Among global regions, the longest-lasting conflicts tend to be in the Middle East, where the roots of conflicts can be traced back over millennia and where the basis of disagreement and hatred can be traced to tribal differences, often influenced by religious factors that have defined and deepened the disagreements across time. In these circumstances, the divisions have festered for a very long time and have been punctuated by unpleasant national experiences that are part of national myths and are chronicled, even justified, on divine grounds. All these add to the irony that the Middle East, the cradle of three of the world's greatest monotheistic religions, is rent by the deepest enmity, and, at times, the most uncivilized behavior on the globe.

Two conflicts exemplify this condition and are worthy of comment both because of their unique characteristics, because they are both major irritants to regional and world peace, and because they each represent the territorial issue of being contests in which at least one aspirant is a stateless nation. They differ in the context in which the claim to statehood is based and in the structure of the problem and alternative solutions. They join the fight for national self-determination being waged more obscurely by the Pashtuns of Afghanistan and Pakistan as the most obvious instances of territorial disputes over sovereign state status by nations that desire their own state.

The two are different in important factual ways. The Palestinian quest for statehood has deep historical roots in the more or less constant struggle for possession of the various territories included in the Levant, but their current dilemma has its roots in post–World War II events, notably the establishment of the state of Israel and the Israeli occupation of territory formerly part of Jordan on the West Bank of the Jordan River that the Palestinians (and most of the international community) have claimed as the site of Palestine. Structurally, it is primarily a dispute between Israel and the Palestinians. The Kurdish desire for statehood, on the other hand, is much more long-standing, and is one in which the Kurds have consistently been denied the right to self-determination. The current problem has its roots in the settlement of World War I, where Kurdistan was made part of several other states. Structurally, it is a contest between the Kurds and those states, notably Turkey, Iraq, Iran, and Syria. In a sense, Kurdistan already exists, but it does as an area within those four states, none of which is willing to allow the Kurds to unite those areas into their ultimate dream, the sovereign state of Kurdistan.

The Case of Palestine: The Irresolvable Conflict?

What to do about the Palestinians has been a major conflict with no apparent resolution acceptable to the major claimants, Israel and the Palestinian Arabs, at least since the end of World War II and even before. In its simplest terms, it is a territorial dispute between the Jewish people who dominate the State of Israel and the mostly Sunni Muslim Arabs who think of themselves as Palestinians. Israel, defined as the area formally accepted as a state before 1967, is an accepted sovereign state. For centuries, the Jews were a stateless nation with a difficult, often tragic history punctuated by Hitler's attempted extinction of the Jewish people in the 1930s and 1940s. Many surviving European Jews heeded the call for a Zionist exodus and ended up in what was then considered Palestine, part of the British mandated zone from the breakup of the Ottoman Empire. Already living in that area (largely in peace with the Jewish settlers already there) were the Palestinian Arabs, another classic stateless nation that sought a sovereign home in the same region. Historic Palestine was the area both wished to claim as their own. Those claims, however, could not be successfully reconciled and came to a head after Israel was designated a sovereign state in part of Palestine in 1948; the two sides have been at odds ever since.

The Arena and the Contestants

There is no universal agreement on exactly what territory definitively delineates Palestine, a common regional malady in the Middle East due to the many states and empires that have ruled all or parts of the region since antiquity. In a general sense, the area is thought of in contemporary times as being composed of Israel (pre-1967), the West Bank (including East Jerusalem) and the Gaza Strip. It is not a physically large area: internationally accepted (pre-1967) Israel is about the size of New Jersey, the West Bank is about the size of Delaware, and Gaza is a narrow peninsula along the eastern Mediterranean coast northward from the Sinai Peninsula of Egypt. The third part of the region, Gaza, is about twice the size of Washington, DC.

The major source of the territorial dispute is the West Bank, which before the 1967 war between Israel and neighboring Muslim states was part of the Kingdom of Jordan. Israel occupied the West Bank (along with the Syrian Golan Heights and Egyptian Sinai) after the war. The Sinai was returned to Egypt as part of a major agreement with Israel implemented in 1982 as part of a comprehensive peace between the two states. The Golan Heights and the West Bank remain under Israeli control. The official Israeli rationale for what most outsiders (but not the Israelis) call an occupation is based in the existential security threat posed by hostile control of both areas. In the West Bank, that threat is that at its narrowest point, Israel is only about ten miles wide from the West Bank to the Mediterranean Sea, raising the prospect of national destruction. Informally, possession of the West Bank allows Israel to attract foreign Jewish settlers to "Greater Israel."

The two basic territories are distinct in terms of population. The population size of pre-1967 Israel is approximately six million, of whom about five million are Jewish and rest are mostly Palestinian Arabs and a small number of Christians. The West Bank, on the other hand, has a Palestinian majority of about three million and, including East Jerusalem, a Jewish population of nearly a half million settlers. Gaza has a population of about 1.75 million, virtually all of whom are Palestinian Arabs. The detailed numbers are not precise, but when the three parts of historic Palestine are combined, there are slightly more Palestinian Arabs than Jews in that population. Demographic trends are unfavorable to the Israelis (the Arab population is growing at a faster rate than the Jewish population), and this fact also affects the attractiveness of various solutions to the territorial dispute.

History of the Conflict: 1948 to the Present

Although virtually anything that happens in the Middle East can be (and usually is) traced back hundreds and even thousands of years, the current Israeli-Palestinian conflict can usefully be thought of as a post–World War II phenomenon. After the war, internal conflict broke out in the British mandate of Palestine. The major precipitant was the movement by increasing numbers of Jewish settlers and immigrants to establish the state of Israel in some part of the Palestinian area. This movement, which included atrocities and arguable terrorism on all sides against one another and the British, sought to drive the British out and to establish Palestinian and Jewish territories for independence. A war-weary Britain did not have the will or desire to quash these movements, and in 1948, the state of Israel was declared in the United Nations in a U.S.-USSR joint resolution. Surrounding Arab states conducted an ill-conceived and poorly conducted campaign to destroy the nascent Israeli state, the net result of which was to increase Israeli territory.

The birth of the Israeli state was also the genesis of the Palestinian condition of statelessness. After the initial "war," many Palestinians, fearing Israeli retribution, fled the new state into refugee status, including residents of areas annexed by Israel. They scattered to refugee camps and enclaves in most of the surrounding states, but especially to the West Bank and Gaza, where many have remained ever since.

The conflict has evolved through three additional wars that help define the current impasse. In 1956, a joint Anglo-French and Israeli campaign sought to regain control of the Suez Canal from the Egyptians, who had nationalized it the previous year. They failed, and the fact that the United States refused to support its allies drove a wedge between them. More importantly, the Six Days' War of 1967 was an overwhelming Israeli victory that resulted in the occupation of the West Bank (as well as Golan and Sinai/Gaza); the West Bank (including East Jerusalem) occupation has defined the territorial dispute between them, since both claim the territory as their own. In 1973, the Arab states attacked Israel and enjoyed early success, which led the Israelis to activate their clandestine nuclear arsenal, including the implicit threat to use those weapons if Israeli existence was threatened.

This sequence had two important effects for present purposes. The outcome of the 1967 war established continuing military and political Israeli possession over the territory the Palestinians claim for their state, a situation that, with some moderation, continues to this day. The outcome of the 1973 Yom Kippur War convinced the Muslim states that they could not defeat or destroy Israel without risking their own destruction, and they have not tried since.

Heart of the Conflict: What Land Is the Palestinian State?

Stripped of its historical and religious trappings, the dispute between the Israelis and Palestinians over the West Bank is conceptually relatively straightforward: who has the superior claim to sovereign domain over Palestine? Part of the question has been effectively decided. There is no question about Israeli sovereignty over territories ceded to the Jewish state in 1948 and as expanded up until the 1967 war. There are many individual property claims by former Palestinian land and homeowners over the rightful ownership of property that they abandoned when they fled and that was subsequently claimed by Israelis, who have lived there since, and demands for restitution constitute much of the basis for the "right of return" for those displaced persons. At heart, however, the question of Israeli sovereignty over the internationally recognized (i.e., pre-1967) boundaries of Israel have been established. Similarly, when Israel ceded total control over the Gaza Strip to the Palestinian authority in 2006, that territorial question was solved as well.

That leaves the West Bank, which is an ongoing problem for two basic reasons. The first is the general question of Israeli settlements on the West Bank. These settlements are enclaves (generally on the best land, which effectively means land with adequate water under it) and are residential areas reserved for Jews, often immigrants. They are not claimed as sovereign territory, but they have become increasingly permanent-looking enclaves that it is increasingly difficult to see Israel abandoning to a Palestinian state. Arab control over the West Bank would likely entail displacement of the settlers, a politically dicey proposition in Israel (especially given the trauma that eviction of approximately 10,000 Jews from Gaza created in 2006). Moreover, these settlements are about the only places in or near Israel to accommodate immigration from the Jewish diaspora to the country (a government priority): the territory uninhabited in Israel proper is almost all effectively uninhabitable.

The other problem is the old city of East Jerusalem. It is a place of historic and religious significance to both sides (as well as Christians), and both Israel and the Palestinians claim it as their national capital. It rests along the border between Israel and the West Bank, and has been the destination of much Jewish settlement outside the pre-1967 boundaries. Both sides have religious sites in the city, and when it has been in the possession of either, that side has denied or threatened to deny access to members of both religions. The religious and political significance of Jerusalem makes it possibly the most intractable part of the territorial dispute.

Possible Solutions: One State, Two States, or Conflict without End?

The question of Palestinian statehood and where to locate a sovereign Palestinian state has been one of the most nettlesome international problems of the last half-century. Because of the special relationship between the United States and Israel, every American president since 1948 has become involved in its solution, and despite some notable efforts at obtaining an agreement between the parties, all have failed. In his first pronouncement on the subject, President Trump intoned that he could live with either a one-state or a two-state solution (the only viable alternatives), whichever the parties could agree to. His pronouncement was immediately dismissed as disingenuous: the heart of the problem is that both sides have been unable to agree on *any* solution.

The two alternatives are easy to state but have proven impossibly difficult to achieve. The first is a one-state solution, where all three of the constituent parts of greater Palestine (Israel, the West Bank, and Gaza) are incorporated into a single state. The Palestinians, who are convinced that the Israelis would dominate such a state, and some Israelis, who fear that demographics ensure they will become a minority in that state, oppose this solution. It would, however, solve the problem of Jewish immigration onto the West Bank and of the status of East Jerusalem, which would become the capital of the unified state. The two-state solution, which has the backing of virtually all the international community outside the U.S.-Israeli axis, calls for an independent Palestine on the West Bank and Gaza and an independent Israel consisting of the pre-1967 territory, some settlements along the border, and presumably some part of East Jerusalem. Most of the opposition comes from factions (including the Netanyahu regime) who favor a concept of Greater Israel (effectively all of Palestine except Gaza) and who fear that a sovereign Palestine would be a launching pad for terrorist activities against the Jewish state. In the absence of any agreement based on one of these alternatives, there is little prospect of any territorial solution to the dispute.

Three pivotal considerations affect disposition of the conflict. The first is Israel's demographic dilemma. Israel was established and prides itself as a state that is both democratic and Jewish. The problem is how to remain both under different territorial solutions. If there is a single-state solution, demographics work in their disfavor. As noted earlier, the Palestinian-Jewish balance in overall Palestine is almost fifty-fifty, and with a higher population growth rate among Muslims, they will soon be a majority of the population of overall Palestine. In that case, Jews would be in a minority, raising the dilemma. If Israel remains democratic, the Arabs will outnumber Jews at the polls, leaving the outcome a democratic but non-Jewish state. If the Jews renounce democracy or qualify it (e.g., weighted voting by groups), the state can remain Jewish, but not fully democratic. On the other hand, the two-state solution may reduce Israel geographically to something like its pre-1967 size, but it will remain solidly Jewish (a five-to-one ratio of Jews in the population), allowing Israel to remain *both* Jewish and democratic.

The second is Israeli security, and it has two parts. The first, already discussed, is the vulnerability Israel faces of being cut in two by hostile forces attacking west from the West Bank. The second is the fear that a hostile West Bank sovereign Palestine will serve as a sanctuary for terrorists attacking Israel, a contingency considerably more dangerous to the Israelis than it is in current circumstances, with Israeli Defense Forces (IDF) on the scene in the occupied areas. This fear also motivated Israel to build a barrier fence along the West Bank frontier to regulate Palestinian movement in and out of Israel (on the model of a similar fence walling off Gaza). This fence has been highly controversial because of its impact on human movement from one jurisdiction to the other and for its symbolism. Palestinians discount this scenario, and their supporters maintain that a sovereign Palestine will have the incentive not to suborn that behavior. Some Israelis disagree. The only definitive way to know is to create Palestine, and see if the Palestinian government is honorable on this issue. Doing so, of course, involves a substantial risk to Israel if the Palestinians are not telling the truth.

The third, and ultimately most vexing, problem is East Jerusalem. It cannot be the capital of two countries, and neither is willing to accept their exclusion while it becomes the other's capital. Given the emotional ties both have to religious sites, neither can abandon it. That leaves two unhappy options. One is to partition the city so part is in Israel and part in Palestine. Conceivably, one zone could become the capital of Israel and the other the capital of Palestine. There have been numerous attempts to divide the city, but none has proven acceptable to both sides. The other possibility is either to declare Jerusalem a neutral city-state, possibly under international jurisdiction (which has been tried unsuccessfully) or to declare that it will not be the capital of either country. Neither country finds this outcome satisfactory.

The Israeli-Palestinian land dispute is an extraordinarily complex, convoluted, and emotional divide that I have called "irresolvable" in previous editions of this text. The enmity and distrust between the two sides on virtually all issues makes an amicable settlement of a dispute over a parcel of land the size of Delaware (the West Bank) a major international issue, and until one side (or preferably both) decide that resolution and the hoped-for peace that will follow are more important than what divides them, it will continue to roil the politics of the Middle East.

The Case of Kurdistan

The Kurdish quest to end its long statelessness is physically more imposing than the Israeli-Palestinian conflict, in that it spans a longer period of time, involves territory and people in four Middle Eastern states, and has been and continues to be a major source of geopolitical struggle between the Kurds and all of those countries where the Kurds live and in which they claim statehood for Kurdistan. The issue appears and then disappears from the global spotlight: it arose in the early 1990s when Iraq's threats of genocidal retribution drove thousands of Iraqi Kurds into uneasy exile in Turkey. It has resurfaced with the prominent role that Kurdish *pesh merga* territory-protecting militias have played in the campaign against the Islamic State.

The Kurds have been a long-time part of the tapestry of Middle Eastern history, although there is no agreed time when they ruled any sizable part of western Asia, which is where most Kurds reside. One of the signal elements of Kurdish history came in 1514, when the Kurds entered into a formal arrange-ment with the Ottoman Turks and thus became part of the Ottoman Empire. Their active quest for statehood came into focus at the end of World War I and the dissolution of that empire.

The Kurds are concentrated in western Asia, principally in four countries. They are most numerous in eastern and southeastern Turkey (northern Kurd-istan), their second largest concentration is in northern Iraq (southern or Iraqi Kurdistan), northern Syria (western Kurdistan or Rojava), and western Iran (east-ern or Iranian Kurdistan). Census figures are not very precise, but the number of Kurds within territories claimed as part of a Kurdish state is in the range of thirty to thirty-two million, which means that were Kurdistan to come into being, its population would be roughly that of Saudi Arabia and greater than Iraq (after the Kurds currently counted as Iraqi were subtracted from the Iraqi population). The Kurds are overwhelmingly Sunni Muslim, but they are ethnically and cul-turally closer to the Iranians than their Arab neighbors. The Kurds clearly meet the criteria of being a stateless nation, and like others (including the Palestinians) are in active pursuit of their quest for full sovereign statehood. As is so often the case, the territory that would form Kurdistan is part of the sovereign states of the four major concentrations of Kurds, and each—with varying intensity and for somewhat different reasons—seeks to deny Kurdish self-determination.

The Dream of and Demand for a Kurdistan

The concerted movement toward Kurdish statehood emerged in the early twen-tieth century, and its progress (or lack thereof) has been highlighted by three major events, the Versailles peace negotiations of 1919, the plight of the Iraqi Kurds after Saddam Hussein threatened their slaughter in 1991, and most recently, the prominent role of the Kurdish *pesh merga* in the military effort to roll back the IS Caliphate. These calendar highlights do not define the lon-ger-standing desire of the Kurds for statehood so much as they provide road markers of international awareness of the Kurdish situation.

Each is significant for a different reason. A Kurdish delegation petitioned the peacemakers in Paris in 1919 to create a sovereign state of Kurdistan in the Kurdish area as part of the carving up of the Ottoman Empire. However, there were multiple claimants to the areas, including European powers such as Britain and France, former regional powers such as Persia, and the Turkish successor state to the empire that had contrary claims, and ultimately their claims pre-vailed. The precedent of denying the Kurds what they viewed as their destiny was established, but at least a greater part of the world became aware of their fate. In 1991, after his stunning eviction from Kuwait and rebellions against him (in, among other places, the Kurdish region of Iraq), Saddam Hussein threatened to renew chemical warfare and other attacks against the Kurds in reprisal. Fearing their extinction at the hands of their own president, thousands of Kurds fled across the border into Turkey for asylum. They were not especially welcome in Turkey, but their plight was widely reported on global television, and the United States, in order to please the Turks, announced a no-fly zone in the Kurdish region from which Iraqi forces were excluded to entice the Kurds to go home. Kurdish suffering and desire for the security of their own sovereign state was the dividend of their suffering on Turkish mountainsides.

The final element has been the Kurdish role in the fight against the Caliphate. Iraqi and Syrian Kurdistan was a prominent part of the land initially conquered by IS as it spread eastward toward Baghdad, and especially in the early going, Iraqi *pesh merga* militia forces were the most effective (for a time virtually the *only* effective) barriers to the IS offensive. This experience called for much further Western reliance on the Kurds as a way to push back the Caliphate. Now that the Caliphate is effectively disassembled, the Kurds are bound to expect some territorial compensation for their efforts (their 2017 independence referendum is a precedent), and the international system will have difficulty denying it to them.

The Geopolitical Resistance

Kurdish irredentism is opposed by all four of the existing states from which Kurdistan would be forged. Resistance to the idea is highest in the two states, Turkey and Iraq, where the Kurds are most numerous and where secession would be most harmful to the existing state. The geopolitics of the region plays into these considerations, and although there is considerable support for the Kurdish cause, it is difficult to find outsiders who can or will offer their wholehearted support for the Kurds, whose desires continue to languish.

Turkey: Opposition to Kurdish self-determination is strongest in Turkey for several reasons. Between eighteen and twenty million Kurds, roughly 20 percent of the Turkish population, are Kurds, making them numerically close to two-thirds of the population of a future Kurdistan. Kurdish majority territories are concentrated in the eastern part of the country, including the Anatolia region that has been developed for its water resources and as a tourist destination by the Turkish government. The Kurdish area is about the size of the state of Washington in a country that is slightly larger than Texas. In addition, the Kurds, principally under the leadership of the Kurdish Workers Party (PKK) have waged a civil war/terrorist campaign against the government in Ankara that was formally ended in 2013. The PKK, however, is Marxist and the Turks accuse them of collusion with Russia, also a Turkish rival.

Turkish Kurdistan is crucial to a comprehensive Kurdish state, but the Turks oppose *any* Kurdistan more than any other regional country. Their motivation arises from the belief that a Kurdish state anywhere would be a platform for encouraging secession by the Turkish Kurds, which is almost certainly true. As a result, the Turks have not been particularly supportive of Iraqi *pesh merga* military efforts against IS, which they feel would be a launching pad to establish an Iraqi Kurdish state along their border. A similar rationale exists toward Syrian Kurdistan, and the Turks, who are fundamentally opposed to the Caliphate, find themselves in the anomalous situation of opposing (or not supporting) a primary opponent (Iraqi Kurds) of an enemy they would like to see defeated (the Caliphate).

Iraq: Since Saddam Hussein's atrocities against the Kurds and especially since the American invasion and occupation, the epicenter of attention to Kurdistan has centered on the Kurdish Autonomous Region of northern Iraq. The region is home to roughly five million Kurds (according to figures provided by The Kurdish Project in 2016), and since the 2003 war, they have been increasingly self-reliant and independent of the central government in Baghdad. Their territory abuts the Kurdish regions of all the other candidate countries and contains significant petroleum reserves in the Zagros Mountain region that makes it valuable to Iraq. The Kurds are linguistically and ethnically distinct from the Sunni and Shiite Arabs of the rest of the country. Moreover, there have been predictions that Iraq, which is an absolutely artificial country, could break apart into three countries, and there is little doubt that the Kurds would be the first out the door of Iraq. This possibility is opposed on the basis that an Iraq splintered would be less of a barrier to other trends in the area (mostly the spread of Iranian influence) and that the largest remaining part of Iraq would be the Shiite southern region, which shares a religious affinity with those Iraqis. The Turks, of course, are in the greatest opposition to Kurdish secession, but the Kurdish region of Iraq has acted increasingly like a de facto independent state. The *pesh merga* clearly considers its primary role as defense of Iraqi Kurdistan, not of Iraq as a whole.

Iran and Syria: Iran has the second most Kurds (about eight million) and the second most territory that is potentially part of any Kurdish state. It contrasts with the others in that it is not Arab or Sunni. Its people are ethnically similar to the Kurds (whose language is akin to Persian), but they share different religious traditions. In popular discourse, there have been far fewer publicized separatist pronouncements coming from eastern Kurdistan than from Turkey or Iraq, although the emergence of an independent Kurdistan in Iraq would certainly arouse demands to join the new state. The Kurds are least numerous in Syria (about two million), and they live in remote, lightly populated parts of eastern Syria contiguous with Turkey about which the Syrians have shown little interest given the demands of their civil war. Liberating territory in Syria occupied by the Caliphate would benefit Syrian Kurds and would likely stimulate demands for an independent state that would accompany the expulsion of IS from the region.

Conclusion

Territorial disputes are among the most difficult, vexing problems that confront the international system in a world of imperfectly drawn sovereign state boundaries that divide people who want to live together or aggregate people who do not. The problem of multinational states and their trials has been the cause of many ongoing and potential violent conflicts, the dynamics of some of which are highlighted in the next chapter. The situations where a particular piece of territory is coveted by more than one party (Palestine) and where sovereign boundaries keep nationalities in separate jurisdictions when they yearn for a common national home (Kurdistan) demonstrate the desperation and furtiveness of these difficulties.

What is striking about territorial disputes is that they have mutually exclusive outcomes preferred by the contesting parties, and there is little, if any, willingness on either (or all) sides to compromise. They are truly zero-sum situations where one side "wins" at the expense of the other. Like sovereign states, their interests are vital to them, meaning they are unwilling voluntarily to compromise on them. Their determination makes the sides impervious to reason or outside influence: the outcomes are simply too important.

If one thinks of Palestine in the broad generic sense (Gaza, Israel, and the West Bank), a compromise is possible, and that is exactly what the two-state solution proposes. Those in power in Israel, however, are unwilling to forfeit their de facto jurisdiction over the West Bank for security and other reasons. Compromise is rejected, and the Palestinians remain formally stateless. The Kurdish irredentist desire is conceptually simpler, but it faces opposition from all four states from which Kurdistan would be carved. Turkey is the biggest barrier, and Turkey's geopolitical importance makes outsiders unwilling to put great pressure on it. Iraqi Kurdish independence is probably the most likely first step in a movement toward a full Kurdish state, but it could leave Iraq a nonviable state (if it is viable now). These cases illustrate the extreme intractability of these territorial problems in a world organized as sovereign states.

Study/Discussion Questions

1. What is at the heart of the problem of territorial disputes? Discuss the problem in terms of colonialism, decolonization, and the emergence of developing world internal conflicts (DWICs).

2. What are multinationalism and irredentism? Discuss these as outcomes of the post–World War I and II worlds. With regard to the Middle East, include the dissolution of the Ottoman Empire.

3. Why are territorial disputes important phenomena in contemporary international relations, especially given changes in the overall pattern of violence in the world?

4. Why are territorial disputes so difficult to resolve? How do the Israeli-Palestinian and Kurdish problems illustrate this difficulty?

5. Discuss the structure of the Israeli-Palestinian dispute. Include a discussion of overall Palestine on the structure of this conflict.

6. What are the possible outcomes to the Israeli-Palestine dispute? Describe each. Why has it proven so difficult to reach an agreement?

7. Who are the Kurds? Where do they live? Why do they desire the creation of a Kurdistan, and from where would it be carved?

8. Who opposes the creation of a Kurdish state, and what is the basis of their objections? Given the resistance that exists, what are the prospects for an independent Kurdistan?

Bibliography

Allsop, Harriet. *The Kurds of Syria: Political Parties and Identity in the Middle East.* London: I. B. Tauris, 2015.

Ambrosio, Thomas. *Irredentism: Ethnic Conflict and International Politics.* Westport, CT: Praeger, 2001.

Atef, Maged. "Sinai Suffering: The Peninsula Has Become a Breeding Ground for Terror." *Foreign Affairs Snapshot* (online), March 13, 2017.

Benn, Auf. "The End of the Old Israel: Now Netanyahu Has Transformed the Nation." *Foreign Affairs* 95, no. 4 (July/August 2016): 16–27.

Bregman, Ahron. *Cursed Victory: A History of Israel and the Occupied Territories, 1967 to the Present.* Trenton, TX: Pegasus, 2015.

Brown, Nathan J. "The Palestinians' Receding Dream of Statehood." *Current History* 110, no. 740 (December 2011): 345–51.

Carter, Jimmy. *Peace Not Apartheid.* New York: Simon & Schuster, 2006.

Chaliland, Gerard, and Michael Pallis. *A People without a Country: The Kurds and Kurdistan.* Northampton, MA: Interlink, 1993.

Chazam, Naomi, ed. *Irredentism and International Politics.* Boulder, CO: Lynne Rienner, 1991.

Clausewitz, Carl von. *On War.* Rev. ed. Translated and edited by Michael Howard and Peter Paret. Princeton, NJ: Princeton University Press, 1984.

Della Pergola, Sergio. "Israel's Existential Predicament: Population, Territory, and Identity." *Current History* 109, no. 731 (December 2010): 383–89.

Ehrenreich, Ben. *The Way to the Spring: Life and Death in Palestine.* New York: Penguin, 2016.

Eppel, Michael. *A People without a State: The Kurds from the Rise of Islam to the Dawn of Nationalism.* Austin: University of Texas Press, 2016.

Gunter, M. Michael. *The Kurds: A Modern History.* Princeton, NJ: Markus Weiner, 2015.

Hammond, Jeremy R. *Obstacle to Peace: The U.S. Role in the Israeli-Palestine Conflict.* New York: Worldview, 2016.

"Kurds in Iraq." The Kurdish Project. https://thekurdishproject.org.

Livni, Tzipi. "Anger and Hope: A Conversation with Tzipi Livni." *Foreign Affairs* 95, no. 4 (July/August 2016): 10–15.

Muravchik, Joshua. *Making David into Goliath: How the World Turned against Israel.* New York: Encounter, 2015.

Peleg, Ilan. *The Democratization of the Hegemonic State.* Cambridge, UK: Cambridge University Press, 2007.

Phillips, David L. Foreword by Bernard Kouchner. *The Kurdish Spring: A New Map of the Middle East.* New York: Transaction, 2015.

Said, Edward W. *The Question of Palestine.* Reissue ed. New York: Vintage, 2015.

Ross, Dennis. *Doomed to Succeed: The U.S.-Israeli Relationship from Truman to Obama.* New York: Farrar, Straus & Giroux, 2015.

Shaked, Ayelet. "Ministering Justice: A Conversation." *Foreign Affairs* 95, no. 4 (July/August 2016): 2–8.

Shavit, Ari. *My Promised Land: The Triumph and Tragedy of Israel.* New York: Spiegel and Grau, 2015.

Smith, Charles D. *Palestine and the Arab-Israeli Conflict: A History with Documents.* 9th ed. New York: St. Martin's, 2016.

Snow, Donald M. *The Case Against Military Intervention: Why We Do It and Why It Fails.* New York and London: Routledge, 2016.

————. *Cases in International Relations.* 6th ed. New York: Pearson, 2015.

————. *The Middle East, Oil, and the U.S. National Security Policy.* Lanham, MD: Rowman & Littlefield, 2016.

————. *National Security.* 6th ed. New York and London: Routledge, 2017.

Van Creveld, Martin L. *The Land of Blood and Honey: The Rise of Modern Israel.* New York: Thomas Dunne, 2010.

Welsh, David. "Domestic Politics and Ethnic Conflict," in *Ethnic Conflict and International Security*, edited by Michael E. Brown. Princeton, NJ: Princeton University Press, 1993.

5

Asymmetrical Warfare
The Never-Ending Case of Afghanistan

One of the most obvious ways in which international relations has changed since the middle of the twentieth century is in the ways that wars are fought. The first half of the century was characterized by the ultimate applications of Western-style warfare in the form of the two world wars: state-sanctioned and directed violence conducted by large, heavily armed military configurations engaging in massive combat seeking to defeat the enemy by destroying its armed forces and in the process destroying the opponent's ability and will to continue. That pattern produced carnage on a quantitatively unprecedented scale, and the Cold War offered the prospect of a continuation of the pattern. The possibility of major-power clashes made much more potentially ghastly by nuclear weapons gradually tipped the balance, and major-power conventional war has essentially disappeared from the fabric of organized armed violence—at least for now.

Conventional European warfare has been replaced by another dominant form, asymmetrical warfare, a methodology more fitting and applicable to the places where fighting now occurs: in the internal affairs of the developing states that emerged from decolonization but suffer from some or all of the woes described in chapter 4. The purposes of asymmetrical warfare—enforcing or imposing the "national" interests of various groups within or between states—has not changed so much as have the ways in which it is conducted. What is now called asymmetrical warfare is certainly not new, with roots in antiquity and tactics and strategies traceable at least back as far as Sun Tzu, the ancient Chinese military philosopher. In important ways, it is Eastern-style warfare that represents the application of principles that allow a militarily inferior force to compete with a larger and more conventionally superior force. As such, it shares commonalities with the other major form of contemporary violence, terrorism. Asymmetrical warfare is such a pervasive form of war that outside powers seeking to influence the events in developing world situations find themselves drawn into developing world internal conflicts (DWICs) that they do not understand, are unprepared to fight, and lack sufficient interest to sustain the effort in these wars, which are usually protracted. The results are poor outcomes for those who intervene.

The long internal war in Afghanistan illustrates this phenomenon. Unconventional, asymmetrical warfare is a long-standing part of the pattern of endemic Afghan instability, and at the time of the September 11, 2001, terrorist attacks against the United States, one of the periodic Afghan civil wars was raging. The Taliban government, under attack by a coalition of rival tribal groups, was providing sanctuary to the Al Qaeda terrorists who committed these attacks, creating an American interest in what was happening in the rugged, forbidding landscape of Afghanistan where virtually no interest had previously existed. When the Taliban refused to remand the Al Qaeda terrorists to American custody, the United States intervened to try to capture them. The attempt failed, but the United States had become involved in an asymmetrical war against the Taliban that has now lasted for almost two decades.

Principle: Asymmetrical Warfare

The phenomenon that is currently called asymmetrical warfare is by no means new. Wars have been fought since bands of humans who were strangers to one another first encountered those others and, for one reason or another, felt threatened enough by the strangers to try either to drive them away or eliminate them. As human groups became larger and more complex, armed conflict became more common and structured, and the result was war in the modern sense of organized violence between groups defined nationally, politically, or both.

A basic dynamic of warfare has always been the balance or imbalance of forces possessed by the warring parties. The dictum attributed to Napoleon that "God favors the big battalions" reflects that concern and the inherent assumption that in a clash between hostile military forces, the larger and better equipped force has the deadly advantage. Whenever a force inferior in numbers or quality and quantity of armaments has faced a superior force so defined, the question of how the inferior force can nullify the advantages of the superior force to the point that it has a chance of defeating or at least avoiding defeat at the hands of the superior force has arisen.

That is the same question that the contemporary asymmetrical warrior contemplates. It is certainly not a new question, and the style of war being waged in most contemporary DWICs is the current variant of the answer to the problem. Because the circumstances are different now than they were when the Indians of the western American plains sought to ward off the U.S. Army's mounted cavalry in the nineteenth century, the actual manifestation at the tactical and even strategic levels are different today than they were then. Modern asymmetrical warfare may *look* different than it did a century or a millennium ago. The motivations and problems it addresses, however, are timeless.

The remainder of this chapter is devoted to understanding the challenge of asymmetrical warfare—its purposes, its conduct, and its outcomes. It will proceed in two sequential parts. First, it will examine the evolving, often amorphous nature of asymmetrical warfare. The discussion will move from a definition and examination of the dynamics to its comparison with terrorism to the difficulties that an outside conventionally armed state has in intervening in these wars. Second, it will apply those observations to one of the international system's most prominent current instance of asymmetrical warfare, the war in Afghanistan.

New/Old War

If asymmetrical warfare is ancient, its modern prevalence combines perennial and contemporary influences and causes. Warfare has changed enormously since the end of the Cold War, for essentially two obvious reasons. The first is the collapse of militarily based major power rivalry. Unlike the Cold War confrontation between the world's two most militarily powerful countries, such rivalry has receded to economic competition with very little potential to escalate to armed violence. The large, heavy conventional (symmetrical) armed forces and accompanying purposes for war have been made arguably obsolete in the process. Russia may represent a partial exception to this trend. Second, the remaining conflicts in the world are mostly developing-world internal conflicts (DWICs), internal conflicts within countries in which the major powers may have a limited interest. Internal conflicts in the least stable parts of the developing world have become the major source of military conflict in the contemporary world, and there seems little prospect that that condition will change anytime soon.

The result is the rising dominance of asymmetrical warfare in the pantheon of modern warfare. Before exploring this phenomenon, however, it is worth repeating two preliminary observations. On one hand, what some have called the "new" way of war is not new or, in general principle, all that innovative. Asymmetrical warfare features the adaptations an inferior force makes when it is faced with a more powerful force with which it cannot compete successfully on the terms preferred by the superior force. The tactics and means that are used may change due to altered circumstances, but the core rationale has endured. Put another way, asymmetrical warfare is an approach to warfare, not a form of war or combat. On the other hand, it is a methodology, a way to organize the problem, not a method or set of battlefield or theater instructions. No two asymmetrical wars are the same, although their purposes may be. The result is that thinking about and planning either to conduct or to counter asymmetrical situations requires considerable adaptability and openness to change, a characteristic not entirely common in conventional military thinking.

The result is a very different contemporary global conflict environment that affects both the places where conflicts occur and which parties are involved in two distinct ways. First, the imbalance in conventional capability between the United States and the rest of the world means that no one is likely to confront the United States in large-scale conventional warfare, making necessary the adoption of different approaches or means to negate that advantage. As Bruce Berkowitz puts it, "Our adversaries know they cannot match the United States in tanks, planes, and warships. They know they will most likely lose any war with us if they play according to the traditional rules." This innovation is the second new characteristic of the environment: the adoption and adaptation of asymmetrical ways to negate the advantages of overwhelming military capability and thus to reduce the military leverage that greater power seems to convey. Asymmetrical approaches are intended, in Berkowitz's terms, "to change the rules to strategies and tactics that avoid our strength head-on and instead hit us where we are weak." This problem is progressive, because the core of asymmetrical warfare is constant adaptation, whereas conventional war (the kind at which the United

States excels) is incremental, seeking better doctrinal solutions to standard problems. Moreover, traditional warfare is directed at state-based sovereign political opponents, whereas territorial tenancy is not so universal in asymmetrical warfare.

The Context and Meaning of Asymmetrical War

Understanding asymmetrical warfare begins by putting it in context. In some ways, asymmetrical wars are better understood as reversions to very old wars. The Thirty Years' War, for instance, featured marauding bands that would now be called nonstate actors, and the nineteenth-century resistance to colonialism certainly featured highly mismatched forces. It is different in terms of the problems for which it is conducted—how those who carry it out think and act— and in terms of the motives of the asymmetrical warrior. Asymmetrical warfare is not only militarily unconventional but it is also intellectually unconventional, for those who both practice and oppose its application. It can also be fought for conventional purposes such as overthrowing governments or to influence the politics within and between states. It is a methodology, not an ideology.

The first large-scale U.S. encounter with asymmetrical warfare was in Vietnam. The country had previous limited experience in places such as the American Southwest in the nineteenth century and in the Philippines at the turn of the twentieth century, but on a much smaller scale. Vietnam mixed symmetrical and asymmetrical characteristics. Its purposes were quite conventional: the North Vietnamese and their Viet Cong allies sought to unify Vietnam as a communist country, and the South Vietnamese and the Americans sought to avoid that outcome. In terms of conduct, however, the war was unconventional. The North Vietnamese concluded early in the American phase of the war that they could not compete with the United States in symmetrical warfare because of visibly superior American firepower. Instead, they reverted to tactics of harassment, ambush, and attrition, the purpose of which was to produce sufficient American casualties to convince the American people that the cost of war was not worth the projected benefits. The North Vietnamese could not have succeeded fighting by the American rules. Their only hope was to change the rules and fight in a way that minimized American advantage and gave them a chance. It worked.

The heart of asymmetrical warfare is a mindset. The potential asymmetrical warrior always begins from a position of military inferiority, and the problem, as Berkowitz points out, is how to negate that disadvantage. Adaptability is at the heart of asymmetrical approaches to warfare. If one asymmetrical tactic does not work, try another. Vietnam was a primer for those who may want to confront American power, but an organization such as Al Qaeda or the Taliban could not succeed simply by adopting Vietnamese methods (for one thing, they had no mountainous jungles into which to retreat after engagements). Instead, the asymmetrical warrior learns from what works and discards what does not. Iraq is a case in point.

In 1990–1991, Iraq attempted to confront the United States conventionally in Kuwait and was crushed for its effort. It learned from this experience that a future conflict with the United States, the prospects of which Iraq faced after September 11, 2001, could not be conducted in the same manner as before without equally devastating results, which included the decimation of Iraqi armed forces.

What to do? The answer, largely unanticipated by the United States, was to offer only enough resistance to American symmetrical force application to make the Americans think they were prevailing, while regrouping to resist an occupation that they were powerless to prevent except in other, asymmetrical ways. Thus, the limited form of irregular warfare (ambushes, car bombings, and suicide terror attacks) became the primary method of resisting the Americans, apparently aimed at the same goal the Vietnamese attained thirty years earlier—convincing the Americans that the costs of occupation were not worth the costs in lives lost and treasure expended.

Whether this was some carefully modulated plan formulated in advance of the invasion by the Iraqis or not is not the point (and it is a point for which adequate evidence is not available anyway). What is hardly arguable is that the United States underestimated the likelihood of such an asymmetrical response in planning the invasion in the first place. In postinvasion analysis, the argument is frequently made that American planning was flawed in, among other ways, its failure to allocate sufficient troops to the effort. The criticism is valid but somewhat misses the point. The troop numbers were clearly adequate for a symmetrical invasion and conquest, which is all that was anticipated. The troop levels were inadequate for a protracted resistance to occupation, which was an unanticipated asymmetrical response.

These experiences introduce an important aspect about how the asymmetrical warrior can achieve his or her goals against an opponent it has no chance of defeating by sheer force of arms. The contrast between asymmetrical objectives in entirely internal wars (DWICs) and those in which outsiders interject themselves illustrate the point. Asymmetrical warfare works in some situations but not in all. The secret, as in so many other things, lies in understanding what the problem is and how to approach it.

Most asymmetrical wars occur in DWICs in former colonies. One group or another is displeased with its situation to the point that it believes the situation can only be rectified by recourse to force. Normally, the insurgents begin their campaign at a disadvantage, less well armed and facing a government with much larger, usually conventionally armed, forces. It cannot confront its opponents on their terms, and so it resorts to strategy and tactics that will allow them to shift the balance of power in their direction. This was the basic approach of the North Vietnamese against American interveners, and it worked. The various groups opposing the Assad regime in Syria have not had so much luck.

The problem is fundamentally different when an outsider intervenes to influence the outcome. The intervening party (often the United States) is likely to be so militarily superior that defeating it is unthinkable. At the same time, its Achilles' heel is likely to be that it has lesser interests in the outcome and will, if engaged in protracted conflict including intervener casualties, tire of the contest and leave. This phenomenon is known as overcoming cost-tolerance and is discussed in the next section.

The Lure of Asymmetrical Warfare

Asymmetrical warfare is attractive to participants in DWICs because it works a good deal of the time when the recourse to more conventional approaches almost always fails. The Iraqi experience with the United States provides an instructive allegory. In 1990–1991 (the Persian Gulf War), a conventional Iraqi army supposedly hardened by its eight-year conflict with Iran between 1980 and 1988 invaded and occupied Kuwait. When the United States organized and led a coalition to push the Iraqis from Kuwait, the conventional armed forces of the two states collided, and the Iraqi asymmetrical army was routed by a far superior American counterpart. When the Americans invaded Iraq in 2003, the Iraqis put up a token conventional resistance and then faded away, especially to the Sunni stronghold of Anbar Province, where they formed an unconventional resistance that spawned Al Qaeda in Iraq (AQI), which in turn morphed into the Islamic State in 2014, a much better outcome from their perspective.

The lure is enhanced by the difficulty of finding a conceptual frame for dealing with the permutation of future asymmetrical situations, a problem with which asymmetrical opponents continue to grapple. Writing in 1995, the then U.S. Army Chief of Staff Gordon Sullivan and Anthony M. Coroalles analogized the problem to "seeing the elephant," a phrase borrowed from the American Civil War (the idea of describing what combat was like from the accounts of others analogized to having an elephant described in the abstract). They wrote, "Our elephant is the complexity, ambiguity, and uncertainty of tomorrow's battlefield. We are trying to see the elephant of the future. But trying to draw that metaphorical elephant is infinitely harder than drawing a real one. We don't know what we don't know; none of us has a clear view of what the elephant will look like this time around."

Modern asymmetrical warfare is today's elephant. As a U.S. Marines officer in Iraq was quoted as saying: "The enemy has gone asymmetric on us. There's treachery. There are ambushes. It's not straight-up conventional fighting." In other words, asymmetrical warfare does not conform to the accepted rules of symmetrical warfare for which the U.S. Marines had prepared themselves. It is a continuing difficulty because of the changing shape of the elephant in each new instance of asymmetrical warfare. One can begin by looking at predictable problems that the asymmetrical warrior will present in the future. With no pretense of being exhaustive, at least five stand out.

First, political and military aspects of these conflicts will continue to merge, and distinctions between military and civilian targets and assets will continue to dissolve. The asymmetrical warrior will continue to muddy the distinction for two reasons. One is that he is likely to see conflicts as pitting societies against societies, so there is no meaningful distinction between combatants and noncombatants, whereas traditional symmetrical warfare draws sharp distinctions between those who fight and those who do not, including prohibitions against attacking noncombatants. The other reason is that embedding conflict within the fabric of society removes some of the advantage of the symmetrical warrior. Urban warfare, for instance, can only be waged symmetrically by concentrating firepower intensity on areas where civilians and opponents are intermingled, where traditional rules of war prohibit actions aimed at civilians, thereby inhibiting some actions, and where the problem of collateral damage (killing noncombatants) is a concern under conventional laws of war. The asymmetrical warrior likely rejects these distinctions, leaving him free either to attack or fight among civilians.

Second, the opposition in these kinds of conflicts often consists of nonstate actors acting out of nonstate motivations and without state bases of operation. International terrorist organizations, for instance, often carry out operations that cannot be tied to any state, and are not clearly based in any state. This creates a problem of response for the symmetrical warrior. Whom does he go after? Whom does he attack and punish? If the asymmetrical warrior remains in the shadows (or mountains or desert) and the government plausibly denies affiliation or association, then using force against the opponent's base is complicated because one cannot attack the opponent's soil. This is a major problem the United States has faced in dealing with Al Qaeda and the Taliban in Pakistan: one cannot attack the enemy without attacking the sovereign territory of an ally.

Third, the opposition posed by asymmetrical warriors will almost certainly be protracted, effectively testing the cost-tolerance of the opponent. The reason for protraction flows from the weakness of the asymmetrical warrior compared to his symmetrical foe. Because direct confrontation is suicidal, the alternative is patient, measured application of force not designed to destroy the enemy, but instead to drag out the conflict, testing the opponent's will and patience. The United States first confronted this dynamic in Vietnam, saw it reprised in Iraq, and most recently has encountered it in Afghanistan. The problem is perseverance in situations where the outcomes are more important to the natives than they are to the outsider, which they almost always are. The goal is to convince the outsider that continued fighting is not worth the effort and thus to leave, unvanquished but frustrated and unfulfilled. The antidote is recognition of the tactic and a considerable degree of patience, generally not the long suit of the United States or other political democracies.

Fourth, these conflicts will often occur in the most fractured, failed states, where conditions are ripe for people to engage in acts of desperation such as suicide bombing. Where high desperation and deprivation exist, the systemic roots of conflict will be extraordinarily difficult to address and solve. The problem is recognizing the multifaceted nature of the wants and needs of the people. Rectifying these situations requires the patience and level of physical (including financial) commitment to removing the festering problems that is often missing or in short supply. As of 2010, the United States, according to Haass, had invested about one trillion dollars in directly accountable costs in Iraq, but hardly any resources to helping build a stable Iraqi state, a goal that remains elusive. Studies in 2013 from Harvard University and Brown University estimated the total, including long-term, costs of American involvement in Iraq and Afghanistan at four to six *trillion* dollars. The tab is still rising with no discernible end in sight.

Fifth, asymmetrical warfare will change in the future. The problem of Iraq was more than overcoming the Iraqi resistance; it was a matter of defeating and discrediting its methods, so it would not form the basis for the opposition of others in the future. From the vantage point of potential asymmetrical warriors, the Iraqi resistance had already succeeded enough that parts of it will be imitated. Can anyone doubt the next asymmetrical warriors will come armed with improvised explosive devices (IEDs) to be detonated against symmetrical opponents? But what else?

The Asymmetrical Warfare-Terrorism Nexus

There is a dynamic relationship between asymmetrical warfare and terrorism. The relationship is reciprocal and intimate: terrorism is, in some ways, a form of asymmetrical warfare, and asymmetrical warriors (as well as their symmetrical counterparts) often use terror as part of their operational tactics and strategy. As a tactical tool, terrorizing an enemy or a hostile target population may be an attractive way to weaken the resolve or strength of that opponent, either military or civilian. It is in this sense that terror is a tool of both conventional and unconventional warriors. A terrorist attack in a major city may be intended to soften the resolve of the target to continue resistance, and air attacks against enemy leadership have the dual purposes of eliminating important enemies and of frightening others in the vicinity.

The strategic relationship is somewhat more complicated and reflects the strength of particular asymmetrical warriors. Terrorism is, as noted more fully in chapter 14, generally a method of the very weak, who can mount no serious campaign to overcome an opponent but hope to gain limited objectives by frightening a target population to the point that its cost-tolerance is exceeded and it acquiesces to some terrorist demand rather than living under the threat of continued attack. Purely terrorist attacks never do and are generally not intended to achieve larger political goals, and their commission may be intended as no more than a reminder to those attacked that the organization is still around and capable of mayhem. Asymmetrical warfare, on the other hand, is the tool of the more robust insurgent, who may not have the military strength to stand toe-to-toe with a conventional force, but whose strength is sufficient to engage in military campaigns of attrition to wear down or discourage the opposition. The choice between the two techniques is a reflection of comparative weakness.

One can draw too fine a distinction between the two kinds of organization. It is possible, for instance, for a terrorist organization to grow into an asymmetrical warfare force, as the former AQI did when it became IS in 2014. At the same time, if an asymmetrical force suffers enough setbacks and is visibly weakened to the point it can no longer compete in an unconventional warfare role, it may revert to the relatively less demanding role of terrorist. The retreat of the Caliphate suggests that that may be happening to IS. Once again, this ability to change shape and mission is nothing new. The writings of strategists such as China's Mao Zedung and North Vietnam's Vo Nguyen Giap suggest that guerrilla and conventional forces could alternate roles and methods depending on their relative situations.

Terrorism and asymmetrical warfare can be thought of as part of a continuum of forms of warfare with the common purpose of trying to prevail against a materially superior opponent. Terrorists operate at the lower end of the scale in terms of both ambition and capability, and asymmetrical warriors aim at gradually taking a position of inferiority and transforming it into a situation where they can prevail, up to and including gaining sovereign political authority. Ironically, terrorism is often "showier" in the sense that its results are often more spectacular and visually horrific, even if they have less effect on the final outcomes of conflicts. Asymmetrical warfare approaches, on the other hand, have more serious and long-term consequences that include the overthrow and replacement of governments and territories where outsiders may have perceived interests. This latter dynamic, common to DWICs, is why outsiders—including the United States—sometimes feel the need to intervene in these situations. Doing so is fraught with dangers and pitfalls that are often unrecognized at the time they are contemplated.

The Perils of Outside Involvement

Involvement in asymmetrical DWICs is the most likely form that major-power involvement in military conflict will take for the foreseeable future. Such involvements are almost always problematical, and, as I have argued most extensively in *The Case against Military Intervention*, likely to be unsuccessful and very frustrating and expensive; the Afghanistan case application clearly demonstrates these possible results. Committing forces to these wars is often like following Alice down the rabbit's hole. Experience has shown this outcome repeatedly, and yet it is a lesson largely unlearned and an experience repeated.

There are at least two reasons that the use of Western, including American, force in DWICs is the most likely form of military employment. First, these wars are essentially "the only game in town," in the sense that there are very few other wars that can attract the involvement of outsiders. Second, there are at least some Western/American interests that are involved in most of these, making their favorable resolution of some salience to the major power contemplating involvement. Usually, however, the outside interests do not unambiguously reach vitality, instead being at a somewhat lower level such as major interests as described in chapter 2. Deciding to insert American or other outside force thus requires a relaxation of the realist guideline of employing force only when vital interests are engaged. It also means that the eventual outcome is almost inevitably more important to the indigenous contestants than it is to the outsiders, affecting adversely the outsiders' stamina in pursuing its goals.

The problem of involvement is that it tends to be open-ended; these internally based conflicts drag on in a protracted manner that is exacerbated when outsiders do become involved. It is not a coincidence that the rise of asymmetrical warfare and most of the longest wars in American history have coincided. The modern era of asymmetrical warfare in the American experience was ushered in with the eight-year involvement in Vietnam between 1965 and 1973, followed by the eight-years-plus invasion and occupation of Iraq (2003–2011) and currently culminated by the sixteen years (and counting) of American involvement in Afghanistan (2001–present).

The peril of involvement arises from the attempt to insert American (or other Western) military might into a situation for which it is unsuited. Militarily, the whole point of asymmetrical warfare is to blunt and foil the intrusion of superior conventional forces into situations, and it is an approach that has been successful. Politically, the situations where involvement may be contemplated tend to be difficult, convoluted, and opaque in terms of the motives of the contestants, and outsiders have not shown great talent in identifying the "side of the angels" in these encounters.

The Military Dimension

Any military force contemplating insertion into a DWIC must face certain uncomfortable and unfamiliar realities. The first concerns the nature of the opponent, its methods, and its goals. DWICs occur in locales very unlike North America and Europe, for which most major-power armed forces were designed, and this makes a difference. The "natives" in DWICs recognize that they cannot fight major-power militaries head-on, and so they can only compete by changing the rules and methods of the "game." Asymmetrical forces avoid the kinds of engagement at which they know they will lose, preferring instead more indirect forms of warfare such as ambushes and improvised explosive devices (IEDs) against conventional foes. They consciously change the rules of engagement (ROEs) so they are uncomfortable for conventional forces. Declaring that there are no noncombatants allows them to embed themselves in civilian populations, forcing the enemy to avoid attacking them or risk causing collateral damage that violates the intervener's ROEs. The symmetrical warrior's goal is not to bring the enemy forces to their knees, but rather to frustrate the enemy and overcome its cost-tolerance.

The goal is achieved by frustrating the opponent to the point that it tires of the contest and leaves. In one construction, the yardstick of success for symmetrical warriors is the military defeat of its enemy as preface to imposing a settlement on it. It wins by winning. By contrast, the asymmetrical warrior's strategy of attrition seeks to get the opponent to leave on its own. The opponent is not vanquished on the field of battle; it leaves voluntarily. The asymmetrical warrior's goal is to keep on the pressure until this occurs: it wins by not losing.

On the battlefield, the major values are innovation and adaptability. Asymmetrical wars are never the same, and thus they are difficult to prepare for. What are the proper doctrinal preparations for an enemy whose major purpose is to surprise and frustrate the best-trained opponents? It is not an easy task, and Western (including American) militaries have not demonstrated that they have mastered it.

The Political Dimension

Two major political dilemmas face the potential intruder into DWICs. The first problem is in understanding them—and thus what and whom to support in them. In most DWIC situations, outsiders do not fully understand the nuances of the situations and whom—if anyone—is worth supporting. DWICs tend to be about loyalty to the sides fighting, and it is often difficult to determine which side represents the aspirations of the population—which side represents the "good guys." Failing to choose the virtuous side and the side likely to prevail is a crucial problem.

The other problem surrounds the lack of intense outsider interest in the outcomes of the conflict. Was there, for instance, anything about any outcome that justified an eight-year commitment and the loss of over 58,000 American lives in Vietnam? Of eight years of combat and commitment in Iraq? Of a decade and a half's military commitment to Afghanistan? Cases can be made on either side of all these, but they are not so overwhelmingly compelling as to gather universal agreement. The lack of vital interests is the culprit.

Application: The Never-Ending Afghanistan War

Unless one counts long occupations such as the U.S. Marines' two decades in Haiti between 1915 and 1934, the American military effort in Afghanistan now represents America's longest war. A definitive outcome seems no more imminent than it did at the beginning. Those who committed the first American forces to Afghanistan did not envision a war without end when they dispatched the first Americans there in October 2001. Spurred by the 9/11 attacks by an Al Qaeda whose principal sanctuary was in Afghanistan and protected by the Taliban government, the overt purpose was to attack, capture, and destroy the terrorist organization and its leader, Osama bin Laden. That action, however, enmeshed the United States in a conventional civil war between the Taliban and insurgents under the banner of the Northern Alliance, and this lingering asymmetrical war has kept the United States and its allies there.

The campaign against bin Laden and Al Qaeda, of course, failed, as the terrorist leader and his followers managed to elude their pursuers and slip across the border into areas of Pakistan not under effective control by the Pakistani government, where they remained and continue to operate. Despite this inability to accomplish the primary—and universally supported—goal of destroying Al Qaeda, the United States has stayed in Afghanistan. When the Taliban returned to reassert their lost domain in 2003, this made the United States part of the Afghan civil war, which was not part of the original purpose but which became justified as necessary to prevent an Al Qaeda return. In that same year, the United States also began a heavy military involvement in Iraq that sapped attention and resources away from Afghanistan for the remainder of the decade.

Afghanistan is a classic asymmetrical war. On one side is the Afghan government, aided by a NATO-based coalition and the United States. Thanks to outside assistance, the Afghan government possesses clearly superior conventional force. On the other side is the insurgent Taliban, whose forces are clearly inferior to those of the United States and its allies (NATO and the Afghan government) in physical terms. In these circumstances, the Taliban had no choice but to adopt the methodology of asymmetrical force.

The Afghan Maelstrom

By virtually any measure and for virtually any purpose, Afghanistan is one of the most forbidding, unforgiving, and difficult countries in the world. It is an ancient land with a discernible history dating back three to four millennia. It has always been a harsh and contentious place with a history punctuated by occasions in which its people have united to repel foreign invaders and then fallen back into fractious disunity and violent rivalry once the outsider had been repulsed. Afghans always seem to be fighting, either against hated outsiders or among themselves. Since 2001, it has been both.

Historic interest in Afghanistan has largely geographic bases. The country has few natural resources to exploit or physical bases for development, and it is one of the poorest countries in the world. In 2016, for instance, the *CIA World Factbook* listed its three largest exports (in order) as opium, fruits, and nuts. It does have a strategic location in the heart of Asia that has made it a junction point, what the U.S. government has called a "land bridge," for travelers and traders throughout history. East–West commerce from the Orient to the Middle East and Europe traversed the country, and the north–south axis from Central Asia to the Asian subcontinent has modern Afghanistan in its path as well.

This strategic location has placed Afghanistan on the transit route or made it the object of some of history's greatest conquerors. Alexander the Great passed through what is now Afghanistan in both directions as he sought to subdue India, and Genghis Khan's Golden Horde swept through and for a time occupied this rugged land of barren mountains and high mountain valleys. More recently, independent Afghanistan (it originally achieved its independence in 1747) was occupied and partially subdued by Great Britain, which fought three wars there in the nineteenth and early twentieth centuries. In the nineteenth century, indeed, Afghanistan was the object of the "Great Game" between the British and the Russians, as the Russians sought to extend their influence southward toward the British Raj in India and the British wanted to retain influence over Afghanistan and part of what is now Pakistan as a buffer area protecting the British domain on the subcontinent. The Soviet Union invaded Afghanistan in December 1979 in a feckless attempt to shore up a communist regime in Kabul. Like virtually all the conquerors that had come before them, the Soviets retreated ignominiously in 1988, having failed utterly in their quest and having weakened themselves to the point that it was a contributory factor in the disintegration and downfall of Soviet communism that began in 1989.

The Afghan experience has been enigmatic and difficult. For most of its history, Afghanistan has been a deeply divided society, with loyalty to tribal affiliations rather than the state. Afghanistan has never evolved a strong, stable central government, and its attempts to create one have been fleeting and ultimately unsuccessful. This misery has been compounded by epidemic corruption over the sparse wealth, which continues to this day. As a March 10, 2017, *New York Times* editorial summarized the situation: "Afghanistan remains in the grip of a resolute insurgency and a kleptocratic, dysfunctional governing elite."

What passes for unity and peacefulness normally has occurred when geographically based, ethnic tribal groups have had substantial autonomy and where such central regulation as existed was the result of *loya jirgas*, extensive meetings of tribal elders from around the country. Whenever a central government in Kabul has attempted to assert its authority outside the tribal council system, it has been actively resisted, often violently. The exception has generally been when Afghanistan has been invaded by outsiders, at which time the various Afghan tribes have temporarily set aside their differences just long enough to expel the foreigners.

The result is an Afghan society that is dominated by its tribal parts and that has a xenophobic dislike and suspicion of outsiders. Within the tribal structure of the country, however, one tribal entity has traditionally been most prominent. The Pashtuns are the largest ethnic group in the country. They are divided into competing subunits, the most prominent of which are the Durrani and the Gilzai Pashtuns. Throughout most of Afghan history, Pashtuns were in the majority in the country, and for a time the terms "Afghan" and "Pashtun" were used synonymously. Forced migration—largely to Pakistan—has cost the Pashtuns their majority status, but they retain a plurality (currently estimated as about 42 percent). Traditional Pashtun lands are concentrated in the southern and eastern parts of the country adjacent to and overlapping the Durand Line (the legal boundary between Afghanistan and Pakistan that many Pashtuns reject as invalid). The Pashtuns are also the second largest ethnic group in Pakistan (behind the Punjabis), and the territory dominated by the Pashtuns on both sides of the border is also known as Pashtunistan. A sovereign state by that name remains the goal of some tribal members. By some measures, the Pashtuns are a stateless nation like the Kurds.

The Pashtuns are important in the current context for two reasons. First, virtually all Afghan governments have been headed by a Pashtun and have had the active support of the Pashtuns. Hamid Karzai, the president of Afghanistan from 2004 to 2014, is an urban Durrani Pashtun, but his support among the rural Gilzais who are the core supporters of the Taliban was always suspect. He was succeeded by Dr. Ashraf Ghani, a former chancellor of Kabul University and an urban Pashtun. He has been unable to stanch the chronic cronyism and corruption that has haunted the country. The Gilzai support base of the Taliban comes almost exclusively from rural-based Pashtuns, and most of the hotbeds of Taliban activity and control are in traditional Pashtun lands. All Pashtuns are by no means Taliban, but virtually all the Taliban are Pashtuns. Second, much of the very strong identity and values of Pashtuns derive from Pashtunwali, a code of morals and proper behavior. Among the central tenets of this code is hospitality and protection of honored guests. Arising from their collaboration in the anti-Soviet resistance, one of the recipients of this protection was Al Qaeda.

Roots and Evolution of War and U.S. Involvement

The structure and issues underlying the current war in Afghanistan are the direct result of the Afghan resistance to the Soviet occupation during 1979–1988 and its aftermath. In predictable fashion, the Soviet invasion produced a fierce resistance by the various Afghan tribes, aided by, among others, the Americans and the Pakistanis. The mujahidin, as the resisters were collectively known, had two distinct elements: native Afghan tribe members who, in typical Afghan fashion, formed a loose coalition to repel the Soviets that dissolved when the Soviets departed; and foreign fighters, mostly from other Islamic countries. Native Afghans formed the basis for both sides in the later civil war between the Taliban and the Northern Alliance. Many foreign fighters, some recruited by a then-obscure Saudi activist named Osama bin Laden, became members of Al Qaeda.

The expulsion of the Soviets ended communist rule in Afghanistan. Between 1988 and 1996, a number of governments came and went in Kabul, but they were equally inept, corrupt, and unpopular. In reaction, a new movement primarily comprising students (talibs) from religious schools (madrassas) largely in Pakistan formed and swept across Afghanistan. In 1996, the Taliban became the government of the country. That same year, Al Qaeda was expelled from Sudan, partly because of pressure from the U.S. government. Looking for a new sanctuary, bin Laden and his followers appealed to their old allies in the new Afghan government, who welcomed them and, under the tenets of Pashtunwali, provided them with protection.

The Taliban government's rule—or misrule—is well documented (e.g., tyrannical fundamentalist excesses, including the draconian suppression of women) and this perhaps inevitably spawned its own opposition. Gradually, a coalition of primarily non-Pashtun tribes formed under the banner of the Northern Alliance. By 9/11, the Northern Alliance and the Taliban were locked in a full-scale civil war, the outcome of which was very much in doubt. Meanwhile, Al Qaeda continued to operate training facilities in Afghanistan, planning, among other things, the 9/11 attacks.

While decrying the Taliban's policies and providing some small amount of assistance to the opposition, the United States stayed on the sidelines of this conflict before 9/11. The public face of the American decision to intervene physically in Afghanistan was the "war on terror," with Al Qaeda as its centerpiece. When U.S. forces entered the country, they in effect created a second conflict with its own objectives and conduct separate from and independent of the ongoing civil war. Although bin Laden's flight from the country effectively ended the military effort against Al Qaeda in Afghanistan (since the terrorists were now in Pakistan), that did not end NATO and American military involvement. Rather, outside assistance had helped drive the Taliban out of power and into Pakistani exile, and the result was the formation of the new Karzai government as the representative of the victorious Northern Alliance, with American blessing. When the Taliban left, the United States and NATO remained to help mop up residual Al Qaeda and Taliban resistance and to ensure that they did not return. The effect was to bifurcate the fighting into a limited and failed effort to capture Al Qaeda, a goal in the highest American interest, and a continuing civil war in which the only American interest was to maintain in power a regime that would oppose Al Qaeda's return. The United States declared Operation Enduring Freedom, recruited allies into the NATO-sponsored International Security Assistance Force (ISAF), and thus set itself up as part of the renewed civil war that was to come. The U.S. interest in that war, of debatable vitality, has remained the basic rationale for the U.S. role ever since.

The Taliban did, of course, begin to infiltrate back into the country and to launch a new phase of the civil war with the pre-9/11 roles reversed: The Karzai-led Northern Alliance formed the core of the government and the Taliban were the insurgents. Now reconfigured as the Afghan National Army (ANA), the Northern Alliance was no more capable of defeating the Taliban than they had been before. As the returning Taliban gradually reasserted its authority over increasing parts of Afghanistan (especially traditional Gilzai Pashtun territories), opposition to the Taliban gradually fell to NATO. The current civil war was thus engaged.

It has become a classic asymmetrical war. The Taliban are a formidable match for the ANA if they do not have outside help, but they are far less powerful than and incapable of defeating the NATO/American forces in symmetrical warfare. The Taliban thus adopted an unconventional, asymmetrical approach to the war, aiming most clearly at overcoming American cost-tolerance by prolonging the conflict sufficiently that American public opinion will turn against the effort and force a withdrawal. This is, of course, a classic insurgent strategic approach against an outside occupier and is consistent with the historical Afghan treatment of outsiders. The American response has been that of counterinsurgency (COIN) as outlined in the Petraeus-inspired FM 3-24, which seeks to liberate Taliban territory and engage in a successful campaign for the "hearts and minds" of the Afghan people to turn their loyalty away from the Taliban and toward the government. At the same time, the strategy calls for expanding the size and quality of Afghan government forces to the point that they eventually can defeat the insurgency on their own.

Never-Ending Conflict

The civil war in Afghanistan between the central government of Ghani (aided or—depending on one's view—propped up) by ISAF, continues, and no one is publicly predicting a conclusion anytime soon. In one sense, the protraction and lack of visible success of either side is not unusual for an asymmetrical war where neither side can vanquish the opponent and impose the kind of peace that marks conventional wars. It is even more a war of attrition than most asymmetrical wars, as its inconclusive length is a testament.

This war would hardly be of interest to the West, and specifically to the United States, were it not for the 9/11-Afghan connection. American interests in Afghanistan before the terrorist attacks were decidedly marginal, and had a country other than Afghanistan provided the sanctuary for Al Qaeda, it is almost impossible to imagine that the United States (or its NATO allies) would have cared enough about the outcome of the war between the Northern Alliance and the Taliban to insert itself to affect the outcome in one direction or the other. The clear American interest was in capturing bin Laden and his cohorts, and it failed. What was left was the internal war, in which the only discernible American interest was in victory for the side that would most oppose Al Qaeda's return. That basically remains the rationale for the ongoing involvement. Whether it has been worth the costs the United States has absorbed is another question. The Al Qaeda problem is now dealt with in different ways; what is left is helping the Kabul government cope with the Taliban.

Opposing the Taliban insurgency is a different, but in many ways a more familiar, problem. The Taliban are conducting an asymmetrical campaign using largely guerrilla tactics and insurgent goals, and the Americans have responded with counterinsurgency strategy. The effort, however, is plagued by at least three difficulties. One is that the Taliban have proven to be tough, adept, and adaptive fighters defending harsh territory with which they are more familiar and comfortable than their opponents: the going is very difficult. The second problem is that the outsiders find themselves aligned with what many Afghans view as an anti-Pashtun coalition. The leadership from Karzai to Ghani are Durrani Pashtuns who have aligned themselves with other ethnic minorities such as the Tajiks, who are the historic enemies of the rural Afghans who compose and support the Taliban. Afghan history has been remarkably consistent in the sense that no government that is opposed by the Pashtun plurality has much chance of succeeding, and when a government is perceived to be an adjunct of urbanites in Kabul, it is doubly suspicious among Afghans from remote parts of the country. Third, the outsiders are exactly that—outsiders—and their presence is resented because they are foreigners and unwelcome guests (or at least guests who have overstayed their welcome). Resistance to foreign military occupation is a universal human instinct, and it is especially strong among the Afghans. The fact that ISAF no longer engages in overt offensive operations without ANA units in the lead has not reduced their unacceptability in a country where outsiders are always suspect.

The war in Afghanistan became an asymmetrical war and continues to be one because of the outside intervention of the United States and its NATO allies. Prior to that involvement, there had been a fairly conventional civil war going on against the Taliban (a not unusual circumstance) that would likely have continued with some internal resolution at some point. Interfering in that internal affair was not a prominent part of the rationale for intervention in the first place, but it has become the de facto reason for staying. Destroying Al Qaeda was the real goal, and the Taliban were in the way. Operationally, the anti–Al Qaeda mission in Afghanistan ended when Al Qaeda fled. The outside mission remained; it became the shield behind which the anti-Taliban government of Karzai was formed, and by staying, it became the protector and sponsor of the new regime. It still is sixteen years later.

How the Afghanistan War will end is a matter of speculation. Historically, one Afghan faction would prevail, govern for a while, and then be overthrown. This war, however, is made more complicated by two factors that speak more to the interests of outsiders than the Afghans themselves. The first, of course, is the Al Qaeda factor. If Al Qaeda is otherwise destroyed or its return to Afghanistan successfully precluded, there is little reason for the outside world to worry about the civil war. The other is the outside (and especially the American) role, which is an enigma. Afghanistan is the longest American war in history, and it has not been cheap. American casualties have been relatively light: 2939 dead of 3529 ISAF deaths, but the monetary costs have been enormous. Officially, $686 billion was appropriated for the conflict between 2001 and 2014, and no one thinks that was the total bill. Most unofficial estimates fall in the $2–4 trillion range for outcomes that are hardly discernible. President Obama announced early in his presidency the intention to get the U.S. out of Afghanistan by 2014, and he failed. The Trump administration has opted for an incremental increase in American military presence.

Where does the effort stand? Analysts disagree, but none are wildly optimistic. The *New York Times* March 10, 2017, editorial argues that "The challenges that have stymied American generals in Afghanistan for years—including havens for insurgents in Pakistan, endemic corruption and poor leadership in the Afghan military—remain unsolved." Alleged but largely unpublicized Pakistani aid to the Taliban is, according to Fair, resulting in a dismal outlook: "the situation in Afghanistan is spiraling downward as the Taliban continues to make new gains while consolidating older ones. Hopes that Pakistan would bring the Taliban to the negotiating table continue to fizzle. The reason for this is simple: Pakistan and its proxy, the Taliban, are winning." The 2017 policy response in Washington, summarized by Jones, is dismal: "aggressively pursue terrorists that threaten the United States, prevent Taliban forces from overthrowing the Afghan government, and encourage a more sustainable and effective Afghan government." Is this not the policy of the last sixteen years—which has not worked?

Conclusion

Warfare is both an ever-changing and never-changing human endeavor. The opponents change, the purposes for which wars are fought change, and the methods and tools of war change. At the same time, the fact that groups of humans find reasons to fight and kill other groups of humans seems ubiquitous, one of history's true constants.

What is now called asymmetrical warfare is part of this larger march of history. The basic ideas, and even some of the methods, underlying this kind of war are as old as warfare itself and have been a recurring part of the historic pattern. What is arguably different is that differential fighting capabilities among and between countries and groups have widened to the point that asymmetrical warfare has become much more necessary for weaker participants than it was in the past. The ongoing war in Afghanistan is only the latest and most currently obvious example of this form of warfare. How it ends will, in turn, have some effect on the form this warfare will take in a future where asymmetrical opponents are the only likely foes for major powers such as the United States.

Study/Discussion Questions

1. The nature and dynamics of warfare have changed markedly since the end of the Cold War. What are the nature and causes of that change? Discuss.

2. What is asymmetrical warfare? Contrast it with symmetrical warfare. Why has it arisen as the major military problem of the twenty-first century? Why is it likely to continue to be the dominant problem?

3. Discuss the problem posed by asymmetrical warfare. Why is it called New/Old War? In what kinds of conflicts and by what kind of groups is it practiced?

4. Why has involvement in asymmetrical warfare become such a large enterprise for the United States? What has the experience been? What political and military problems does it create?

5. Discuss the background and evolution of the Afghanistan War, beginning with its roots in the Afghan resistance to the Soviet occupation and leading to the 9/11 attacks. Why does the war have two distinct facets? What are they? Explain.

6. Building on the dual nature of the conflict, describe Afghanistan as an asymmetrical war. Put your discussion in the context of the Afghan historical experience.

7. How did the United States get involved in Afghanistan? What changes have occurred since the initial involvement that could or should have changed the nature of that involvement?

8. What do you think the lessons of Afghanistan should be for the United States? Discuss.

Bibliography

Ansary, Tamim. *Game without Rules: The Often-Interrupted History of Afghanistan*. New York: PublicAffairs, 2012.

Badkhen, Anna. "Afghanistan: Cold and Violent." *Foreign Policy* (online), March 9, 2011.

Barfield, Thomas. *Afghanistan: A Cultural and Political History*. Princeton, NJ: Princeton University Press, 2010.

Barnett, Roger W. *Asymmetrical Warfare: Today's Challenge to U.S. Military Power*. Issues in Twenty-First Century Warfare. Washington, DC: Potomac, 2013.

Belasco, Amy. *The Cost of Iraq, Afghanistan and Other Global Terrorist Operations since 9/11*. Washington, DC: Congressional Research Service, December 8, 2014.

Berkowitz, Bruce. *The New Face of War: How War Will Be Fought in the 21st Century*. New York: Free Press, 2003.

Biddle, Stephen, Fotini Christia, and Alexander Thier. "Defining Success in Afghanistan: What Can the United States Accept?" *Foreign Affairs* 89, no. 4 (July/August 2011): 48–60.

Blackwill, Robert D. "Plan B in Afghanistan: Why a De Facto Partition Is the Least Bad Option." *Foreign Affairs* 90, no. 1 (January/February 2012): 43–50.

Central Intelligence Agency. *CIA World Factbook, 2016*. Washington, DC: Central Intelligence Agency, 2016.

Coll, Steve. *Ghost Wars: The Secret History of the CIA, Afghanistan, and bin Laden from the Soviet Invasion to September 10, 2001*. New York: Penguin, 2004.

Crews, Robert D., and Amin Tarzi, eds. *The Taliban and the Crisis of Afghanistan*. Cambridge, MA: Harvard University Press, 2008.

Editorial Board. "Afghanistan Is Now Trump's War." *New York Times* (online). March 10, 2017.

Ewans, Martin. *Afghanistan: A Short History of Its People and Politics*. New York: Harper-Collins Perennial, 2002.

Fair, C. Christine. "Pakistan's Deadly Grip on Afghanistan." *Current History* 116, no. 789 (April 2017): 136–41.

Galula, David. *Counterinsurgency Warfare: Theory and Practice*. Westport, CT: Praeger (Praeger Classics of the Counterinsurgency Era), 2006.

Giap, Vo Nguyen. *People's War, People's Army*. New York: Praeger, 1962.

Haass, Richard N. *War of Necessity, War of Choice: A Memoir of Two Iraq Wars*. New York: Simon & Schuster, 2009.

Jalali, Ali A. "The Future of Afghanistan." *Parameters* XXXVI, no. 1 (Spring 2006): 4–19.

Jones, Seth G. "How Trump Should Manage Afghanistan: A Realistic Set of Goals for the New Administration." *Foreign Affairs Snapshot* (online), March 21, 2017.

———. *In the Graveyard of Empires: America's War in Afghanistan*. New York: Norton, 2009.

Kaplan, Robert D. "Man versus Afghanistan." *Atlantic* 305, no. 3 (April 2010): 60–71.

Kaurin, Pauline M. *The Warrior, Military Ethics and Contemporary Warfare: Achilles Goes Asymmetrical*. New York and London: Routledge, 2016.

Lowther, Adam B. *Americans and Asymmetrical Warfare: Lebanon, Somalia, and Afghanistan*. Westport, CT: Praeger Security International, 2007.

Mao Zedung. *The Collected Works of Mao Zedung*. Vols. 1–4. Beijing, China: Foreign Languages Press, 1967.

O'Hanlon, Michael. "Staying Power: The U.S. Mission in Afghanistan After 2011." *Foreign Affairs* 89, no. 5 (September/October 2010): 63–79.

Rashid, Ahmed. *Taliban: Militant Islam, Oil, and Fundamentalism in Central Asia*. 2nd ed. New Haven, CT: Yale University Press, 2010.

Scales, Robert H. Jr. *Future War: Anthology*. Carlisle Barracks, PA: Strategic Studies Institute, 1999.

Snow, Donald M. *The Case against Military Intervention: Why We Do It and Why It Fails*. New York and London: Routledge, 2016.

———. *National Security*, 6th ed. New York and London: Routledge, 2017.

Snow, Donald M., and Dennis M. Drew. *From Lexington to Baghdad and Beyond: War and Politics in the American Experience*. 3rd ed. Armonk, NY: M. E. Sharpe, 2009.

Sullivan, Gordon R., and Anthony M. Coroalles. *Seeing the Elephant: Leading America's Army into the Twenty-First Century*. Boston: Institute for Foreign Policy Analysis, 1995.

Tomsen, Peter. *The Wars of Afghanistan: Messianic Terrorism, Tribal Conflicts, and the Failure of Great Powers*. New York: PublicAffairs, 2013.

U.S. Army and U.S. Marine Corps. *Counterinsurgency Field Manual* (U.S. Army Field Manual No. 3-24, Marine Corps Warfighting Publication No. 3-33.5). Chicago: University of Chicago Press, 2007.

U.S. Marine Corps. *Afghanistan: Operational Culture for Deploying Personnel*. Quantico, VA: Center for Operational Cultural Learning, 2009.

Van Creveld, Martin. *The Transformation of War*. New York: Free Press, 1991.

Weston, J. Kael. *The Mirror Test: America at War in Iraq and Afghanistan*. New York: Vintage, 2016.

6

Nuclear Proliferation

The Contrasting Cases of North Korea and Iran

Avoiding the spread of nuclear weapons to countries that do not currently possess them has been a global problem and policy goal since the United States exploded the first nuclear device in 1945. This priority arises from two sources: the enormous destructive power of the weapons and the fear that *someone else* in possession of these weapons might use them against you. Actual proliferation first occurred when the Soviet Union exploded a nuclear bomb in 1949. Despite efforts by the nuclear "club" of weapons possessors, it has continued to the present, although at a more modest pace than early doomsayers feared. The flip side of proliferation is arms control—a process that has had some successes but that has been plagued by contradictions and condescension in its advocacies. The argument for avoiding proliferation is that those states seeking the capability are less stable than current possessors and thus more likely to start a nuclear war.

The current concern focuses on two states that are or may become nuclear possessors: North Korea and Iran. Both are autocratic developing world states, occupy strategic locations, and have been expressly anti-Western and anti-American. They are also different. North Korea has broken out of the proliferation regime, has been aggressively pursuing weapons and delivery system development, and has threatened to use its arsenal against neighbors and the United States. Iran maintains it has no interest in weapons development, and has entered a controversial treaty eschewing its right to build the weapons. The two states thus form a contrast on the subject.

The spread of different categories of weapons to states that do not possess them and whose possession concerns other states is not a new phenomenon. In the modern world, trying to place limits on the numbers and types of weapons that states possess goes back to the period between the world wars in modern times; the Washington Conference on naval fleet sizes and the Kellogg–Briand Pact, both of which were negotiated in the 1920s, were early prototypes of the concern that is now called proliferation. Dealing with the spread of nuclear weapons has been a concern since the late 1940s.

The post–World War II concern with the spread of nuclear weapons reached a crescendo with the negotiation of the Nuclear Nonproliferation Treaty (NPT) of 1968. The NPT prohibited additional states that did not already have nuclear weapons from acquiring (or trying to acquire) them. It also required current possessors not to aid in the spread of nuclear weapons and made them promise to reduce and eliminate their own arsenals. The NPT has enjoyed a mixed level of success.

Concern about proliferation has ebbed and flowed. When the membership in the nuclear "club" (the countries that possess the weapons) was very small during the 1950s and 1960s, there was great concern that many countries would acquire them, and nuclear proliferation thought was developed to deal with that contingency. During the 1970s and 1980s, concern became more muted, both because the number of nuclear weapons states did not grow perceptibly, and because of concern with other matters, notably the end of the Cold War.

Interest in proliferation has returned since the turn of the millennium. It has been tied closely to the problem of international terrorism, because of the fear that terrorists might acquire and use nuclear or other deadly weapons (so-called weapons of mass destruction or WMDs), a concern important enough that the 2006 National Security Strategy of the United States stated, "There are few greater threats than a terrorist attack with WMD."

The current concern with WMDs has two basic sources tied to possible terrorist acquisition and use of proscribed weapons. The first worry is over the countries that might acquire such weapons, and it focuses currently on countries such as the Democratic People's Republic of Korea (DPRK, or North Korea) and Iran. The second source of concern is the various types of WMDs that might be acquired. Ultimately, the WMDs that most matter are nuclear weapons because of their enormous destructive capacity, but other forms such as biological and chemical weapons are of importance as well, as the Syrian crises of 2013 and 2017 have demonstrated.

This case study describes the problem of proliferation. It begins with a discussion of the general problem as it has evolved, including the dynamics of the problem and how the international system has attempted to deal with it. Proliferation is a real and vital current problem, and the application contrasts the two major examples of the problem. It concentrates on the DPRK, looking at both attempts to prevent North Korea from joining the nuclear club and the dynamics that have made such conformance impossible to achieve. It contrasts this problem with the Iranian agreement to abandon a weapons program through a multilateral treaty.

Principle: Nuclear Proliferation

Proliferation is a delicate international problem, in large measure because its underlying aim is both discriminatory and condescending to those at whom it is aimed. The desire to limit possession of nuclear weapons and other WMDs has largely come from countries that already possess those weapons and is aimed at those who do not. Thus, the strongest current efforts to reverse the DPRK's program come from countries such as the United States, Britain, and China, which already have them.

The delicacy of the situation arises from rationalizing why it is all right for some states to have nuclear weapons when others should not. The assertions and arguments are inherently discriminatory, and the question that must be answered is why some but not others? Invariably, the answer to that question comes back to an assumption regarding responsibility: those who have the weapons, it is argued by those countries that have them, can be trusted to act responsibly with the weapons (which basically means they will not use them). Others, however, are not necessarily so trustworthy and, by definition, have no track record of responsible possession. This reasoning is convincing to countries already possessing the weapons but not necessarily to those that do not. Some nonpossessors feel that the assertion is unjustifiably condescending and effectively aims at denying the sovereign right to defend themselves.

The proliferation problem is structurally complex. To understand it, one can look at three questions: What is the nature of the problem? Why is it a problem? And what can be done about it? The answers collectively form the context for analyzing the case application to North Korea and Iran.

The Nature of the Proliferation Problem

The roots of the contemporary proliferation problem lie in the Cold War fear of nuclear war. The major purposes were to prevent the spread of nuclear weapons to states that did not have them, and to limit the size and destructiveness of the arsenals of possessing states. These two intents were related. In addition, there was concern about the destabilizing impact of burgeoning nuclear possession, which in turn spawned two additional concerns. One was about the kind of capability that countries were attempting to proliferate (what forms of WMD), and the other was the mechanics of how proliferation could occur (and thus what steps had to be taken to prevent it from happening).

Two basic forms of proliferation were identified and targeted during the Cold War: vertical and horizontal. Vertical proliferation refers to incremental additions of weapons systems by a state (or states) that already has the weapon. It is a concern both because additional increments of weapons add to the potential deadliness of confrontations and because those increments can spawn arms races in which additions by one side cause the other to build more, resulting in a potentially destabilizing arms spiral. Efforts to control vertical proliferation generally aim at curbing or reducing levels of different kinds of arms and are the traditional object of arms control. Most of the nuclear arms treaties negotiated by the United States and the Soviet Union during the Cold War (such as the Strategic Arms Limitations Talks—SALT—and the Strategic Arms Reduction Talks—START) were attempts to limit vertical proliferation.

Contemporary proliferation efforts center on horizontal proliferation: the spread of nuclear or other weapons to states that currently do not possess them; generally, when the term *proliferation* is used in contemporary discussions, it is shorthand for horizontal proliferation. The two forms are linked because many of the calls for limiting horizontal proliferation have come from states (such as the United States and the former Soviet Union) that have been engaged in vertical proliferation (nuclear arms races) that made their entreaties to others to self-abnegate attempts to gain the weapons seem disingenuous and created demands to link the two (see the following discussion of the NPT).

The kinds of capabilities being proliferated were also a concern that led to independent efforts to curb each phenomenon. The categories of weapons that may be proliferated are WMDs, which generally are categorized into three types captured by the abbreviation NBC: nuclear, biological, and chemical weapons. Though all are of concern, the dangers they pose differ. Nuclear weapons are arguably the only unambiguous weapons of mass destruction, because of the size and destructiveness of nuclear explosions. Biological (or agents of biological origin, ABO) and chemical weapons can cause large numbers of deaths that are often particularly hideous, but their extensiveness of destruction is more limited. On the other hand, biological and especially chemical weapons are much easier to construct and conceal than nuclear weapons, making terrorist possession and use a major concern. Chemical and biological weapons take on added importance because the Syrians—and earlier the Iraqis—have shown that taboos against their use are lower than those of employing nuclear weapons. Proliferation efforts have centered on nuclear weapons, although they have been extended to other forms of WMDs. In addition, there is concern about how WMDs might be delivered to targets. The most dramatic form of delivery is by ballistic missiles, because at present there are no foolproof means of engaging in highly effective defenses against ballistic missile attacks.

How to produce and avoid the production of these capabilities have also been matters of major concern, centering particularly on nuclear weapons and ways to get them to target. The problem of nuclear weapons production is straightforward and has two components. The first is the knowledge of how to fabricate a nuclear device. Nuclear physics has been taught openly for over sixty years now in the world's (and notably American) universities, so that knowledge is widely available both to most governments and undoubtedly to many private groups. The knowledge genie is clearly out of the bottle. The other requirement for building nuclear weapons is possession of adequate supplies of weapons-grade (i.e., highly enriched) isotopes of uranium/plutonium, which generally are byproducts of nuclear reactions in certain types of power generators. Access to such materials is highly guarded and restricted, and aspirants to nuclear weapons must either possess nuclear reactors that produce weapons-grade materials or be able to purchase or steal such material from those who possess it. Nonproliferation efforts have been concentrated on denying access to weapons-grade material to potential proliferators.

The other, and until recently less publicized, aspect of nuclear proliferation surrounds the ability to deliver those weapons to targets—specifically to targets in the United States and other Western countries. Terrorist horror scenarios center on clandestine shipment of assembled bombs via cargo ship and the like to places such as New York or the dispatch of so-called suitcase bombs (small nuclear devices contained in luggage or other parcels) or dirty bombs (conventional explosives coated with radioactive materials dispersed with detonation of the bomb). More conventional analyses deal with the ability of nuclear pretenders to build or buy ballistic missiles to deliver these weapons. The question of ballistic delivery systems has been a developing problem in dealing with the DPRK.

The Problem Proliferation Poses

The short answer to why proliferation is a problem is that one has much less to fear from a weapons capability that one's actual or potential adversaries do not possess than from a capability that they do possess. In the classic Cold War seedbed of thinking about nuclear proliferation, the problem was the difficulty of keeping additional sovereign states from achieving nuclear capability. The more such additional countries obtained the weapons, the more "fingers" there would be on the nuclear "button," and thus as a matter of probability, the more likely someone would push the button and start a nuclear war. That problem remains central to the contemporary problem, but is augmented by the fear that some of the potential proliferating states might share their capabilities with terrorist non-state actors, who would allegedly be more difficult to dissuade from using those weapons than state actors.

In classic terms, the problem of the spread of nuclear (or other) weapons to nonpossessing states is known as the $N+1$ problem. The idea is straightforward. In the formulation, N stands for the number of states that currently possess nuclear weapons and refers to the dynamics among them; $+1$, on the other hand, refers to the added problems that would be created for the international system (notably the states that form N) by the addition of new $(+1)$ states to the nuclear club.

Current members (N) and potential proliferators $(+1)$ see the problem essentially from opposite ends of the conceptual spectrum. The current members generally believe that the current "club" represents a stable, reliable membership (even if earlier members opposed the addition of some current members before they "joined"). Viewed this way, the emphasis of the club is on the problems created by new members, and the criterion for concern is the likelihood of destabilization of the system created by new members. From this perspective, it is not surprising that members of N tend to look for and find sources of destabilization that should be opposed and want to restrict membership to existing levels.

Members of $+1$, however, see the problem differently. Nonmembers do not see their own acquisition of nuclear weapons as destabilizing and are righteously indignant at the notion that their acquisition would destabilize the system. The accusation by "club" members is a backhanded way of suggesting that new members would be less responsible possessors than those who already have the weapons. Put more bluntly, the imputation that a new state would destabilize amounts to accusing such a state of a greater likelihood of starting a nuclear war than those who already have them and have refrained from doing so. If you are a member of the government of North Korea, for instance, you would like an explanation of exactly why the United States, which maintains over 28,000 troops and until 1991 numerous nuclear warheads on the soil of your next-door neighbor (South Korea), should be treated as more responsible with weapons of mass destruction than you are. It is not an easy sell.

Indeed, in the current context, nonpossessors are more likely to make the argument that their membership in the nuclear club will stabilize their situations and even global politics generally, because it is a fact (even if the causality is arguable) that no state that possesses nuclear weapons has ever been the victim of an aggression against it. Indeed, one of the arguments that both the Iranians and North Koreans (among others) have made in recent years is that gaining nuclear weapons capability is a useful—even necessary—means to avoid being attacked by an aggressive United States. Would, for instance, the United States have attacked Iraq it had possessed, rather than being accused of trying to get, nuclear weapons? Some nonpossessing countries argue that the American attack would have been less likely and that Saddam Hussein's major error was in not getting a nuclear capability that might have deterred the United States from invading the country. Some even argue that had he not abandoned his nuclear weapons program, he might still be alive and in power.

There is a further irony that attaches to the $N+1$ problem—it is generally viewed as a problem by the current nuclear club. Ironically, a country that aspires to become a member (a $+1$ country) may be viewed as a problem before it gets the capability, but once it has and has demonstrated its "responsible possession" of the capability, it becomes part of the club and views other aspirants as part of the problem. Thus, for instance, when only the United States and the Soviet Union had nuclear weapons, they viewed the addition of the third member (Britain) as a potential problem. When Britain obtained the weapons, it ceased to be a problem, but viewed the addition of other countries (France, China) as destabilizing prospects. When those countries joined the club, they became part of N and thus looked at other prospective members as part of the problem.

By definition, the nuclear problem is qualitatively worse when there are more nuclear powers, but one obstacle to sustaining international momentum behind proliferation control has been that it has not occurred at the pace envisioned by those who most feared the prospects. The nuclear club was pretty well established by 1964, when China obtained nuclear weapons and pushed the number to five—in order of acquisition: United States, the Soviet Union, Great Britain, France, and China. At the time, there were fears that without restraint the number might jump to twenty, thirty, or even more nuclear states, but that simply has not happened. Since the 1960s, five states have gained nuclear capability. One state (Israel) does not formally admit it has the weapons (it also does not deny it), one state obtained and then renounced and destroyed its weapons (South Africa), two countries openly joined the club in 1998 (India and Pakistan), and North Korea exploded a nuclear device in 2006. The total number of currently acknowledged nuclear states thus stands at nine, which is far less than the doomsayers predicted. In the current debate, three states have been mentioned with varying levels of likelihood of attempting to join the club: Iran, Iraq, and Syria. The American invasion of Iraq precluded that country's membership for the foreseeable future, and international pressures and internal chaos effectively curb any Syrian ambitions. That leaves Iran and North Korea as the current problems.

Solving or Containing the Problem

Because the roots of thinking about the control of nuclear weapons have their origins in the Cold War, so too does thinking about how to prevent proliferation. The key concept in dealing with nuclear weapons in the Cold War context was deterrence, and that concept dominates historic and contemporary discussions of proliferation as well.

The problem of deterrence has changed with the end of the Cold War system. In the past, nuclear deterrence existed among states with very large arsenals of nuclear weapons—principally the United States and the Soviet Union—and the dynamic of deterrence, captured in the idea of assured destruction, was that any nuclear attack against a nuclear-armed superpower would be suicidal, because the attacked state would retain such devastating capabilities even after absorbing an attack as to be able to retaliate against the attacker and destroy it, making any "victory" decidedly pyrrhic (costing far more than it was worth). Because potential attackers were presumably rational (or at least not suicidal), the prospects of a counterattack that would certainly immolate them was enough to dissuade (or deter) an attack in the first place. The same logic applies to the continuing viability of the NPT, the major international regime on proliferation.

The Contemporary Problem of Proliferation

The proliferation situation has changed in two important respects. First, nuclear arsenals and the policies that supported them have changed. All the major weapons states maintain nuclear arsenals, but they are far smaller than they used to be. The primary Cold War antagonists, the United States and the Soviet Union/Russia had arsenals of 10,000–12,000 warheads capable of reaching the other's territory; the number today is closer to 2,000. China, the rising nuclear power, is moving toward a similar arsenal size. Second, and more important in the current context, the threats in the contemporary environment come from states that will, at best, have a small number of nuclear weapons at their disposal but may not be dissuaded by the same threats that deterred the Soviets during the Cold War. Thus, as Joseph Pilat puts it, "There are real questions about whether old, Cold War–vintage concepts . . . really address the needs of today."

What was the structure of deterrent threats that were available both to dissuade states from acquiring nuclear weapons and to convince states that had those weapons not to use them during the Cold War? Answering that question is logically a precondition to assessing whether such mechanisms will work today.

In a text published originally in 1996, Eugene Brown and I laid out a reasonably comprehensive framework for categorizing types of mechanisms that could be used to deter unwanted nuclear behavior. Within this framework, arms proliferation can be dealt with in two ways: acquisition (or front-end) and employment (or back-end) deterrence. Acquisition deterrence, as the name implies, consists of efforts to keep states from obtaining nuclear weapons in the first place. The effort consists of two related and, for many purposes, sequential activities. Persuasion, or convincing states that gaining nuclear weapons is not in their best interests (often accompanied by the promise of related rewards for nonproliferation or punitive threats if compliance does not occur), seeks to cajole possible proliferating states into not doing so. In contemporary terms, successful multilateral efforts through the United Nations and in other forums to dissuade Iran from making a positive nuclear weapons decision fall into this category. If persuasion does not work, then coercion (threatening or taking punitive—

including military—action to prevent proliferation) may occur. The attacks by Israel against an Iraqi nuclear reactor in 1981 and more recently against Syria are extreme examples of coercive options.

The success of acquisition deterrence has been mixed. These efforts were most successful during the Cold War, when the potential negative consequences of proliferation—the possibility of a general, civilization-destroying war—were greatest. In that circumstance, the leaders of the opposing coalitions could and did bring pressure on the states within their orbits to refrain from gaining nuclear weapons. The leading supporting members of the coalitions on both sides—Great Britain and France in the West and China in the East—did proceed with nuclear weapons programs, but they were the exceptions.

The current focus on proliferation has become the spread of nuclear weapons to countries—and especially unstable countries—in the developing world. The stalking horses of this concern were Israel and South Africa, both of which conducted highly clandestine weapons development programs that led to their acquisition of nuclear capability. Both countries developed their programs outside the Cold War context: Israel because of its fear that its Islamic neighbors might destroy it; South Africa because of the alleged threat posed by neighboring black states (the "frontline" states). When South Africa dismantled its apartheid system, it also destroyed its nuclear weapons. Israel continues to maintain, and even to expand, its nuclear arsenal.

Israel and South Africa form a bridge of sorts to the present concern because both are instances where the attempt to restrain proliferation by the major powers was unsuccessful. Developing-world states have proven less prone to geopolitical constraint than were Cold War allies. India and Pakistan ignored dissuasion and joined the nuclear "club" in 1998, for instance. One of the major commonalities of George W. Bush's 2002 "Axis of Evil" designation of Iraq, Iran, and North Korea was their aspiration to nuclear status.

The other form of dissuasion is employment deterrence. If efforts to keep states from gaining nuclear weapons fail, then one must turn to efforts to keeping them from using the weapons they do acquire. Once again, two mechanisms can be employed. One is the threat of retaliation against any nuclear possessor that may choose to use its weapons against another state (and particularly the United States). The threat is to retaliate with such devastating—including assured destruction—force that it would not only be suicidal for an attacking state to use its weapons, but the suicide would not necessarily be mutual because of different sizes of arsenals. Thus, the horror scenario of a possible future North Korean attack against the United States might consist of lobbing a handful of weapons against American targets and inflicting severe but not fatal damage; North Korea would be destroyed in the U.S. retaliation. The question that is raised about the extension of this form of deterrence in the current context is whether potential proliferating states' leadership is sufficiently rational (i.e., nonsuicidal) that this form of threat will be effective against them. The other form of employment deterrence threat is denial, the promise that if an attack is launched, it will fail because the potential attacked state has the capability to defend itself from an attack. The question here is whether the claim to be able to deny an attack is credible given the wide variety of means by which someone could attack, say, the United States with nuclear weapons. Both concerns are present in the current U.S.-DPRK situation.

Employment deterrence efforts have, to this point, been 100 percent effective, in that no state has used nuclear weapons in anger since 1945. Although one cannot state with certainty that deterrence threats have been the reason for this, nonetheless the record remains perfect. From a proliferation perspective, of course, keeping the number of states that could "break" this record as small as possible is the most compelling concern.

The major mechanism by which nonproliferation has been enforced is the Nonproliferation Treaty. The NPT was negotiated in 1968 and went into effect in 1970. Most countries of the world are or have been members of the regime—Iran and North Korea, for instance—and the question is whether the treaty will remain a viable means to avoid more proliferation in the future.

The Role of the NPT

The NPT was, and still is, the most dramatic, open international attempt to prevent and reverse the spread of weapons of mass destruction around the world. Conventions exist that ban the production, use, and sale of chemical and biological weapons and their components, and the Missile Technology Control Regime (MTCR) represents an effort by the major powers (initiated by the G-7 economic powers) to control the spread of missile delivery technology. All have been reasonable but not unqualified successes: Syria and the chemical weapons ban and North Korea and the MTCR. The crown jewel of proliferation control, however, has been the effort to prevent the spread of nuclear weapons in the world, and the instrument has been the NPT.

The NPT was not the first international agreement that addressed horizontal proliferation, but it was the first treaty to have proliferation as its sole purpose. In 1963, the United States, the Soviet Union, and Great Britain negotiated the Limited Test Ban Treaty (LTBT), which prohibited the atmospheric testing of nuclear devices, and this had a secondary proliferation effect, because the technology at the time virtually required nuclear weapons aspirants to explode a nuclear device in the atmosphere to achieve adequate confidence that its device would work.

The same three states cosponsored the NPT. Its major purpose was to create a nuclear caste system based on nuclear weapons possession. Nuclear-weapons-possessing states party to the NPT can keep their nuclear weapons, but agree not to share nuclear technology with nonpossessing states and to work toward disarmament of their arsenals. These provisions, one should quickly note, require very little action on the part of possessors, and are thus generally innocuous and painless. Nonpossessing states, on the other hand, incur real obligations, because they agree that as long as they are members of the treaty (and there are provisions to renounce one's membership), they will not build or seek to build nuclear weapons. Among the nonpossessors that have signed the NPT, this creates a varying obligation. Some states (Sweden, for instance) have never had any intentions to build nuclear weapons and so could join the treaty regime without noticeable effect. Other states (most of the states of sub-Saharan Africa, for instance) lack the wherewithal to even think of developing the weapons, and thus they sacrifice little by joining either.

There is, however, a third category of states: countries that do not have nuclear weapons but might want the ability to exercise the option sometime in the future. For these states, the NPT creates a real potential problem, because ratifying it means giving away the right to exercise the nuclear option while one is a member. Although states can withdraw and thus free themselves from NPT restrictions, doing so is traumatic and would brand whoever did so as a potential aggressor. As a result, only one state that has signed NPT has ever left it (North Korea in 2003), joining Israel, Cuba, India, and Pakistan as nonmembers among the world's major countries.

States desiring to retain the nuclear option have two ways to deal with the NPT. One is not to sign it, thereby avoiding its restrictions. Other states with potential nuclear aspirations have signed the agreement and either complied fully with it or have engaged in activities that come close to noncompliance but stop short of that level.

The nonproliferation enterprise remains a work in progress. Since the NPT was launched nearly a half-century ago, there has been little overt nuclear weapons proliferation (India, Pakistan, and North Korea have been added, South Africa subtracted from the list). Yet, proliferation has emerged in the post–September 11 world as a major concern, fueled by the fear that some rogue state—some members of the "Axis of Evil"—might acquire such weapons and use them either personally or through some terrorist surrogate. Whether this fear is real or fanciful is not the point; that this perception fuels international concern is the point. North Korea and Iran are the two states about which proliferation fears are the greatest.

Application: North Korea and Iran

The general problem of proliferation gains meaning in the specific context of individual states that might be or are suspected of attempting to exercise the nuclear weapons option. The distinction of North Korea is that it has physically gone through the proliferation process and is now a nuclear power. It is, as noted, the only country physically to withdraw from the NPT, an action it undertook and completed in 2003. It is also the only new member of the nuclear club that has conducted nuclear weapons tests since India and Pakistan. Its testing program dates to 2003, and since Kim Jong-un succeeded his father in 2011, the program has accelerated quantitatively and qualitatively. DPRK weapons testing has become progressively aggressive, especially in the mid-2010s, and the North Koreans possess a small arsenal, some of which is reportedly wedded to short-range, portable missile launchers. It is also testing missiles capable of delivering a nuclear weapon over an intercontinental range. Estimates vary about when it may achieve that status.

The other state that has been mentioned prominently in proliferation concerns is Iran. It shares several characteristics with North Korea. First, it has significant foreign policy differences with the United States (although of a different nature and for different reasons than the DPRK) and has been categorized as among America's adversaries. Second, Iran possesses the technology and expertise to produce nuclear weapons and could reasonably easily gain access to the weapons-grade plutonium necessary for bomb construction. Third, and a point of contention, Iran denies any interest or desire to build, and especially to use, nuclear weapons, but these claims are widely disbelieved in policy circles, especially in the United States. Fourth, although Iran is a member of NPT, it has been deemed to be an untrustworthy rogue regime whose word cannot be trusted at face value by prominent political elements in the United States, notably President Trump.

Iran is also different in an important respect already identified. Iran is not a nuclear power and has by treaty obligation forfeited its right to become one. As such, Iran poses a problem of acquisition (or front-end) deterrence. North Korea is different. According to former assistant secretary of defense Ashton Carter and former secretary of defense William J. Perry (both under President Clinton) in a June 22, 2006, column in the *Washington Post*, the DPRK "openly boasts of its nuclear deterrent, has obtained six to eight bombs' worth of plutonium since 2003 and is plunging ahead to make more." Delury summarizes the current situation in a 2017 *Foreign Affairs* article: "The regime already possesses a modest nuclear arsenal and the means to hit targets in Guam, Japan, and South Korea." Thus, the problem posed by North Korea is one of employment (or back-end) deterrence.

Background of the DPRK Problem

North Korea's relentless drive to become a consequential nuclear weapons state is the major face of the proliferation problem today, as it has been for a decade or more. The major protagonists have been the United States and North Korea, and in some ways, it is the latest manifestation of a long conflict between the two countries that now spans two-thirds of a century. America's adversarial relationship with the DPRK dates to the Korean War of 1950–1953. The DPRK nuclear weapons program dates to the 1950s, when a nuclear-armed United States remained the occupying power in South Korea and had nuclear weapons deployed in South Korea to deter another DPRK invasion. This coincidence created a circumstance that some argue helps explain the DPRK's perceived need for weapons of its own. In addition, the United States has been the loudest proponent of nonproliferation, especially when potential proliferators are American adversaries.

The United States is the original *N* state, and it has consistently opposed almost all other attempts at proliferation. Great Britain's attainment of membership is the most notable exception, and the United States has generally not been an overt opponent of the Israeli program, the existence of which is rarely raised by American officials. The long-standing animosity between the DPRK and the United States combine with the advanced status of the DPRK program to give it special relevance for the United States, and the strategic location of the DPRK in

East Asia adds to the poignancy of the problem, since major East Asian powers and the balance between them are also affected.

The proliferation problem posed by North Korea has ebbed and flowed. In the early 1990s it seemed to be settled. In 1994, the Clinton administration made a deal with the DPRK (the Framework Agreement), under which the United States would furnish the North Koreans food, fuel oil, and light (non-weapons-grade) nuclear fuel in return for the DPRK abandoning its nuclear weapons program. That agreement held until the George W. Bush administration, deeply suspicious and arguably ignorant of the North Koreans, threatened to and did renege on the deal. Cumings states the case regarding the Bush administration dramatically: "Bush combined utter ignorance with a visceral hatred for his counterpart in Pyongyang." This action led the North Koreans to remove themselves from the NPT in 2003 and to resume their nuclear program, and it has continued to grow ever since.

The Nature of the North Korean Threat

The proliferation problem regarding the DPRK is distinctive. North Korea, of course, poses a more advanced problem than nuclear pretenders such as Iran, because it possesses nuclear weapons and because of its development of long-range missile systems that it advertises will be able to reach the United States. This stature means antiproliferation efforts must be based in employment deterrence or convincing the DPRK to disarm its arsenal, a less likely prospect.

The North Korean case is also distinctive in that it has been, at various times, in the process of being resolved through negotiation. After several years of off-again, on-again negotiations between the DPRK and the other countries involved in the so-called six-nations talks (the United States, Russia, China, Japan, and North and South Korea), a breakthrough occurred in summer 2008 that would have resulted in North Korean disassembly of nuclear facilities capable of producing bomb-grade plutonium, destruction of nuclear bomb materials, and re-accession to the NPT. In return, the DPRK was to be removed from the U.S. State Department's list of terrorist states and the "Axis of Evil," and some provisions of the American Trading with the Enemy Act pertinent to the DPRK have been lifted. Full implementation was interrupted in late 2008 by the apparent serious illness suffered by Kim Jong-il, leaving DPRK leadership in limbo.

The DPRK problem began to move toward its current crisis proportions shortly after 2008. The North Koreans have always disliked the six-power approach to negotiations, arguing that they are demeaning and stacked against them. They insist that real negotiations should be bilateral with the Americans and that the larger format makes discussions difficult because all the other five countries oppose the DPRK nuclear program. The situation was made even worse when twenty-nine-year-old Kim Jong-un succeeded his father in 2011. The young Kim brought with him a fierce determination to increase his country's security, and he apparently felt this imperative would best be served with a nuclear deterrent threatening the region and especially the United States.

The rift between Pyongyang and Washington is geopolitical and multifaceted, combining proliferation with other concerns. The DPRK has been much more recalcitrant about its weapons programs, including both nuclear weapons and ballistic delivery systems, than other potential nuclear states. Moreover, the Korean peninsula's location in the heart of East Asia gives it a great deal of geopolitical importance. At the same time, North Korea is one of the most destitute countries on the globe, relies heavily on Chinese assistance to maintain its meager standard of living, and would be almost totally ignorable and inconsequential were it not for possessing nuclear weapons.

The DPRK's unique situation cuts both ways in terms of trying to deal with them. The country's extreme poverty and lack of developmental prospects has made it receptive to outside assistance, as was part of the 1994 agreement. The regime is anxious to avoid letting the population know just how miserable their condition and prospects are, particularly compared to the circumstances of surrounding countries like South Korea, but this is an ever-increasingly difficult condition to maintain. Moreover, as Lankov notes, the nuclear program serves to ameliorate some of the country's woes: "Pyongyang cannot do away with these programs. That would mean losing a powerful military deterrent and a time-tested tool of extortion. It would also relegate North Korea to being a third-rate country, on a par with Mozambique or Uganda."

The history of the North Korean nuclear program—and concerns about it— is long-standing and, as noted, is framed largely in terms of U.S.–North Korean relations. The United States and the DPRK have, of course, been antagonists since the 1950s, when they were primary opponents. Aside from the general antagonism this confrontation created, it may have provided the impetus for North Korean nuclear pretensions. As Robert Norris put it in his 2003 *Bulletin of the Atomic Scientists* article, "The fact that North Korea was threatened with nuclear weapons during the Korean War, and that for decades thereafter U.S. weapons were deployed in the South, may have helped motivate former President Kim Il Sung to launch a nuclear weapons program of his own." Regardless of whether one accepts this explanation at face value, the North Koreans have consistently asserted their need to maintain the nuclear weapons option.

The genesis of the ongoing crisis goes back to the Clinton administration. A May 1992 inspection of North Korean nuclear facilities by the International Atomic Energy Agency (IAEA) inspectors headed by Hans Blix concluded that the North Koreans might be engaged in weapons activity (converting spent nuclear fuel into weapons-grade plutonium). This precipitated a crisis in which the North Koreans threatened the until-then-unprecedented step of withdrawing from the NPT in March 1993 (they had joined the treaty in 1984). At this point the Clinton administration intervened, entering into direct talks that produced a negotiated settlement to the problem, the Framework Agreement. Under its provisions, the North Koreans agreed to freeze and eventually to dismantle their nuclear weapons program under IAEA supervision. In turn, North Korea would accept light water nuclear reactors to replace those capable of producing weapons-grade materials and would receive heavy fuel oil for electricity and heating purposes. In addition, Norris adds, "political and economic relations would be normalized, and both countries would work toward a nuclear weapons-free Korean peninsula and to strengthen the nuclear proliferation regime." Despite some controversies, however, the basic policy survived until the George W. Bush administration.

The current, ongoing crisis was precipitated when the Bush administration cut off the flow of heating oil to North Korea and terminated the Framework Agreement in December 2002. The DPRK responded by announcing on January 10, 2003, that it was withdrawing from the NPT, which it did after the mandatory ninety-day waiting period following the announcement of intent. Saber rattling on both sides followed in the ensuing months, and six-party negotiations between the DPRK, South Korea, Japan, Russia, China, and the United States opened on August 28, 2003, at which point North Korea announced it was prepared "to declare itself formally as a nuclear weapons state" (which it did in December 2006) and added that it possessed the capability to deliver these weapons to target by ballistic means.

The North Koreans, as noted, have always viewed the six-party format for negotiations (an American construct) as undesirable, preferring bilateral negotiations that the Bush administration refused to accept. On September 9, 2004, an explosion occurred at a nuclear site (Ryanggang) in North Korea that may have been a nuclear test, although the North Koreans denied that the test was of a nuclear device. The North Koreans announced on February 10, 2005, that they had developed nuclear weapons for self-defense purposes and suspended participation in the six-party talks. In a direct reversal that illustrates some of the flavor of the ongoing relationship, the six-party talks resumed in September 2005 and produced an agreement whereby the DPRK agreed to dismantle its nuclear weapons program in return for economic assistance. In June 2006, as the Taepodong crisis (tests of North Korean Taepodong missiles, some of which flew over Japanese territory) unfolded, critics Carter and Perry declared that "the six-party talks . . . have collapsed." The summer 2006 brouhaha over North Korean missile tests emerged from this context and foreshadowed the tenor and content of the contemporary crisis.

The breakdown of the six-power talks has largely extinguished formal negotiations with the North Koreans in a proliferation context. The acknowledgment that the DPRK has produced and possesses nuclear weapons and that missile development efforts are under way effectively removed the issue from the realm of acquisition deterrence, which had failed. As such, the DPRK is no longer a nonproliferation issue, and it cannot become one again until (or unless) the North Koreans decide to dismantle the forces and to reenter the NPT regime. The prospects of their doing so under the rule of the mercurial Kim Jong-un are not, to put it mildly, very encouraging. This means that the problem conceptually has become a matter of keeping them from using those weapons (employment deterrence). The dynamics of the two forms of discouragement are different. In the current context, the problem is largely one of containing a volatile North Korea whose behavior and threats are difficult to measure.

In this light, one is left with what to make of the North Korean nuclear "threat." Given that the North Koreans are nuclear-capable, the question is, what would keep them from using their weapons? It is difficult to conjure reasons why North Korea would launch an offensive, preemptive nuclear strike against anyone, given the certain response would be its own utter and certain destruction. Despite this reality, the DPRK leader continues to threaten a nuclear strike against the United States that would destroy his country. The threat is less nonsensical if North Korea truly believes it helps deter the United States from attacking the DPRK. The idea that the United States needs to be deterred may seem outlandish to most Americans, but not to the North Koreans. As Cumings puts it, "it seems irrational for Pyongyang to give up its handful of nukes when the United States still threatens to attack." North Korea is, after all, a small country in a Far East dominated by China, Japan, South Korea, and the United States, and its sole source of power and leverage is its nuclear arsenal. Getting them to change course is very difficult and almost certainly requires the intercession of the other major powers. The problem is that all the affected parties have contradictory interests that make their cooperation in confronting the North Koreans extremely difficult. They all agree that a nonnuclear DPRK is preferable to a nuclear one, but they have different positions on how to get there and on the consequences *for them* of different outcomes.

The 800-pound gorilla in all calculations is how to get the North Koreans to give up their nuclear weapons and aspirations. Because they view their program as a source of prestige and standing in their region in the world as well as a deterrent against predators such as the United States, the regime is unlikely to do so voluntarily. That means the DPRK must be coerced into that decision, and operationally, that almost certainly means regime change (toppling the government). Should that occur, the fate of an independent North Korea comes into play, and that affects others in the region, notably China.

It is generally conceded that China is the key actor in cajoling or coercing the DPRK into moderating its nuclear stance. The People's Republic of China (PRC) joins North Korea as the only remaining communist states in the region; the longest land border the DPRK has with any country is with China; the PRC is overwhelmingly the largest trading partner and broker of the DPRK; and according to Shirk, "some 85 percent" of North Korean trade "goes to or through" China. In addition, many North Koreans commute to factories on the Chinese side of the frontier to augment their meager existences, and China provides the DPRK with a large amount of foreign assistance without which existence in the Hermit Kingdom would be even grimmer than it is. Despite these sources of leverage, however, the Chinese have not been major contributors to reining in their neighbors. China has the levers to induce North Korea to negotiate its program, and as Cha (2017) puts it, "China's diplomatic pique is likely to be part of any successful attempt to get North Korea back to the denuclearization negotiating table."

China does not support the DPRK nuclear program, but it does support what it views as the need for an independent North Korea, for which that program is the major prop. Without nuclear weapons, the peninsular debate would quickly return to reunification, which had support in the early 2000s. From the Chinese vantage point, the Westernized, democratic South Koreans would dominate a unified Korea (much as the West Germans have dominated Germany since reunification), and this raises the specter of a potentially hostile country on China's border. That prospect propelled China into the Korean War in 1951, and it is a prospect they feel would violate their basic national interest. For that reason alone, they have been reluctant to pressure Kim Jong-un hard enough to force a sea change in the DPRK nuclear weapons program—which is one of its chief claims to fame—and regime support.

South Korea also has mixed motives. Their fundamental problem with the DPRK is that some of the weapons are aimed at them, and in the event of war that the North Koreans periodically threaten, the Republic of Korea (ROK) would be obliterated. Reunification would solve that problem if it could be accomplished without war, although the Chinese oppose this progression. Although they have little stake in the question of Korean reunification, Japan is also menaced by North Korean nuclear threats, including the repeated overflight of Japan by DPRK missile tests.

The United States is the final outside actor in this mix. The United States opposes proliferation generally, of which the DPRK is currently the most advanced problem and thus the highest priority to contain or reverse. The United States has very substantial interests in the region's politics and economics that are threatened by destabilization caused by DPRK saber rattling or worse, and the direct threats that Kim Jong-un has made about menacing or attacking the American homeland in the future will become greater in the future as the attainment of that capability moves closer.

The pivot of the problem of outside pressure on the DPRK is the possible inexorable movement toward peninsular reunification under ROK control and the geopolitical effect that would have on China. That dynamic is not, in the strictest sense, a proliferation concern, although a unified Korea would almost certainly abandon the DPRK program, a proliferation effect. The major geopolitical challenge is how to facilitate such an outcome in a manner that placates China's fear of a hostile neighbor enough to buy in to the solution. Until that occurs, North Korea will remain a case of failed proliferation policy.

The Iranian Contrast

The other state that is mentioned prominently in proliferation discussions is Iran. Like North Korea, Iran is a politically controversial place and has, since 1979, been at major odds with the United States. In 2002, then president George W. Bush included both countries (as well as Iraq) on his "Axis of Evil" list. One of the bases of that list has been that each of those countries at one time or another had nuclear programs with weapons potential. The DPRK obviously fulfilled that ambition; Iran and Iraq have not.

Whether Iran has (or has had) proliferation ambitions is a matter of disagreement. The Iranians have consistently denied that their nuclear program has any pretensions of gaining weapons status, but other countries, led by the United States and Israel, have voiced great skepticism about those claims. The American suspicion is part of the aftermath of the Iranian Revolution of 1979, which overthrew the American-backed Shah, captured the U.S. embassy in Tehran and held its personnel hostage for 444 days, and declared a fundamentalist Islamic Repub-lic of Iran, the chief enemy of which was the "Great Satan" (the United States). The two countries have not had formal relations since. Any Iraqi pretensions were ended by the U.S. invasion and conquest of 2003, part of the rationale for which was destroying Iraq's WMD, including nuclear, program—which the invaders never demonstrated existed.

The main contrast in the two experiences is that Iran signed an agreement in 2015 with the 5+1 powers (the permanent members of the United Nations Security Council plus Germany) in which they abjured any right to build nuclear weapons and agreed to international inspection of its nuclear facilities. This agreement has been denounced by Israel and some Americans, led by President Trump, who do not trust the Iranians, do not believe they will honor their bar-gain, and want to rescind American participation in it. Nonetheless, it remains in force, and there have been no major demonstrated instances of Iran violating its provisions. Even if the United States dropped out of the agreement, it would still be binding due to the adherence of the other parties. If nothing else, how-ever, the agreement does demonstrate that it is possible successfully to engage in proliferation control efforts: North Korea has been a negative precedent for the future, but it is at least partly countermanded by Iran's restraint.

Conclusion

Is the North Korean case study or its Iranian counterpart the potential harbin-ger for other proliferation cases? The DPRK has defied the proliferation regime and gotten away with it to this point, but its nuclear program had sufficient momentum and resolve to allow it to maintain control of its nuclear fate and a regional situation that did not force a negative decision on them. The DPRK case demonstrates that if a state is determined enough to "go nuclear," interna-tional restraints such as the NPT may not be robust enough to stop them.

No one, except potential proliferating countries that are part of +1, argues that the spread of nuclear and other weapons of mass destruction to nonpossess-ing states is in principle a good idea that should be encouraged. On the other hand, the empirical evidence of the impact of individual proliferations (when individual countries joined the nuclear weapons "club") hardly provides incon-trovertible proof of the dire perils that have been predicted. What is the evi-dence, for instance, that the world is a less stable place because Israel, India, or Pakistan possesses the bomb? One can contend that it would be better if they did not, but the peril remains theoretical, not demonstrated. Is the DPRK qualita-tively different?

How should future proliferators view the scene? Should they conclude that their attempts to attain nuclear weapons status will be viewed as internationally dangerous and destabilizing enough to prompt an international response that will reduce their security if they do not eschew proliferation? Or will they decide a positive nuclear weapons decision will protect them—provide them a deterrent—from attacks by predators, thereby increasing their security?

Nuclear-possessing states have one answer to that question, but recent experience may offer a different interpretation. When they ask themselves (as the North Koreans apparently have) if Saddam Hussein would have been immune from an American invasion had he not stopped pursuing nuclear weapons, many believe he made the wrong choice. At the same time, its nuclear weapons may have won the DPRK a ticket off the "Axis of Evil" by presenting the world (and especially the United States) with a threat that harsh rhetoric alone could not solve. At a minimum, recent experience does not unambiguously tell potential proliferators not to pursue the nuclear option, and the experience of the DPRK in attracting world attention to this ongoing crisis with South Korea and the United States demonstrates that "going nuclear" still provides some leverage and has some attraction in international politics.

Study/Discussion Questions

1. What is proliferation? Why is proliferation a "delicate" problem? Distinguish between types of proliferation, including what kinds of materials and capabilities are being proliferated and what difference each makes.
2. What is the *N+1* problem? Define it and explain why it illustrates the delicacy of the proliferation problem. Why is it so difficult to resolve?
3. What means are available to deal with proliferation? Distinguish between acquisition and employment deterrence. How does each work?
4. What is the Nuclear Nonproliferation Treaty (NPT)? How does it work? What categories of states are party to the treaty? How are they different?
5. Define the DPRK in proliferation terms. What is its status? How has it evolved to where it is? What special geopolitical circumstances have affected its status and what can be done to contain its weapons program?
6. Put yourself in the position of a country contemplating nuclear proliferation. Does recent experience suggest that pursuit of the nuclear option will enhance or detract from your security? Why?
7. If you were representing a country contemplating gaining nuclear weapons but in an adversarial relationship with the United States, how would that fact influence your decision process? Elaborate.

Bibliography

Bluth, Christoph. "North Korea: How Will It End?" *Current History* 109, no. 728 (September 2010): 237–43.

Carter, Ashton B., and William J. Perry. "If Necessary, Strike and Destroy." *Washington Post*, June 22, 2006, A29.

Cha, Victor. "Making China Pay on North Korea: Why Beijing's Coal Ban Isn't Enough." *Foreign Affairs Snapshot* (online), March 21, 2017.

Cha, Victor D., and David C. Kang. *Nuclear North Korea: A Debate on Engagement Strategies.* New York: Columbia University Press, 2008.

Cumings, Bruce. "The North Korea Problem: Dealing with Irrationality." *Current History* 108, no. 719 (September 2009): 284–90.

Debs, Alexandre, and Numo P. Mantiero. *Nuclear Politics: The Strategic Case of Proliferation.* (Cambridge Studies in International Relations). Cambridge, UK: Cambridge University Press, 2017.

Delury, John. "Trump and North Korea: Reviving the Art of the Deal." *Foreign Affairs* 96, no. 2 (March/April 2017): 46–51.

Demick, Barbara. "Few Moves Left with N. Korea." *Los Angeles Times* (online), June 21, 2006.

Harrison, Selig S. "Did North Korea Cheat?" *Foreign Affairs* 84, no. 1 (January/February 2005): 99–110.

Haynes, Susan Turner. *Chinese Nuclear Proliferation: How Global Politics Is Transforming China's Weapons Buildup and Modernization.* Washington, DC: Potomac, 2016.

Kim, Sung Chull, and Michael D. Cohen. *North Korea and Nuclear Weapons: Entering the New Era Deterrence.* Washington, DC: Georgetown University Press, 2017.

Lankov, Andrei. "Changing North Korea." *Foreign Affairs* 88, no. 6 (November–December 2009): 95–105.

Lieber, Kier A., and David G. Press. "The Rise of U.S. Nuclear Supremacy." *Foreign Affairs* 85, no. 2 (March/April 2006): 42–54.

Mendelsohn, Jack. "The New Threats: Nuclear Amnesia, Nuclear Legitimacy." *Current History* 105, no. 694 (November 2006): 385–90.

The National Security Strategy of the United States of America. Washington, DC: White House, March 2006.

Norris, Robert S. "North Korea's Nuclear Program, 2003." *Bulletin of the Atomic Scientists* 59, no. 2 (March/April 2003): 74–77.

Oberdorfer, Don, and Robert Carlin. *The Two Koreas: A Contemporary History.* 3rd ed. New York: Basic, 2014.

Onishi, Norimitsu, and Edward Wong. "U.S. to Take North Korea Off Terrorist List." *New York Times* (online), June 27, 2008.

O'Reilly, Kelly P. *Nuclear Weapons and the Psychology of Political Leadership: Beliefs, Motivations, and Perceptions.* New York and London: Routledge, 2016.

Perkowich, George. "The End of the Proliferation Regime." *Current History* 105, no. 694 (November 2006): 355–62.

Pilat, Joseph F. "Reassessing Security Assurances in a Unipolar World." *Washington Quarterly* 28, no. 2 (Spring 2005): 59–70.

Ratcliff, Jonathan E. B. *Nuclear Proliferation: Overview, History, and Reference Guide.* New York: CreateSpace Independent Publishing, 2016.

Sagan, Scott, and Kenneth N. Waltz. *The Spread of Nuclear Weapons: An Enduring Debate.* New York: Norton, 2012.

Shirk, Susan. "Trump and China: Getting to Yes with Beijing." *Foreign Affairs* 96, no. 2 (March/April 2017): 20–27.

Sigal, Leon V. "The Lessons of North Korea's Test." *Current History* 105, no. 694 (November 2006): 364–65.

Snow, Donald M. *Cases in American Foreign Policy.* 1st ed. New York: Pearson, 2013, especially chapter 4.

Snow, Donald M., and Eugene Brown. *The Contours of Power: An Introduction to Contemporary International Relations.* New York: St. Martin's, 1996.

Specter, Arlen, and Christopher Walsh. "Dialogue with Adversaries." *Washington Quarterly* 30, no. 1 (Winter 2006/2007): 9–26.

Winner, Andrew C. "The Proliferation Security Initiative: The New Face of Interdiction." *Washington Quarterly* 28, no. 2 (Spring 2005): 129–43.

Wit, Joel S., Daniel Poneman, and Robert Gallucci. *Going Critical: The First North Korean Nuclear Crisis.* Washington, DC: Brookings Institution Press, 2004.

7

War Crimes and Enforcing International Norms

Reciprocity, the International Criminal Court, and Syrian Chemicals

The traumatic events of World War II, and most prominently German genocide in the Holocaust, shook an important pillar of international relations. Assaults on the absolute nature of sovereignty and its implications for how states could treat their citizens and their enemies had progressed since Westphalia, but the gruesome Nazi actions created a growing conviction that there were limits to what people could do to one other people both within sovereign states and in the relations between these sovereign entities. Largely focused around the new United Nations, the postwar world turned its attention to the need to fashion and agree upon legal norms to limit man's inhumanity to humankind. The effect—in some cases the intent—has been to limit the prerogatives of those who wield sovereign authority. Its most obvious manifestation has been in the laws of war. The result is an ongoing process to develop and enforce evolving norms.

These efforts have proceeded along two tracks explored in this chapter. These focus on what are sometimes called the negative or political rights: what states are obligated to do or prohibited from doing to their citizens and to other countries. These efforts have been concentrated on the conduct of hostilities and are best exemplified in areas such as war crimes and efforts to control it. The applications are the positive innovation of the International Criminal Court and the negative violation of chemical weapons bans by Syria. Chapter 10 deals with the so-called positive rights, which are highlighted by those obligations humankind has for ensuring the quality of human life.

People engaging in violence against one another individually or in groups is certainly nothing new in human history, although increases in the number of people and the efficiency with which they can kill one another may be intensifying as a global trait. At the same time, sovereignty, which has been the principle by which violence has been justified, does not cause human violence, even if it rationalizes it. These excuses were stretched to and beyond the breaking point by excesses in World War II, and the end of the war provided a watershed in thinking about this problem and its containment.

Efforts to address the subject of war crimes are also not new and have historically centered on the laws of war—rules of permissible and impermissible ways of making war. The most obvious contemporary case was the war crimes trials against German and Japanese defendants at the end of World War II, discussed later in the chapter. The subject lay largely fallow during the Cold War, but in the early 1990s, outrageous instances of war crimes occurred in places like Bosnia and Rwanda and reinvigorated interest in the war crimes issue. The major result was the negotiation of the International Criminal Court (ICC) through the Rome Treaty of 1998. The jurisdiction of the ICC is accepted by many states today, but exceptions (including the United States) remain.

The evolution of these efforts demonstrates, in important ways and for reasons worth noting, the limits of international cooperation in sovereignty, war crimes terms. As of 2015, only 120 of the 190 or so countries of the world had ratified the ICC statute and become parties to the treaty. The nonmembers include five of the six most populous states in the world (China, India, the United States, Indonesia, and Pakistan), which between them have a population of 3.393 billion of a world population estimated at 7.256 billion (about 47 percent of world population), according to 2015 *CIA World Factbook* estimates. Of the six largest states, only Brazil has ratified the ICC treaty. When other nonsignatories' populations are added to the total, over half the people living in the world are not covered by the international regime forbidding war crimes. Within the volatile Middle East where violence and atrocity are widespread, the only signatories of the ICC are Afghanistan and Jordan.

The purpose of this case is to study the problem of war crimes as a microcosm of the global problem of international cooperation on political rights. At a commonsensical level, the idea that war crimes should be condemned and perpetrators punished seems obvious—a "no-brainer." Yet, within the more byzantine workings of international relations, other concerns such as the protection of state sovereignty may come into conflict with apparently consensual concerns that would seem to militate toward cooperation between states. War crimes are not the only place where this anomaly appears, but they are one of the most dramatic.

War crimes reentered the international dialogue during the 1990s. The immediate precipitant had been a rash of so-called humanitarian disasters, in which intolerable acts against groups within states, often grouped under the name "ethnic cleansing," occurred. The worst of these occurred in Bosnia during the early 1990s and in Rwanda in 1994. A somewhat more limited case occurred in Kosovo in 1998–1999.

The result, according to one source, was a paradox: "Humanitarian law and international human rights has never been more developed, yet never before have human rights been violated more frequently. This state of affairs will not improve absent a mechanism to enforce those laws and the norms they embody." The ongoing and historical tragedy in Syria accentuates these concerns.

This quote suggests that the contemporary concern with strengthening war crimes regimes stems from two parallel developments. One is the assertion that there are universal human rights to which people and groups are entitled, violations of which should be subject to penalty. The second is an interest in some form of international mechanism for dealing with violators of these norms. In the absence of such mechanisms, self-help and reciprocity are the major means by which states, and groups within states, can protect themselves.

The ideas of defining criminal behavior and enforcement of laws in international, universal terms are of recent origin in international affairs. The idea of universal human rights transcending sovereign state boundaries is really a post–World War II phenomenon; the primary crime that has been identified in war crimes, genocide, was not identified until the word was coined by Richard Lemkin in 1944, and the United Nations Convention on Genocide, which bans its commission, was not passed until 1948. The term war crimes, which now refers to a broad range of activities associated with war, was basically linked with violations of the so-called laws of war until war crimes trials were convened in Nuremberg and Tokyo to prosecute accused Nazi and Japanese violators after World War II.

The subject of war crimes is unlikely to disappear from international discourse, for at least five reasons. First, acts now defined as war crimes continue to be committed in many places. Exclusionary nationalism (when national groups persecute nonmembers) in some developing-world states may increase the number of savage acts that are now considered war crimes. Second, the war crimes trials involving Bosnia and Rwanda held in the early 1990s have set a precedent for how such outrages will be treated the future. Third, definitions are rapidly evolving. Rape, for instance, has only recently been added to the list of punishable crimes against humanity. Terrorist mass murders almost certainly qualify as well. The trial and execution of Saddam Hussein gave wide publicity to these phenomena. Fourth, one outcome of the concern for war crimes has been the establishment of a controversial permanent International Criminal Court with legal jurisdiction over war crimes. Fifth, accusations of war crimes in places like Syria ensure that the subject does not disappear from public awareness. The commission of atrocities seems to occur most frequently in internal violence within states, and such conflicts are the most common form of violence and instability in the contemporary world.

This statement of the problem suggests the direction this case study will take. It begins with a brief historical overview of the evolution of war crimes concerns. Its major point is that whereas the idea of crimes of war has long been part of international concerns, war crimes as they are now defined are of recent vintage. The case will then look at the various categories of war crimes that arose from the experience of the war crimes trials at the end of World War II, and how the existence of well-documented atrocities in places like Bosnia and Rwanda rekindled interest in the subject. The case will be applied to mechanisms that states have traditionally used to deal with violence against them and with how norms and regimes in areas like torture have changed behavior. It concludes with the special case of Syrian chemical weapons use and what to do about it.

Principle: War Crimes and International Enforcement

Throughout most of history, the term *war crimes* has been associated with conformity to the so-called laws of war, a use traceable as far back as 200 BC, when a code of the permissible behavior in war was formulated in the Hindu Code of

Manu. Acceptable codes of warfare were part of Roman law and were later practiced throughout Europe. These rules began to be codified into international law following the Thirty Years' War (1618–1648), when most of Europe was swept up in very brutal religiously based warfare. The first definitive international law text, Hugo Grotius's *On the Law of War and Peace*, was published in 1625 and included the admonition that "war ought not to be undertaken except for the enforcement of rights; when once undertaken, it should be carried on only within the bounds of law and good faith." Definitions of the laws of war, and hence violations of those laws, developed gradually during the eighteenth and nineteenth centuries, culminating in the Geneva and Hague Conventions of 1899 and 1907.

The idea of war crimes expanded to cover other areas of conduct in war in the twentieth century. The precipitant for this expansion was World War II and wartime atrocities committed by the Axis powers (notably Germany and Japan). Some of the crimes fit traditional definitions of war crimes—the mistreatment of American and other prisoners of war (POWs) by the Japanese during the infamous Bataan death march, for instance. Many actions, however, went well beyond the conduct of war per se, as in the systematic extermination of Jews, Gypsies, and other groups in the Holocaust by Germany and the so-called Rape of Nanking, in which Japanese soldiers went on a rampage and reportedly slaughtered nearly 300,000 citizens of that Chinese city (some Japanese sources dispute the numbers) on the pretext that some of them were soldiers hiding among the civilians.

Contemporary Evolution of War Crimes

World War II thus provided the impetus for change. It was a truly global and brutal war, and one of its major "innovations" was to extend to civilian population what the American general William Tecumseh Sherman called the "hard hand of war" during the Civil War. The Allies discussed the problem throughout the war. The first formal statement on the subject was the Moscow declaration of 1943, which stated that Nazi officials guilty of "atrocities, massacres, and executions" would be sent to the countries in which they committed their crimes for trial and appropriate punishment after the war ended.

The document that defined modern war crimes precedent was the London Agreement of August 8, 1945. It did two major things. First, it established the International Military Tribunal as the court that would try alleged war crimes and thereby set the precedent for a formal, permanent body at a later date. At the time, it specifically set the groundwork for the Nuremberg and Tokyo tribunals. Second, the agreement established the boundaries of its jurisdiction, which have become the standard means for defining war crimes.

The London Agreement defined three kinds of war crimes. The first is *crimes against peace*, "namely, planning, preparation, initiation, or waging of a war of aggression, or a war in violation of international treaties, agreements or assurances, or participation in a common plan or conspiracy for the accomplishment of any of the foregoing." This admonition was reinforced by the United Nations

Charter that same year, in which the signatories relinquished the "right" to initiate war. The North Korean invasion of South Korea in 1950 qualifies as a crime against peace, as does the U.S. invasion of Iraq in 2003.

The second category reiterates the traditional usage of the concept. *War crimes* are defined as "violations of the laws or customs of war. Such violations shall include, but not be limited to, murder, ill-treatment or deportation to slave labor or for any other purpose of civilian population of or in occupied territory, murder or ill-treatment of prisoners of war or persons on the seas, killing of hostages, plunder of public or private property, wanton destruction of cities, towns or villages, or devastation not justified by military necessity." This enumeration, of course, was a virtual laundry list of accusations against the Germans and the Japanese (although the Allies arguably committed some of the same acts). The crimes enumerated are limited to mistreatment of general civilian populations rather than their systematic extension to individuals and segments of the population.

The third category was the most innovative and controversial. It is also the type of war crimes with which the concept is now most closely associated. *Crimes against humanity* are defined as "murder, extermination, enslavement, deportation, and other inhumane acts committed against any civilian population, before or during the war; or persecutions on political, racial or religious grounds in execution of or in connection with any crime . . . whether or not in violation of the domestic law where perpetrated." The statute goes further, establishing the basis of responsibility and thus vulnerability to prosecution. "Leaders, organizers, instigators, or accomplices participating in the formulation or execution of a common plan or conspiracy to commit any of the foregoing crimes are responsible for all acts performed by any persons in execution of such plan." This latter enumeration of responsibility justified the indictment of former Yugoslav president Slobodan Milosevic, who was never accused of personally carrying out acts qualifying as war crimes, and against Saddam Hussein. It would also undoubtedly be included in an indictment against Syrian President Bashar al-Assad and possibly against some leaders of the opposition against him.

These expansions of the concept of war crimes are intended as part of the binding obligations that states party to them incur. As such, they represent expansions of international jurisdiction, and at the time, they were radical expansions of international obligations. First, wars against humanity criminalized actions by states (or groups within states) that had previously not been thought of as criminal. Imagine, for instance, Genghis Khan and the leaders of the Golden Horde being placed in the docket for their brutal actions while conquering much of Eurasia in the thirteenth century. The same applies to the Ottoman Turk executors of the genocidal campaign against the Armenians early in the twentieth century.

The second radical idea contained in the definition is that of jurisdiction. By stating that crimes against humanity are enforceable "whether or not in violation of the domestic law" in the places they occur, the definition adds a universality to its delineation that seems to transcend the sovereign rights of states within their territory. That assertion remains at the base of controversy about the institutionalization of war crimes, because it entwines war criminal behavior (the reprehensibility of which is agreed upon) with the controversy over sovereignty (about which there is considerable disagreement). Third, the statute seeks to remove the defense that crimes against humanity can be justified on the basis that they were committed on orders from a superior.

The statute does not address the issue of "victor's law," the idea that norms that have been broken by both or all sides are only enforced against the losers, and that the winners are not punished for similar infractions. The recognition that any trial enforcing war crimes may represent an application of victor's law has been an ongoing concern about war crimes is reflected in the jurisdiction of the International Criminal Court (ICC), discussed in the applications section.

This concern carried over into the postwar world. In 1948, the General Assembly of the United Nations passed the International Convention on the Prevention and Punishment of the Crime of Genocide, known more compactly as the Convention on Genocide. Building on the assertion of crimes against humanity, the Convention on Genocide provided clarification and codification of what constituted acts of genocide. According to the convention, any of the following actions, when committed with the intent of eliminating a particular national, ethnic, racial, or religious group, constitute genocide: (1) killing members of the group; (2) causing conditions of life calculated to kill; (3) imposing measures intended to prevent births within a group; and (4) forcibly transferring children out of a group.

In important ways, enunciating the Convention on Genocide and the UN Declaration on Human Rights was a form of international atonement for Axis excesses, and especially for the Holocaust. Most countries signed and ratified the Convention, which took force—without, one might quickly add, any real form of enforcement. A few countries, notably the United States, refused to ratify the document for reasons based in infringement of sovereignty discussed later. This dichotomy reflects that although there are international *norms* (accepted canons or values within the international community) regarding certain forms of behavior, they have not been elevated to international *law* (agreed upon and universally enforceable codes of behavior).

The Cold War Pause

The momentum that was created by the surge of war crimes sentiment stimulated by World War II and its war crimes trial aftermath and as reflected in UN declarations went into hibernation with the outbreak of the Cold War in the late 1940s. That confrontation dominated international politics for over forty years, and virtually anything that happened became a Cold War matter viewed through the lens of that conflict. War crimes was no exception.

Why was this the case? It is not because crimes against humanity became less unacceptable; those kinds of acts and traditional war crimes certainly continued to occur, at least on a smaller scale than had happened during World War II. Rather, the more likely explanation is that the subject matter became a victim of the Cold War, as did other initiatives such as the aggressive promotion of human rights.

It is almost certainly not a coincidence that the emergence of a broad international interest in war crimes emerged at a time of U.S.-Soviet cooperation right after World War II, that concern and progress ground to an effective halt during the ideological and geopolitical confrontation between them, and that the subject has resurfaced and been revitalized since the cessation of that competition.

Why would the Cold War competition hamstring progress on a subject that would, on the face of it, seem above the ideological fray of that competition? No one, after all, officially condones war crimes, and yet, in the Cold War context, neither was their clarification or codification aggressively pursued internationally.

In the Cold War context, issues such as war crimes tended to become caught up in the propaganda war between the superpowers. Both sides tended to assume that the advocacy of certain principles was championed to embarrass the other, and that apparent violations would be blamed on the other for propaganda advantage—a charge not without merit on either side.

Had the Soviets, for instance, decided to push for greater progress on war crimes during the American participation in the Vietnam War between 1965 and 1973, the United States would have quite rightly assumed the purpose was to embarrass American service members and discredit the American military effort. The My Lai incident of March 16, 1968 (in which a platoon of U.S. servicemen destroyed a Vietnamese village and slaughtered its residents), illustrates this dynamic. Innocent civilians were slaughtered at My Lai in what was a clear crime against humanity, but dispassionate consideration was drowned out by wartime propaganda duels over Cold War issues. For Soviet propagandists, the incident provided proof of the imperialist savagery of the American invaders and demonstrated to other developing countries why they should support them and oppose the Americans. The principle of war crimes per se became lost in the shuffle.

The communist side had its equivalent episode in Cambodia in 1975. In that small country adjacent to Vietnam, a civil war raged between communist groups supported by China and Russia. The side sponsored by the Chinese won, bringing the Khmer Rouge and its infamous leader Pol Pot to power. During his murderous four-year reign between 1975 and 1979, the Khmer Rouge murdered between 1.5 and 3 million of their own citizens, roughly 25 percent of the population for racial reasons (Vietnamese, Chinese, and Thais were especially targeted) and against virtually anyone else who opposed the regime. Cold war politics muted international response to this clear genocide. The slaughter was, after all, in some ways an intramural communist event between followers of the two major communist powers, and any attempt to publicize it was dismissed as Western propaganda. The slaughter finally ended with the overthrow of Pol Pot by Vietnamese-supported rebels, but at a horrific toll from which Cambodia is still recovering.

There was a second problem with extending the idea of war crimes, and especially the codification of the idea into some enforcement regime, that has been a sticking point for the U.S. government: the issue of sovereignty. As noted in chapter 1, the United States and China have been among the staunchest supporters of the doctrine of state sovereignty. Because the Convention on Genocide and other war crimes agreements are universally applicable to all states that have signed and ratified it and thus have acceded to them, they have been viewed by powerful political elements in the United States with suspicion and opposition as an infringement of the authority of the U.S. government to regulate its own affairs. This argument may seem strained in areas such as genocide: one way of looking at the objection is that it preserves the right of the United States to commit genocide. Nonetheless, the argument against diluting American national sovereignty was sufficient politically to prevent the U.S. Senate from ratifying the genocide convention until 1993 (after the end of the Cold War, when it was submitted to the Senate by President Clinton and approved by the necessary two-thirds majority). The issue had not changed, but the surrounding circumstances had.

Two other things had changed between the 1970s and the revived international concern about crimes against humanity in the 1990s, and they help explain earlier international indifference and international activism in the 1990s. The first change was the emergence of much more aggressive global electronic media with the physical capability to expose and publicize apparent atrocities. During most of the Cold War, there was no such thing as global television; Cable News Network (CNN), for instance, was not launched until 1980 and did not become a prominent force for some time thereafter. Moreover, media tools such as hand-held camcorders and satellite uplinks were theoretical ideas, not the everyday equipment of reporters and members of the general global public. Telephones with video cameras were a science fiction or a cartoon fantasy (the oldest popular version was a wristwatch camera phone in the cartoon *Dick Tracy*). In this atmosphere, governments could and did obscure some of their most atrocious behavior, a practice that has become much more difficult, as social media have made most citizens effectively journalistic publicists of world events, up to and including the commission of war crimes. The government of Syria could have plausibly denied that its citizens were the victims of sarin gas attacks by Syrian forces a generation ago, because the atrocity was not recorded and rebroadcast in real time. It could not be covered up in 2017.

The other change has been the growing de facto (in practice) if not de jure (in law) acceptance of the permissibility of international intervention in the internal affairs of states or factions within states that grossly abuse other people or groups—in other words, commit various crimes against humanity. Without an elaborate statement of the principle of humanitarian intervention (see chapter 10), this is what the United Nations authorized when it sent UN forces into Somalia in 1992. More recently, this "principle" has been called the "responsibility to protect (R2P)." By the early 1990s, the dynamics affecting international politics had changed sufficiently to raise the prospects of dealing with war crimes onto the international agenda. The end of the Cold War meant atrocities were less likely to be hidden or accusations about them suppressed on ideological or propagandistic grounds. A more aggressive and technologically empowered electronic media with global reach was available to report and publicize atrocities wherever they occurred. At the same time, the UN operation in Somalia had established something like a precedent about the notion of international responses to war crimes. Two particularly egregious cases during the 1990s, in

Bosnia and Rwanda, drew attention to the problem and its solution. The trend has continued.

Individually and in combination, Bosnia and Rwanda thrust two unavoidable imperatives before the international community. First, they made the subject and horror of war crimes so public that it could no longer be ignored. Second, it created the need for some mechanism to prosecute those accused of committing war crimes, and the result was the formation of ad hoc war crimes tribunals to deal with each case. A major outgrowth of this process was a growing belief that there should be a permanent international institution both to deter potential future war criminals and to try future undeterred perpetrators.

Application: The International Criminal Court and Syria

The precedent of the Bosnian and Rwandan special war crimes tribunals stimulated and energized momentum for a permanent court. It was increasingly clear from atrocities being committed in other countries that there would be no shortage of situations in which allegations of crimes against humanity would emerge. Internal conflicts in places as widely separated as Sierra Leone in Africa, Kosovo in Europe, and East Timor on the Indonesian archipelago provided evidence of both geographic diversity and numerous opportunities to enforce sanctions against a new breed of war criminals perpetrating despicable crimes against their fellow citizens. There appeared to be a "market" for a permanent structure. It was also the hope of proponents that the existence of such a court and the knowledge that it could bring criminals to justice might deter some future crimes against humanity. But how should the international community react?

One aspect of the evolving debate over war crimes stands out in the contemporary international scene, and it is a matter of special interest to the United States. That concern is the desirability of a permanent institution (the ICC) with mandatory jurisdiction both to determine instances of war crimes and to prosecute them. The heart of that concern is the mandatory nature of jurisdiction and thus authority over accused war criminals. Sovereignty-based concerns have made the United States the world's most vocal and prominent opponent of international institutionalized efforts to foster international cooperation in this area. An examination of the ICC thus illustrates the limits of international cooperation in what might initially seem an area of obvious need and appeal.

Proposals for a Permanent War Crimes Tribunal

The initial advocacy of a permanent court to adjudicate war crimes accompanied the flurry of activity surrounding Nuremberg and Tokyo and the adoption of the Convention on Genocide. In 1948, the UN General Assembly commissioned the International Law Commission (a private body) to study the possibility of establishing an ICC. The commission examined this problem until 1954 and produced a draft statute for the ICC. Unfortunately, it appeared during the darkest days of the Cold War; there were objections from both sides of the Iron Curtain, and the United Nations dropped the proposal.

The idea of an ICC lay dormant until 1989, when the tiny Caribbean island country of Trinidad and Tobago revived the proposal within the United Nations. Trinidad and Tobago's motive, oddly enough, was to provide an instrument in its struggle against drug traffickers from South America. Nonetheless, the events in Bosnia and Rwanda revived broader interest that suggested the wisdom of a permanent body to provide a more effective, timely response to war crimes.

The idea of a permanent war crimes tribunal illustrated dramatically the clash between order and disorder inherent in the world system of sovereign states. No country endorses the right to commit war crimes, but some states and groups or individuals within states from time to time violate the moral and legal norms that constitute war crimes. At the same time, accusing a country or group of crimes against humanity can be a political tool to embarrass or stigmatize the country or group unfairly. One way to avoid that possibility is to not create or empower a unit that can make or endorse such accusations.

The proposal for an ICC has been controversial, especially surrounding the matter of jurisdiction. Champions contend that the court must have mandatory jurisdiction over all accused instances of war crimes and that its jurisdiction must supersede national sovereignty to be effective. Sovereignty, in other words, should not be a shield behind which war criminals can hide. Opponents object that this infringement on national sovereignty is unwarranted and could form the basis for future abuses of sovereignty. Sovereignty may also provide protection against unfair and unjust accusations against those who are innocent.

The Case for the ICC

The idea of an ICC flowed from renewed interest in dealing with war crimes and the belief that a permanent war crimes institution had several advantages over impaneling ad hoc tribunals. First, a permanent body would avoid having to start essentially from scratch each time suspected war crimes are uncovered. A permanent ICC would have, among other things, a permanent staff of investigators and prosecutors, and its staff would have the authority and jurisdiction to ascertain when crimes against humanity have indeed occurred.

Second, and related to the first point, a permanent ICC could be much more responsive to the occurrence—or even perhaps the possibility—of war crimes in the future. Not only would permanent staff members have or develop the expertise for efficient identification of war crimes situations, they could be mobilized rapidly and applied to the problem rather than being recruited and activated after the fact.

Third, it was hoped that a permanent ICC would deter future potential war criminals. Would, for instance, the Bosnian Serb leaders indicted (mostly in absentia) for authorizing ethnic cleansing in Bosnia have been dissuaded from doing so if they knew there was an international criminal authority to bring them to justice for their deeds? What influence would a permanent ICC have had on the planners and implementers of the slaughter in Rwanda? This claim is fundamentally the same as the asserted deterrent value of police forces. Although no one can know the answers to these questions, the existence of the ICC might have made a difference.

Fourth, the idea emerged at a time when international cooperation was being instituted on a broad range of vexing issues, from human and women's rights to free trade. The end of the Cold War seemed to usher in an atmosphere where the narrow, conflict-driven paradigm of world politics was being replaced by a more open and cooperative atmosphere. The time for an ICC seemed ripe.

As a result, pressure to negotiate a treaty to create an ICC grew during the 1990s. As early as 1995, the Clinton administration became an activist in the movement supporting the idea. The movement culminated with the Rome Conference of 1998 (technically the United Nations Diplomatic Conference on the Establishment of a Permanent International Criminal Court). The conference produced a draft treaty to establish the ICC as a permanent body for trying individuals accused of committing genocide, war crimes, or crimes against humanity and gave the court jurisdiction over individuals accused of these crimes. When the draft was put to a vote, it passed by a vote of 120 states in favor, seven opposed, and twenty-one abstentions. For the treaty to come into force, at least sixty states had to ratify it. It reached that level in 2002 and came into official existence on July 1, 2002. As of April 2017, there were 124 members. Burundi, which is under formal investigation by the ICC, has given formal notice of its intention to withdraw. In a similar vein, Russia withdrew as a signatory in 2016. It is also party to a "preliminary investigation" of events in Ukraine regarding its part in events in 2014 (the "Maidan protests") and "events in Crimea and Eastern Ukraine" according to the ICC official website on April 19, 2017.

In what would prove a harbinger of future difficulties, the U.S. government was one of the seven states to vote against the treaty in Rome and has neither signed nor ratified the document, despite the Clinton administration's involvement in promoting and drafting its statute. In one of his final acts in office, President Clinton signed the statute in December 2000. In February 2001, Secretary of State Colin S. Powell announced that President George W. Bush had no intention of submitting it to the Senate for ratification; and the Bush administration subsequently announced that it was "unsigning" the treaty, an ambiguous international legal act punctuating its high level of opposition.

Objections to the ICC

The United States advocating and then opposing the ICC statute may seem anomalous, but it is not entirely unusual. The apparent schizophrenia represents different views of America's place in the world, the American attitude toward the world, and especially the question of sovereignty. The Clinton administration saw the ICC statute as a way both to demonstrate responsible U.S. leadership and to improve the quality of the international environment, and thus became a champion of a war crimes court with "teeth." Other powerful political forces, however, feared the loss of sovereignty that joining the treaty might entail and opposed U.S. formal participation as a member. The problem came to focus on the potential loss of control of the U.S. government over its own forces in the field. This objection has been the basis of American refusals to turn over service members accused of war crimes to international authorities or authorities in countries where the alleged acts occurred, an issue on which many Americans were adamant. To accede would effectively subject those forces to prosecution by foreign authorities over which the United States would have no formal influence. The March 2012 American refusal to relinquish control of an American soldier accused of killing sixteen Afghan villagers and to try him instead in an American military court is an example.

David Sheffer, head of the American delegation, delivered the heart of the U.S. objection at the end of the Rome Conference. He began by pointing out that the ICC would have jurisdiction only in countries that were parties to the treaty and noted that countries accused of war crimes could and would evade prosecution by simply not joining the treaty. Iraq was an example then, and Syria is today. The qualifying point of this objection was that a UN Security Council Resolution (UNSCR) can extend that jurisdiction to a given case.

The heart of the objection was that the treaty forces countries to relinquish their sovereign jurisdiction over their forces and leaves those forces vulnerable to international prosecution with no U.S. ability to come to their aid when the United States participates in UN-sponsored peacekeeping operations, such as those in Bosnia and Kosovo or in Iraq or Afghanistan. As Sheffer put it, "Thus, the treaty purports to establish an arrangement whereby U.S. armed forces operating overseas could be conceivably prosecuted by the international court even if the U.S. has not agreed to be bound by the treaty. Not only is this contrary to the most fundamental principles of treaty law, it could inhibit the ability of the U.S. to use its military to meet alliance obligations and participate in multinational operations, including humanitarian interventions to save civilian lives." Jennifer Elsea summarized U.S. objections in a 2006 Congressional Research Service study, the gist of which remains American policy. "The ICC purports to its jurisdiction citizens of non-member nations," she wrote. Moreover, lack of adequate due process to argue against jurisdiction in specific instances "will not offer accused Americans the due process guaranteed them under the U.S. constitution." The sovereign control of American forces potentially accused of war crimes thus stands at the base of the U.S. refusal to sign off on the ICC statute.

To circumvent the problem of sovereignty forfeiture, the United States has dredged up a tactic it used after World War II to ensure Senate ratification of the statute of the International Court of Justice (ICJ, or World Court), with which the ICC is affiliated. In the case of the ICJ, the United States insisted that the statute include the provision that the court would only have jurisdiction in individual cases if both (or all) parties granted jurisdiction for that action alone. In other words, countries, including the United States, can only be sued and have judgments made against them in situations in which they have given their permission: Sovereign control is only abrogated by explicit consent. The same argument is incorporated in the American approach to the question of the jurisdiction of the ICC. The American-proposed "supplement" to the Rome Treaty read: "The United Nations and the International Criminal Court agree that the Court may seek the surrender or accept custody of a national who acts within the overall direction of a U.N. Member State, and such directing State has so acknowledged only in the event (a) the directing State is a State Party to the Statute or the Court obtains the consent of the directing State, or (b) measures have been authorized pursuant to Chapter VII of the U.N. Charter against the directing State in relation to the situation or actions giving rise to alleged crime or crimes." Parties to the statute have consistently rejected this American position.

The U.S. position, which was formulated by the Bush administration but was neither modified nor renounced by its successor, goes on to add other objections based in the expansion of international authority contained in the ICC statute. Elsea cited two: an "unacceptable prosecutor" who would have "unchecked discretion to initiate cases," and the "usurpation of the role of the UN Security Council" in regulating ICC initiatives. Both find their base in the sovereignty issue: checks would presumably be exercised by states through the effective veto of prosecution of individual cases, and the Security Council's authority is based in the veto power of the permanent members, including the United States.

These distinctions are more than academic. The question of mandatory jurisdiction forces the United States to join a virtual rogues' gallery of other states that also have not ratified the ICC statute. This list contains both the world's most populous states (of which the United States is one) some of its worst human rights abusers (membership in which the United States would deny), and other states vulnerable to prosecution (such as Burundi and Russia) by the ICC. The motivation of many (but not all) of these states, which are concentrated in the Middle East and Africa, is to avoid the ICC's reach in cases where they or their top officials might be defendants. One of these states is Syria.

The Specific, Frustrating Case of Syria

Despite considerable publicity of the continuing practice of war crimes, they do occur, and international efforts to curb them and to punish perpetrators have been no more than moderately successful. The ICC is the international focal point against accused international war criminals, and its website reveals that it is engaged in investigations of most global accusations. Most of those under investigation have not been brought in front of the ICC for trial and potential conviction, and the existence of the ICC has not apparently deterred new violations. One is left to ask, "why not?"

The Syrian civil war is the current "poster child" for unpunished commission of crimes against humanity. As of April 20, 2017, there was no active examination or investigation into allegations of Syrian crimes against humanity committed against its own population, despite a publicized sarin gas attack on April 4, 2017 against a town controlled by rebels that was eerily reminiscent of similar attacks in 2013. Reactions to those attacks forced Syria to join the Chemical Weapons Convention (CWC, technically the Convention on the Prohibition of the Development, Production, Stockpiling and Use of Chemical Weapons and on Their Destruction) in October 2013.

The formal title indicates the obligations Syria accepted by joining the CWC. Their accession was part of a negotiated agreement to avoid prosecution of Assad by the ICC (among other things), and by its provisions, Syria was to destroy all its chemical weapons and promise not to acquire any more. They apparently lied, although the Assad regime denies complicity and blames the rebels for the attacks against their own stronghold. Russia supported the Assad position.

The proportions of this tragedy are staggering. Syria is a small country with a 2015 population of slightly more than seventeen million, of whom about 87 percent are Muslim, mostly Sunni (about 70 percent). The government and the military are controlled by the Alawite minority (about 10 percent of the population), who are Shiite and of which Assad is a member. The Shiite connection makes Iran a supporter of the regime. The lines in the civil war are largely defined by Sunni-Shia differences, but the Sunni majority is so divided that it cannot mount an effective, coordinated resistance against the government. No overarching leader has arisen to unite the antigovernment forces, nor has any faction demonstrated the competence and vigilance to attract major outside assistance.

It is against this backdrop that the tragedy has unfolded. The chemical weapons attacks have been the most obvious symbol, but Syrian suffering has extended far beyond that. Al Jazeera estimated in April 2017, for instance, that 465,000 Syrians had been killed between 2011 (when the civil war began) and 2017. The civil war was an extension of the abortive Arab Spring that began because a teenager scribbling anti-Assad graffiti on a Damascus wall was arrested and killed by police. More shocking has been the number of refugees resulting from the war. Al Jazeera, once again, estimated their 2017 numbers as upwards of twelve million citizens. As many as 6.6 million are internal displaced persons; most of the rest have fled the country and form the core of the ongoing worldwide refugee crisis (see chapter 11).

Outrage over Syrian actions has been cumulative and is growing, but it has not translated into effective action against the Assad regime. The U.S. government has for some time been at the forefront of these accusations. On February 28, 2012, American Secretary of State Hillary Clinton argued in a speech (quoted in Spence), "Based on definitions of war crimes and crimes against humanity, there ought to be an argument that he [al-Assad] fits into that category." There were outpourings of agreement from Western capitals, including Great Britain and France (whose governments volunteered to take an indictment of Assad to the ICC) and in a few Middle Eastern states, notably neighboring Turkey.

There are two contradictory precedents about how to deal with Assad. In the 1990s, Serbian president Slobodan Milosevic was accused of war crimes in Kosovo as part of the disintegration of Yugoslavia. His successor's government turned him in to the ICC; he was convicted, and he is serving a life sentence for crimes against humanity. Sudanese president Omar al-Bashir, on the other hand, has been indicted by the ICC in absentia for crimes in Darfur and South Sudan. Sudan has denied requests for his extradition, and he remains free and in power. Assad has so far succeeded in following the Sudanese precedent.

Although there are firm bases for dealing with the Syrian case as a war crime within ICC jurisdiction, there are also at least two objections. One of these, which Clinton raised, is that indicting al-Bashar would make efforts to convince him to step down more difficult. As a former leader, he would be much more vulnerable to arrest and deportation to an ICC tribunal (the Milosevic precedent) than if he remains in power (the al-Bashir precedent).

The other objection arises from the ICC's claimed jurisdiction over accused war criminals from states that are not party to the ICC. Because Syria is not a member, such jurisdiction must be established for the ICC to have a claim of authority over Assad. It is, however, the heart of the American (and Israeli and others') objection to the ICC to deny this extension of authority. This obviously puts the United States in an arguably hypocritical position of accusing Assad of crimes but denying the authority of the body specifically entrusted with trying him. The potential trial of Assad thus raises important legal questions regarding the universality of laws against war crimes.

The February 2013 report of the commission of the UN Human Rights Council (a 131-page document) widened the accusation to include war crimes accusations of leaders of the opposition as well. The report, as described in the *New York Times* (see Cummings-Bruce) and elsewhere, argued that alleged violence by both sides is worsening, "aggravated by increasing sectarianism," and made even worse by a growing influx of foreign fighters into the country. Speaking for the commission, Carla del Ponte, described as a "UN human rights investigator," summarized what the report views as the necessary international response. "It's incredible the Security Council doesn't take a decision," she says. "Crimes are continuing, and the number of victims is increasing every day." The report recommends sending the case to the ICC, but two of the permanent members of the Security Council with veto power, China and the United States, are also nonmembers of the ICC.

The issue came to a head in mid-2013 with the accusation of chemical weapons use against Syrian civilians by the government. The attacks clearly constituted a crime against humanity and placed the perpetrators under the jurisdiction of the ICC. Preferring charges would have required a direct accusation against the regime and Assad and created a dilemma for the world community. If the norm has any teeth, it would have to be enforced. Assad, along with supporters such as Russia, would have resisted, and in all probability the only way to enforce the norms would have been through the application of force, including the capture of Assad.

The problem was resolved in 2013 by a UN Security Council Resolution (UNSCR 2118) that demanded Syrian disarmament of its chemical weapons under international supervision, but with no mention of or blame assigned to chemical uses against civilians. The international community was thus able to enforce the ban on chemical weapons without needing to enforce the ban on crimes against humanity.

The 2017 crisis has unfolded within this context. When accusations were made about the most recent gassing after it was beamed globally on television, Syria and its Russian ally quickly denied all guilt, and Russian support ensured that any anti-Syrian UN Security Council action would be vetoed. The outcome, for as long as it holds, demonstrates the clear limits on international cooperation in a world of sovereign states some of which reserve the "right" to use controversial force to protect their interests.

Conclusion and Dilemmas

War crimes and their elimination are not likely to go away as a concern in international relations. In a gradually democratizing world in which authoritarianism is still practiced but rarely extolled, there is no longer any organized, principled objection to the notion that there are limits on both the conduct of war and how individuals and groups can be treated. The development of something like a consensus is quite recent in historical terms (particularly the idea of crimes against peace and humanity), and objections to the idea are now indirectly couched in terms such as sovereignty.

The major remaining barrier is institutionalization of war crimes enforcement. The development of anti–war crimes norms far out-distances efforts to create mechanisms to enforce that consensus. States agree that war crimes are bad, but they are reluctant to create enforcers who might be employed against them. It is an extension of the argument for sovereignty introduced in chapter 1. Syria is the current symbol of man's inhumanity to humanity, and it also demonstrates the difficulty of adjudicating such inhumanity due the limited reach of the ICC.

Is the ICC the answer? Clearly, it would solve some problems and have some advantages. It would certainly be more responsive when problems arise; it would maximize whatever deterrent value a potential violator would experience knowing the court was waiting for him or her; and it would insulate the system from accusations of victors' law in future cases. Moreover, it would contribute at least marginally to the general promotion of lawfulness in the international system and, in specific cases, might help defuse public passions by removing trials from the places in which alleged crimes took place and in which there was universal international support for action, a limit in the Syrian case. To its proponents, these are powerful and compelling justifications for the ICC.

Then there is the American position. The U.S. objection to the ICC is neither a defense of war crimes nor an explicit defense of international disorder. Rather, it stems from a long-standing American fixation with state sovereignty and the need for the American government to have sole jurisdiction over its citizens. In practice, this policy puts the United States at cross-purposes with most of the international community, including most of its closest allies, and on the same side as some rogue states on this and similar issues. The result can be schizophrenic. The Clinton administration championed the ICC, and the Bush administration backed away and opposed it.

In the end, the international debate is not about war crimes or the establishment of a court. No one is for war crimes or against a tribunal to prosecute offenders. The debate is over the nature of the court's jurisdiction and how that jurisdiction applies to individual countries. More specifically, it is a question of whether a country is willing to forfeit some of its independent control over its territory and citizens in the pursuit of a common value, violation of which could be turned on them. Some countries are willing to do so; some are not.

The result is a clash between advocacies of war crimes prosecution and defenders of sovereignty. Which is more important? At one level, international cooperation against crimes against humanity is clearly virtuous and praiseworthy, but what if such cooperation is detrimental to the ability of the state to protect itself from evils being committed in it, including evils committed using those very acts the cooperation attempts to prevent? More concretely, can states advocate the imposition of mandatory war crimes jurisdiction against others but not against themselves?

At another level, the dilemma is over the rule of law versus the primal right of self-protection. International cooperation in adjudicating war crimes, after all, is about self-interest. One reason that crimes against humanity are outlawed is based in reciprocity: If I do not commit these acts, you cannot justify using them either, so it is in both of our interests to outlaw them.

But there will always be exceptions. Some people will always break the law, and in the case of war crimes, doing so can endanger the people of sovereign states. Syria is the latest dramatic illustration. What should the state do in these circumstances? It is easy to delineate the extremes: The cooperative rule of law should triumph regardless of the human consequences, or states should do whatever they feel they must to defend themselves, regardless of the impact on law and even civilization. But most cases in the real world lie between the extremes, where the choices are neither so stark nor clear-cut.

Study/Discussion Questions

1. The commission of war crimes is universally condemned, and international cooperation to end and punish these acts seems to be the obvious solution, but this has not always been the case. Why?

2. Discuss the evolution of the war crimes concept. What was the impact of the end of the Cold War and the tragedies of Bosnia and Rwanda on that evolution? How is the International Criminal Court the product of that evolution?

3. How are war crimes prosecution and sovereignty related? How does this relationship create anomalous, even hypocritical, situations for some states?

4. What are the various categories of war crimes? Discuss them histori-

cally and in terms of their current importance.

5. What is the ICC? Are the arguments in favor of it compelling? How much of the American objection to the question of automatic, overriding jurisdiction should be accommodated? If you were the representative of another government, what would you think about the American position?

6. What are the supposed virtues of a permanent, rather than an ad hoc, tribunal on war crimes? Using the cases of Slobodan Milosevic and Omar al-Bashir as examples, has experience validated this assumption of virtue?

7. What is the war crimes case against Syria? What rules have

they violated? Trace these violations through the Syrian civil war, the 2013 case of chemical weapons use, and the Russian factor in the current situation. Discuss.

8. What should the international system do about Syrian war crimes and the crimes of Bashar al-Assad?

Should the ICC take on the lead role in this process? If this case ends up violating the sovereignty of Syria and this is viewed as a precedent for dealing with other countries, is the principle worth the sacrifice? Why or why not?

Bibliography

Allison, William Thomas. *My Lai: An American Atrocity in the Vietnam War*. Witness to History. Baltimore, MD: Johns Hopkins University Press, 2012.

Bosco, David. *Rough Justice: The International Criminal Court in a World of Power Politics*. New York: Cambridge University Press, 2014.

Brinkley, Joel. *Cambodia's Curse: The Modern History of a Troubled Land*. New York: PublicAffairs, 2011.

Central Intelligence Agency. *CIA World Factbook, 2015*. Washington, DC: Central Intelligence Agency, 2015.

Cobban, Helena. "Think Again: International Courts." *Foreign Policy*, March/April 2006, 22–28.

Cummings-Bruce, Nick. "U.N. Rights Panel on Syria Urges War Crimes Charges." *New York Times* (online), February 18, 2013.

Dempsey, Gary. *Reasonable Doubt: The Case Against the Proposed International Criminal Court*. Cato Policy Analysis No. 311. Washington, DC: Cato Institute, 1998.

Elsea, Jennifer K. *U.S. Policy Regarding the International Criminal Court*. Washington, DC: Congressional Research Service, August 29, 2006.

Greenberg, Karen Joy. *The Torture Debate in America*. Cambridge, MA: MIT Press, 2005.

Grotius, Hugo. *On the Law of War and Peace*. New York: Cambridge University Press, 2012 (originally published 1625).

Gutman, Roy, and David Rieff, eds. *Crimes of War*. New York: Norton, 1999.

Hersh, Seymour. *Chain of Command: The Road from 9/11 to Abu Ghraib*. New York: HarperCollins, 2004.

Jones, Howard. *My Lai: Vietnam, 1968, and the Descent into Darkness*. Moments in American History. New York: Oxford University Press, 2017.

Kahn, Leo. *Nuremberg Trials*. New York: Ballantine, 1972.

Kersten, Mark. *Justice in Conflict: The Effect of the International Criminal Court's Interventions on Ending Wars and Building Peace*. Oxford, UK: Oxford University Press, 2016.

Kiernan, Ben. *The Pol Pot Regime: Race, Power, and Genocide in Cambodia under the Khmer Rouge, 1975–1979*. New Haven, CT: Yale University Press, 2008.

Lister, Charles. *The Syrian Jihad: Al Qaeda, the Islamic State, and the Evolution of an Insurgency*. Oxford, UK: Oxford University Press, 2016.

Malek, Alia. *The Home That Was Our Country: A Memoir of Syria*. New York: Nation, 2017.

Phillips, Christopher. *The Battle for Syria: International Rivalry in the New Middle East*. New Haven, CT: Yale University Press, 2016.

Schabas, William A. *An Introduction to the International Criminal Court.* 5th ed. New York: Cambridge University Press, 2017.

Sewell, Sarah, and Carl Kaysen, eds. *The United States and the International Criminal Court: National Security and International Law.* Lanham, MD: Rowman & Littlefield, 2000.

Short, Philip. *Pol Pot: Anatomy of a Nightmare.* New York: Henry Hol, 2007.

Spence, Richard. "Syria: Bashar al-Assad Could Be Regarded as a War Criminal, Says Hillary Clinton." *Telegraph* (online), February 28, 2012.

Tusa, Ann, and John Tusa. *The Nuremberg Trial.* New York: Atheneum, 1983.

Wegner, Patrick. *The International Criminal Court in Ongoing Intrastate Conflicts: Navigating the Peace-Justice Divide.* New York: Cambridge University Press, 2015.

Welsh, Jennifer. "The Responsibility to Protect: Dilemmas of a New Norm." *Current History* 111, no. 748 (November 2012): 291–98.

PART II
Continuing Issues and Problems

8

Globalization and Terms of International Trade

The Case of the WTO and NAFTA

The exchange of goods and services among people and political units is as old as human interaction generally, and as it has evolved, it has become a main emphasis of economics and a major part of internal and international politics. Economic protectionism was a major factor in the slide toward World War II in Europe under the banner of mercantilism, and the emergence of what amounted to two separate and incompatible sectional economies in the United States in the early nineteenth century helped pave the road to the Civil War. Trade has clear economic consequences, but it also has political impacts. Sometimes these effects are exaggerated by both champions and opponents, which has arguably been the case in contemporary discussions. The realization of political effects led planners of the post–World War II international system to place economic cooperation high on their list of priorities. This process began in the 1940s and blossomed into economic globalization and a series of free-trade-based agreements since the end of the Cold War.

Events such as the global economic recession of 2008 and growing European concerns over aspects of the European Union (see chapter 9) have dampened international enthusiasm over free trade. The North American Free Trade Agreement (NAFTA), which came into force in 1994, has been a focal point of free trade criticism, especially since the 2016 election of Donald J. Trump as president of the United States. The fate of NAFTA, the impact of which is more symbolic than physical, was widely extolled until recently, and its fate may serve as an important harbinger in the international terms of trade debate.

Trading goods and services has been one of humankind's oldest forms of interchange with other peoples and communities, and it is at the heart of the contemporary emphasis in international relations on economic globalization and reactions to it. In ancient times, the purpose of trade was generally to acquire goods that did not exist or grow, or could not be produced, locally; a major source of pride and prestige surrounded the successful acquisition of commodities such as exotic fabrics like silk, spices, or precious metals. As the ability of political communities to span greater distances in shorter periods increased, trade expanded both in extent and in terms of what was and was not traded.

The modern issue of trade probably congealed over whether to import goods and services that were also produced domestically, especially if foreign goods were cheaper and of comparable or better quality. That question is near the top of the agenda in contemporary discussions of trade and is manifested in most disagreements on the subject, from questions of barriers to trade to environmental impacts of importation versus domestic production. Since the economic downturn of 2008, the contribution of trade to prosperity has been a point of concern, particularly in areas such as employment and fairness of competition in the United States and elsewhere. Both were major themes of the Trump campaign and have carried over into his presidency. The World Trade Organization (WTO) and NAFTA, featured in the application section of this chapter, have been lightning rods in this debate. Given accusations that the trade practices of some countries provided them artificial, unfair advantages during the difficult economic times of the past few years, free trade has been under increasing levels of criticism that continue to grow. It has become a virtually basic element of the contemporary global economic environment.

The debate over the impact of trade is not new, either internationally or in the United States. The emergence of the capitalist system first in Europe and then worldwide pitted global traders against what are now called protectionists in the form of mercantilists seeking to protect new, infant industries from destructive outside competition. In the United States, advocacy and opposition have been sectional historically and remain as part of the contemporary landscape. As Michael Lind explains, "From the eighteenth century on, the Southern plantation oligarchy was content for the United States to specialize in exporting agricultural goods and raw materials to more industrial nations, importing manufactured goods in return. Thanks to the dominance of the South and Southwest, what was once the foreign economic policy of the Confederate States of America has become the trade policy of the United States as a whole." In turn, he argues, this has caused the United States to lead "the campaign to reduce or eliminate tariffs worldwide."

Whether to allow the unfettered movement of goods and services internationally (free trade) or to place restrictions of one kind or another on that flow is a central element in contemporary international relations. The removal of barriers to trade emerged as the centerpiece of the economic globalization movement of the 1990s, one of the engines designed to draw countries into closer collaboration by entwining them in the global prosperity of that decade. The global economic downturn at the turn of the millennium and the rise of the global war on terror took some of the luster from the free trade issue and relegated it to a less prominent place on the international political agenda. Yet, while attention is diverted elsewhere, globalization has continued, and proponents and opponents continue to fight over whether to expand or constrict free trade arrangements. Its dynamics are foundational for understanding contemporary international politics.

Principle: Globalization and Terms of Trade

The basic poles in the free trade debate have been between those seeking to expand trade (free traders) and those seeking to restrict trade (protectionists). Nestled between the extremes are those who advocate freer, but not necessarily totally free, trade (who often portray themselves as fair traders). All three emphases are vibrant parts of contemporary arguments. As some debates have become increasingly adversarial, the internal manipulation of competitive pricing by some governments has become an additional concern.

While the Industrial Revolution was raging in Europe and later North America, the need to buffer nascent industries from outside competition militated toward restriction, largely under the intellectual banner of mercantilism. During the period leading to World War II, protectionism ran rampant in a Great Depression–riddled Europe, and economic restrictions were partially blamed for the bloodiest war in human history. The "lessons" of interwar economics, in turn, helped frame the international political debate and its institutionalization, and especially in greater cooperation and interdependence.

Because it deals with people's prosperity and conditions of living, the debate tends to be very emotional and hyperbolic. A major conjunction in the emotional side of the debate is between trade practices and jobs, a clearly critical concern for almost everyone. From both economic and political perspectives, a key question is whether policies promoting one or another trading philosophy create, destroy, or have no effect on employment generally or on individual categories of jobs. The result is to add a clearly emotional element to the debate that will be exploited by partisans on all sides of the issue. These discussions tend to exaggerate effects and to make calm consideration of what may be quite marginal economic impacts politically difficult.

Trade Advocacies

The economic aspect of the trade debate has been, and is, asymmetrical, and proponents on one side or the other tend to talk past one another, meaning interchange often devolves into monologues. The arguments promoting free and expanded trade tend to be mainly abstract, impersonal, and macroeconomic. Free trade is argued to be beneficial because it unleashes basic economic principles like comparative advantage that make overall economies (national or international) stronger and economic conditions within and between countries more vital and prosperous. Advocates maintain that arrangements promoting trade have had a net positive impact on the global economy, and because they expand production, they promote closer, friendlier relations between the participants. Additionally, they intertwine the economies of trade partners in ways that make conflict between them impractical and self-destructive.

Anti–free trade arguments, on the other hand, tend to be specific, personal, and microeconomic. Cries to restrict trade tend to be posed in terms of the adverse impact that expanding trade opportunities has on individuals, groups, industrial sectors, and even geographical regions within countries. Trade is not about economic theories; rather, it is about peoples' jobs and livelihoods. Thus, opponents home in on things such as jobs lost by individuals in particular industries to make their points. The "theory" of comparative advantage suggests that macroeconomic prosperity and growth is the result of specialization: those who make a good or service of better quality and lower price should be encouraged to expand production. This may expand the overall economy, but it means those who lack comparative advantage can lose their livelihoods. For them, microeconomic loss outweighs macroeconomic benefits.

Fair trade is a third alternative. Fair traders seek a compromise somewhere between the extremes, advocating selective trade reductions in conformance with the principle of free trade but seeking to minimize negative microeconomic impact. Frequently, fair traders emphasize the need for compensatory actions for those individuals adversely affected by what they basically see as the beneficial impacts from free trade. They also oppose actions by trade partners that artificially inflate their competitive advantage at the expense of others.

The argument over textiles illustrates the asymmetry in this debate. To pro–free traders, moving clothing manufacturing overseas, where labor costs are lower, makes economic sense. Clothes are cheaper, and the economies of new textile producers are stimulated. Uncompetitive textile manufacturers can redirect their efforts to other production areas in which they can produce better products at lower costs. Moreover, all consumers benefit, because goods are produced at the lowest possible costs, and the savings are passed along to consumers. In the end, it is a macroeconomic win-win situation that draws countries closer together, thus promoting greater cooperation and reduced international tension.

From the anti–free trade viewpoint, these abstractions are unconvincing, because moving textile manufacturing overseas costs domestic textile workers their jobs. It is a concern centered on the impact on individuals, not on the systemic impact. Thus, when free traders extol the removal of barriers and anti–free traders deride that possibility, they are actually not talking about the same thing. Fair traders add that providing training and the like for displaced workers so they can find competitive jobs is an answer, but one not always available.

The debate is intensely political at both the domestic and international levels. Within American national politics, the asymmetry is reflected between branches of the federal government. Historically, the executive branch of government, more concerned with the overall health of the economy and somewhat more removed from the impact on specific individuals or groups (as opposed to the whole country), tends to be more free trade–oriented and macroeconomic. Members of Congress, whose constituents are the people whose jobs are endangered when foreign goods and services are allowed to enter the country more freely, tend to be more microeconomic and opposed.

At the international level, the debate tends to become intermingled with preferences for the general orientation toward political interactions with the world. Broadly speaking, two positions have dominated the global argument. *Internationalists* generally advocate a maximum involvement in the international system, because such involvement is systemically beneficial and promotes cooperative interactions among states. Advocacy of free trade and globalization are the economic manifestation of that reasoning.

The other position, *isolationism*, advocates a minimal level of involvement in the world. This position reached its institutionalized zenith between the world wars, when "splendid isolationism" sought to keep the United States entirely separated from world, and especially European, politics, an economic exclusionary preference that spread to Europe during the 1930s. "America First" movements in the 1930s and more recently reflect this orientation. In its pure economic form, isolationists are also protectionist, because protectionism limits international economic interactions by placing prohibitive barriers on incoming trade.

The terms of the debate are not purely economic. Pro-trade advocates of the 1990s, for instance, argued that the globalization process of which free trade is the centerpiece produces political as well as economic benefits. As noted in chapter 3, one of the major reasons for promoting trade with China is to draw that country more intimately into the global political system. At the same time, anti–free trade arguments have expanded to include strictly noneconomic concerns ranging from environmental degradation to compromises of sovereignty, as well as politico-economic arguments about the effects on different groups within societies, all arguments that also arise in the China context.

This introduction frames the structure of the section, which has three purposes. The first purpose is historical, tracing the process whereby free trade has been institutionalized in the international system since the end of World War II. That process has crystallized the principal reasons for advocating and opposing free trade, a discussion of which is the second purpose of the discussion. Finally, it will attempt to apply this institutional framework and the positions of the two sides to the current, ongoing debate on the issue. These discussions provide a framework for examining NAFTA.

Institutionalizing Trade

The genesis of the contemporary debate over trade was the period leading to World War II, the war's traumatic impact, and the determination to ensure that it did not recur. Planners agreed that a major reason for the war was economic conditions during the Great Depression that nurtured protectionism and produced economic chaos that facilitated the descent into the maelstrom of global war.

Economic nationalism and protectionism were identified as the chief culprits for this situation. As the Great Depression took hold across Europe and North America, governments scrambled to minimize the effects on their own economies and peoples. One solution was to protect national industries from foreign competition by erecting prohibitively high trade barriers to keep foreign goods and services out and thus to keep domestic industries (and the jobs they created) alive. These tariffs and other barriers spawned retaliation and counter-retaliation that brought European trade to a virtual standstill. At the same time, currency fluctuations and devaluations became commonplace to prop up failing enterprises. The resulting destabilization was felt especially strongly in Germany, which faced stiff reparations requirements exacted at the Versailles Peace Conference that ended World War I. Unable to meet reparations schedules with foreign exchange from trade that had dried up, the German economy spun out of control as the depression hit that country harder than any other. In that atmosphere, Adolf Hitler arose, promising, among other things, to restore prosperity.

The process of rebuilding the postwar world began early during the war itself, largely through British and American collaboration. The purpose was to ensure that the structure of postwar peace would prevent a recurrence of global war. Politically, this collaboration produced thoroughly internationalist constructs such as the United Nations Charter and the North Atlantic Treaty Organization (NATO). Economically, it produced a series of agreements known as the Bretton Woods system.

The Bretton Woods System and Free Trade

Encouraged and cajoled by the governments of Great Britain and the United States, representatives of forty-four countries met in the White Mountains resort town of Bretton Woods, New Hampshire, in July 1944 to plan for the postwar economic peace. At that conference, the participants hammered out a series of agreements that produced international economic institutions that have endured into the twenty-first century and have become staple parts of the system of globalization.

They agreed that the heart of the prewar economic problem was protectionism, manifested in international financial and economic practices such as large fluctuation in exchange rates of currencies, chronic balance-of-payments difficulties, and prohibitively high tariffs. All had contributed to restricting international commerce, and the conferees agreed that a major antidote was to encourage much freer trade among countries. This explicitly free trade preference was held most strongly by the U.S. delegation to Bretton Woods. This preference came from the Roosevelt administration and had some opposition domestically from conservative members of Congress and private organizations such as the U.S. Chamber of Commerce (a close ally of American businesses that benefited from protectionism).

The Bretton Woods process more successfully confronted some priorities than others. Two international organizations were created, the International Monetary Fund (IMF) and the International Bank for Reconstruction and Development (IBRD, or World Bank). The IMF was chartered to deal with the problem of currency fluctuations by authorizing the granting of credits to shore up weak currencies, thus contributing to economic stabilization. The IMF has gradually widened its purview to a variety of other economic matters. The World Bank was to assist in economic stabilization by granting loans for reconstruction of war-torn countries and later for the development of the emerging Third World.

The priority of freeing trade did not enjoy as successful a fate. Although Bretton Woods produced two organizations, it failed to see the third pillar of its vision institutionalized, an international organization devoted explicitly to the promotion of free trade. Instead, that process was gradual and convoluted, not reaching fruition until the 1990s.

From Bretton Woods to ITO, GATT, and WTO

There was a clear sentiment for creating a parallel free trade–promoting international organization at Bretton Woods, but there was enough opposition to the idea both internationally and domestically in the United States to prevent such an organization from being included in the Bretton Woods package. The American position was crucial because the United States dominated the early postwar international economic system so thoroughly that it had an effective veto over economic matters. The problem was the familiar ambivalence of American politics relating to foreign affairs. As a result, the United States found itself alternately championing and opposing the creation of an organization to promote free trade, depending on whether free trade or anti–free trade elements held sway in the domestic decision process.

During and shortly after the war, the idea of the International Trade Organization (ITO) surfaced within the executive branch of the American government, and especially the U.S. Department of State. When Harry S. Truman succeeded Franklin Delano Roosevelt as president in 1945, he adopted the ITO as his own project. His administration took the leadership role in proposing a United Nations Conference on Trade and Development (UNCTAD) in 1946, a major purpose of which was to draft a charter for the ITO. That proposal was, however, opposed by powerful elements in the U.S. Congress, and as a result, a meeting was held in Geneva, Switzerland, in 1947 to lay out the principles of a General Agreement on Tariffs and Trade (GATT), as an interim, partial solution to the free trade issue. The proposal for GATT was to be a temporary "fix," on the road to creating the ITO at a meeting scheduled for Havana, Cuba, in 1947.

Then American domestic politics intervened. The ITO, like other free trade institutions since, would have done two things of varying controversy. The first was to provide an institutional basis for promoting reduction of barriers to trade, which was the less controversial aspect. The second, and more divisive, purpose was to create an instrument with jurisdiction and authority to enforce trade agreements, including the capability to levy enforceable penalties against sovereign governments. Opponents of the ITO complained that this enforcement provision represented an unacceptable infringement on American sovereignty, a familiar American refrain.

The ITO proposal was undermined by political actions in the United States in 1948. A coalition of powerful elements in the Congress led the way. The major players in this array against the ITO included conservative Republicans backed by protectionist agricultural and manufacturing interests, liberal Democrats who viewed the ITO document as too timid an approach, and conservatives who feared the sovereignty infringement that ITO enforcement provisions proposed.

This congressional array faced a Truman administration that favored ratification of the ITO statute but that was unwilling to expend scarce political capital in the process. Competing on the foreign policy agenda was the North Atlantic Treaty Organization (NATO) proposal. As an initiative to create the first peacetime military alliance in American history, NATO was also controversial. The Truman administration reasoned that it could muster support for one but not both treaties, and that of the two, NATO was the more critical (the Cold War was heating up at the time). Thus, the Truman administration backed away from its advocacy of the ITO, and the proposal died. The United States had, not uncharacteristically, both enthusiastically endorsed and helped develop the charter for the ITO and then destroyed it.

The demise of the ITO elevated GATT to a prominence and permanence that those who had originally proposed it had not envisioned. GATT survived as the flag bearer for international free trade from 1948 until the WTO came into existence in 1995. Those who oppose free trade in principle or effect were unenthused by GATT, but felt less threatened by it than by the ITO.

GATT was less objectionable than the ITO because it lacked an enforcement capability. GATT, in effect, was not an organization at all, but rather a series of negotiating sessions called "rounds" among the sovereign members. These sessions created international agreements on different free trade issues, but they were less threatening than the ITO. GATT was not an organization and thus lacked more than a modest staff; therefore, it had no investigating capability. It was never granted any enforcement authority, and all agreements had to be ratified by all participating countries before their provisions affected them. Those who feared institutionalizing free trade on sovereignty grounds had little to fear from the GATT process.

Although it was not a permanent international organization, GATT was not useless. The outcomes of the various rounds did produce a series of principles and practices that have been incorporated into the WTO. The principal thrust of GATT action was centered on the *most favored nation* (MFN) principle: the idea of providing to all trading partners the same customs and tariff treatment enjoyed by a country given the greatest trade privilege—the most favored country. Thus, if one country lowers its tariffs on goods to another country, it should extend that same tariff treatment to all GATT members.

The last, or Uruguay, round of GATT included proposals to establish the World Trade Organization (WTO). In a very real sense, the WTO is the ITO reincarnated, because it combines the two basic elements of the ITO again within a permanent international organization: the promotion of free trade, *and* mechanisms to enforce trade agreements including the legal authority to penalize members of the organization that violate international trade agreements.

First proposed in 1993, the WTO did not produce the same volume of objection that the ITO did in 1948. The same basic opposed interests, if with different representatives, were against the WTO in the United States. Protectionists disfavored the principle of free trade; in 1948, these were mostly business-related Republicans, but in 1993 they were mostly union-supporting Democrats. Some again objected that the organization was too timid—in this case the objectors were principally environmentalists concerned that the WTO would not aggressively protect the environment. Others raised objections on the grounds of infringements of national sovereignty. The U.S. Congress ratified the WTO statute on December 1, 1994. It was not submitted as a treaty (requiring the advice and consent of two-thirds of the Senate), but instead as an economic agreement under the provisions of so-called *fast track* procedures (also known as trade promotion authority). Treating the WTO as an economic agreement meant that it had to pass both houses of Congress, but with only a simple, rather than a weighted, majority. Designating it under fast track (a provision to facilitate the passage of trade agreements) meant there were limits on congressional debate on the matter and that it could only be voted up or down in its entirety (the authority to amend it was removed). Nearly fifty years after its principles were first proposed, institutionalized free trade became reality in 1995.

The WTO has now existed for over two decades. Its membership has increased from approximately seventy in 1995 to 164 as of July 29, 2016 (according to its website). In addition, twenty-one nonmember countries participate in the organization (observers have five years to apply for full membership), including Iraq, Iran, and Afghanistan. The headquarters, including the secretariat, are in Lausanne, Switzerland. The WTO has established itself as a leading international economic organization in the process.

Its brief tenure has been filled with more controversy and a great deal more publicity than functional international organizations (those that deal with a specific policy area rather than generalist organizations such as the United Nations) usually attract or desire. In some ways, the acceptance of or opposition to the WTO reflects the status of globalization, whose central principle of free trade it exemplifies. When the charter came into effect in 1995, globalization was at its apex and the new WTO only activated its most ardent opponents. After 9/11, international attention shifted to the problem of terrorism, taking the spotlight off globalization and the WTO. Free trade has continued to grow, but the acceptance of its values and their institutionalization has become more controversial. For different reasons, NAFTA and the European Union (the case in chapter 9) are examples of these reactions. As a result, that continued momentum is a matter of some contention.

Application: Free Trade, the WTO, and NAFTA

The movement to promote greater international trade has had two related thrusts, one economic and one political, since it burst upon the global scene as a dominant theme in the 1990s. Both underlay the postwar evolution of trade promotion and share two assumptions: that greater trade will increase productivity and prosperity, and that the resulting economic globalization will also promote economically induced interdependence that will contribute to political stability and peace.

These assumptions were largely unquestioned during the balance of the 1990s. In the aftermath of the end of the Cold War, the 1990s were relatively tranquil politically and prosperous economically, and much of the credit (rightly or wrongly) was attributed to growing globalization, the signature symbol of which was freeing trade. The major champion was the United States, which possessed the world's most vibrant economy and administration led by one of the world's most vocal and visible champions of globalization, President Bill Clinton. It is no coincidence that American participation in both WTO and NAFTA occurred in 1994, his second year in office.

The political tranquility, of course, was shattered by 9/11. Terrorism replaced globalization as the global political mantra, and the global economy was disrupted by the attacks on New York. Globalization was not implicated in the tragedy and continued at a lower level of awareness. Globalization and free trade became more closely associated with the global recession of 2008 that began on Wall Street and spread like a computer virus worldwide. The recession demonstrated that globalization not only contributed to prosperity but could also worsen and universalize economic downturns.

During the "boom" years of trade promotion and expansion, the phenomenon moved along two tracks. One, represented by the WTO, was to champion free trade through internationalist advocacy and regulation. The other, symbolized by NAFTA, was regional, seeking to deepen economic interaction by specific agreements between generally neighboring states. Both experiences are relevant in assessing whether trade promotion is a "good" idea.

The virtue of greater trade has become controversial, based on two questions. One question is whether free trade itself is a worthy goal, and it has as a subtext the question of whether free trade *as it is currently defined and being pursued* is a good idea. One can, for instance, believe that the general principle of removing barriers to trade is a good idea, but disagree that the overarching implementing principle of removing "barriers to trade" should override other principles, such as promoting equities in the fairness of the resulting relationship for all or some parties. The other question is whether to institutionalize free trade advocacy and implementation. That question has the subtexts of whether the WTO *as it is currently organized and with the authority it has* is a good idea and whether regional organizations perform well for all participants.

The WTO, and more recently NAFTA, have become lightning rods on the free trade issue. Those who oppose free trade, generally on the basis that its effects are not as desirable for individuals or societies as its advocates suggest, clearly oppose advocating institutions. Proponents of free trade generally support the idea of an institutional base from which to promote their advocacy, but may not like the structure that exists.

Free Trade or Not Free Trade?

The generalized defense of free trade rests on the macroeconomic benefits it brings to countries and the microeconomic benefits it accords to individuals and groups. Both are controversial. Citing the international application of the Ricardian principle of comparative advantage, free traders argue that removing barriers to the movement of goods and services across national boundaries means the most efficient producers of goods and providers of services will dominate the markets in the areas of their advantage, to the benefit of consumers who will receive the best goods and services at the lowest prices from these providers. Presuming that all countries have products or services where they have such advantages, all will find markets, and the result will be a general and growing specialization and prosperity. International free trade is the handmaiden of the process of economic globalization, because the result should be widening of participation in the global economy, as more and more countries find and exploit areas in which they have or can develop a comparative advantage.

According to its champions, free trade promotes a more cooperative, peaceful environment through *complex interdependence*, the idea that as countries become increasingly reliant on one another for essential goods and services, their ability and desire to engage in conflict, and especially war, becomes more problematical—either because the desire to fight is decreased by proximity and acquaintance, or because the intertwining of economies makes it impractical or impossible to fight.

This macroeconomic argument is abstract and intellectual, and its dynamics are not universally accepted. It argues that free trade improves the general lot of peoples, and thus increases the prosperity of individuals: "a rising tide lifts all boats," to borrow a phrase that advocates often invoke. As an abstract formulation presented in this way, it is difficult to argue with the virtue of free trade. At a slightly less abstract level, proponents of free trade also point to largely macroeconomic indicators, especially from the mid-1990s, to demonstrate growth in the global economy and within individual countries, phenomena they attribute to free trade–driven globalization. When these statistics are applied at more specific levels—to those of individuals or even sectors of economies within countries—the case is not as clearly positive.

The major objections to free trade come not over these abstract principles, but from their application. A key element in opposition arises from the presumption that all countries (or whatever entities are part of a free trading arrangement) will in fact find areas of production at which they have a comparative advantage. This is not always the case, and countries lacking comparative advantage (generally the least developed countries) thus tend to avoid involvement to the extent that they can. It also presumes that areas of uncompetitive production can be replaced with compensatory equivalent areas where comparative advantage can be developed to replace uncompetitive enterprises. It is central to microeconomic objections to free trade that this is also not always the case.

This contrast in macro-level versus micro-level benefits helps explain why free trade is more popular among economic elites than the general population and why the issue becomes a flash point in economic debates during political campaigns such as 2016 in the United States. The economic elites—investors, entrepreneurs, and the like—are all more likely to be insulated from negative micro-level impacts but more affected by broader, macro-level effects such as the overall impact on the stock market. If these macro-level indicators are expanding, then those who benefit personally are likely to be supportive. Negative micro-level effects have a direct impact on the jobs of individual voters, and candidates for public office are likely to reflect the suffering that displaced individuals and industries feel. Thus, it is not surprising to see opposition to globalization in areas where globalization has produced declines in noncompetitive industries, from the textile workers of the Carolinas to automobile workers in Michigan or steelworkers in Pennsylvania.

An international example of negative effects is the impact of institutionalized free trade on the economic development of poor countries. Because the basis of free trade is the most favored nation (MFN) principle, opponents argue that poor countries are disadvantaged: they are at a comparative disadvantage at producing nearly everything (a major reason they are less developed), and they are vulnerable to a flooding of cheaper foreign goods and services across the range of economic activity if they are part of a free trade system. Their inability to protect nascent economic activities means that indigenous development will be undercut systematically by participation in the free trade regime and thus development will be retarded. The net impact of being exposed to MFN has thus been, according to critics, to contribute to greater economic inequality between the rich and poor countries, the very opposite of what the proponents of free trade argue.

For the "turtles," as Thomas Friedman labels the countries that cannot compete in the free trade environment, there are two options. One is to stay outside the globalization framework to minimize negative impacts. Almost all the countries that have not joined the WTO, for instance, are extremely poor, and outreach programs to these outsiders have not been entirely successful at overcoming these objections. The other alternative is to join the global system and suffer the consequences of assault on the domestic economy in the hopes that doing so will help "lift" the national boat.

Like all economic ideas and their institutionalization, trade arrangements are inextricably economic and political, and attempts to argue them exclusively on one ground or the other are fundamentally feckless. Politics at heart involves the authoritative allocation of scarce resources, and economic resources such as wealth and economic power are prime subjects for politically determined decisions with both political and economic consequences. To argue the case for or against trade arrangements on "purely" economic criteria distorts reality. Whether macroeconomic or microeconomic consequences should be supreme, for instance, is a political determination, since some of those consequences affect who gains scarce economic benefits. Politics and economics are intertwined inextricably, and this is true of both WTO and NAFTA.

The WTO: Problem or Solution?

The WTO is the final fulfillment of the dreams of the Bretton Woods planners, completing the troika of the IMF, IBRD, and itself as centerpieces of the postwar effort to harmonize economic concerns with the political goal of peace. Assessing whether the WTO helps or hinders free trade can be broken into three separate concerns. The first is the kind of free trade that the WTO advocates. To its opponents, the WTO is little more than a handmaiden to the large multinational corporations (MNCs). Global Exchange, a web-based research organization that is very critical of the WTO, calls it an "unaccountable, corporate-based government" that reflects the values of the MNCs at the expense of virtually everyone else. At least to some extent, this should come as little surprise. The globalization process of which free trade is an implementing device is based in the promotion of capitalist, free market economics, of which corporations are a prominent core part. Moreover, much of the economic resources on which the spread of globalization is based comes in the form of foreign direct investment (FDI) by private sources, and entities such as international banks and multinational corporations provide most of the FDI. Because they do so out of a profit motive and not from a sense of philanthropy, it follows that these entities would have an interest in helping to shape the philosophies and policies the WTO promotes. As indirect evidence of the success of the MNCs in this regard, it might be remembered that corporations within the United States were major opponents of the ITO because of protectionist motives, but have by and large been equally strong supporters of the WTO.

The advocacy of free trade and the promotion of its implementation through the WTO thus include two substantive judgments. One is whether an alternative economic philosophy could be attached to free trade that would make it more palatable to those who oppose the idea or its consequences. Is there some alternative to a market-economy-based, free trade–driven, globalized economy? The second judgment flows from the first: If there is no acceptable alternative underpinning, are the positive outcomes of institutionalized free trade better or worse than the absence of such a system? The analogy of the rising tide and the boat is sometimes used to frame this question. Pro–free traders admit that not everyone benefits equally from free trade, but that everyone does benefit to some extent and thus everyone is better off under a free trade regime (the tide lifts all boats). Opponents argue that the benefits are so inequitably distributed that gaps are widened to the point that some are left relatively worse off (some boats become swamped).

The second disagreement concerns the structure of the WTO itself. The organization has two basic functions: the promotion of free trade and the enforcement of free trade agreements. Because of the possibility of sovereignty infringements, the enforcement mandate is and always has been the more controversial aspect of the WTO. The mechanism for enforcement was agreed on during the Uruguay round of GATT in the form of something called the Dispute Settlement Understanding (DSU). Under the DSU, the WTO is authorized to establish and convene the Dispute Settlement Body (DSB). The *Geneva Briefing Book* describes the considerable authority of the DSB, "which has the sole authority to establish such panels to adjudicate disputes between members and to accept or reject the findings of panels and the Appellate Body, a standing appeals body of seven independent experts. The DSB also . . . has the power to authorize retaliation when a member does not comply with DSB recommendations and rulings."

These powers are listed because they are not inconsiderable and include the power to identify alleged violations; to convene and prosecute those alleged violations; and then to issue binding rulings and penalties and to enforce those penalties, ostensibly without recourse to an outside, independent source of appeal (all appeals are internal to the process).

To critics that span the ITO–WTO debate, a chief objection to this arrangement is its effect on national sovereignty. The rulings of the DSU process have the effect of treaty law on the countries against which they are levied, which means that member governments cannot unilaterally overturn or ignore them. This is particularly troubling in the United States, which is notably sensitive over intrusions on state sovereignty. In the specific case of WTO rulings, these have disproportionately affected the United States. According to the *Geneva Briefing*

Book, "From the advent of the WTO, in January 1995, until October 1, 2003, the United States has been a party in 56 out of 93 WTO dispute settlement panel reports and 36 out of 56 Appellate Body reports." The source does not indicate how many of these involved judgments against the United States, but it is likely that at least some of them did.

The third concern regards what unforeseen consequences the institutionalization of free trade has had, and whether those consequences are acceptable. As one might expect, most unforeseen outcomes that have been identified are negative and are expressed most vocally by opponents of the process and its outcomes. Two areas stand out as examples: the alleged antilabor bias of the WTO, and its negative environmental impacts. Both are chestnuts in trade debates and specifically addressed in NAFTA protocols.

Objections to free trade as antilabor contain both macroeconomic and microeconomic elements. At the microeconomic level, free trade is the culprit among those people working in industries and services that do not enjoy comparative advantage and can only compete if protected by some form of trade barrier. The textile industry cited earlier is a prime example. Labor unions contend that the ways in which the WTO operates to remove barriers to trade provide incentives for corporations to move their businesses to places that engage in unfair labor practices (everything from low wages and benefits to child labor), thereby creating an unfair environment within which to compete. Moreover, they believe that the corporatist mentality they say reigns within the WTO encourages foreign direct investors to nurture and create these unfair practices as ways to create and sustain comparative advantage. These allegations are parallel to older domestic arguments about union busting and scab labor practices, and, in the United States, to "right-to-work" laws that restrain organized labor activity and jurisdiction. Because these are extremely emotional issues among trade unionists, it helps explain the depth of their animosity toward the WTO and the prevalence of trade unionists in anti–free trade, anti-WTO activities.

Environmentalists' objections to free trade and the WTO are parallel. The need to establish conditions of comparative advantage drives some countries to rescind environmental regulations that add to the cost of production (e.g., dumping hazardous chemicals used in processing materials into the environment rather than rendering these chemicals harmless before release), thereby making their industries more competitive than industries in the United States that must meet environmental standards that add to production costs. Critics cite cases in Latin America (especially Mexico) in which environmental standards have indeed been relaxed or done away with to attract industry.

The environmentalist objection is also applied directly to the WTO. Environmentalists contend that most corporations resist environmental restraints philosophically and only accede to environmental regulation reluctantly and unenthusiastically. Because the WTO is alleged to be controlled largely by corporate interests and reflects corporate values, they are thus predisposed to be suspicious of the organization on those grounds. Environmentalists are also generally conspicuous at demonstrations against the WTO because it allegedly condones environmental degradation.

The North American Free Trade Agreement (NAFTA)

NAFTA is a free trading agreement between the governments of the United States, Canada, and Mexico. It is a follow-on agreement to a similar obligation entered into by Canada and the United States negotiated between the Reagan administration and the administration of Canadian Prime Minister Brian Mulroney in 1987, the Canada-United States Free Trade Agreement (CUSFTA). That agreement was formally signed and implemented in 1988 with very little public fanfare, especially in the United States, where 40 percent of the public was unaware of its existence at the time it went into effect.

The CUSFTA treaty was the prototype for NAFTA, negotiations for which began in 1990. The agreement listed five purposes, each of which was incorporated in the expanded free trade arrangement. These included the elimination of barriers to trade in goods and services between the two countries, facilitation of fair competition within the free-trade area, liberalized conditions for investment across national boundaries, establishment of procedures to administer the agreement and to resolve disputes, and, in a preview of things to come, to "lay the foundation for further bilateral and multilateral cooperation." The agreement between the two states was quite literally the blueprint for NAFTA.

The major dynamic change introduced by NAFTA was, of course, the addition of Mexico to the North American association. If CUSFTA laid the groundwork by producing a working draft for NAFTA, the addition of Mexico represented something more than a simple expansion. The U.S.-Canadian agreement was between two countries with similar economies, cultures, histories, and levels of economic development. Mexico represented a qualitatively different physical and economic entity. Beyond language and history, Mexico and the United States have long-standing and ongoing disputes. The two countries fought a war (1846–1848) over where the boundary between them would be located, the outcome of which still troubles some Mexicans. Their 1,933-mile border, the subject of considerable political controversy in the United States, is the world's longest boundary between a developed and a developing world state, and that coincidence creates tensions in areas such as immigration and the movement of illicit items (notably drugs) across the frontier. Many of the problems predate NAFTA (drugs such as cocaine have come across the border since the end of the U.S. Civil War, for instance), but have either increased in intensity or become intertwined with other problems for which NAFTA has become a lightning rod. Likewise, advocacy or opposition to NAFTA (and especially any expansion) also becomes amplified as part of the terms of trade debate.

It is important to note what NAFTA is in terms of international trade arrangements. Chapter 9 presents a sequential set of distinctions in terms of the depth of interrelationship any trading agreement creates among its members. Free trade agreements stand at the bottom of that pyramid, which extends all the way to economic unions such as the EU. As stated in the CUSFTA agreement, the principal goal is to promote greater trade by reducing barriers to trade between the members. Operationally, that means a removal of tariffs and quotas on trade across those borders, subject to negotiation in the case of individual categories of items: agricultural goods are a prime example. In terms of basic economic obligations incurred by the members, this is basically all that a free trade arrangement does, which is why it is considered the most elemental and, for some purposes, ineffective form of international trade arrangement.

The major thing that a free trade area does *not* do is to establish common standards such as a uniform set of economic standards for goods and services entering individual countries from outside the area. NAFTA has successfully removed almost all barriers to trade among its three members, but it does not regulate the conditions of those same goods or services coming into the members from outside. This allows outsiders to evade barriers to trade with individual members through what is known as "indirect exportation." As an example, if the United States has a higher tariff against a class of goods entering the country from China and Mexico has a lower tariff on those same goods, China can avoid the American impediment by exporting the good to Mexico, then allowing it to enter the United States across the U.S.-Mexican border, where there are no tariffs. Since the purposes of tariffs are generally protectionist, this dynamic creates some of the basis of opposition to NAFTA.

NAFTA has been the subject of criticism, some of it arguably unfair, since it was instituted. The criticisms are not partisan. NAFTA's predecessor was negotiated by a Republican (Reagan), as was the NAFTA agreement itself (George H. W. Bush). Bush's term expired before he could sign the agreement himself, a task Democrat Clinton performed. In the new century, GOP president George W. Bush and Democrat Barack Obama supported NAFTA. President Donald Trump is the first sitting chief executive to raise questions about its continuation.

NAFTA has become entangled with the highly emotional, often distorting dialogue of trade positions. As trading arrangements go, NAFTA is basically innocuous. Its structure and provisions contain no major controversial additions to the trading dialogue, and the emotional disagreements that do exist tend to arise from other dynamics such as the interaction between the developed United States and developing Mexico. It has, however, gained visibility as part of the domestic political debate in the United States over jobs, and especially the effort to repatriate jobs allegedly lost to Mexico because of its existence. Free trading arrangements do have microeconomic consequences, of which job dislocations are the most obvious and public. An example that has become virtually a mantra of how NAFTA has become a whipping boy when it may not deserve to be in NAFTA terms is the case of assembly plants across the border in Mexico—most famously automobile assembly plants, the maquiladoras. In terms of American job losses, the maquiladoras are a problem; their conjunction with NAFTA represents a distortion of how important NAFTA is.

The maquiladoras have attracted the most recent attention because they are associated with job losses in what were crucial American "rust belt" states during the 2016 American election. The maquiladoras are foreign-owned assembly plants located just across the border in Mexico that employ cheaper Mexican labor to produce goods and services than would be the case if assembly occurred in the United States. The reason American corporations have opened these factories in places such as Toluca, Leon, and Pueblo is to avoid having to pay American union wages for the assembly of products such as automobiles and trucks and, since NAFTA, to avoid American duties on parts imported from other places.

These operations unquestionably have cost American workers well-paying jobs, and the unions have every reason to oppose them on that ground, which they do. Indeed, the WTO-like annexes to NAFTA reflect this concern. The North American Agreement on Environmental Cooperation (NAAEC) and the parallel Agreement on Labor Cooperation (NAALC) were both motivated by this factor. The environmental accord was aimed at preventing Mexico from dumping hazardous residues from these factories to lower costs but potentially causing pollution on both sides of the border. The labor agreement covered labor practices (such as child labor) to avoid unfair advantages for the operations in Mexico.

Two fantasies surround the issue. One fantasy of the maquiladoras is that they are the result of NAFTA. Since NAFTA has been in force, these plants have indeed increased in size, jobs, and profitability for Mexico, but the problem is not an artifact of NAFTA. As Cowie has pointed out, American factories "popped up like mushrooms" in Mexico between the 1960s and 1980s, well before anyone had ever thought of NAFTA. He adds that "prior to official trade liberalization with Mexico, there had long been tariff loopholes that allowed assembly work to be done abroad." In fact, by the mid-1980s, the operations of the maquiladoras had become the second-largest source of Mexican export income after oil. During the 1992 election campaign in the United States, third-party candidate Ross Perot had warned ominously that NAFTA would result in the "great sucking sound" of American jobs disappearing across the Mexican boundary, an analogy Trump implicitly adopted. The problem was that the drinking straw that produced that sound had been crafted decades earlier.

The second fantasy is an exaggeration of their jobs impact, and especially the positive effect of closing them down, either by forcing American corporations to shutter them and return home or face steep penalties or by dropping out of NAFTA. The premise is that if there were no maquiladoras, jobs would return to the United States, but that is only partly true. Some jobs would come back to places such as Michigan, but a lot of the manufacturing return would be in terms of automated factories employing far fewer people than the champions of job growth from this source admit.

Conclusion

Advocacy of or opposition to free trade and its institutionalization has never been an easy or straightforward proposition. At the abstract, theoretical level of international macroeconomics, the case for free trade is very convincing, and it is not surprising that many of the defenses of free trade spring from these theoretical arguments. At the applied level of the impact of free trade on individuals and groups (the microeconomic level), the proposition creates more ambivalence. Individual consumers benefit when comparative advantage produces goods and services at lower cost and higher quality through free trade than they otherwise would. Imagine, for instance, the impact on Christmas gift spending if all goods made in China were eliminated. At the same time, removing protection can terminate employment for those in the less efficient industries. The theory of comparative advantage says that displaced people should find alternative employment in more competitive fields, but that outcome is almost always easier to accomplish in the abstract than it really is. Theory and reality often collide.

Institutionalizing free trade is a related but not synonymous question. One can reasonably take one of three positions on the desirability of free trade per se: one can favor free trade unconditionally, one can oppose it equally unconditionally, or one can favor free trade with some restrictions, the heart of fair trade. For the "pure" positions, the answer to whether to establish some organization to promote and enforce free trade is straightforward and flows directly from one's basic position—virtually regardless of empirical circumstances. From either extreme, debate is pointless and the facts almost beside the point.

That leaves the "fair traders" in the middle. They support expansions in trade through the reduction of barriers to trade, but they believe there should be exclusions or limitations on the extent and degree of trade promotion. Such an advocacy attempts to finesse the dichotomy between free trade and protectionism by advocating some of both, depending on the context. The WTO and NAFTA compromises on environmental impact and labor are examples of this greater pragmatism.

The free trade movement is under some level of siege that is partly the result of excessive expectations when it burst upon the scene toward the end of the last century. Its virtues and positive impacts were exaggerated, as were its negative effects. Stimulating economic activity by reducing barriers to trade across state boundaries became the mantra of the 1990s, and it did produce positive outcomes. The hype, however, was greater than the dynamics of trade deserved or could sustain.

That overselling is apparent in the institutions created in trade's name. The WTO made some waves in the 1990s when it took several countries, including the United States, before it on alleged violations. It continues, but at a much lower level of visibility. The hype was especially excessive over NAFTA, partly because its economic effects have been less than its more publicized political intertwining with the immigration issue in the United States. As Cowie concludes, "The economic impact of the trade deal is far more ambiguous and significantly less interesting than its political impact. Indeed, it is less of a trade deal than an icon to be smashed or revered." Globalization, in Naim's 2009 phrase, is "here to stay." The question is in what form. The next chapter explores one of those forms.

Study/Discussion Questions

1. What is trade? Discuss its origins and historical development. What basic positions on trade have evolved? Describe them, including a discussion of comparative advantage and its role in the debate.

2. What are the three contemporary positions on trade? Describe each, including its genesis and relationship to basic foreign policy schools of thought.

3. How did World War II affect thinking about trade? Trace the evolution through Bretton Woods and the institutions it created.

4. How did free trade fit into the overall Bretton Woods discussions? Discuss why it failed to be institutionalized at Bretton Woods but was later enacted.

5. Free trade is more than simple economics. Discuss it as an economic and a political phenomenon, including macroeconomic and microeconomic effects and basic arguments for and against it.

6. What is the WTO? Discuss its origins, structure, and functions, and the controversies associated with it.

7. What is NAFTA? What are its history and purposes, the controversies surrounding it, and distortions in discussions about it? Include the maquiladora controversy in your answer.

8. The issues of globalization and free trade have become less prominent in contemporary discussions than they were a decade or more ago. Why is this? Include in your answer the possibility that the phenomenon was oversold (or hyped).

Bibliography

Barshefsky, Charlene. "Trade Policy in a Networked World." *Foreign Affairs* 80, no. 2 (March/April 2001): 134–46.

Bauman, Zygmunt. *Globalization: The Human Consequences.* New York: Columbia University Press, 1998.

Boskin, Michael J. *NAFTA at 20: The North American Free Trade Agreement's Achievements and Challenges.* Palo Alto, CA: Hoover Institution Press, 2014.

Cowie, Jefferson. "What Trump Gets Wrong about NAFTA: The Deal Is Not the Source of America's Problems." *Foreign Affairs Snapshot* (online), May 4, 2017.

Dierks, Rosa Gomez. *Introduction to Globalization: Political and Economic Perspectives for a New Era.* Chicago: Burnham, 2001.

Drezner, Daniel W. *U.S. Trade Strategy: Free Versus Fair.* New York: Council on Foreign Relations Press, 2006.

Friedman, Thomas L. *The Lexus and the Olive Tree: Understanding Globalization.* New York: Farrar, Straus & Giroux, 1999.

———. *The World Is Flat: A Brief History of the Twenty-First Century.* New York: Farrar, Straus & Giroux, 2005.

Irwin, Douglas A. "The False Promise of Protectionism: Trump's Trade Policy Could Backfire." *Foreign Affairs* 96, no. 3 (May/June 2017): 56–65.

———. *Free Trade Under Fire.* 4th ed. Princeton, NJ: Princeton University Press, 2015.

Landau, Alice. *Redrawing the Global Economy: Elements of Integration and Fragmentation.* New York: Palgrave, 2001.

Lind, Michael. *Made in Texas: George W. Bush and the Southern Takeover of American Politics.* New York: New America Books, 2003.

McBride, Stephen, and John Wiseman, eds. *Globalization and Its Discontents.* New York: St. Martin's, 2000.

"Measuring Globalization." *Foreign Policy*, March/April 2004, 46–53.

Naim, Moises. "Think Again: Globalization." *Foreign Policy*, March/April 2009, 28–34.

O'Connor, David E. *Demystifying the Global Economy: A Guide for Students*. Westport, CT: Greenwood, 2002.

Panagariya, Arvind. "Think Again: International Trade." *Foreign Policy*, November/December 2003, 20–29.

Park, Jacob. "Globalization After Seattle." *Washington Quarterly* 23, no. 2 (Spring 2000): 13–16.

Ricardo, David. *On the Principles of Political Economy and Taxation*. Edited and introduction by R. M. Hartwell. New York: Penguin Classics, 1971.

Rodrik, Dani. *The Globalization Paradox: Democracy and the Future of the World Economy*. New York: Norton, 2010.

Rothgeb, John M. J. *Trade Policy: Balancing Economic Dreams and Political Realities*. Washington, DC: CQ, 2001.

Schaeffer, Robert K. *Understanding Globalization: The Social Consequences of Political, Economic, and Environmental Change*. Lanham, MD: Rowman & Littlefield, 2003.

Shah, Anup. "Free Trade and Globalization." *Global Issues* (online), July 25, 2009.

Villareal, M. Angeles, and Ian F. Fergusson. *NAFTA at 20: Overview and Trade Effects*. Washington, DC: Congressional Research Service, 2014.

World Trade Organization. *The Geneva Briefing Book*. Lausanne, Switzerland: World Trade Organization, 2004.

———. WTO website (www.wto.org), 2017.

9

Regional Integration
The European Union, Sovereign Debt, and Brexit

The process of economic integration is multidimensional. Economically, it involves different degrees of integration. It is also political in its consequences, which may be its Achilles' heel. It began in Europe shortly after World War II through the establishment of a small group of institutions that have evolved into the European Union (EU). They represent a geographically limited area but have achieved a far greater degree of integration than any other schemes and proposals. The EU has moved from being a limited-scale free trading arrangement to a true economic union with strong political implications, controversies, and problems. The evolution of the EU offers some reasonable precedents about at least one way in which the movement toward globalization may evolve. This case will concentrate on the growing dynamic evolution of the EU physically and conceptually. It will also highlight, in the application section, problems and tensions represented by the sovereign debt crisis and British withdrawal (Brexit). It will also examine how the resolution of that crisis will affect the further development of the EU as an experiment in integration.

The European Union celebrates its sixtieth birthday in 2018. It came into being with the implementation of the Treaty of Rome in 1958 among six states that expanded to twenty-eight in 2013 and will contract to twenty-seven with the departure of the United Kingdom. Regional economic integration of the nature and scale of the European Common Market, as it was known then, was unprecedented, and it had both political and economic motivations. The underlying political goal was to create a Europe in which a repetition of the century of warfare centering on Germany and France would be eliminated, and the institutions that became the core of the EU had this purpose fully in mind as they sought an institutional setting to make war between the major European powers impossible. Economically, the process proposed to stimulate the economies of its members through integration that would apply the principles of the theory of comparative advantage to the continent.

The history of the EU has not been one of smooth sailing. The ambitious idea of international integration was controversial when the Treaty of Rome was negotiated, but despite many disagreements, it has been an enormous success. A Europe devastated by World War II and in a state of postwar economic doldrums was rapidly transformed into an economic force in the world that could compete on a global scale with the United States and Japan and as a political equal to the

Soviet Union. Moravcsik in 2010 called it "the most ambitious and successful international organization of all time." The EU has grown from a free trading arrangement between six adjacent continental states to an evolving economic union, with more states waiting in the queue. At the same time, expansion has entailed a process of political integration and extension to countries unlike the original members that has created a crisis of sovereignty-based concern as the organization moves further into the twenty-first century. Brexit is its symbol.

Strains have emerged between the more and less prosperous members, reflecting the economic heterogeneity that has accompanied expansion. Northern European countries such as Germany are the most stable, prosperous states in the EU, and they have been called upon with increasing frequency to cover economic deficiencies and excesses in the less prosperous members' economies. These problems have been most glaring in Mediterranean countries such as Greece, Italy, Spain, and most recently Cyprus (but also in Ireland). Collectively, they form the core of the EU debt crisis.

The EU has been the most positive regional symbol of globalization. As Foroohar put it in a 2013 article, "The E.U. is perhaps the most benign example of globalization. As a global phenomenon, this process maximizes the number of states that participate in globalization but not the depth or extent of participation that EU does." The EU is an important symbol of how far global integration can proceed on a regional basis, but also of the political complications of integration. EU is thus the gauge for measuring the prospects for globalization worldwide.

All economic integration schemes are not the same, differing in at least two salient characteristics. One is the *physical dimensions* of the unit. In the evolving history of globalization, there have been two major geographical foci of economic integration: regional approaches and worldwide applications. The second dimension is the *extent* of integration being sought. The admixture of economic and political purposes tends to grow as the extent of the integrating unit expands, and in some cases, political integration may even be the coequal or overriding purpose of the economic integration effort.

Extent of integration goes beyond the incorporation of political integration, and indeed, most economists tend to downplay the political implications and instead look at the extent of economic integration proposed. In rough terms, integration spans a range of ever-closer association and commitment that begins with the establishment of free trade among the members and moves through stages such as a customs union, a common or single market, a monetary union, and a true economic union. Most global schemes have proposed no more than a free trade area level of integration: NAFTA and the Asia-Pacific Economic Cooperation (APEC) are examples. The EU is unique in that it has traveled through all the steps of economic integration.

Because it has traversed more fully the path of economic integration than any other contemporary economic set of institutions, the EU provides the best available model for judging the desirability, opportunities, and pitfalls associated with regional attempts at integration. To understand the dynamics of the regional economic integration process, the discussion will begin with a general overview of the dynamics and forms of regional integration and how the political and economic dynamics intertwine. These observations will then be applied to the evolving case of the EU. The travails of the EU are particularly important for this process because, as Foroohar puts it, "If it [the EU] fails, that has big consequences."

Principle: The Regional Integration Process

Regional integration—binding together the economies of physically proximate states—is simultaneously simpler and more difficult than global approaches to integration. It is simpler because of smaller geographical reach and jurisdiction and because regional groupings are likely to contain peoples of similar culture and history with some understanding and history of interaction. The Germans and the French, in other words, have known each other for a long time. However, this very familiarity can breed contempt and animosity among regional actors that make their cooperation more rather than less difficult. One reason Germans and Frenchmen know each other so well is that they have been fighting for so long. Within regions, there may be dissimilarities between potential members (the United States and Mexico within NAFTA, for instance) that create unique problems and circumstances.

To describe regional integration, the discussion will be centered on two major benchmarks, both of which are applicable to the global and regional levels but are particularly poignant when dealing with a highly integrated regional structure like the EU. One is the degree of integration involved in any proposed or existing scheme. A taxonomy of gradually increasing levels of integration will be laid out. The other concern is the degree of political and economic integration and controversy involved, and the relationship between existing or potential economic and political goals. Generally, the more complex and extensive an economic association, the more political concerns arise that may underpin or undermine the effort. Familiarity can breed both attachment and contempt, and deepening association can accentuate points of difference and conflict.

Forms of Integration

The process of economic integration, pursued at any level, can produce greater or lesser degrees of interdependence and interpenetration among parties. In the general discussion of globalization, most goals are stated in terms of the pursuit of *free trade*, as introduced and discussed in chapter 8. Agreements like that creating the WTO or regional arrangements like NAFTA have the promotion of free trade as their primary, even sole, focus. The principal objectives of *free trading agreements* are to encourage greater trade among members by reducing barriers to trade—tariffs, quotas, and the like—among the members. Such arrangements represent the initial, and least binding or formal, means to approach greater economic—or political—integration.

Free trade agreements stand at the base of integration schemes. As noted in chapter 8, such arrangements lower or eliminate barriers to trade among the signatories, but stop short of creating uniform standards on trade coming into the area from outside its boundaries, thereby allowing indirect importation into the area. They are thus the tentative first step in the integration process.

The next step is a *customs union*. In this form of arrangement, the members add a common external tariff toward all goods and services entering any of the member countries to the free trade area. The effect is greater unity among the members and the need to negotiate a united trading front to the outside world on which all members can agree. One result is the need for greater political agreement, since members' preferences will vary on different standards.

When a free trade area and customs union are created for the same physical area, the result is the creation of a *single* or *common market*. The goal of a common market is to create the free circulation of goods, capital, people, and services within the geographic constraints of the common market region. This is done by reducing, preferably to zero, all trade barriers among the members (the basis of a free trade area) and by creating a common external barrier against goods and services imported anywhere within the region (a customs union). The result is to create an economic area that maximizes the flow of goods, services, capital, and people within the single market area while excluding or making more difficult the entry of items produced outside the area. This was the original form that the European Economic Community assumed in the 1960s and beyond, and it was a huge success in stimulating the economies of the member states and in attracting the interest of other states that wanted to join the process. This form of association goes far beyond most current conceptions of integration outside Europe.

As the integration process progresses, it also become more political. Broadening jurisdiction and economic impact create more areas of responsibility and issues over which the contracting parties can disagree. This collision is most obvious in two general areas. One is differing microeconomic effects on various parts of the area, which generally means conflicts between countries and regions over differential effects of actions on national populations. The sovereign debt problem in the application section is an example. The other politicizing factor is the need to expand and restructure political jurisdictions, making economic decisions affecting the unit. Discussions of such adjustments are necessary to reach the ultimate form of integration, *economic union*. Monetary union is the first, controversial step in that process. Brexit demonstrates what happens when further steps can go further than some members want.

A common market's level of integration is circumscribed if its members maintain their individual currencies, because commerce is slowed by the necessity of establishing and enforcing exchange rates, and translating transactions from one currency to another. The solution to this barrier is the establishment of a *monetary union*, a financial institution that can issue a common currency and make monetary policy that is binding on all the political units. The EU has established a monetary union, but it is one of the most controversial aspects of the EU. The reason is that a monetary union requires fashioning a common monetary policy among the members, and this requires a political body that has the authority to make such policy. This authority comes at the expense of national legislatures and is, in some cases, a major source of political concern on sovereignty grounds. One way to attenuate the national sovereignty problem created by a monetary union is to leave the setting of fiscal policy (such as taxation) under national control, as is done in the EU. As Gros explains, "Monetary union was not intended to lead to a transfer of power in the fiscal field." The euro is the most visible manifestation of the monetary union, and resistance to adopting the euro in countries such as Great Britain is a symbol of the controversy.

The ultimate form of economic integration is the *economic union*, an arrangement that combines a single or common market and a monetary union. This is the form of association that was created originally by the EU in 1993, and it remains a major source of controversy surrounding the organization. At the purely economic level, the creation of an economic union culminates the process of economic integration, because the formation of the monetary union removes the last barrier to economic activity across political boundaries. If economic integration is the goal, economic union is its zenith.

The movement toward an economic union, however, also creates the strongest possible political reverberations. Economic and political unions are, in theory, separable, because one deals with what can be viewed as purely economic consequences and benefits, whereas political union implies an arrangement or rearrangement of political authority in the proposed unit. Economic associations at lower levels of integration have tended to be less controversial, because their economic benefits tend to overwhelm political concerns and to have less obvious negative implications. That has been the case throughout most of the process of European economic integration until recently. As integration has proceeded, it has become more politicized as its champions labor to create union-wide institutions to make it more efficient. One effect has been to collide with the sovereignty wall in some member states.

Political and Economic Integration

Separating politics and economics in any real situation is always difficult. The realm of politics is authoritative (normally governmental) decision making. I define politics as "the process by which conflicts of interest over scarce resources are resolved." The definition is accepted in general terms and suggests that politics is both a process (a set of rules for making authoritative allocations of resources) and a substantive concern over those resources being allocated (the conflicts of interest over scarce resources). Many scarce resources require allocation, but the most common and prominent are economic resources, thereby making politics an integral component in economic integration schemes.

Economic resources are so important that deciding how they should be divided becomes a major concern in designating who can make political decisions and the decisions they render. One concern is which political authorities have the right to levy taxes and spend money; who has that authority influences which resources are allocated for what purposes (fiscal policy). As integration moves toward an economic union, a major political question is thus which political authority will have the jurisdiction over matters such as monetary policy (including currency regulation). Because of the centrality of monetary policy to the overall operation of any political or economic unit, determining the political authority controlling that function is fundamental to the political equation. National governments have possessed and continue to covet autonomous power over monetary policy, setting up a conflict with the union and those who assert its primacy.

The reasons for entering economic associations also have a political underpinning. Economic associations are supposed to stimulate economic activity and create prosperity, and those who propose and construct those associations expect political support for having done so. When the European Common Market was first instituted, for instance, it was wildly successful and overwhelmingly popular. Part of the political reason for forming the organization was to strengthen governments to discourage support for communism within Western Europe. Economic success worked to undermine communist appeal, a direct political effect of economic action.

Political and economic aspects of economic schemes are often so inextricable as to be impossible to disaggregate altogether. Again, the EU is a prime example. The roots of what has become the EU go back to World War II and the attempt to reconstruct the European economic system after the war. The impetus was what most believed to have been the root cause of the European world wars—Franco-German rivalry for control of Europe. World War II, in effect, was the fourth violent round in that competition that began with the Napoleonic wars and continued through the Franco-Prussian War of 1870 and World War I. The first four rounds had proven inconclusive, and there was a strong desire to avoid the possibility of a fifth round. But how?

The answer, devised through allied consultation during the war in which the Frenchman Jean Monnet played a very prominent role, was to make future warfare between Germany and France functionally impossible. The planners began from the assumption that modern, symmetrical warfare as practiced by Europeans required the ability to produce steel and thus the implements of war. If a country could not independently produce steel, it could not go to war. Thus, the planners sought to see if they could create an international political unit that would deprive France and Germany of the ability to produce the wherewithal of war independently of one another. The result was the European Coal and Steel Community (ECSC) of 1951, the first institution in what evolved into the EU.

The ECSC was the model and inspiration for the integration that followed; the movement leading to the EU thus had both distinctly political and economic roots impossible to disentangle over time. The great successes of and support for the movement have been economic and seen in expanding economies and prosperity and the impatient demands of European countries outside the association to be included. At the same time, the political intents have never been far below the surface. Those who planned the progression of the EU recognized that economic integration would create increasing pressures for political unification as well, and this was the intention of the earliest planners of the regional economic integration prototype that the EU represents. For Monnet and many others, a *real* underlying goal was political integration of the European continent into something like a United States of Europe, with the fruits of economic integration providing the impetus and demand for that outcome.

This political goal was mixed with a more politically tinged economic goal. As noted already in chapter 8, most of the planners at Bretton Woods agreed that economic policies had played a large role in the economic nationalism that facilitated the breakdown of commerce among European states and fueled the animosities leading to war. The Bretton Woods institutions responded to this perceived problem, but so did the movement toward European economic integration. A Europe that was politically united could not be economically divided, and vice versa.

Much of the evolution of the EU thus has been an attempt to maximize the economic benefits that form the popular base for integration while deferring or trying to soften political consequences that were viewed as equally necessary but that might rouse political opposition. Most of the potential political opposition was based in the dilution of national sovereignty that an expanding integration movement created. Common economic policies inevitably point to common political institutions transcending national boundaries and encroaching upon purely national political prerogatives. That movement has always been controversial and thus a matter not to be confronted directly by the organization until that confrontation can no longer be finessed or avoided. That approach was possible until the fateful step was taken to create a full economic union; since that step was taken in 1993, the *politics* of European regional economic integration have largely been about how to deal with the political implications of union, especially those surrounding national sovereignty. The final ratification of the Lisbon Treaty in 2009 represents an important watershed in that process.

The synergism between economic and political dynamics works in both directions. The momentum and support for greater integration has always been driven by the increasing benefits that integration has produced, and support for political integration has largely derived from and followed economic success. Because of these dynamics, the EU stands apart from other efforts aimed at achieving the general goal of globalization or economic integration. In the current debate, none of the proposed or actual forms have gone beyond proposals for free trade areas, which can be and are negotiated by national governments that can retain control over them.

Application: The European Union Experience: Sovereign Debt and Brexit

The EU is by far the most successful experiment in cross-national economic integration. It began modestly in 1951 as an association of six continental states, France, Germany, Italy, and the Benelux countries (Belgium, the Netherlands, and Luxembourg), with a limited agenda and limited integration goals. From the beginning, it was wildly successful and popular, consistently exceeding expectations in the amount of growth and prosperity it created. That very success in turn led to demands for expansion in two simultaneous directions: horizontally by adding new members and vertically through greater integration of the economies of the member states. These two directions have been reflected in long-standing debates between so-called *wideners*, who believe the primary focus should be to bring as many European states as possible under the EU umbrella (widening membership), and so-called *deepeners*, who believe that primary energy should be on maximum integration of the economic systems of the members (deepening relationships between existing members).

From its modest beginning, the EU has grown to a membership of twenty-seven states (including the withdrawal of the United Kingdom) incorporating most of Western and Eastern Europe. At that, most of the states in or contiguous to the EU have sought membership because of the perceived economic boost membership would bring. The result of that growth has been to make the EU a major competitive force in the world's economy with a size, economic strength, and market rivaling that of the United States. According to the *CIA World Factbook* for 2016 (which reflects British membership), for instance, the population of the EU stood at 509 million (July 2013 estimate), compared to about 319 million for the United States that year. The gross domestic product (GDP) per capita of EU members is $34,500 (2013 estimate); the comparable figure for the United States is $52,800. The physical area of the EU is a little less than half that of the United States.

The EU is a unique phenomenon. It is the most far-reaching of all the attempts at international economic integration. Moravcsik summarizes its achievements as of 2010: "The EU has enjoyed an astonishingly successful run: It has completed the single market; established a single currency; created a zone without internal boundaries; launched common defense, foreign and internal security policies; promulgated a constitutional treaty; and most importantly, expanded from 12 to 27 members." The uniqueness of the EU reflects its birth in the immediate post–World War II environment and the mandates for change those times created. The fact that the European continent was a more homogeneous cultural, historical, and developmental area than other parts of the world has undoubtedly contributed to a degree of success that would be much more difficult or impossible in more diverse, heterogeneous regions.

Birth and Early Evolution

At the end of World War II, Europe lay in tatters. It had been the center of world civilization for over 300 years, but the two great wars left the major European powers prostrate. To the east, the Soviet Union stood as a giant military and ideological opponent that had also been devastated economically by the war but retained a huge armed force with which it occupied most of Eastern Europe and menaced the rest. To the west, an ideologically compatible but upstart United States stood as the only country physically strengthened by the war.

The question was how to revive Europe—to make it strong enough to withstand Soviet military power and prosperous enough to rebuff the ideological promises of communism. Militarily, the North Atlantic Treaty Organization (NATO) was formed in 1949 to provide an American-led bulwark against Soviet military expansion. In that same year, the first political association of Western European states—the Council of Europe—formed to link the countries culturally, socially, and economically.

The process leading to European economic integration began in 1950. At the suggestion of Monnet, French Foreign Minister Robert Schuman proposed the pooling of French and German coal and steel resources. This initiative, known as the Schuman Plan, was the basis for negotiating the first European Union institution, the ECSC, in 1951. With the six core members (France, Germany, Italy, and the Benelux countries), the ECSC began operating in 1952, and it was so successful that it spawned interest in a wider form of association. The result was the negotiation of the Treaties of Rome in 1957, which created the European Atomic Energy Community (EURATOM) and, more importantly, the European Economic Community (EEC) among the six members of the ECSC. The EEC expanded the previous degree of economic cooperation among the ECSC members by creating both a common or single market and a customs union. Thus, the integration process was begun toward both the free circulation of goods, services, people, and capital among the states of the EEC area and erecting a common external tariff for the rest of the world.

The Rome Treaty was the platform from which the EU evolved. It has followed two basic tracks. One has concerned membership. The primary emphasis of the wideners (and their most ardent outside supporters, notably the United States) has been to expand EU participation to its current membership. The momentum toward expanded membership is now overshadowed by the debt crisis and British withdrawal. The other form has been deeper integration of the membership, through movement to the economic union that was created by the Treaty of Maastricht in 1992 and more deeply implemented by the Lisbon Treaty. How much further the EU will progress toward a full political union has been a matter of considerable contention since the original days of the EEC—conflict accentuated by Brexit.

Ongoing Processes: Widening

Expanding EU membership into new countries has been a major priority since the process began. The wideners believe that the EU (and the rest of the world) is best served by extending membership, drawing as many formerly contentious states and regions of Europe under the common banner of the EU as possible and thereby reducing the prospect of renewed conflict in Europe. In addition, many wideners have seen widening as an *alternative* to creating deeper institutional bonds that restrict national sovereignty and sacrifice aspects of national identity. As Rachman puts it, "the wideners believed that the larger the EU was, the more diverse it would become, and the more difficult it would be to achieve the deepeners' goal of a united Europe."

Membership in the EU has expanded through a series of what the organization calls rounds. To date, there have been six identified rounds of membership accretion, taking the organization from its core of six members to its

Table 9.1. EU Membership Expansion by Rounds

Round 1	Round 2	Round 3	Round 4	Round 5	Round 6
1958	1973	1981	1995	2004	2007
Belgium	Denmark	Greece	Austria	Cyprus	Bulgaria
France	Ireland	**1986**	Finland	Czech	Romania
Germany	U.K.	Spain	Sweden	Republic	**2013**
Italy		Portugal		Estonia	Croatia
Luxembourg				Hungary	
Netherlands				Latvia	
				Lithuania	
				Malta	
				Poland	
				Slovakia	
				Slovenia	

Source: Wikipedia, European Union.

current complement of twenty-seven. This membership process is summarized in table 9.1.

The table requires a little explanation. Rounds 1, 2, 4, and 5 consisted of single actions on membership in a single year (1957, 1973, 1995, and 2004). The other rounds consisted of actions in more than one year. Thus, the first accession of Round 3 was Greece in 1981, followed by the addition of Portugal and Spain five years later. Round 6 also has consisted of actions in two different years, with two states admitted in 2007 and one in 2013.

The pattern of membership growth reflects the debate about who should be members of the organization. In the first two rounds, all the countries were essentially similar: market democracies of relatively long standing, Western in their political and security orientations, with vibrant, similar levels of economic development (Ireland at the time was a partial exception).

Round 3 introduced the question of who should be allowed into the union. Greece had a long tradition of political democracy that had been interrupted by authoritarian interludes, and it was not as developed as the other members, meaning there would have to be a developmental effort by the existing members to bring the Greeks up to the economic standards of the rest. Portugal and Spain represented this same problem even more starkly. As a result, their membership applications were delayed. The introduction of new kinds of states and the end of the Cold War caused the EU to formalize the bases for new membership. In 1993, the union adopted the so-called Copenhagen criteria (so named because they were agreed to in the Danish capital). There were four criteria established:

1. It must be a stable democracy.
2. It must demonstrate respect for human rights and the rule of law.
3. It must possess a functioning, market economy.
4. It must be willing to accept all membership obligations.

The first accession under these rules occurred in 1995 and was relatively straightforward. The three new members (Austria, Finland, and Sweden) had all been Cold War neutrals which, had they joined earlier, might have caused Cold War consternation because of their proximity to the Soviet Union.

The fifth round is in some ways the most interesting and most indicative of the problems the EU will face in the future. A total of ten states were added over two accessions in 2004 and 2007. Most are formerly communist states that were either members of the old Warsaw Pact (the Czech Republic, Hungary, Poland, and Slovakia), former Soviet republics (Estonia, Latvia, and Lithuania), parts of Yugoslavia (Slovenia), or Mediterranean island countries (Cyprus and Malta). None unambiguously meets the criterion of long-standing political democracies, and most have economies far less vibrant than those of the older, more traditional members. The sixth round added formerly communist states as well: Bulgaria and Romania in 2007, and Croatia in 2013.

Not all European states are members. Two states, Norway and Switzerland, have declined the invitation to join. Switzerland's reasons include its long tradition of neutrality (the Swiss have not been combatants in a foreign war since 1515) and the possibility that membership in the organization would subject the Swiss banking system to international regulation, thus undermining its unique and sometimes controversial place in the world. Norway voted down membership in 1994 because of the fear that its national identity would be compromised (Norway is a relatively young European state, having broken away from the Kingdom of Sweden in 1905), and many Norwegians were unwilling to forfeit their hard-won national independence. Two other countries have candidate status for membership: Macedonia and Turkey. In the past, all states that have been candidates have become full members; however, the application of Turkey has been controversial for some time. In addition, several former republics of the Soviet Union (notably Ukraine) and western Balkans states (former parts of Yugoslavia—Serbia, Bosnia and Herzegovina, and Montenegro, for instance) are still in the queue for membership consideration.

The worldwide economic crisis that engulfed the global economy in 2008 did not spare the countries of the EU and raised questions about the continuing pace of membership expansion. As Cohen explains, because of the economic downturn, "EU elites and publics have been forced to revisit whether they can afford the costs of both EU enlargement and a more centralized and activist union." Some even wonder about the continuing viability of the EU as an institution.

The Sovereign Debt Crisis and EU Deepening

The political implications of increasing levels of integration are the source of some distress in the EU area. The problem is straightforward: the more deeply the economies of the members of the union become intertwined, the greater is the need for common political decision-making bodies to make political decisions on community-wide economic issues. Policies regarding common monetary policy, for instance, may be economic, but they reflect political decisions derived through political processes. For policy to be fashioned in the most efficient and effective way, the political body that makes that decision should be coequal in authority to the physical area for which it is making policy. A union-wide set of policies thus implies the need for a union-wide political set of institutions with union-wide authority. Policies made by such a body could override, even replace, decisions made by national political bodies, so the result can be a loss of national political power. That means, in turn, the loss of sovereign political control by the member states to the union. For those with primary allegiance to the state, the trade-off of political power for economic advantage becomes an increasingly problematical bargain.

This is not a new problem for the European integration movement. The British, for instance, opted out of participation in the process until 1973, when economic considerations seemed to overcome political objections. But these concerns have made the British supporters of widening rather than deepening since 1973 to limit the increasing power of the union. This fear of lost sovereignty has played a large role in British withdrawal from the EU.

The sovereign debt crisis in several EU member states is a current source of strain. It is a problem of what political levels should be able to influence or dictate budgetary decisions for member states that have the effect of weakening other members. The issue divides the more and less wealthy members. The substantive issue is the extent and accumulation of national indebtedness, or sovereign debt.

What is sovereign debt? The term is more imposing than its meaning, probably because the adjective "sovereign" is attached to it. As the *Financial Times* points out, however, sovereign debt is "debt that is issued by a national government." All governments incur some level of sovereign debt, borrowing money whenever their current assets do not adequately cover obligations that must be met. Borrowing is a universal phenomenon, and as the *Financial Times* further states, "It is theoretically considered to be risk-free, as the government can employ different measures to guarantee repayment, e.g., raise taxes or print money."

Sovereign debt is ubiquitous in the international economic system, but it has been elevated to the level of a "crisis" within the EU and elsewhere in recent years. The concern has been the *amount* of debt that some states have incurred and the negative impact increasing levels of debt have on the economies that are running them up. The issue has had at least two facets that are also reflected in the EU debate. One is the amount of debt that annual deficits are accumulating. Among the most dramatic and publicized indicators of the debt accumulation is debt as a percentage of the size of the national economy expressed as a percentage of gross domestic product (GDP). The rule of thumb is that the lower the ratio between debt and GDP (the lower the percentage of debt compared to GDP), the healthier the economy is thought to be. Within the United States, concern became great when the ratio achieved unity (debt equaled GDP), which occurred in early 2013. To critics, this unity represented a kind of tipping point indicating that the debt problem had reached critical proportions. Other economists disagreed, and the *Economist*, in an assessment in January 2013, argued that "economists do not know how much debt is too much."

The second concern is with the ability of government to honor (or "service") the debts they have. Can the issuing government cover the obligations it incurs with lenders in terms of repayment, and what can be done to improve that situation? This dimension is both physical and psychological. The physical inability to process debt can lead eventually to government default on its debts, with consequences that investors who have bought debt can lose those investments. Questions about the ability or willingness of governments to repay have the psychological effect of making potential purchasers of future debt reluctant to invest further.

The most pernicious effects of both aspects of the debt problem create the sovereign debt crisis in the EU. Countries that are members of the "euro zone" (the countries that use the euro as their currency) are required to maintain a debt-to-GDP ratio of 60 percent (debt is no more than three-fifths of GDP). Many states have long since exceeded that ratio, and many members of the euro zone and elsewhere have passed unity (debt exceeds GDP), and this creates problems within the EU. Although, as the *Economist* points out, "Many countries may be able to afford to have significantly higher ratios of government debt to national income," there is also general agreement that the ratio can become too high. There is no consensus about when the ratio is intolerable: fiscal conservatives begin to worry before the ratio reaches unity, whereas more liberal economists are comfortable with higher ratios. There is agreement that a "too high" or "too much" point exists, but not where it is.

At some point, a growing debt ratio raises concern about the ability of a government to repay it. Debt ratios tend to be highest in countries with relatively weak economies. This characterization is not universally true: Japan, for instance, has a very high debt ratio. Nevertheless, a combination of a weak economy and growing debt raises questions about the ability of states to use traditional tools such as taxing or printing more money to service current debt, and thus raises potential lender concern about buying additional debt from the offending country. At some point, confidence in a country's solvency may collapse to the point that no one will lend it more at a time when government spending still exceeds revenue and it is too politically difficult to impose fiscal austerity. At this point, a crisis emerges in which insolvency and even discussions of national bankruptcy can occur.

This is the frightening point at which the euro zone has found itself, notably in Greece and Cyprus and potentially in places such as Spain and Italy. The only recourse has been the injection of capital from other countries into the ailing economy—a bailout in popular, if pejorative, terms. That prospect is particularly irksome to some countries—which are generally prosperous and have maintained debt ratios below unity—that must provide the funds to underwrite the bailouts of those whose fiscal policies have caused the crisis. Within the contemporary EU, most of the countries in crisis are Mediterranean states, while the potential saviors are from northern Europe.

Germany is the linchpin, and its patience and willingness to continue propping up weak euro zone economies has been tested by the ongoing sovereign debt crisis. As Foroohar puts it, the Germans "feel they have done everything right—worked hard, liberalized their economy, kept debt and unemployment low—why should they support spendthrift southern European nations?" Beyond that arguably self-righteous vantage point is the more basic question of what they can do to keep the problem from recurring. The current answer is not very much, which brings the discussion back to the issue of EU deepening.

The reason there are large economic problems in some EU countries but not in others is that the monetary union has not progressed to the point of being able to legislate and enforce common fiscal policies (such as levels of government spending) across the membership. The basic reason for the problem reflects the ambivalence the members have always had toward deepening toward a full political union. Creating a full union swamps national sovereign decision-making power over policies regulating the lives of citizens, and ultimately threatens national identity. Those who seek added EU authority (known as unionists) do not necessarily have such insidious underlying motives or intents, but their proposed intrusions raise suspicions that they do, or that diluting national sovereignty will be an outgrowth of such policy changes. The result is further resistance to deepening.

Seen in this light, the sovereign debt crisis is the latest substantive example of the dilemmas of deepening. The debt crisis and its solution are part of the same cloth. As the *Washington Post* explained it in a March 2013 editorial, the current EU "is a currency union absent the usual political, legal, and regulatory infrastructure. Until that inherently confusing and unstable situation changes, Europe's policy-makers will continue to make it up as they go." Ad hoc solutions are almost certainly not the best answer to the debt crisis, but creating a comprehensive, union-wide authority that could solve them in an orderly way requires resolving the deepening disagreement, a solution that remains elusive. This dynamic—national sovereignty versus a deeper union—more recently was the basis for British withdrawal from the EU.

Reverse Integration: Brexit

In June 2016, the regional integration process in Europe underwent a course adjustment, as the voters of the United Kingdom chose in a national referendum to leave the EU. The outcome of the vote was not widely expected despite evidence that parts of the UK were more committed to membership than other areas. Support for the EU was strongest in London, which benefited financially from its connections to the EU, and also in Scotland and Northern Ireland, whose people, among other things, saw the EU connection as a mechanism for loosening their control by London. Opposition was strongest in the rest of England (including Wales), which had not bounced back well from the 2008 recession and which saw immigrants flowing into the country as a threat to their jobs. Immediately after the vote, there was even some suspicion that its outcome might revive secessionist sentiments within both Scotland and Ulster (Northern Ireland).

The actual Brexit referendum was put to the vote on June 23, 2016. The outcome was very close, as pollsters had predicted, but in the opposite direction of most prognostications. Roughly 72 percent of registered voters turned out, and those favoring withdrawal got 17.4 million ballots (52 percent), whereas pro-unionists cast 16.1 million votes (48 percent). The government of David Cameron announced that it would invoke Article 50 of the EU Treaty to initiate withdrawal, a process that can take up to two years. Cameron's successor, Theresa May, has continued the process, which is expected to be completed sometime in 2018.

Why did Brexit come up and succeed? Its basic dynamics combine elements of the crisis of EU that has been under way since the provisions of the Lisbon Treaty have begun to be felt, primarily in shifts of authority in some policy areas from the member states to the central EU mechanisms in Brussels. The sovereign debt crisis is not directly related to the Brexit, since it was primarily a contest over fiscal responsibility between the northern and southern continental members of the EU, in which the British had a peripheral role. There is, however, a symbolic link that probably motivated anti-union forces in Britain, because proponents of greater fiscal responsibility did appeal to central EU institutions for help in trying to force economic reforms on the poorer southern members. Such advocacies provided evidence of attempts to accumulate greater political power to the central EU mechanisms at the expense of member sovereignty, a matter on which the British have always voiced concern.

The added ingredient in helping to create Brexit was immigration into the EU, and specifically the perceived loss of control of who entered European countries because the ability to regulate who came into member countries had largely been captured by the proponents of greater union in the months prior to the Brexit vote. The Brexit appeal thus admixed opposition to the dilution of British sovereignty with the feeling that the EU had stolen the British ability to determine who could and could not live in the UK.

As has been argued in numerous analyses, the apparent motivations that underlay support for Brexit mirrored election dynamics in the United States in 2016 in some ways. A major issue in both countries was economic performance, with voters in both countries who felt their economic futures to be under siege leading the charge for change (i.e., being pro-Trump or anti-EU). This anxiety was expressed in general opposition to immigration into the two countries. This sentiment was more general in the United States, whereas in Britain (and other parts of the EU) it was more complex and encompassing, adding anxiety over terrorists being allowed to migrate and circulate freely among EU states and what many nationalists in the UK and elsewhere saw as the usurpation of the ability to regulate who could and could not enter the country by the pro-deepeners in Brussels. This latter concern was a direct clash between those who treasured British sovereignty over the economic benefits but political loss of power that the EU provides. In the UK, at least, the nationalists won.

Control of immigration was the fuse of Brexit. The immigration problem is especially difficult. Virtually all European countries have small population growth rates and thus need immigrants. The basic dynamic is demographic. European birth rates are low, and if Europe wants to avoid population decline, it has no other option than to accept massive immigration, a process that is already happening. Part of this mandate arises from the real need to provide young workers for the workforce and thus prosperity. The problem is that the migrant population for Europe is largely from the Middle East and North Africa, which is also where terrorists have bred in recent years, creating legitimate fears that some immigrants are or will become terrorists (many of them do not assimilate well and live in ghetto areas that foster radicalization). The result is a desire to maintain some national control over immigrants, a power usurped by the Union and the fuse that lit the powder keg of Brexit.

If this issue were to kindle and explode anywhere in Europe, the UK was its most likely site. Because the EU permits full and unfettered movement of people within the area, the only way to restrain who enters any EU country is to restrict who enters the EU at all. The EU, through the European Border and Coast Guard Agency—Frontex (a French acronym for "external borders")—was established in 2004 to aid members in this filtering function, but in 2015–2016, the Union expanded its role in response to the refugee crisis from Syria. On December 18, 2015, the European Council voted a new European Border and Coast Guard to supplant national authorities. The new effort came into effect on October 6, 2016. The Brexit fuse was lit.

Brexit became reality in the country that had the longest tradition of aloofness from the European continent. It has been British policy for centuries to remain on the outside, acting as a balancer when continental affairs got out of control and it could move in to straighten matters out, retreating beyond the English Channel when their mission was accomplished. Many Britishers cringed when the channel tunnel under the English Channel (the "Chunnel") was opened in 1994, since it tied the islands physically to the continent in ways many citizens of the UK found uncomfortable, and the threat of uncontrollable immigration simply was too much for many who voted to leave. This symbol of deepening has "led to an unprecedented politicization of the EU," according to Müller. Luedtke adds, "European integration cannot be separated, institutionally or politically, from issues of immigration." Brexit is the best evidence.

Conclusion

The EU is by far the most comprehensive, successful experiment in voluntary economic integration in the contemporary world, probably in human history. It has been a far more ambitious effort than any other attempt to transcend national boundaries economically, and it has moved much further along than other international proposals and actions, none of which has moved past the initial stage of forming free trading areas. The EU has marched through free trade status to customs union, to single market, and now to full economic union with strong political implications. It has done this on a regional basis among countries that share a common civilization and were in common economic straits after World War II. Its uniqueness reflects partly the circumstances in which it was born and in which it has subsequently thrived. Whether the lessons of the EU are transferable to other geographic areas is debatable, as is the union's future shape and nature and extent of operation. Europe is a unique place where integration could flourish in ways and to an extent difficult to imagine anywhere else. But does the sovereign debt crisis and Brexit suggest it may have gone too far?

What kind of future does the EU have? It can develop in two directions—economically or politically and by increasing membership (widening) or making the union more encompassing (deepening)—but will it do both, or either? The economic dimension involves the completion of the economic union process, which means the inclusion of all members within the currency union and other economic obligations that the debt crisis has shown will be difficult—possibly even too hard to accomplish. Some new members admitted under Rounds 5 and 6 have substantially less developed economies than those of the pre-expansion core.

Leavening economic standards has strained and will continue to strain the union and to compromise support for greater deepening. In turn, potential new members will be anxiously watching the way the EU handles these dynamics. All the potential members are poorer than the most developed current members. The attraction of membership in an EU that is wider or deeper will depend greatly on how the sovereign debt problem is resolved.

A political perspective leads to different problems raised most dramatically by Brexit. Essentially, there are two political questions. The first is the political evolution of the EU itself: will the EU move toward becoming a full political union? Great Britain has answered that question negatively for itself, reflecting British predilections against being too integral a part of Europe, from which they prefer a certain separation. In the past, countries that very much favored and enjoyed the benefits of further integration became very skittish when the political consequences of moving forward had potentially erosive effects on national identity and prerogatives. The loss of national control over who crosses its borders to central control by the EU central authority in Brussels is the current pivotal issue dividing national and unionist supporters. Will there be more sources of disagreement?

The resolution of the debt and Brexit dilemmas will certainly influence the ultimate potential impact of integration on the global system. The EU is at a crossroads where it must decide if it will become a full political and economic union or remain a somewhat looser institution wherein its members retain sovereign control. It is a question that Europeans have been asking themselves and one another since the process began in 1958 and before, and they have not reached an EU-wide consensus. So far, Brexit has not proven infectious, as many analysts feared in 2016 when the British vote occurred. The French presidential election of May 6, 2017, in which pro-EU political novice Emmanuel Macron trounced anti-unionist Marine Le Pen (who advocated a French Brexit) by thirty-two percentage points in national voting, has arrested disunion sentiment for now. A continuation of the IS-inspired terrorist campaign within the EU could revive that emotion. In the meantime, the EU is likely to punish the UK for leaving, partly out of pique but also to send a message to anyone else who might contemplate following suit. Müller suggests in a 2017 *Foreign Affairs* article that punishment will take the form of high tariffs on post-separation British goods entering the EU that will add $7 billion a year to the added price of buying British goods in union countries.

Eventually, Europeans will have to decide on the basic question of integration. They can maintain the status quo that retains sovereign state control of important monetary and fiscal functions but that virtually guarantees that crises like those over sovereign debt and British withdrawal continue. They can create a true monetary union that effectively becomes a political union, in the process undermining national sovereignty and threatening national identity. To this point, the members have been unwilling to forfeit or threaten their national identities; nationalism and adherence to sovereignty remain stronger forces than economic efficiency for many European members. Until or unless the champions of great deepening can accommodate or surmount that dynamic, one can expect crises like that associated with sovereign debt to continue.

Study/Discussion Questions

1. How does European integration differ from economic schemes in other parts of the world, such as those discussed in chapter 8? Describe those differences in general terms.

2. Discuss the physical steps in the EU process, including how each step changed the nature of the regional integration movement. What forms has economic integration taken? How does each stage build on the others? How does the balance between economic and political aspects change in various steps in the process? Describe the evolution of the EU in these terms.

3. How have the birth and evolution of the EU been influenced by both economic and political motives? How have they commingled at each step? Elaborate.

4. What are "widening" and "deepening" in European Union terms? Define and discuss the evolution

of each dynamic in the EU experience.

5. How has widening changed the nature of the EU in both economic and political terms? What have been the consequences of these changes for greater deepening of the union? Why have some countries such as the UK used widening and deepening as alternative directions for the EU?

6. What is sovereign debt? What is its nature, and when does it become a "problem"? Why has the European sovereign debt situation been described as a "crisis"? How does it relate to greater tensions between those who want to expand the authority of EU and those who do not?

7. What is Brexit? Why did it arise? What issues underlay its appeal to some UK citizens? How is it part of the larger debate on widening and deepening? What have its consequences been?

8. What is the future of the European Union, based on the material to which you have been exposed? What kind of indicator was the outcome of the 2017 French presidential election for the process? Are there likely to be more challenges to union? What continuing role will national sovereignty play in those debates?

Bibliography

Alesino, Alberto, and Francesca Giavazzi. *The Future of Europe: Reform or Decline*. Cambridge, MA: MIT Press, 2006.

Algieri, Franco. "A Weakened EU's Prospects of Global Leadership." *Washington Quarterly* 30, no. 3 (Winter 2006–2007): 106–15.

Bache, Ian, and Stephen George. *Politics in the European Union*. 2nd ed. Oxford, UK: Oxford University Press, 2006.

Brickerton, Chris. *The European Union: A Citizen's Guide*. New York: Pelican, 2016.

Central Intelligence Agency. *CIA World Factbook, 2016*. Washington, DC: Central Intelligence Agency, 2016.

Clarke, Harold D., Michael Goodwin, and Paul Whiteley. *Brexit: Why Britain Voted to Leave the European Union*. Cambridge, UK: Cambridge University Press, 2017.

Cohen, Leonard J. "Detours on the Balkan Road to EU Integration." *Current History* 108, no. 716 (March 2009): 124–30.

Delanty, Gerard. "The EU's Indistinct Identity." *Current History* 115, no. 779 (March 2016): 117–19.

Dinan, Desmond. *Europe Recast: A History of the European Union*. Boulder, CO: Lynne Rienner, 2014.

Dunt, Jan. *Brexit: What the Hell Happens Now? Everything You Need to Know about Britain's Divorce from Europe*. London: Canbury, 2016.

Foroohar, Rana. "Continental Commitment Issues." *Time*, April 1, 2013, 16.

"Government Debt: How Much Is Too Much?" *Economist* (online), January 2, 2013.

Gros, Daniel. "The Dogs That Didn't Bark: The EU and the Financial Crisis." *Current History* 108, no. 716 (March 2009): 105–9.

"In Cyprus, Making a European Solution on the Fly." *Washington Post* (online), March 26, 2013.

Janes, Jackson, and Stephen Szabo. "Angela Merkel's Germany." *Current History* 106, no. 698 (March 2007): 106–11.

Kauppi, Niilo. *Democracy, Social Resources, and Political Power in the European Union*. Manchester, UK: Manchester University Press, 2005.

Luedtke, Adam. "Crisis and Reality in European Immigration Policy." *Current History* 114, no. 770 (March 2015): 89–94.

Matthijs, Matthias. "Europe after Brexit: A Less Perfect Union." *Foreign Affairs* 96, no. 1 (January/February 2017), 85–95.

McCormick, John. *European Union Politics*. London: Palgrave Macmillan, 2015.

———. *Understanding the European Union: A Concise Introduction*. New York: Palgrave Macmillan, 2002.

Moravcsik, Andrew. "Europe, the Second Superpower." *Current History* 109, no. 725 (March 2010): 91–98.

Müller, Jan-Werner. "The EU's Democratic Deficit and the Public Sphere." *Current History* 115, no. 779 (March 2016): 83–88.

Oliver, Craig. *Unleashing Demons: The Inside Story of Brexit.* London: Hodder and Stoughton, 2016.

"Q&A: The Lisbon Treaty." *BBC News* (online), February 5, 2010.

Rachman, Gideon. "The Death of Enlargement." *Washington Quarterly* 29, no. 3 (Summer 2006): 51–65.

Shepherd, Robin. "Romania, Bulgaria, and the EU's Future." *Current History* 106, no. 698 (March 2007): 117–22.

Shipman, Tim. *All Out War: The Full Story of How Brexit Sank Britain's Political Class.* New York: HarperCollins, 2016.

Soros, George. *The Tragedy of the European Union: Disintegration or Revival.* New York: PublicAffairs, 2014.

"Sovereign Debt." *Financial Times Lexicon* (online), February 2, 2013.

Watts, Duncan. *The European Union.* Edinburgh: Edinburgh University Press, 2010.

Wood, Steve, and Wolfgang Quaisser. *The New European Union: Confronting the Challenges of Integration.* Boulder, CO: Lynne Rienner, 2007.

10

International Efforts to Promote Well-Being and Development

The Tragic Case of South Sudan

The same post–World War II environment that dictated international efforts to outlaw the worst excesses of the Nazi regime in the form of war crimes did not stop there, extending its ideals to the notion that there should be standards of human existence that also promoted basic human entitlements and conditions of life. Some of these overlapped the negative political rights discussed in chapter 7, because removing politically induced deprivation is often the prerequisite for promoting more positive values and conditions. The positive rights were first articulated in 1948 in the UN Declaration on Human Rights (UNDHR). Efforts to promote the UNDHR's promises included positive actions such as developmental initiatives in the developing world and punitive calls for humanitarian intervention where conditions preclude those initiatives from being implemented. Development remains a goal, and many international efforts have centered on efforts to ameliorate tragic conditions and violence that accompany great deprivation and inequality. The principles section looks at several of these efforts, including efforts at development and attempts to alleviate human-caused suffering in the developing world under the rubric of humanitarian intervention, the responsibility to protect, and peacekeeping. The application section deals with one especially thorny and intractable case where these kinds of efforts have yet to bear fruit: the tragic case of the Republic of South Sudan.

The United Nations Universal Declaration of Human Rights was proclaimed by the UN General Assembly in Paris in December 1948. Its preamble states clearly its premise about positive rights in the postwar world, saying "recognition of the inherent dignity and of the equal and inalienable rights of all members of the human family is the foundation of freedom, justice and peace in the world." It goes on to assert its basic underlying belief that "disregard and contempt for human rights have resulted in barbarous acts which have enraged the conscience of mankind and the advent of a world in which human beings shall enjoy freedom of speech and belief and freedom from want has been proclaimed as the highest aspiration of the common people." These goals have clearly not been achieved universally, as suggested by the kinds of ongoing world problems chronicled in chapter 7, but those who framed the declaration warned that "it is essential, if man is not compelled to have recourse, as a last resort, to rebellion against tyranny and oppression, that human rights should be protected by the rule of law."

The UNDHR is implicitly divided into two concepts. The first encompasses the so-called political or negative rights, an iteration of political freedoms that states are prohibited from breaching (Articles 1–15), and includes matters as diverse as freedom from being enslaved, equal protection under the law (including legal and juridical rights such as the presumption of innocence in trials), and privileges associated with political democracy. The second category encompasses the so-called social and economic or positive rights (Articles 16–30). The rights are a list of human entitlements, from the right to own property, to "marry and to found a family," to free education, to freedom of assembly and speech. In most ways, the rights in the document reflect the U.S. Bill of Rights (on which they were largely based), but go beyond that document in some of the positive entitlements it contains.

The negative and positive rights are also sequential in important ways. Clearly, all the rights encompassed in the document have not been reached for a large part of the world's population over seven decades after its adoption, and for literally billions of humans trapped in wretched conditions of life, they represent no more than an abstract aspiration unlikely to be achieved during their lifetimes. As world population continues to grow and the numbers of people who do not enjoy the rights contained in the declaration expand as a result, the prospects of realizing the declaration's promise contracts or is made longer and more difficult as well.

There are numerous barriers to spreading the declaration's promise, and the nature and content of those difficulties vary among the world's areas and states. The basic underlying need in almost all cases, however, is for economic development to create the kind of wealth and economic conditions that allow the declaration's promises to be realized. One cannot, for instance, provide a free universal education if there is not enough money from somewhere to build, staff, or equip schools. The developmental imperative is foundational but difficult to achieve. At the same time, poverty and despair are factors in violence and instability that is often internal in nature, and there is a question about whether solutions to these kinds of instability represent any kind of obligation to the world at large.

Principle: International Efforts to Promote Well-Being and Development

In the abstract, virtually no one denies the desirability of improving the human condition for the large number of humans who do not enjoy the positive benefits of a safe and commodious life. There are wide disparities in the quality of life experienced by people in different parts of the world. Since World War II, the cleaving characteristic distinguishing the "haves" from the "have-nots" has been the side of the colonial divide on which they stand. The most powerful and prosperous countries have been the countries of Europe, North America, and peripheries such as Australia and New Zealand, effectively the membership of the

Organization of Economic Cooperation and Development (OECD). They share the common characteristics of being wealthy and mostly politically democratic (the essential indicators of development) and either having been colonial powers or at least having avoided being colonized in the twentieth century. On the other side of the divide are the countries of Africa, Asia, and parts of Latin America. Large parts of these areas were subject to colonial rule and did not emerge from the colonial "yoke" until after the second world conflict. These "developing" countries are less economically advanced than their developed world counterparts and generally have fewer democratic and more unstable political systems marked by great disparities in wealth and power. They are the parts of the world where the UNDHR's promise is least realized and are thus the focus on development in the quest for human well-being asserted by the UNDHR.

The Problem of Development

The idea that the richest countries of the world should help uplift the peoples of the less wealthy countries and regions has been an ongoing humanitarian theme at least since the UNDHR's list of aspirations was passed in 1948. No one denies the desirability of a world of more equal opportunity and prosperity on humanitarian grounds, and there is little disagreement that a more uniformly prosperous environment would reduce the incidence of violence and insecurity in the world. Hardly anyone questions the laudability of development.

The rhetorical, exhortatory support for development has not translated into a major global operational priority to alleviate the problem aggressively. Development is a topic that is talked about a lot, but it is not an imperative on which there is widespread action. Part of the reason for this is that the problem is enormous and would be very—some would argue impossibly—expensive to attack in any systematic way. Even the wealthiest countries have competing priorities for the resources they might devote to the developmental effort that their citizens deem to be more important than helping the developing countries develop. The perpetual debate and criticism of "foreign aid" in the United States emphasized by the Trump administration is emblematic of this problem. Should, for instance, the United States devote its limited resources to rebuilding its own crumbling infrastructure or help other countries build theirs in the first place (assuming it cannot do both)? The other problem is conceptual. There is a belief in some parts of the donor world that developmental assistance is a giant black hole into which resources are dumped without prospects of visible positive outcomes. Political scientists and others have been studying the problem of how to "do" development since the latter 1940s, and there is still a consensus neither on how to do it nor what, if anything, works to achieve the goal.

This discouraging picture helps frame the effort to realize the UNDHR's promise. The influence of that 1948 entreaty is largely implicit: it states ideals and aspirations that are certainly part of the Western liberal tradition, but there are large parts of the world in which these values are assigned a comparatively minor position in governmental philosophy and priorities. The values incorporated into the promotion of human rights are decidedly Western, reflecting

Western social and political philosophies as they evolved in a Western experience that emphasized expanding political participation (democratization) and economic expansion (development). For many in the developing world, these ideals are abstractions in an environment of great material deprivation, maldistribution of resources, and political turmoil where development does not mean the same thing as it does to Westerners and where the absence of developmental achievements is viewed as normal.

Beyond the humanitarian side of the UNDHR's call, there is also a geopolitical argument that may play an even greater role for advocating development in a tumultuous international system. As noted in earlier chapters, most of the violence and physical instability in the current international system occurs in the developing world, which is also the target of developmental efforts. The connection is not coincidental or spurious and begins from the empirical proposition that misery and deprivation are the seeds from which violence and instability sprout in forms such as developing world internal conflicts (DWICs). If this connection has causal elements, as hypothesized, then one way to reduce global violence might be through political and economic development. This idea forms part of the central premise of the democratic peace argument that democracies do not fight one another, from which one can extrapolate that greater democratization (a hypothetical concomitant of economic development) could lead to greater world peace.

Much of the difficulty of arguing either for or against development is that most of the supporting observations and premises are hypothetical and not the product of sound theoretical knowledge in any scientifically acceptable sense. If one accepts the premises of the developmental argument, then it follows that the members of the international system should devote considerable efforts to alleviating developmental inequalities. If one questions either the basic argument or its imperatives, the case for developmental assistance is much weaker. In a sense, the structure of argumentation resembles that over climate change described in chapter 12. If one accepts the premises and evidence surrounding climate change, then the call for action seems virtually inexorable. If one questions those premises, the imperative fades or disappears. The same is largely true for developmental efforts: if developmental deprivations are at the root of violence and instability, the case for reducing those inequalities by raising the standards of the deprived is stronger than if one disbelieves or is skeptical of the premise. The major difference between the two arguments is that the scientific evidence supporting the climate change hypothesis is much stronger and more direct than the argumentation and support for developmental prescriptions and their consequences.

There is an important conundrum in the argument. Political and other social scientists have been studying and writing about development since the 1940s, and have devised some elaborate and well-thought-out constructs about how to facilitate the movement from underdeveloped status to something better (see Latham for a good summary). The problem is that most of the propositions and constructs have not been tested. All of them are premised on sizable investments in the developmental enterprise, and it has proven impossible to attract the levels of capital necessary to test the propositions. South Korea is a signal exception, but funds were available because of the Korean War, not as a way to test the developmental argument. Aside from a paucity of available funds, the conundrum is that it has proven impossible to attract the levels of funding necessary to test these propositions mostly because there is very little empirical evidence that the money will not be wasted or not have the desired effects.

The Development Debate

No one seriously questions whether developmental disparities exist and impede the realization of the positive rights included in the UNDHR, or that a world in which developmental conditions were uniformly high worldwide would probably be a more harmonious and generally better world environment. One question concerns who is responsible for creating the disparities and thus who bears the resulting burden for taking the lead in dealing with them. Both of these concerns are international. The other question bears on who should proceed with development and how, which is partially a philosophical debate over economic and political imperatives and the most efficient way to promote and maximize developmental impacts. Included in the debate is also the implicit question and assumption regarding the outcomes of different developmental strategies in geopolitical terms.

Responsibility

Who caused the great disparity in developmental levels? As noted, the primary factor cleaving the developed and developing worlds was on which side of the colonial equation a country resided. The developed world contained the countries who were the colonizers, whereas most of the developing countries were colonies, and as a result, the assignment of blame tends to be between advocates from the developing and developed worlds. The major arguments for blame assignment come from developmental efforts that go back into the 1950s. Both arguments proceed from the assumption that the other bears primary responsibility and thus blame, and both are partially valid. The position of those who were colonized is that the colonizers who invaded and occupied their territories were primarily motivated by greed and power and that they suppressed what would otherwise have been the development of colonial societies. This position is not without merit, although some colonizing powers were harsher and arguably more venal than others. The colonizing powers respond that most of the areas they conquered were highly stagnant, traditional societies and that the innovations and levels of advancement they introduced raised the standards of existence of those colonized, in the process whetting appetites for more, a position that also has merit. The shared truth is that colonizers did enter traditional societies and create awareness and desires for better living standards, which the colonizers did not fulfill.

The arguments are important because they help form the basis for answering the question, "who should do something about the disparities?" Is it the responsibility of the colonizing powers who created the problem or the desire for greater equality (the developing world position)? Or does the responsibility rest with those in the developing world to act primarily on their own with some outside assistance (the colonial position)? The former colonizers have, by and large, accepted some responsibility for not doing more to alleviate disparities, but they have not been successful in finding or investing adequate resources to "solving" them.

Philosophical Differences

If there is limited agreement on the desirability of development but differences about who is to blame, there is also disagreement on how to proceed to create development in economic terms. The major question, deriving from differences in economic philosophy, is between those who believe that the primary emphasis should be on public, government-to-government funding of developmental efforts and those who believe that private sources are best and most effective.

Much of the difference is a matter of sequencing. A major problem facing most developing countries is in *infrastructure*, the existence of basic developmental building blocks to allow and facilitate economic growth. Power sources and grids, roads, railroads, and airports, and an educational system that can produce appropriately skilled workers are examples of necessary prerequisites to enable economic expansion, whether it be the development of indigenous forms of development or to attract private outside investment and jobs.

The basic problem is that basic infrastructural investments (e.g., financing the dredging of a port) are not *self-liquidating* in the sense of directly producing revenue to pay off the debts that are incurred building them, and this makes such projects unattractive to private lenders. These investments are crucial to creating the underpinning for advancement (education is an example), but only public spending that does not have a strict fiscal connection can be used for such necessary expenses, the traditional rationale for "foreign aid." Once these underlying conditions are in place, then societies become attractive to the private sector for investments that have positive developmental consequences.

Geopolitical Implications

There are two general ways in which the outcomes of developmental efforts may have salutary international political effects. One is if the democratic peace hypothesis is correct. In its most basic form, this Kantian construct maintains that democratic states are less likely to fight, mostly because free people do not freely choose war, especially with other politically like-minded countries. This does not mean that democratic states will not and do not fight, because the thesis does not extend unambiguously to relations between democracies and non-democratic states. Its implication, however, is that a world in which politically democratic states are expanding (which is currently not the case) would be more peaceful because there would be fewer countries that would go to war with one another. If, as developmental advocates argue, economic development is likely to lead to political democratization, then development is related to peace logically.

Second, even if development does not lead inexorably to democratization, it is related to participation in the global economy (see chapter 8). States that become part of the globalization system tend to develop ties between them that make conflict impractical even when geopolitical differences persist. Before China emerged as a major part of the world economy, for instance, its relations with the United States were much more negative than they are today. Before the Four Modernizations of Deng Xiaoping (see chapter 3), China was a very poor country that was a more appropriate recipient of assistance than a donor, a role it plays today. Clearly, the relationship between development and peace is more complicated than a simple correlation in a place as large, complex, and powerful as China, but it is at least arguably a contributing factor.

Barriers and Status

Development is clearly a work in progress. Poverty and its concomitant miseries continue to dominate the lives of most people in different parts of the world. The situation is worst in Africa, but it is also significant in the Middle East and parts of Asia. Annual World Bank statistics reveal that disparities are shrinking slowly, but translate into miserable living conditions, poverty, and deprivation for many people around the world. It shows many faces: a child born into poverty in the developing world, for instance, is four times less likely to receive even a rudimentary primary education than a child in the developed world, according to the World Bank. That disadvantaged beginning cascades through the child's life.

There is simply inadequate support or resources to deal comprehensively with this problem. The idea of developmental assistance is often dismissed in places such as the United States under the pejorative heading of "foreign aid," and although private benefactors attempt to fill part of the void, it is too great to make more than a selective dent into a global problem. That condition means poverty, deprivation, and misery will be the plight of a large part of the global population.

Inevitably, the result will be frustration in some places that will result in violence which, in many cases, makes matters worse than they already are and add to the problem of global violence and instability that makes lives even more wretched than they would be otherwise. This cycle is present in many parts of the less developed world; the deteriorating situation in South Sudan highlighted in the application section is a vivid example. When faced with this additional source of misery, the question arises as to what, if anything, the international community can or should do to influence the situation. One answer falls under the rubric of "humanitarian intervention" and the responsibility to protect (R2P) as operationalized through various forms of peacekeeping discussed in the next section.

Finally, there is the intangible political context. Development is not only an uncertain business; it is also a long-term process that often has little immediate positive impact. Developmental efforts involve long-term planning and implementation, and politicians and political processes are much better at confronting

and solving short-term emergencies and exigencies. They are notoriously inef-
fectual in dealing with long-term problems, which tend to be put off until they
reach crisis proportions. Developing the Republic of Korea achieved crisis status
because of the war on the Korean peninsula in the 1950s, the aftermath of which
allowed massive investment in what has become the South Korean economic
miracle. Lesser crises do not achieve these same levels of immediacy and thus
can be consigned to the "back burner" of political priorities. One result, however, can be increased instability and violence because developmental needs go
untended, which raises the question of what can and should be done to deal with
those crises before developmental efforts seem necessary or immediate enough
to demand attention.

Humanitarian Intervention and the Responsibility to Protect (R2P)

All the violence and instability found in DWICs are not the result of developmental differences and inequalities, but such contrasts are often present and are
at least a part of the complex of issues and differences that lead to fighting and
killing. It is not unusual for these situations to proceed for extended periods
without resolution but with growing human consequences and suffering. When
resolutions are possible, they are often zero-sum outcomes where the victor prevails at the overwhelming cost of the losers. Developmental efforts would not
preclude or solve all these tragedies, but they might play a role in attenuating
them or making them easier to resolve. They are, however, sources of human
misery of the proximate nature of developmental deprivations.

The same basic question must be asked in these situations that applies to aid-
ing in development: what obligation, if any, does humankind have to prevent or
to interfere in these situations? As in the developmental equation, a hard-headed
geopolitical analysis is likely to conclude that interests basic enough to take deci-
sive, including military, action are simply not present and to conclude that while
these situations may be tragic and regrettable, they go beyond the interests of
states to try to solve. The world, after all, has done very little to relieve the misery of the Syrian people since 2011, as described in chapter 7, and strict nationalist or isolationist sentiments found in some Western countries reinforce this
reluctance to engage.

The premise and arguments for humanitarian intervention are thus controversial. The basic premise is that there is a universal vital interest in protecting
people from man-made disasters. As Weiss puts it in *Humanitarian Intervention*,
"The issue is not the right but the responsibility of every state to play its appropriate role, with the objective not being intervention as such but the protection
of men, women, and children threatened by the horror of mass violence." How
convincing or compelling this assertion is depends critically on how important the interest underlying the possible intrusion. States must perform acts of
humanitarian intervention, and the precipitants must be important enough *to
them* to activate that state interest.

There are several arguments in support or effective opposition to this position. It clearly asserts that states have a responsibility to protect that its supporters refer to by the acronym R2P. Walzer makes this case explicitly in terms of the kinds of often atrocious behavior associated with DWICs. "The greatest danger that most people face in the modern world comes from their own states," he writes, "and the chief dilemma of international politics is whether people in danger should be rescued by *military forces from outside*" (emphasis added). This statement, published originally in 1976 and updated in 2006, certainly presages the current world situation. His conclusion, of course, supports this basis for humanitarian intervention and reflects then president Clinton's justification for intervening in Kosovo in the 1990s: "Doing the right thing." Clinton's epiphany reflects his regret at not taking similar action in the face of the Rwandan genocide of 1994 and was intended to prevent such tragedies in the future.

The debate over whether there is a responsibility to protect through humanitarian intervention represents a moral judgment that flies in the face of the traditional amorality of sovereignty-based international politics. Notions of morality as a limiting factor in international behavior are not new to the contemporary environment. Nardin summarizes the historic tradition of concerns like R2P: "What we now call humanitarian intervention was conceived by moralists, theologians, and philosophers writing before the emergence of international law." Built into the evolving nature of international law was the positivist idea of absolute sovereignty under which, Evans argues, sovereignty implied "immunity from outside scrutiny or sanction."

This dichotomy frames the disagreement over whether an undeniable mandate to engage in humanitarian intervention exists and how compelling it may be. The notion that the international community has no interest or mandate to involve itself when governments or groups within countries do inhuman atrocious things to one another has largely disappeared since World War II, as discussed in chapter 6. This change has not, however, extended to a full embrace of something like R2P, because so many of the humanitarian problems do not appear to have the kinds of immediate consequences with which political processes in developed countries deal most effectively. Occasionally, abuses are so terrible that they cannot be ignored entirely, as the Syrian case indicates, but that does not mean effective action will be taken. In many cases, the humanitarian intervention mandate is "satisfied" by limited, symbolic actions that do not solve the problems but which can be justified in sovereignty terms.

Finally, there is the question of how much obligation outsiders have given the expense and physical dangers that interference may entail. Nardin, once again, offers the common wisdom on this point based in general terms: "It is consistent with common morality to argue that humanitarian intervention is justified in a wide range of situations, but that prudential considerations override this justification." Humanitarian disasters happening half a world away, in other words, may not violate vital interest enough to impel a robust response. The result, as Bellamy (2009) concludes, is that "all too often the world's response . . . has been slow, timid, and disjointed."

Peacekeeping

As is has been used in efforts to contain violence in the developing world, the term peacekeeping has had two distinct contexts, each with different meaning and content. The term was originally coined to describe UN interposition between formerly warring parties and thus literally to keep the peace. The UN mission in the Sinai Desert between 1956 and 1967 (the United Nations Emergency Force or UNEF) is a classic example of this usage. The definitive statement of UN-based peacekeeping is found in former UN secretary-general Boutros Boutros-Ghali's 1992 *An Agenda for Peace*. The UN is still in the peacekeeping business, although at a much lower level of visibility.

There is a second, and more generic, meaning to the idea of peacekeeping, which is the sense of the idea used here. I have described this usage in, among other places, *National Security* (Sixth Edition), and it refers generically to the process by which outsiders may seek to intrude in the violence within countries to bring a cessation to ongoing hostilities and move gradually to a situation of reliable, self-sustaining peace in the target country or region. This process consists of three distinct phases that describe a given situation, the goal of outsiders trying to influence it, and the different kinds of outside forces necessary for different actions. The steps are sequential and reversible, depending on the state of given situations at any point in time.

Generic peacekeeping situations begin during states of "war," violent campaigns that may never be declared as war in the international legal sense but which involve military action including violence against civilians. Most of them occur within multinational or irredentist states between indigenous populations with deep divisions and hatreds that ignite violence and make its resolution by the parties involved difficult or impossible. Tragically for the participants, these situations remain under the global radar unless there is widely publicized evidence of atrocity and suffering that includes the slaughter of innocents, massive population displacement, migration, highly visible refugee crises, or suggestions or evidence of war crimes. If some of these characteristics are present and sufficiently visible, they may trigger a peacekeeping response by the UN or a regional organization (the African Union, for instance).

The first step in this process is to stop the fighting, an activity I call *peace imposition* (PI). The term suggests two things. The first is that fighting is ongoing and that one or both parties has proven incapable or unwilling to end the bloodshed but instead prefers its continuation and will take active military steps to avoid having an end to violence imposed upon them. This leads to the second observation, which is that active warfighting soldiers are necessary as "peacekeepers," because the purpose is to create a peace that can be kept. The inability of the parties to do so indicates that they cannot do this themselves, meaning someone must do it for them. The need to impose peace distinguishes this use of the term peacekeeping from the historical UN model, which presumes both that fighting between combatants has ceased and that the parties prefer peace to the continuation of war, a presumption that is false in PI situations. The goal in this phase is to bring a cessation to physical hostilities—to impose a peace. Doing so does not solve the problems that caused the violence in the first place, which requires reconciliation once fighting has stopped. It can be a very difficult and lengthy process. It is also one for which it may be difficult, sometimes impossible, to recruit adequate outside force to achieve its goals. If successful, however, it may move the situation from one of war to an unstable peace.

If the absence of violence can be imposed successfully, the model suggests movement to a second phase, *peace enforcement* (PE). The PE phase suggests that PI has stopped the fighting but has not necessarily overcome the will to continue the armed conflict. The absence of fighting is tenuous, and the purpose of PE is to keep the former combatants apart so that war does not return. During this phase, there are really two purposes. One is to physically separate and restrain the former combatants so that a calmer atmosphere exists within which negotiations can proceed. The second purpose is to provide for the safety of the population, allowing a return to some form of normalcy. These purposes mean that two kinds of skills are necessary for the peacekeepers: there still must be active warfighters to protect against a reversion to violence, and there must be peacekeepers skilled in monitoring the absence of hostilities and nurturing law-abiding behavior (essentially a policing function). During this phase, the overall goal is to calm the situation and gradually to move from a condition of unstable to one of stable peace, the difference being in whether peace is self-sustaining or must continue to be imposed.

The difference between unstable and stable peace is the acceptance by former combatants of a preference for the absence of violent solutions to their problems. It is a process of reconciliation that gradually creates a civil order that can be self-sustaining. Nurturing this condition is the goal of actual *peacekeeping* (PK). This phase involves monitoring of the condition of peace that both sides have essentially accepted and nurturing attitudes that will allow the internal situation to stabilize to the point that it becomes self-sustaining. If the process succeeds, the need for humanitarian intervention that triggers PI is replaced by a civic condition in which developmental efforts may begin. This third phase of the modified model is basically what traditional forms of UN peacekeeping are designed to create and sustain.

Application: The Tragedy of South Sudan

The tragic situation in the Republic of South Sudan, a small east African country that has been racked by ongoing, separate civil wars episodically for more than sixty years illustrates all the difficulties associated with realizing humankind's prospects and the extreme difficulties that surround such efforts. It is the territory on which the 2003 movie *Lost Boys of Sudan* was set, a film that chronicled the wandering of members of the country's two largest tribes, the Dinka and the Nuer, in the face of the ravages of one of the area's earlier civil wars when South Sudan was part of the Republic of Sudan. Those two tribes are now the central antagonists in the ongoing civil war in the independent Republic of South Sudan.

From (Sudanese) Independence to (South Sudanese) Independence

The history of this tortured and enormously backward and poor country has been filled with confusion and tragedy. South Sudan was part of the original Sudan when it achieved independence in 1956. That country was a totally artificial, multinational state that was divided into a northern region encompassing the southern Sahara and inhabited by Muslims, most of whom were fundamentalist and considered themselves Arabs ethnically. Co-religion was not enough to guarantee unity in Islamic Sudan, as the rebellion in Darfur province that has been going on episodically since the 1990s demonstrates. The contrast between the Muslim north and the south was even more stark. The southerners are racially distinct from the northerners, consider themselves African, and practice either Christianity or animism as their religious preference. The south was exploited as a major source of slaves during the period of colonial rule.

The political marriage of the two regions was incongruous and unsuccessful from the beginning. The major theme of north-south relations was attempts by religiously conservative Islamic regimes in Khartoum to try to impose *sharia* law and Arabic language and culture on the south, which the south resisted, followed by temporary reconciliation when the government relaxed Islamic requirements. A more devout regime would then come to power and reinstate objectionable requirements on the non-Muslim south, which would lead to the outbreak of renewed resistance among the southerners. This pattern began almost immediately after Sudanese independence in 1956 and resulting in a civil war that lasted until 1972. A more moderate Muslim regime ruled until 1983, when the fundamentalists returned to power and reinstated objectionable requirements (Omar al-Bashir, currently under indictment for war crimes in Darfur and mentioned in chapter 7, became president during this period). War broke out in that year and continued until 2005, when the rebellious south and the Khartoum regime signed the momentous Comprehensive Peace Agreement (CPA) that formed the basis for South Sudanese secession from Sudan. It was the cause of much rejoicing and celebration at the time.

The extent of the violence and suffering are hard to ignore, although most of the world has tried. Pre-2011 data on Sudan (from the *CIA World Factbook*) show that a slight majority of Sudanese considered themselves African (52 percent to 39 percent who considered themselves Arab), but most of the regime violence was directed against the majority. Statistics regarding deaths are not terribly reliable, but estimates are that upward of 2.4 million perished in the two civil wars before the CPA (compared to about 300,000 deaths in the much more widely chronicled Darfur war). The formal end of those hostilities and the prospects of leading to secession of the south brought considerable optimism to what became South Sudan. Unfortunately, violence in the independent Republic of South Sudan since its July 9, 2011, birth has attenuated that joy.

The CPA did several things that led the process of divorcing the two regions. First, it created a "government of national unity" for all of Sudan and an autonomous Government of South Sudan (GOSS) that provided a political framework for independence. Second, it rescinded the more objectionable aspects of

Islamic law in the south. Third, it called for countrywide free elections in 2009 (they were held in 2010). Fourth, it set a January 2011 date for a referendum in the south on continued union with Sudan. Finally, it attempted to deal with the special status of places such as Abyei that were near what became the border between the two.

While this process was unfolding, events conspired to put Sudan in the world spotlight in 2009. The ICC indicted President Bashar for alleged war crimes in Darfur, which triggered a Sudanese retaliation ordering sixteen humanitarian organizations out of the country. That same year, oil prices cratered on the world market, destroying much of Sudan's source of foreign exchange. Finally, the election of an African American president of the United States suggested that Washington might have a more favorable relationship with the south than previously. None of these events put Khartoum in a good position and thus stifled any reluctance it might otherwise have had to resist secession. When the referendum on continued union was held in 2011, 98.6 percent of the 3.5 million registered southerners voted for disunion. It was such an overwhelming majority that it could not be denied.

The July 9, 2011, declaration of independence seemed an auspicious beginning for the new country. National Security Advisor Susan Rice represented the United States at the ceremonies, and American and other world dignitaries were well represented in the streets of the capital of Juba. A new government composed of the factions of the Sudanese Liberation Movement/Army (SPLM/A) seemed ready to unite and move the country forward from the long abyss of its union with Sudan. That optimism, however, proved illusory, and deep problems and schisms have doomed the country since.

The Tragedy Since Independence

Separating the 1956 Republic of Sudan into an essentially Muslim Arab state and a non-Islamic African state removed much of the basic division that bedeviled the first half-century of Sudanese freedom from colonial rule. Rather than creating conditions that would produce human progress in either country, however, the bifurcation simply stripped away one layer of animosity and allowed other conditions in each to come to the surface. In the much larger Republic of Sudan (which is almost three times the size of South Sudan), intra-Islamic strife replaced Arab-African conflict, pitting the fundamentalists around Khartoum who have ruled the country against the more moderate Muslims of the periphery. The Darfur conflict that raged in the 1990s and officially ended in 2006 with outside imposition of force to protect the Darfuris is the classic example. The UN and the African Union sponsored a joint 26,000-man peacekeeping force beginning in 2007 (the UN Mission in Sudan or UNMIS) that kept peace in Darfur for a time, but fighting resumed in 2014–2015.

The euphoria in South Sudan was similarly fleeting. The SPLM/A was a coalition formed around southern tribal units that were assigned to maintain order in the south while it was still part of Sudan, and the dominant tribal factions managed to cooperate when the government in Khartoum provided a convenient negative displacement object for both. Like the dynamics of Hindu-Muslim cooperation to throw the British off the Indian subcontinent in the late 1940s that dissolved after the British left, the removal of oppressive rule from Khartoum stripped away the negative ties that created the façade of southern unity.

The situation got off to a reasonably auspicious beginning. The new Republic of South Sudan (reflected in the composition of the SPLM/A) was dominated by the two largest African tribes in the country. The Dinka, who are mostly Christian, are the largest tribe, with what the CIA estimates is about 35.6 percent of the population, and the new president was tribal member Salva Kiir Mayardit, an SPLM/A military leader who replaced SPLM/A icon John Garang when he was killed in a helicopter accident in 2008. The second largest tribe is the Nuer, who are predominately animist and make up 15.6 percent of the population. Riek Machar, a Nuer SPLM/A leader who has since become extremely controversial, was named vice president. It seemed like a good start; the appearance did not, however, comport with reality, and within two years, civil war had returned *within* the southern region.

The problem for the Republic of South Sudan is a microcosm of the problem of the original country. The original Sudan was a poor, artificial state that had little reason to exist, and so are its successors. Both have deep cleavages typical of multinational states, and both are extremely poor countries whose economies, such as they are, rely on the fickle economics of petroleum that is essentially their only basis for prosperity. Both have had attempts at outside humanitarian assistance through intervention in the form of UN-sponsored peacekeeping mechanisms that have not been successful in improving extremely difficult barriers to prosperity. These problems are especially present in the Republic of South Sudan.

The first problem is economic. The Republic of South Sudan is, according to the 2017 *World Factbook*, "one of the world's poorest countries and ranks among the lowest in many socioeconomic categories." According to 2016 CIA estimates, its gross domestic product (GDP) was $20.88 billion, 146th in the world, and that was one of its highest global ratings. Per capita GDP stands at $1,700, 213th in the world; the GDP growth rate is a *negative* 13.1 percent (224th in the world); and the inflation rate stood at 476 percent (226th in the world). Other measures are indicative of the malaise: only 27 percent of the citizenry is literate despite a constitutional mandate for universal education, and this country nearly the size of Texas is dominated by an enormous wetlands area (the Sudd) and has 200 kilometers of paved roads. Despite this, it spends 10.32 percent of GDP on the military, the highest percentage in the world. It is little surprise that since 2016, South Sudan has ranked second on the Fragile State (formerly Failed State) Index worldwide. How the country can possibly engage, even with considerable outside help, in meaningful economic development in these circumstances is difficult to envision.

The one fungible economic access South Sudan possesses is petroleum, revenues from which are also necessary for the Sudanese economy. The Sudanese oil fields are in the areas along the 2011 border created to separate the two countries, with about 75 percent of the reserves located in South Sudan (confirmed reserves stand at 3.75 billion barrels, twenty-eighth in the world) discovered in 1974 and jointly developed until secession. Both countries have been highly dependent on oil revenues for governmental operations, but since 2013, these have dried up, for two reasons.

One problem has been the decrease in oil prices worldwide, which has affected South Sudan as much as or more than other oil-dependent countries. More importantly, however, has been Sudanese-South Sudanese wrangling over the distribution of oil revenues. Both sides lay claim to most of the monies involved. The South Sudanese believe they should get the lion's share because the oil is located under their territory, but they have no way to get it to market. The only developed pipeline to the world's oceans goes across Sudan to Port Sudan, and the government of Sudan bases its claims to revenues on a transit fee for getting the oil to market. Piqued by Sudanese demands, the South Sudanese initially responded in 2012 by suspending oil production and thus transshipment, a solution that hurt both countries and that continues, with economically deleterious, arguably disastrous, effects for both.

The other major problem arises from multinationalism in South Sudan and is exacerbated by the country's economic ills. As noted earlier, the end of Christian/Muslim conflict did not homogenize South Sudan so much as it changed the mix of conflict. The outbreak of discord between tribal elements accentuated by the Dinka and Nuer was not entirely a surprise; the UN Mission to South Sudan (UNMISS) was commissioned with a potential peacekeeping role on July 8, 2011, the day before independence through United National Security Council Resolution (UNSCR) 68 for that year, and in 2013 a UNMISS force with potential upward limits of 12,500 troops and 1,323 police was authorized if needed. The action, unfortunately, proved clairvoyant.

The Violent Present

The accord between the historic SPLM tribal components lasted until late 2013, when fighting broke out between Dinka and Nuer army units over a Kiir announcement he was sacking his vice president. The precipitant was a falling-out between the two former SPLM/A allies. Kiir fired Machar from his position for alleged plans to overthrow the regime and establish Nuer ascendancy, and the former vice president fled into the South Sudanese bush, from which he leads a continuing resistance. Negotiations brokered by neighboring states such as Uganda and Kenya have tried to reestablish stability and produced a ceasefire in 2015, but it broke down when Machar fled into exile. In 2016, President Kiir replaced Machar with Taban Deng Gai, a Nuer who was a former mining minister and governor of Unity State.

The fighting has produced large-scale death and suffering. Statistical evidence is imprecise, but upwards of 300,000 have been killed since fighting broke out between Dinka and Nuer units in the army over the announcement of Kiir's intention to sack Machar. In addition, as many as three million South Sudanese (out of a total population of twelve million) have been forced from their homes out of fear of the consequences of staying or returning home. Roughly two million of these people have fled into the bush, where they exist as internal displaced persons, and another million have become refugees, mostly in neighboring states such as Kenya, Sudan, and Uganda. In 2015, the neighboring states working through the African Union (of which South Sudan is a member) managed to negotiate an end to the fighting in the form of the Agreement for the Resolution of Conflict in South Sudan (ARCISS). That agreement largely collapsed in early 2016 when Machar's flight into exile reignited fighting. The quest for a durable peace continues.

UNMISS has responded with an international effort aimed at humanitarian intervention, but its extent and success has been limited. The effort has largely been focused on peacekeeping goals such as those described earlier in the chapter. The UNMISS website (part of the UN peacekeeping site) lists four basic mandates:

1. The protection of citizens from physical harm
2. Monitoring human rights and their violation
3. The creation of conditions that will facilitate the provision of humanitarian assistance
4. Support for implementation of the ARCISS and any other agreements to end hostilities

These goals, paraphrased from the UN site but in the same order of presentation, mirror the stages of peacekeeping. Protection of citizens from violence involves providing a physical shield to protect South Sudanese from forces on either side of the fighting and falls under peace imposition. Monitoring human rights abuses and creating conditions to allow humanitarian assistance presumably take place in conditions of unstable peace as examples of peace enforcement. Supporting implementation of peace accords suggests the monitoring function most closely associated with peacekeeping. The current mandate for UNMISS, which expired on December 15, 2017, authorized as many as 7,000 peacekeeping forces and 900 police drawn from member countries and is a very small physical force to stabilize a country the size of Texas with virtually no transportation infrastructure.

The situation in South Sudan remains dire by any measure. The civil war continues with varying levels of killing and atrocity, and the situation is militarily unsettled to the point that those who have fled cannot return to their homes from internal or external exile. The government has ground to a virtual halt, with periodic reports of different agencies going on strike for nonpayment of their wages (South Sudanese overseas diplomats are a May 2017 example). There is some outside help, but it is far from enough to make a dent in the situation.

The humanitarian aspect of the tragedy is even worse in some ways. UNICEF, for instance, advertised in late spring 2017 that 100,000 South Sudanese were in danger of imminent starvation and that another million "were on the brink." Neither public nor private sources seem adequate to improve the human condition in the country materially.

Conclusion

For much of the developing world, poverty and deprivation intermix with political instability and violence to form a toxic condition that contributes to, or in many cases, causes enormously grim conditions of life for much of the world's population. Much of this suffering is in the developing countries of Africa and Asia and takes the form of DWICs and other forms of human tragedy. Doing something about these problems represents a major aspiration in terms of human intervention. It is a work in progress.

The goal of developmental efforts is to muster adequate resources to alleviate suffering and to improve the human condition wherever there is suffering and deprivation. Multilateral efforts are clearly necessary because of the enormity of the task. Developmental efforts must compete within the budget processes of donor states with domestic claims on funds, and in that competition, those calling for international uses of funding are disadvantaged because their cause does not have the same domestic constituency appeal as do efforts to apply funding for domestic needs. To repeat a contemporary American example, the need for major domestic investment in infrastructure repair competes with calls for infrastructure assistance to foreign countries. Foreign assistance will inevitably take on secondary priority in that competition.

The actuality or prospect of violence and instability exacerbates the problem. In conditions of instability, it is more difficult to justify making resources available for humanitarian or developmental purposes if one fears they might be consumed in violence or intergroup intrigue that will keep the resources from reaching those who most need and arguably deserve it. The same is true if peace breaks down and there are calls for humanitarian intervention. Regardless of the poignancy of the situation and the moral claim of a responsibility to protect, can the expense and danger such actions imply or demand be justified among other ways that a country can invest its treasure or blood?

The situation in South Sudan is a microcosm of the problem at its absolute worst. The Republic of South Sudan is the tragic result of two misguided attempts at creating a state, first as part of the Republic of Sudan in 1956 and more recently in its own independence in 2011. Both actions produced extremely poor, unstable political entities that had little justification for independent existence as they were constituted and that were virtually bound to struggle and possibly to fail. South Sudan was declared amid great optimism and hope as the shackles of Islamic rule were broken. Unfortunately for the ill-fated citizens of the country, new forms of tyranny and deprivation imposed by those who remained quickly replaced that liberation.

Economics have deepened the tragedy. The suspension of oil production has harmed both Sudans, but especially the South, which has little other basis of wealth with which to uplift its people and hopefully to provide for increasing human well-being. Economic privation has helped create instability and violence, and that fighting and killing has reinforced and added to the horrible economic suffering of the South Sudanese people.

Happily, not every country in the developing world is in as complex and difficult a situation as South Sudan. If that were the case, the prospects for the relief of human suffering would be much more hopeless than it may appear. Relieving human suffering and privation remains a global humanitarian value of the first order; solving the problem, however, remains an elusive goal.

Study/Discussion Questions

1. What is the UNDHR? Why is it important as an agenda setter and set of goals for the human well-being debate?
2. What are the major categories of effort to improve human well-being? In what parts of the world is the problem greatest? Why is that the case? Describe the categories and how they are interrelated.
3. Discuss development substantively and as a goal. What is the nature of the development problem? Using infrastructure as an example, why is it such a difficult problem to deal with effectively?
4. Describe the nature of the problem of elevating development on the international agenda in terms of responsibility, philosophy, geopolitical implications, and barriers to achievement. What conceptual problems inhibit promoting the developmental agenda?
5. Why is violence, especially in the form of DWICs, a human well-being problem? What are humanitarian intervention and the responsibility to protect (R2P), and how do they relate to this aspect of the well-being problem? Discuss.
6. The text describes a peacekeeping (PK) process different from traditional UN formulations. Describe its phases and how they relate to conventional UN definitions. How do the three stages discussed in the model relate to development and well-being?
7. Why is the Republic of South Sudan an example of the development/violence problem as it affects well-being at its very worst? Discuss the evolution of the problem in South Sudan in both politico-economic and military aspects.
8. What is the ongoing status of the situation in the Republic of South Sudan? How does it highlight the enormous difficulties of dealing with these problems and of the limits of outside assistance, including a discussion of the goals of UNMISS. Is the situation resolvable? Why or why not? How does your conclusion relate to the general nature of solving the human well-being and development problem?

Bibliography

Arnold, Matthew, and Matthew Le Riche. *South Sudan: From Revolution to Independence*. New York: Oxford University Press, 2013.

Bellamy, Alex. *Responsibility to Protect*. Malden, MA: Polity, 2009.

———. *The Responsibility to Protect: A Defense*. Oxford, UK: Oxford University Press, 2014.

Bellamy, Alex, and Tim Dunne. *The Oxford Handbook of Responsibility to Protect*. Oxford, UK: Oxford University Press, 2016.

Bellamy, Alex, and Paul D. Williams. *Understanding Peacekeeping.* 2nd ed. New York: Polity, 2010.

Boutros-Ghali, Boutros. *An Agenda for Peace: Preventive Diplomacy, Peacemaking, and Peacekeeping.* New York: United Nations, 1992.

Collier, Paul. *The Bottom Billion: Why the Poorest Nations Are Failing and What Van Be Done about It.* Oxford, UK: Oxford University Press, 2008.

DeConing, Cedric, and Chiyuki Aoi. *UN Peacekeeping Doctrine in a New Era: Adaptation to Stabilization, Protection, and New Threats.* New York and London: Routledge, 2017.

Evans, Gareth. *The Responsibility to Protect: End Mass Atrocity Crimes Once and For All.* Washington, DC: Brookings Institution Press, 2008.

Fortna, Virginia Page. *Does Peacekeeping Work? Shaping Belligerents' Choices after Civil War.* Princeton, NJ: Princeton University Press, 2008.

Guechenno, Jean-Marie. *The Fog of Peace: A Memoir of Peacekeeping in the 21st Century.* Washington, DC: Brookings Institution Press, 2015.

Hook, Stephen W., ed. *Democratic Peace in Theory and Practice.* Kent, OH: Kent State University Press, 2015.

Johnson, Hilde. *South Sudan: The Untold Story from Independence to the Civil War.* London: I. B. Tauris, 2013.

Junk, Julian, Francesco Mancini, Wolfgang Seibel, and Till Blume. *The Management of United Nations Peacekeeping: Coordination, Learning, and Leadership in Peace Operations.* Boulder, CO: Lynne Rienner, 2017.

Kopps, Joachim, and Norrie McQueen. *The Oxford Handbook of United Nations Peacekeeping.* Oxford, UK: Oxford University Press, 2015.

Latham, Michael E. *The Right Kind of Revolution: Modernization, Development and U.S. Foreign Policy from the Cold War to the Present.* Ithaca, NY: Cornell University Press, 2011.

Manon, Rajan. *The Conceit of Humanitarian Intervention.* Oxford, UK: Oxford University Press, 2016.

Nardin, Terry. "The Moral Basis of Humanitarian Intervention." *Ethics and International Affairs* 16, no. 1 (March 2002): 57–70.

Natsios, Andrew. *Sudan, South Sudan, and Darfur: What Everyone Needs to Know.* New York: Oxford University Press, 2012.

Rapley, John. *Understanding Development: Theory and Practice in the Third World.* Boulder, CO: Lynne Rienner, 2007.

Seligson, Mitchell A., and John T. Passe-Smith. *Development and Underdevelopment: The Political Economy of Global Inequality.* 5th ed. Boulder, CO: Lynne Rienner, 2013.

Snow, Donald M. *National Security.* 6th ed. New York and London: Routledge, 2017.

———. *Thinking about National Security: Strategy, Policy, and Issues.* New York and London: Routledge, 2016.

Thakur, Ramesh, and William Melvey, eds. *Theorizing the Responsibility to Protect.* Cambridge, UK: Cambridge University Press, 2015.

Thomas, Edward. *South Sudan: A Slow Liberation.* London: Zed, 2015.

Walzer, Michael. *Just and Unjust Wars: A Moral Argument with Historical Illustrations.* New York: Basic, 2006 (originally released in 1976).

Weiss, Thomas G. *Humanitarian Intervention* (War and Conflict in the Modern World). New York: Polity, 2016.

World Bank Group. *Taking on Inequality: Poverty and Shared Prosperity 2016.* Washington, DC: International Bank for Reconstruction and Development/World Bank, 2016.

11

International Population Movement

The Contrasting U.S. and European Experiences

The movement of people from one place to another precedes human history. People have moved for many reasons, most frequently hoping to find a better life, but also to avoid distress, suppression, and even extinction. Immigrants, refugees, and asylum seekers are a constant that has been increasing in this century and has reached critical proportions in some places. The influx of distinct waves of new peoples has always created a negative response among some receiving people; that "nativism" is especially prominent today in some parts of the developed world, notably in the European Union and North America.

There are competing, contradictory forces at work in this equation. There are two basic stimuli for migration. One directly involves immigration of people from the developing to the developed world. From an immigrant standpoint, the motive may be both economic and political: seeking prosperity and freedom. For receiving countries, immigrants provide necessary augmentation of shrinking labor forces and stimulate productivity. The result can be positive for both sides, but its synergism is partially upset by the prospects that undesirables—especially terrorists—will infiltrate the immigrants. The other stimulus is largely internal to the developing world in terms of privation and atrocity associated with internal conflicts that produce massive refugee and asylum-seeking populations. The contours of this phenomenon are different in individual cases, and the application section contrasts in general terms American and European experiences with population migration.

Human migration is a two-way proposition. On one hand are the immigrants, refugees, and asylum-seekers who seek to relocate for one reason or another, including out of fear for their lives. On the other are those in the sovereign jurisdictions to which the migrants seek to relocate, who must decide whether to accept them. It is rarely a seamless, smooth process. It is also a difficult, often traumatic and even dangerous experience.

Migration is one of the oldest and most enduring aspects of the human experience. At some level of remove, essentially everyone is an immigrant or the descendant of immigrants; the only humans who can rightfully claim nonimmigrant status are direct descendants of the earliest humans from the Great Rift Valley in Africa (where the ancestors of today's human population are believed first to have emerged) who still live there. The immigrant label is especially true for North Americans: even those peoples to whom the appellation "Native Americans" is applied arrived here from Asia, probably walking across the then-existing land bridge between Asia and North America in the Bering Strait.

Human migration in its various forms is a large, important, and controversial contemporary phenomenon. In 2005, the United Nations (UN) Department of Economic and Social Affairs reported that there were 191 million international immigrants (people residing in countries other than that of their birth). That figure fluctuates from year to year, as some immigrants are repatriated and others leave voluntarily or flee their native lands. The reasons they move are various and complicated, but the net result is a constant flow of people across borders. The arrival of these new peoples has always been a source of controversy of greater or lesser intensity depending on who was trying to settle where, in what numbers, and for what reasons. No two cases are identical.

The immigrant question has always been important for the United States. As the admonition to "bring me your tired, your huddled masses" on the Statue of Liberty heralds, the United States is a quintessential immigrant state, with waves of immigrants from various places arriving at different times in the country's history to constitute one of the world's most nationally and ethnically diverse populations. Sometimes the process of new immigrant waves has been orderly, open, and noncontentious, but it has also been surrounded by considerable disagreement and rancor.

Immigration has become particularly contentious in the United States over the last two decades because of the large-scale movement of Mexicans and Central Americans across the U.S.-Mexico border. The actual numbers involved are difficult to estimate accurately, because many of the immigrants have been so-called irregular or illegal immigrants who, by definition, are unaccounted for when they arrive. UN figures from 2005 estimated that about 20 percent of immigrants in the world are in the United States, over half of whom have entered across the U.S.-Mexico border, mostly illegally. The situation is starker in much of Europe.

Although the American situation is a current manifestation of concern over immigration, it is by no means the only place where the question sits on the public agenda. Europe, for instance, is host to a considerably larger immigrant population than the United States, especially in a few select countries such as Germany. To understand the nature of the concern—and to place the current U.S. debate into a global context—it is necessary to look at the immigration question more broadly.

Principle: Human Population Movement Forms, Dynamics, and Human Suffering

Population movement is a normal, daily occurrence in much of the world. Some countries are more permissive about letting citizens leave (emigrate) or enter from other countries (immigrate), but some population movement is a regular part of international activity, and one that is arguably increasing in a globalizing world in which international commerce of all kinds is increasing. Employing an accepted definition used by Koser that an international immigrant is "a person who stays outside his usual country of residence for at least one year," the global total of immigrants today is over 200 million people. Immigration is, however, only one, if the largest, form of human movement. Understanding the problem in a contemporary context requires beginning by classifying different categories of those who traverse borders.

Forms of Movement

There are various categories of people who seek to leave their homes to go to other locations. Immigration is the historically largest and most generic category, but there are others. Two that will be explored are refugees and asylum seekers, both because of their prominence in contemporary international relations and because they are often the result (or even the cause) of great human suffering.

Immigrants are often subdivided into more or less controversial categories. Legal immigrants are those individuals who have migrated to a country through legal channels, meaning their immigration is recognized and accepted by the host government. Countries allow immigrants into the country for a variety of reasons and in different numbers depending on the needs or uses they may have for such populations. Parts of Europe—notably Germany—have long admitted workers from places such as Turkey to augment shrinking workforces as their populations age, and the United States has historically given priority status to people with particularly needed education and technical skills, such as scientists and engineers from developing countries like India.

There are, however, other, more controversial categories of immigrants. In the contemporary debate, the most controversial are so-called *irregular immigrants*. The UN Department of Economic and Social Affairs defines this class of people as "those who enter a country without proper authorization or who have violated the terms of stay of the authorization they hold, including by overstaying." Other terms for irregular status include illegal, undocumented, and unauthorized immigrants. As Koser points out, "there are around 40 million irregular immigrants worldwide, of whom perhaps one-third are in the United States." The most publicized and largest part of that total are irregular by virtue of illegal entry into the country; some of the most problematical, however, are individuals who have entered the country legally but have overstayed the conditions of their residence, as in not leaving after student or temporary work visas have expired. This latter category is troublesome because of possible connections to anti-American activities such as terrorism.

A special category of immigrants is refugees. Broadly speaking, refugees are the most prominent example of what the UN Commission on Human Rights (UNCHR) calls "forcibly displaced people," who, according to 2017 UNCHR figures, number about sixty-five million. The largest numbers of people within this category are refugees (displaced people living outside their native countries) at about 21.3 million, internally displaced persons or IDPs (refugees within their own countries) at about forty-three million, and asylum seekers (people who have sought international protection but whose applications have not been acted upon). The Refugee Act of 1980 in the United States borrows its definition from the 1951 UN Convention Relating to the Status of Refugees (and its 1967 Protocol), saying a refugee is "a person outside of his or her country of nationality who is unable or unwilling to return because of persecution or a well-grounded fear of persecution on account of race, religion, nationality, membership in a particular social group, or political opinion." Those who seek refugee status often come from developing countries where human misery is both economic and political, meaning that it is sometimes difficult to determine why a particular refugee or group of refugees seeks to migrate. As Koser points out, "though an important legal distinction can be made between people who move for work purposes and those who flee conflict and persecution, in reality the two can be difficult to distinguish."

International and internal refugees are most prominently associated with conflict zones and especially civil conflicts. One of the world's most well-publicized instances of refugee dynamics is taking place in the Middle East, currently highlighted by the estimated 4.9 million refugees of the Syrian civil war in 2016.

The dynamics of immigration as a global issue requires looking at the phenomenon from at least three vantage points. The first is the motivation for immigration: Why do people emigrate from one place to another, and what roles do they fulfill when they become immigrants? The second is where the phenomenon of immigration is the most and least evident on a global scale. Although it is generally true that the global pattern is one of people moving from the developing to the developed world, the pattern is selective and regionally distinctive. The third concern is immigration as a problem, both globally and locally. Are there distinctive problems that are created by current, ongoing patterns, and are these likely to get better or worse in the future? The answers to these questions, in turn, help frame the context of the problems associated with immigration across the Mexican border into the United States.

Immigration Motivations and Functions

One way to think about the reasons for immigration is in terms of "push" and "pull" factors. Push factors are motives to leave a particular political jurisdiction—conditions that make people want to leave or that push them out. Pull factors, on the other hand, refer to perceived positive attributes to attract immigrants to particular destinations—or serve to pull people to different locations. When push and pull factors are in proximity, as is the case with parts of Central America and the United States and with areas of North Africa and the Middle East and the European Union (EU) area—the immigration pipeline is particularly strong.

The most obvious—virtually tautological—push factor is to improve one's living conditions by relocation. People decide to leave for both political and economic reasons: politically to avoid conflict or discrimination in their homeland, and economically in the hope or promise of a materially better life in the country to which they immigrate. This basic statement of motivation has numerous variations, as Choucri and Mistree enumerate: "the most obvious patterns of international migration today include the following: migration for employment; seasonal mobility for employment; permanent settlements; refugees who are forced to migrate; resettlement; state-sponsored movements; tourism and ecotourism; brain drains and 'reversals' of brain drains; smuggled and trafficked people; people returning to their country of origin; environmental migration and refugees from natural shortages or crises; nonlegal migration; and religious pilgrimage."

History's most dramatic migrations have had political upheaval as an underlying theme. As Koser points out, "large movements of people have always been associated with significant global events like revolutions, wars, and the rise and fall of empires; with epochal changes like economic expansion, nation-building, and political transformations; and with enduring challenges like conflict, persecution, and dispossession." These dramatic and tragic events are still obvious in places such as Syria, and they are augmented in places touched by terrorism, notably in Middle Eastern locations where IS has a presence and especially where they are being evicted.

The economic motivation, to move somewhere where economic opportunities are better than those where one lives, is nothing new. As Choucri and Mistree summarize, "during good times people migrate to find better opportunities; during bad times people migrate to escape more difficult circumstances." In either situation, the motivating factor is opportunity, which is manifested in the availability of jobs because, as Choucri and Mistree add, "To the extent that population growth exceeds a society's employment potential, the probability is very high that people will move to other countries in search of jobs."

Demographics also enter the picture. Population growth rates are highest in developing countries, and that means the rising number of job seekers is greatest in these countries relative to the number of available jobs. In the developed world, on the other hand, population growth rates are much lower (in some cases below levels to maintain current population sizes), the overall population is aging, and thus the percentage of citizens in the active workforce is diminishing. Goldstone explains the consequence: "the developed countries' labor forces will substantially age and decline, constraining economic growth in the developed world and raising demands for immigrant workers." Indeed, there are estimates that the developed countries that will be most successful in the future are those that are best able to augment their shrinking workforces with immigrant labor. This simple dynamic dictates pressure for population migration from developing to developed countries globally.

The kinds of talents that immigrants can contribute come in different categories that make their acceptance more or less enthusiastic. The smallest and most welcome category of immigrants is what the United Nations refers to as "highly skilled workers." These workers, generally highly educated and possessing scientific or engineering expertise at the cutting edge of the global economy, are the subject of "brain drains" in one direction or the other.

Far more problematical are the economic immigrants who have comparatively low skill levels. They are a double-edged sword for the countries into which they move. On one hand, they provide labor when it is in short supply, and particularly in low-paying or undesirable areas. Koser refers to these kinds of jobs as "3D jobs: dirty, difficult, or dangerous." He points out that "in the majority of advanced economies, migrant workers are overrepresented in agriculture, construction, heavy industry, manufacturing, and services—especially food, hospitality, and domestic services." Martin adds that these kinds of jobs are "the work magnet that stimulates illegal immigration."

Unskilled immigrants—especially irregular immigrants—pose a particular moral and practical dilemma for receiving states. These immigrants do jobs that the citizens are either unwilling to do or that they will not do at the lower wages that migrants will accept (especially irregular migrants). Thus, without a pool of such laborers, vital services either would not be done or would only be done at higher costs. The alternative to migrant labor is more expensive indigenous labor, which would demand higher wages (federal minimum wages in the United States at least), which would ripple upward through the wage system (there would be relatively fewer laborers for other jobs, making their labor more valuable). The dilemma is that quotas on legal immigration are often far too restrictive to produce an adequate-sized legal migrant pool to do the jobs migrants do, and if the current "underground" economy went aboveboard and hired only legally registered immigrants, employers would have to pay them higher wages, provide benefits, and do other things that would raise the costs of their labor. This dynamic underlies much of the American debate and controversy over irregular immigrants from Mexico and Central America.

Refugees present a separate problem. Generally, they can also be divided into skilled and unskilled groups, with the skilled often constituting professionals from the country from which they flee, and the unskilled composed mainly of subsistence farmers and the like. The skilled parts of the population are more likely to be absorbed into the country to which they flee (although generally at much lower standards of living), whereas the unskilled generally cannot be absorbed and become a burden on the country or on international bodies such as the UNCHR. Moreover, most refugees are from developing countries and flee to adjacent countries, which are also poor and thus lacking the resources to tend to their new citizens. Most of the Syrian refugees, for instance, have fled to adjacent countries such as Turkey, Lebanon, Jordan, and Iraq, which have difficult political and economic problems already.

The World Situation: The Human Tragedy Factor

There are two basic, overlapping continuing trends in worldwide immigration. The first is demographic: the majority of this population movement is from the developing to the developed world, and especially to Europe and North America. This trend is not new, but it has gained greater cogency in light of the terrorist problem that may accompany immigration from some places. In addition, that immigration is increasing numerically: there are more immigrants worldwide than there have been. Part of this latter trend can be at least partially explained by the overall increase in world population. A significant element, however, is demographic, based in aging populations in the developed world and the consequent need to import younger workers both to sustain economic activity and to support an aging and unproductive population.

The other trend is political. Fragile countries in parts of the developing world are disintegrating into violence with a multinational basis along ethnic and religious lines, and the result is the furtive, extremely bloody and gut-wrenching violence against population segments, including innocent and often defenseless civilians, of which Syria and South Sudan are currently the most publicized examples. IS atrocity against occupied population on territories claimed as part of the crumbling Caliphate also provides additional instances of human atrocity against others. The worst cases are currently in the Middle East (see Snow, *The Middle East, Oil, and the U.S. National Security Policy* for examples).

Population movements across political boundaries are always controversial to some extent. Unless the people seeking to move are highly desired and have great contributions to make that are obvious to the recipients (Indian scientists and engineers moving to Silicon Valley, for instance), there will be resistance in the receiving country, if for no other reason than that those who wish or feel compelled to migrate are somehow different from those who already live in the host country. The "pull" in the push-pull relationship will, in other words, generally always be restrained in some way. Germans may need foreign workers to make up for demographic limits, but that does not necessarily mean all Germans welcome them. The same is true for Americans regarding immigrants from across the southern border.

These demographic and political trends are likely to increase in the future. To reiterate Goldstone's points, "the developed countries' labor forces will substantially age and decline, constraining economic growth in the developed world and raising the demand for immigrant workers." The rate at which populations are aging, and how governments respond to this problem, varies greatly, with different consequences. Japan, for instance, has one of the world's most rapidly aging populations and has been very reluctant to allow non-Japanese immigrants into the country, for cultural reasons. This is already having two effects. First, it means that a shrinking portion of the population is part of the productive workforce that produces, among other things, the wealth needed to support older, retired Japanese. Second, it means a contraction in productivity and also population. The cumulative effect of these dynamics is the projection of a smaller and less economically prominent Japan in the future, a fate shared by other countries such as China, as described in chapter 3. The problem is not yet severe in the United States but it could become so if current nativist (e.g., "America First") sentiments dampen the desire of developing world economic immigrants to seek homes in America.

There is, of course, a wild card in the interaction between demographic and political imperatives: terrorism. A detailed discussion of terrorism is reserved for chapter 14, but terror has infected the question of migration, making it an added, and especially volatile and controversial, part of the general discussion of migration. Terrorism is pushing many people out of their homes and into the queue of migrants. It is also creating anti-migrant, including anti-refugee, sentiments in many of the countries where the pull of needing economic immigrants is strong. This dynamic is especially evident in Europe, but it has provided an additional emotional basis to discussions in the United States as well. The bottom line of this phenomenon is the fear that allowing immigrants into a country will increase the likelihood that terrorists will be admitted as part of that influx.

The terrorist phenomenon pervades migration in at least three related ways. First, a great deal of the current surge in migration comes from the Middle East, which is also the source of most world terrorism. Even populations that have historically welcomed migrants from Islamic countries—the Germans and Turkish immigrants, for instance—have become wary of foreign intruders. Second, terrorist activities, and especially the atrocities committed by IS and some of its affiliates in the Middle East and Africa, are the cause of much flight, and especially the flood of refugees seeking to flee to the developed world. Third, the great fear in many European and American locations is that foreign terrorists from the Middle East will penetrate their countries disguised as economic or political refugees or immigrants, thus increasing anxieties. Anxiety over admitting people who are "different" has always been an immigration concern. The fear of increasing terror adds to that concern.

The scale of immigration, from the developing to the developed world, is not going to go away. If anything, it will increase in the future. As Goldstone suggests, "Current levels of immigration from developing to developed countries are paltry compared to those that the forces of supply and demand might soon create across the world." The degree to which this likely trend is a concern depends on whether one views immigration as a problem or not.

Application: The Continuing U.S. and European Experiences

Those on the receiving end of population migration have various, sometimes contradictory reasons for accepting or rejecting the influx of new peoples into their countries. In contemporary international affairs, the largest incentive to add new people from outside is the need for additional sources of labor in developed countries. Humanitarian concerns over the plight of beleaguered people also enter the calculus. On the negative side in the present system, there is the danger that in admitting desirable new individuals and groups, one will also allow undesirable, even dangerous people into the country in the process. The result of this dynamic tension is political controversy that enters into national and international considerations.

The two places where this concern is greatest today are in the United States and in Europe. Both are concerned about the quantity and quality of outsiders who seek entry, although the concerns are both substantively and qualitatively different. The United States has a smaller (but not nonexistent) need for immigrant labor, but is more concerned about the excess volume involved and problems it creates. It has a secondary concern with terrorists entering the country. Europe, on the other hand, has a large need for immigrant labor, which has made it a much larger recipient of that immigration. Since much of that movement comes from the Middle East and North Africa, it has a much larger concern with terrorists entering the EU area. The political challenge in the United States has been how to restrict immigrants, symbolized by the debate over building a fence the length of the U.S.-Mexican border. In the EU, the debate is over the loss of sovereign control of borders due to EU actions to take over the boundary regulation function, the most dramatic example of which is the role of that dispute in the Brexit decision.

The U.S.-Mexican Border Problem

The migration of large numbers of people across the border from Mexico and Central America has been an American political issue since the 1990s, when the U.S. population of irregular immigrants increased from an estimated four million to twelve million. There has always been partisan disagreement about how much of a problem (if any) this migration across the long, porous frontier between the United States and its southern neighbors creates and what to do about it. Especially with the rise of Donald J. Trump, those dedicated to reducing the immigrant population or stanching the flow have gained the ascendancy. The threat of possible terrorist penetration has been added in the form of proposed bans on immigrants and refugees from certain Muslim countries.

The border situation also has its own unique, exacerbating characteristics. As a developed-developing world phenomenon, the U.S.-Mexico border case is intensified by the nature of the border. With 1,933 miles of mostly desolate, rural topography, it is a very long and difficult frontier to "seal," as proponents of "the Wall" advocate. At the same time, the U.S.-Mexico boundary is the world's only direct land border between the developed and developing worlds.

The U.S.-Mexico case is also distinguished by its sheer volume and the accompanying complexity of the problem. No one, of course, knows exactly how many irregular immigrants are in the United States, and those who voice the greatest concern would argue that official estimates of around twelve million cited earlier are probably too low. This is a larger number than for any other country, although there are several countries such as Germany that have a higher percentage of immigrants in the population than the United States. Moreover, the problem is geographically distinct within the United States: About one-quarter of all estimated irregular immigrants in the United States in 2008 were in California (2.85 million), followed by Texas (1.68 million), and Florida (840,000). The issue is also a complex one. The concern about the U.S.-Mexico border not only involves immigration, but the integrity of the frontier also has strong implications for the trafficking of illicit drugs into the United States and potentially for terrorists seeking to penetrate American soil.

The Physical Problem

Almost all the solutions proposed for the U.S.-Mexico border revolve around some better way to "secure" it, which means roughly to make it more difficult for unauthorized people to come across the border into the United States. The most extreme advocacies call for "sealing" the border, which generally equates to making it impossible physically for unwanted outsiders to intrude on American soil. Before examining the desirability of such a policy and what it would entail, it is necessary first to examine the physical problem posed by the unique nature of the American border.

The territorial boundaries of the United States are among the most extensive, complex, and difficult to secure of any country on earth. These borders can be divided into sea and land boundaries, each of which poses different priorities and problems. The borders are extensive. The land border between the United States and Canada, for instance, is slightly more than 5,500 miles long (the boundary between Canada and the forty-eight contiguous states is 3,987 miles and between Canada and Alaska is 1,538 miles). Added to the 1,933-mile land border between the United States and Mexico, the total American land border is 7,358 miles. Most of the U.S.-Canada border is hardly secured at all, particularly the extensive stretch between Lake Superior and the Pacific Ocean and the Alaska-Canada border. The sea borders of the United States are even more extensive. Two measures are normally used to describe these borders: coastline and shoreline. The coastline generally refers to a line drawn along the intersection of the coast and the ocean, not allowing for bays, inlets, and other coastal features and is 12,383 miles. The shoreline measures the topography of the coast, including the shores of bodies of water that empty into the oceans and seas and is 88,633 miles.

Effectively securing these borders is clearly a formidable task. The current effort concentrates on the 1,933-mile Mexican land border and two forms of security: a border fence and larger numbers of Border Patrol and other human assets to monitor activity. Funding has proven difficult to obtain. It is not clear that an "immigrant-proof" solution is possible. As former New Mexico governor Bill Richardson has been quoted as saying, "If we put up a ten-foot fence, somebody is going to build an eleven-foot ladder."

The Border Threats

The difficulty surrounding the U.S.-Mexico border is really more than one problem. Its most prominent feature has been the level and consequences of irregular immigration across the border, and that aspect will be examined most prominently. In addition, there is a question of the movement of illicit narcotics and the consequent criminal behavior they bring, and of the possible penetration of the United States by terrorists. It is not entirely clear that the most extensive and most important of these threats are the same.

Immigration

Immigration is, and always has been, an integral part of the American experience. Although for most times and purposes, it has been one of the proud elements of the American heritage, it has had its dark side in the form of negative reactions to the migration of some people to the United States at different times. Throughout American history, what is now referred to as illegal immigration has always been a part of the pattern, and the history of immigration politics is largely an attempt to regulate both the quantity and quality (measured both in point of origin and in skill levels) of immigration to the country. For Americans, the immigration problem along the U.S.-Mexico border is the most dramatic and contentious manifestation of a worldwide pattern of international immigration.

The sheer volume of irregular immigrants in the United States is the heart of the perceived problem in the American political debate. More specifically, it is about irregular immigration by Mexicans and Central Americans into the country in numbers that exceed ten million and may be much higher. Efforts to secure the border are aimed at reducing or eliminating the flow of irregulars into the country; efforts to apprehend and deport irregular immigrants already in the country are aimed at reducing those numbers.

Why is this immigrant flow a problem? Generally speaking, two reasons are cited, and they help illuminate the parameters of the concern. One concern is the alleged criminality associated with illegal residents. Statistical evidence is ambivalent, but those who hold this concern point particularly to greater incidence of violent crime in places where illegal immigrants are concentrated. The other concern is the demand on social services (e.g., schools and medical facilities) made by irregular immigrants and their families, a concern accentuated by the fact that most irregular immigrants pay only user taxes (e.g., sales tax) but do not contribute to the Social Security fund or through payroll deduction, for instance.

These two distinct problems point to a basic division within the irregular immigrant population. There are, in essence, two groups that make up that community. By far the most numerous are *economic immigrants*. There is no systematic indication that their participation in or contribution to crime is any greater than that of the population at large; indeed, it may be lower. The other group is comprised of *criminal immigrants*, individuals who enter the country to engage in criminal behavior, most notably people engaged in narcotics trafficking in one way or another. This group brings with it the violent crime that has ravaged Mexico in particular, and is the source of virtually all the concern over the impact of immigration on crime.

Dividing the irregular immigrant community into these two categories helps in understanding the problem and what to do about it. One must begin by asking the question, why do immigrants come illegally to the country? In the case of the economic immigrants, the answer is economic opportunity: jobs. This should not be surprising, given the disparity of wealth between the United States and Mexico and Central America, and it is why economic immigrants migrate worldwide.

The vast majority of irregular economic migrants have been displaced Mexicans and Central Americans who have come to the United States in the pursuit of economic advancement, including the accumulation of enough money to send remittances back to their local communities and families at home. Their migration is like economic migration everywhere, moving from where there is no economic opportunity (jobs) to where such opportunities exist.

The immigration problem and its solution take on a different complexion put in these terms. If there are jobs available that irregular immigrants fill, then there must be a labor need that these immigrants fulfill. Generally, this means low-skill, low-paying jobs, often with one or more of the so-called 3D characteristics of being dirty, dangerous, or difficult. If there were Americans willing to do these jobs at wages that employers were willing to pay and that produced services at prices consumers would pay, there would not be jobs, and there would be no incentive for migrants to immigrate. That they have done so and continue to do so indicates not only that such opportunities exist, but that they have not been sated. That is simple supply and demand.

Moreover, the dynamics suggest that there is not only a market for immigrant labor but also a continuing market for irregular immigrant labor. Given the reaction against irregular immigration, this assertion seems anomalous, but it is nonetheless true. The simple fact is that illegal workers have advantages to employers over legal immigrants: They will work at lower wages (they have no bargaining ability on wages), they will work longer (they are covered by no labor laws or contracts), and they do not require employers to pay benefits such as Social Security taxes or health insurance. For highly labor-intensive work such as lawn care, roofing, or garbage collection, hiring irregular laborers has economic advantages for employers that allow them to maximize profits while minimizing costs to themselves and consumers. Moreover, if the kinds of jobs that irregular immigrants typically perform became part of the regular economy, labor costs would increase (to minimum wage, at the least), which in turn would drive up the costs of the services and the wages of other lower-end jobs. A large number of Americans would feel the impact in their wallets. Advocates of tighter border control and the expulsion of illegal immigrants rarely mention these consequences.

This places the problem in a different context than those who simply call for expelling irregular immigrants like to frame the question. Do all the advocates *really* want to get rid of irregular immigrants? Because they are doing jobs that either would not get done at all or only at higher labor costs otherwise, the answer is not clear. If all employees, including current irregulars in the underground economy, were to enter the mainstream, then suddenly these workers would be paying all taxes (rather than just regressive levies such as sales taxes), thereby contributing to things like Social Security and Medicare/Medicaid and making themselves less of a social services burden. But doing so would mean employers would have to increase their own efforts and expenses, which they clearly are reluctant to do. As a result, some people publicly oppose illegal immigration but employ irregular immigrants.

There is some indication that the same demographics that combined to create the immigrant surge may also alleviate it with time. In a June 7, 2010, *Newsweek* article, Campos-Flores points out that fertility rates in Mexico have declined dramatically "from 6.7 children per woman in 1970 to 2.1 today," according to World Bank figures. The result will be a gradual reduction in the number of young people entering the Mexican labor market, from over 850,000 per year in the early 2000s to about 300,000 per year in 2030, a number the Mexican economy can more adequately absorb. Some of this is already occurring (projected new members of the labor force this year are down to 750,000), but with a rub: "Mexican migration will taper off further just as baby boomers begin retiring in 2012," according to Campos-Flores.

Narcotics

The drug trade across the U.S.-Mexico frontier is both an immigration and a narcotics policy problem. Most of the illegal drugs that enter the United States are shipped through Mexico and then across the border, making it a border issue. As Shifter explains, "Mexico is the transit route for roughly 70 to 90 percent of the illegal drugs entering the United States. . . . Along the U.S.-Mexico border, the kidnapping trade, clearly tied to the drug trade, is flourishing." Andreas points out that increased American border security efforts exacerbate the drug problem: "adding thousands of new Border Patrol agents has had the perverse effect of entrenching smugglers rather than deterring immigrants since the problem of breaching the border is more difficult and requires help for some immigrants"; some of that assistance is provided by drug traffickers. Moreover, the drug and immigration efforts come into conflict with one another; they are conducted by different government agencies (e.g., the Border Patrol and the Drug Enforcement Agency) with different priorities and different cultures. Adding National Guard personnel to this mix, as was begun in 2010, only adds to the jurisdictional confusion.

The drug and immigration issues intersect when members of the various drug syndicates move across the border into the United States to better control their illicit operations. There is considerable evidence that Mexican drug cartels are now active in most large American cities and that they bring with them the drug-related violent crime that has become endemic on the Mexican side of the border. The numbers of immigrants who are part of criminal immigration are quite small compared to the economic immigrants, but their presence is amplified because of the spikes in violent crime that occur where they are present. This violence is mostly between members of various drug cartels, but inevitably it spills over into broader communities, inflaming anti-immigrant sentiments that are at least partially misdirected. These kinds of problems have already destabilized Mexican national and local politics, and there is a fear that the same thing could happen on the U.S. side of the border.

A more comprehensive view of drugs breaching the border includes an emphasis on reducing the market for drugs in the United States. Just as the availability of jobs has fueled economic immigration, so too has the demand for drugs fueled the growing flow of drugs into the country. If the demand for illegal drugs among Americans were to decrease (analogous to drying up jobs for irregular immigrants), the supply coming across the border would also likely decrease due to a decreased market. During the height of the "war on drugs" during the late 1980s and early 1990s, this approach was known as "demand-side," and although hardly anyone suggested it was a comprehensive solution to the problem, it could help by making the volume of trafficking across the border more manageable.

The difficulty is disentangling the narcotics and illegal immigration aspects of the effects of border leakage. They really are two almost entirely different problems with different sources, dynamics, and largely unrelated consequences. The only thing linking them is the obvious fact that both drugs and unauthorized immigrants come across the border illegally. Even the dynamics of the two enterprises are different, as are the goals and methods of the officials pursuing each priority.

Terrorism

Although there may be an arguable analogy between the immigration and drug problems, this comparison largely does not extend to the problem posed by the penetration of the United States by terrorists. For one thing, the terrorism threat is not a specifically U.S.-Mexico border problem. Terrorists can enter the United States from Mexico, but also from Canada or at airports or seaports anywhere in the country from different points of origin. Indeed, it is arguable that the greater emphasis placed on the Mexican border may mean a diminution of personnel and effort at other points of entry, making them more likely transit points than they would be in the absence of an immigration emphasis.

The terrorism threat, unlike the other two, is also more of a qualitative than a quantitative problem, and one that is managed in a distinctive way. Irregular economic immigration involves a very large volume of people breaching the border, but each individual poses little if any specific threat to the United States or its citizens. The problem that people perceive is the result of the overwhelming numbers of irregular immigrants and the collective burdens and problems they create. In contrast, there are relatively few terrorists against whose entry the United States must prepare, but the potential havoc that any one poses means that efforts must be essentially perfect or they can yield disastrous results. Thus, for instance, a boundary system that reduces the flow of economic immigrants across the Mexican border by 90 percent would have an enormous impact on the border issue, but the same effectiveness against terrorist penetration might be entirely unacceptable.

What separates the terrorism aspect of the problem in the American case from other components is that there are few, if any, terrorists in the population seeking to enter the country for legitimate economic reasons or criminal, drug-related reasons. This is especially true of Middle Eastern Islamic terrorists. There is no concentration of Muslim extremists in Mexico or Central America from which a pool of potential penetrators could be drawn, and any outsiders who might try to use the pipeline northward would be racially, ethnically, and linguistically distinct from those individuals and groups who move north. It is possible that such a pipeline could develop in the future if other methods of penetration become too forbidding, and in the absence of a major international barrier to crossing (e.g., the Wall), such routes might seem attractive. Taking active measures based in terror at this time, however, would be hard to justify. Terrorism is really *sui generis*, a special problem.

The European Problem

The migration problem for Europe is different. Most of the current concern is specifically related to the problem of terror that has increasingly consumed much of northern, NATO-related Europe, and the substance of migration more often involves refugees and asylum seekers than it does irregular immigrants. Terrorism containment is more pressing and difficult, because of the prior existence of enclaves of people from terrorist-vulnerable societies and the difficulty of monitoring new terrorists who might penetrate the EU area. Immigration by Mediterranean and Middle Eastern people is more established in Europe because of the ongoing need for foreigners across time. At the same time, the continuing influx and EU attempts to take over functions that ultimately affect control of borders has become a highly divisive issue. All these factors contrast with the American situation.

As events over the past two years or so clearly demonstrate, Europe is in the throes of an "epidemic" of limited, but often spectacular and gruesome, terrorist attacks that have caused some divisions both within and between European countries. Some of this debate is covered in chapter 14, but the simple fact is that Europe is more proximate to the Middle East crucible of terrorist activity than is North America, has welcomed and accepted people from these countries for generations, and given European demographics and geography, has a difficult time excluding all those who want to enter the EU area from the Middle East or North Africa. Europe is proximate to the problem, vulnerable to it, and partially as a consequence of economically motivated immigration policies, in a difficult position trying to stanch terrorist penetration.

The mix of immigrants and refugees is different in the American and European situations. This is also a matter of proximity and circumstance. Due to violent instability in the Muslim world, UNCHR statistics for June 2017 show that the three countries with the most refugees are all in the region close to Europe: Syria with 4.9 million, Afghanistan with 2.7 million, and Somalia with 1.5 million. Of these, the victims of the Syrian civil war represent the largest and most compelling problem. The nearly five million refugees are part of a larger IDP problem that more than doubles that number, and the vicious nature of the civil war makes the return of these refugees impossible in the near term. Surveys of Syrians in refugee camps in the region (principally Turkey) indicate all but about 5 percent hope to return to Syria when the civil war ends, but until they can, they are a tragic burden that spreads to Europe. Especially because of their large immigrant populations (the *CIA World Factbook* lists 2.7 percent of people in Germany as of Turkish ethnicity), they have a much more difficult time than do Americans denying them access.

This juxtaposition creates a unique construction of the problem for Europeans. Countries such as Germany both need and already have sizable migrant populations whom they have recruited because of labor shortages and do not want to alienate. In several European countries, these populations have not assimilated well, and the isolated ghetto environments in which they reside are seen as prime recruiting grounds for groups such as IS. Alienating or turning away refugees who might become immigrants is not a good way to build the loyalties that will dampen radicalization of parts of the population.

The recent spate of terrorist attacks in major northern European urban areas has heightened the urgency and salience of the migrant problem. An additional element that makes the identification of potential terrorists difficult lies in the fact that, in many cases, the countries from which the terrorists come are former colonies of the European countries that are their destinations and that, as a result, provide a special status for these individuals. Radicalized Libyans crossing the Mediterranean Sea for destinations in Italy and other southern European locales is one example, as are people from old French Union countries.

A final special circumstance surrounds how immigrants and refugees enter Europe and the ability of individual countries to regulate their movement and especially their ability to enter the sovereign territory of countries without obtaining permission from the governments of those countries. This problem was introduced in chapter 9 and bears some resemblance to the border issue in the United States. As suggested in the earlier discussion, it is probably not a coincidence that this issue is of salience in both the United States and the UK.

The migration dilemma pits the question of population movement against the enduring question of sovereignty. Economic immigration needs create the incentive for much of Europe to make it relatively easy to let people into the EU area and to facilitate their movement. Part of the economic union's structure is free movement of people across sovereign boundaries without restriction or even routine monitoring of who comes and goes, which facilitates the greater integration of the arrangement. That means, however, that anyone who can pass whatever barriers there are to entry into the EU territory cannot be excluded from any part of the union. That, in turn, means that individual states lose control over the gatekeeping function of those borders—a loss of sovereign control. This potential loss has been a rallying cry of those promoting stronger border measures in the United States. The events of 2015–2016 in the EU, depicted in the discussion of Brexit, enlivened that same concern in Great Britain as well. In the clash between a broader and more comprehensive union and British national sovereignty, the union was the clear loser.

Brexit has not spread beyond the British Isles to this point. The election of Emmanuel Macron in France signaled that the anti-immigrant, anti-refugee option exercised by the UK has not spread inexorably to the continent, and the fact that terrorist events have subsequently occurred on both sides of the English Channel further suggests that the connection between population movement and terror is not inexorable. It is almost certainly one IS purpose in its attacks on Europe to stir anti-immigrant sentiment and further to divide the immigrant/refugee population from the "native" populations of European countries. Whether the ploy will work remains to be seen.

Conclusion

Human migration is one of humankind's oldest and often most difficult phenomena. Most individuals prefer to live where they have always lived, and being uprooted and having to move is often a very traumatic and unpleasant experience. The inducement and trauma were probably less severe when there were far fewer people and migration was less encumbered by contact with other peoples who viewed the migrating population with fear, suspicion, even hatred. In a world where there are over seven billion people, places to migrate are far fewer. Moreover, the entire land surface of the world—other than Antarctica—is now under the sovereign control of some political authority, and those migrating must gain the permission of the occupying authority to take up residence.

The different forms of movement create varying problems and emotions, depending on circumstances. Normally immigration, the most generic description of movement, has been the least traumatic unless the migration of people from one locale to another is so massive as to activate nativist reactions in the receiving country. This has been the pattern in the United States, where people from an earlier generation of immigration have objected when people from somewhere else seek to settle in their sovereign space. The migration of Mexicans and other Central Americans across the southern border is just the most recent example. The current distinction may be the sheer volume of immigrants involved.

Controversy and emotion increase when the migration consists solely or in large measure of refugees seeking safety or asylum from disastrous conditions in their countries of origin. The causes of refugee flows are normally disputed by the government of the originating country, which may also consider the refugees radicals or political criminals. The decision to accept or reject refugees is difficult for the receiving country, because it likely strains relations with the government of the country of origin and may entangle it in the dynamics of what caused the refugee problem in the first place. The situation is amplified if there are sizable numbers of political asylum seekers among the fleeing refugees. Humanitarian suffering and deprivation counterbalance these factors, especially when those seeking refuge are part of an even larger population of IDPs in the country of origin. These concerns all swirl around the ongoing tragedy in Syria.

The contemporary situation adds two contradictory factors to the issue: demographic needs and possible terrorist penetration. The demographic imperative is the need for additional young members of the labor force in developed countries where declining birth rates produce inadequate numbers of entrants into the job market and where outside augmentation is necessary to keep the economy operating at peak levels. The "pull" involved is especially great for highly skilled, educated immigrants, but it means that people from economically disadvantaged developing world countries are attractive, needed commodities pulled toward the more prosperous but labor-deficient developed world.

The other side, pushing against this dynamic, arises from the fact that some of the workforce that is needed comes from parts of the world that also produce terrorists. It is a national imperative everywhere in the developed world to exclude from their sovereign territory those who would do it harm. The difficulty is in how to be certain that economic immigrants can be adequately vetted to exclude terrorists from sneaking in along with legitimate and welcome people willing to migrate. This juxtaposition can create a very emotional, volatile political condition in both sending and receiving countries, made even worse when massive numbers of refugees fleeing violence in places such as Syria are added to the mix.

In the contemporary environment, both aspects of this are especially evident in the EU area and less so in the United States. The most prosperous parts of the EU—especially the industrialized countries of northern Europe—both need additions to their workforce and face the reality and prospects of terrorist attacks against them. The American border problem is emotional but less dangerous: some Americans dislike the intrusion on their land by such large numbers of people from south of the border, but other than some drug dealers, it has not been demonstrated that they pose any other major national security problem.

The question of human migration is, as stated at the outset, as old as human inhabitation of territory. It has always been a contentious dynamic, because of fears of the unknown when new people are added to whatever other fears people may possess. In the contemporary environment, the various issues surrounding different forms and motivations have intertwined demographic pulls with terrorist pushes. The result is a dynamic tension likely to be present for some time into the future.

Study/Discussion Questions

1. What is immigration? Into what categories are immigrants normally placed? Define, discuss, and compare each to the others. In particular, define and contrast categories of immigrants.
2. Why do people migrate? Use the "push-pull" analogy to help describe reasons for the differences. Apply this analysis to migration across the U.S.-Mexican frontier.
3. What are the demographic and political factors affecting migration trends worldwide? Describe each factor in detail. What basic trends arise from these observations?
4. Discuss the dynamics of contemporary migration in geographic and human terms. What basic trends arise from these observations, including implications for human suffering?
5. Describe the U.S.-Mexico border problem in physical terms and in terms of the threats posed by irregular immigrants crossing that line.
6. Who and what crosses the Mexican-American border illegally? What is the impact of each on the United States? How much of a problem does penetration by potential terrorists pose?
7. What is the nature of the European immigration problem? Discuss this problem in geographic, demographical, and jurisdictional terms, as well as links to terrorism. How does this problem relate to the Brexit decision?
8. Who has the greatest immigration problem in the world today? Is it receiving countries and areas such as the United States or the European Union, or is it those countries whose citizens wish to or feel they must leave? Compare and contrast the seriousness and consequences of the U.S. and EU cases.

Bibliography

Alden, Edward. *The Closing of the American Border.* New York: HarperCollins, 2009.
Andreas, Peter. "Politics on Edge: Managing the U.S.-Mexico Border." *Current History* 105, no. 688 (February 2006): 64–68.

Berjas, George J. *Heaven's Door: Immigration Policy and the American Economy*. Princeton, NJ: Princeton University Press, 2016.

Campos-Flores, Arian. "Don't Fence Them In: The Arizona of the Future Won't Suffer from Too Many Immigrants—But from Too Few." *Newsweek*, June 7, 2010, 34–35.

Central Intelligence Agency. *CIA World Factbook 2017*. Washington, DC: U.S. Central Intelligence Agency, 2017.

Choucri, Nazli, and Dinsha Mistree. "Globalization, Migration, and New Challenges to Governance." *Current History* 108, no. 717 (April 2009): 173–79.

Collett, Elizabeth. "Destination: Europe: Managing the Migrant Crisis." *Foreign Affairs* 92, no. 2 (March/April 2017): 150–56.

Flynn, Stephen. *America the Vulnerable: How Our Government Is Failing to Protect Us from Terrorism*. New York: Harper Perennials, 2005.

Gest, Justin. *The New Minority: White Working Class Politics in an Age of Inequality*. Oxford, UK: Oxford University Press, 2016.

Goldstone, Jack A. "The New Population Bomb: The Four Megatrends That Will Change the World." *Foreign Affairs* 89, no. 1 (January/February 2010): 31–43.

Haynes, Chris, S. Karthick Ramakrishnan, and Jennifer Merolla. *Framing Immigrants: News Coverage, Public Opinion, and Policy*. Washington, DC: Russell Sage Foundation, 2016.

"International Migration Levels, Trends, and Policies." *International Migration Report 2006: A Global Assessment*. New York: United Nations Department of Economic and Social Affairs/Population Division, 2006.

Jones, Reece. *Border Walls: Security and the War on Terror in the United States, India, and Israel*. New York: Zed, 2012.

Kingsley, Patrick. *The New Odyssey: The Story of the Twenty-First Century Refugee Crisis*. London: Liveright, 2017.

Koser, Khalid. "Why Immigration Matters." *Current History* 108, no. 717 (April 2009): 147–53.

Krauze, Enrique. "Furthering Democracy in Mexico." *Foreign Affairs* 85, no. 1 (January/February 2006): 54–65.

Krikorian, Mark. "Bordering on CAFTA: More Trade, Less Immigration." *National Review Online*, July 28, 2005. http://www.cis.org/CAFTA.

Maril, Robert Lee. *The Fence: National Security, Public Safety, and Illegal Immigration Along the U.S.-Mexican Border*. Lubbock: Texas Tech University Press, 2012.

Martin, Susan F. "Waiting Games: The Politics of US Immigration Reform." *Current History* 108, no. 717 (April 2009): 160–65.

McDonald-Gibson, Charlotte. *Cast Away: True Stories of Survival from Europe's Refugee Crisis*. New York: New Press, 2016.

O'Neil, Shannon. "The Real War in Mexico." *Foreign Affairs* 88, no. 4 (July/August 2009): 66–77.

Payan, Terry. *The Three U.S.–Mexico Border Wars: Drugs, Immigration, and Homeland Security*. Westport, CT: Greenwood, 2006.

Rockenbach, Leslie J. *The Mexican–American Border: NAFTA and Global Linkages*. Abingdon, UK: Routledge, 2001.

Rozenthal, Andres. "The Other Side of Immigration." *Current History* 106, no. 697 (February 2007): 89–90.

Shifter, Michael. "Latin America's Drug Problem." *Current History* 106, no. 697 (February 2007): 58–63.

Snow, Donald M. *Cases in International Relations*. 3rd ed. New York: Pearson Longman, 2008.

————. *The Middle East, Oil, and the U.S. National Security Policy.* Lanham, MD: Rowman & Littlefield, 2016.

2008 Global Trends: Refugees, Asylum-seekers, Returnees, Internally Displaced and Stateless Persons. New York: United Nations High Commission on Refugees, June 16, 2009.

Van Hear, Nicholas. "The Rise of Refugee Diasporas." *Current History* 108, no. 717 (April 2009): 180–85.

12

Global Climate Change

Paris and the Continuing Crisis and Controversy

Global climate change represents one of the clearest, yet most controversial, issues facing the world. It is clearly a problem that cannot be solved by the individual efforts of states, but must be done collectively if it is to be done successfully at all. It is controversial because there is substantial public, if not scientific, disagreement both about the nature and severity of the problem and over the structure and content of proposed solutions to climate change that is the clear byproduct of global warming, the most visible symbol of change. The controversy, centered in the United States, is over what is causing change.

This case study looks at the problem from two related vantage points. The first is the nature and extent of the problem, what does and does not require controlling, and who the most egregious offenders are. The second is an examination of the controversial process surrounding international efforts to deal with global climate change. The original lightning rod for this effort was the Kyoto Protocol of 1997, which expired in 2012. Attempts to implement and move beyond the actions prescribed in that treaty failed until the Paris Climate Agreement of 2015 and the fate and effectiveness of the Trump administration decision to withdraw from it in June 2017.

The issue of climate change—the extent to which the earth's climate is gradually warming due to human actions or natural processes—is one of the most controversial, divisive, and yet consequential problems facing international relations in the twenty-first century. No one, of course, favors a gradual or precipitous change in global climate because the consequences could be catastrophic. The issue contains a perceptual disconnect. Virtually all disinterested scientists (over 97 percent, according to a survey quoted in the May 16, 2013 *International Herald Tribune*) agree that the problem is real. Yet, as Helm points out, "the public gets more indifferent or even skeptical." Most of this skepticism is American.

Whereas some question whether global climate change exists at all, others predict dire consequences unless drastic measures are taken to curb the contributors to warming the earth, mostly through the burning of fossil fuels, and especially coal, in support of a broad variety of human activities. The fact that fossil fuels produce energy links global warming to energy, the subject of chapter 13. There are significant differences on the parameters of the problem (exactly what will be affected and how much), and on the quality of the science underlying claims on either side. As might be expected, projections diverge most when extrapolations are made far into the future.

Regardless of how serious the problem is, global warming is clearly a classic, full-blown transnational issue. As Eileen Claussen and Lisa McNeilly put it, "Climate change is a global problem that demands a global solution because emissions from one country can impact the climate in all other countries." Global warming, in other words, will be curbed internationally or likely it will not be controlled at all.

The underlying dynamic, if not its seriousness, can be easily stated. Global warming, the major manifestation of climate change, is the direct result of the release of so-called greenhouse gases into the atmosphere in volumes that are beyond the capacity of the ecosystem to eliminate naturally. There are several greenhouse gases. The largest part of the problem comes from the burning of fossil fuels such as petroleum, natural gas, coal, and wood, which releases carbon dioxide, methane, and nitrous oxide into the air in large quantities. According to U.S. Environmental Protection Agency (EPA) figures in 2017, emissions from fossil fuel burning and "forestry" account for 76 percent, methane for 16 percent, and nitrous oxides for 6 percent of emissions. The natural method of containing the amount of carbon dioxide and its ultimate damaging residue, carbon, in the atmosphere is the absorption and conversion of that gas in so-called carbon sinks, which separate the two elements (carbon and oxygen) and release them harmlessly back into the atmosphere. In nature, the equatorial rain forests have been where these sinks have historically done most of the work.

The problem of excessive carbon dioxide comes from both sides of the production and elimination process. The burning of fossil fuels, which are the source of much energy production and thus economic activity worldwide, has increased steadily over the last quarter century. Most of the added emissions have come from new contributors: countries entering the developed world by increasing production and their energy usage. China has been the most conspicuous example, because of both its geometrically growing need for and use of energy and its reliance on the dirtiest, most carbon-releasing fossil fuel—coal—to produce that energy. As a result, there is more carbon dioxide in the atmosphere than there used to be, and because carbon dioxide has a half-life of roughly a century, that which is emitted today will be around for a long time. At the same time, cutting down trees in the rain forests has reduced the number and quality of natural sinks, thereby reducing nature's ability to capture and convert carbon dioxide into innocuous elements.

The cumulative effect is that there is more carbon dioxide in the atmosphere than there used to be, and it acts as a greenhouse gas. What this means is that as heat from the sun radiates off the earth and attempts to return in an adequate amount into space to maintain current climate, carbon dioxide acts as a "trap" that retains the heat in the atmosphere rather than allowing it to escape. This blanketing effect keeps excess heat in the atmosphere, and the result is a warmer atmosphere and the phenomenon of global warming—net increases in atmospheric temperatures in specific locales and worldwide.

Responsibility for causing global warming and thus primary liability for doing something about it is also controversial. Significantly, the problem has become a mainstay of the global debate between the more industrially developed countries mostly located in the Northern Hemisphere and the less developed countries, many of which are located in the Southern Hemisphere. One aspect of this debate concerns causation and hence responsibility for the problem. Fossil fuel burning is at the heart of warming; clearly, much of the problem was originally created in the North, which has already gone through an industrializing process for which fossil-fuel-based energy was and remains an important component. From the vantage point of developing countries that aspire to the material success of the developed countries, this creates two points of contention. On one hand, they view developed countries as the cause of the problem and thus believe those countries should solve the problem by reducing emissions. On the other hand, developed countries ask them to refrain from the same kind of fossil-fuel-driven growth that they underwent, because doing so will simply make the greenhouse gas effect worse. The call for self-abnegation (under the banner of "sustainable development") by those countries that were fossil fuel self-indulgers strikes many in the developing world as hypocritical, to say the least. Currently, this aspect of the problem centers primarily on India and more particularly on China, which is now the world's largest producer of carbon dioxide (India is fourth).

The expired Kyoto Protocol of 1997 (so named after the Japanese city where it was finalized) was the most visible symbol of reaction to global warming and has become the lightning rod of the procedural and substantive debate over it. The protocol was a very technical, complicated document, the heart of which was a series of guidelines for the reduction of emissions almost exclusively by the developed countries. The requirements of the agreement raised controversy because of the differential levels of reduction they imposed, especially in the United States. The Kyoto Protocol expired in 2012, creating a sense of concern among supporters of international attempts to control climate change through international regulation and a sense of relief among skeptics. The process of modifying and extending the protocol began formally in Bali, Indonesia, on Kyoto's tenth anniversary on December 1, 2007, which laid out the principles to guide negotiations for a new, stronger agreement in Copenhagen, Denmark, which ultimately failed to produce an accord. The emphasis moved to Paris, where an agreement was reached in December 2015. Like its predecessors, the Paris Climate Agreement has been controversial, and its future effectiveness has been clouded by the announcement by the U.S. administration of its intent to withdraw issued in June 2017, an action far from unprecedented by the United States, which has a history of supporting, even championing, international environmental and other agreements and then denouncing them.

Principle: Global Climate Change

The urgency and importance of the Paris climate accord depends vitally on the urgency and importance of the problem. The debate over climate change is contentious. At least three related factors make a calm, rational debate over the extent and consequences of global warming difficult to conduct. The first is the absence of immediate consequences of whatever change is occurring. Over the past quarter century or more, climate change in the form of warming has indeed been occurring worldwide, but until recently the effects have been so gradual and generally small that either they have gone unnoticed by most people or have not been definitively attributable to the phenomenon. As the frequency of violent climatologically induced events such as tornados and hurricanes and weather fluctuations have increased, the connection is becoming harder to ignore. Global warming is blamed for numerous contemporary events, from the melting of polar ice caps to recent patterns of violent weather, but there is lingering disagreement about whether man-made global warming is the underlying culprit. Superstorm Sandy's effects, for instance, were almost certainly made worse by a rise in sea levels along the Jersey shore, but can that impact be traced to and blamed on global warming? Most people believe there probably is a connection. But a very vocal and well-financed opposition argues the contrary.

Second, there are abundant scientific disagreements about the parameters of the problem and its solution. Some of the disagreement is honest, some possibly self-interested, but for every dire prediction about future consequences, there is a rebuttal from somewhere. This debate often becomes shrill and accusatory, leading to confusion in the public about what to believe. In this confusion, the citizenry has a difficult time making reasoned assessments and consequent demands on policy makers to adopt standards.

Third, almost all the projections have until recently been sufficiently far in the future to allow considerable disagreement and to discourage resolution. One can argue that the scientific evidence to date is very strong one way or the other on various consequences of warming; the actual consequences are distant enough, however, that the extrapolation is subject to sufficient variation that scientists can take the same data and reach diametrically opposed conclusions. These extrapolations are often fifty or even one hundred years in the future, when most of the people at whom they are aimed will not even be alive to witness or be held accountable for them. Sea levels may indeed be rising, and if the trend is not arrested or reversed, some very expensive waterfront properties may find themselves submerged. Most of the owners (who also tend to be skeptics) will not be alive to get their feet wet when the rising ocean laps at their doorsteps.

The acrimonious debate over the melting of polar ice caps provides an example of this disagreement on rising ocean levels. There is no disagreement that ice caps are melting; the disagreement is about why and what this means. Those most worried about the global warming effects of climate change argue that the burning of fossil fuels is the culprit, and the consequences include rising ocean levels (mostly from melting in Antarctica) and ecological change (especially in the Arctic). Critics contend there is little evidence that the changes are not natural and dispute the notion of an accelerated rise in sea levels.

Parameters of Debate

That global climate is changing is not contested on any side of the debate over global warming. The Intergovernmental Panel on Climate Change (IPCC) has investigated the extent to which this has happened in the past and has concluded that the average surface temperature of the earth increased by about one degree Fahrenheit during the twentieth century and "that most of the warming observed over the past 50 years is attributable to human activities." (Much of the IPCC material in this section is from the 2001 report of Groups I–III of the IPCC, cited in the bibliography.) Extrapolating from trends in the last century, the IPCC predicted additional warming between 2.2 and 10 degrees Fahrenheit (1.4 and 5.8 degrees Celsius) in this century. The primary culprits are the greenhouse gases cited in the Kyoto Protocol that result from deforestation (and its destruction of carbon sinks), energy production from the combustion of fossil fuels (natural gas, oil, and coal), transportation (primarily cars and trucks, but also trains and other modes), cattle production (methane gases), rice farming, and cement production. Factors such as conservation and the increasing use and economic competitiveness of nonfossil fuels are altering projections somewhat (see chapter 13), but the basic parameters and dynamics hold.

A variety of effects has been observed and attributed to these changes. In some areas, birds are laying eggs a few weeks earlier than they used to, butterflies are moving their habitats farther up mountains to avoid lowland heat, and trees are blooming earlier in the spring and losing their leaves later in the fall. Any of these changes can be dismissed as of low relative concern, but there are more fundamental changes alleged with more obvious consequences. Warming, the IPCC II reports, shows that snow accumulation is decreasing worldwide, as is the global supply of ice pack. At the same time, glaciers are retreating worldwide (some of the most dramatic American examples are in places like Glacier National Park in Montana), sea levels and ocean temperatures have risen, and rainfall patterns in many regions have changed as well. In addition, there is evidence that permafrost is thawing in the polar areas, that lakes are freezing later and thawing earlier, and that even some plant and animal species have declined and may disappear due to changes in climate.

Some of the most dramatic examples involve the effects on coastal regions. The projected problems arise from both the gradual rise of oceanic levels and the warming of ocean waters. Both are a concern because of the large and growing portion of populations residing in coastal locations (it is, for instance, a major demographic reality in the United States that the population is gradually moving out of the central parts of the country toward more temperate coastal regions).

The extent of these effects, of course, depends on the amount of change caused by global warming. IPCC II data project an average rise of between six and thirty-six inches in sea levels by 2100. Using the higher figure, the impact on some countries would be dramatic. A thirty-six-inch rise would inundate territory in which ten million people live in Bangladesh alone, forcing their relocation to scarce higher land. The same increase would cover 12 percent of the arable land of the Nile River delta in Egypt, which produces crops on which over seven million people are dependent. Some estimates suggest the island country of Vanuatu in the South Pacific would simply disappear under the rising waters. Many resort and retirement communities along the American Atlantic shoreline and the Florida peninsula could be affected catastrophically. Some already have been. Worldwide, it is estimated that forty-five million people would be displaced.

Warming ocean water could also have dramatic effects, for instance, by affecting ocean currents that now have an influence on climate in various parts of the world. The Atlantic Gulf Stream, for instance, could be affected by warmer water coming from polar areas, changing patterns for the coastal United States and Europe. As an example, Gulf Stream effects that tend to keep major hurricanes off parts of the American coast (e.g., the South Carolina Lowcountry) could and in some instances have been diverted, resulting in new patterns of hurricane, tornado, and storm impacts. Large-scale changes in patterns of ocean circulation are possible worldwide. The cumulative effect, according to the IPCC, could be "a widespread increase in the risk of flooding for human settlements (tens of millions of inhabitants in settlements studied) from both increased heavy precipitation and sea level rise" (IPCC II).

The Skeptics

The consensus on climate change is not shared universally. As weather patterns have become more volatile and the effects of climate-based events have become increasingly frequent and calamitous, it has become impossible to deny that climate is changing for the worse. The thrust of counterarguments has drifted from denial of change to causation and the accuracy of apocalyptical projections if something is not done to arrest and reverse current trends.

The newer thrust, most vociferously associated with the current American administration, raises questions about whether fluctuations are natural historical anomalies or are "man-made," a euphemism for change as the result of human activity. Since the human activity most often associated with warming is CO_2 emissions caused by fossil fuel burning, skepticism of man-made causes is mostly associated with champions of the fossil-fuel-producing industries. The critics also question the accuracy and severity of some long-term projections.

Some scientists—admittedly, a relative few—disagree with the accuracy of these projections and the direness of the consequences that they project. There is little disagreement about the historical record (i.e., the amount of climate change in the last century) because that is based on observable data that can be examined for accuracy. There is, however, some disagreement on the precise causes of change (e.g., scientists affiliated with the power industry tend to downplay the impact of energy production as part of denying man-made culpability).

There is also disagreement on projections of trends and effects extrapolated into the future. The main source of this disagreement is the fact that projections are based not in observations of effects in a future that has not yet occurred, but are instead based on projections of historically grounded observations into a future the exact dimensions of which cannot be known or entirely predicted. It is, in other words, easier to predict things that have happened than things that have not and may not happen. Extrapolation becomes more uncertain the further predictions are cast into the future, and thus there is an increased level of disagreement the further into the future one goes. Because the deleterious effects of global warming are argued to be cumulative and thus more serious the further into the future one makes projections, the basis for lively, at times acrimonious, discussions is thus built into the scientific debate.

There tend to be three criticisms of climate change that scientists can phrase in terms of questions. The first is the factual content of the warnings: How much effect will global warming have? A second, corollary question is how much will those effects accumulate under different assumptions about natural and man-made adjustments to these effects? Third, how difficult are the solutions?

The problem, of course, is that there is strenuous disagreement on all these matters. Consider, for instance, the projections on how much average surface temperatures will increase in this century if action is not taken. Estimates range from one to ten degrees Fahrenheit, and that is a considerable range in terms of the consequences to the world and humankind. If the actual figure is at the upper end of that spectrum, then problems such as snow pack, glacier, and polar ice cap melting will be considerable, with oceans rising at the upper limits of predictions (around three feet). Parts of Tampa Bay and New Orleans, among other places, will be underwater unless levees are constructed to keep the water out, and Vanuatu may become the next Lost City of Atlantis (an analogy often made by climate change scientists). If the rise in mean surface temperature is closer to or at the lower extreme (a degree or so), however, the consequences are probably far less dire. Nobody, of course, knows how much less.

Who knows which part of the range is correct? The answer is that with any scientific certitude, no one does. The amount of warming is necessarily an extrapolation into a future that does not exist, after all, not an observation of something that does. Clearly, it is in the interests of those who either do not believe in the more severe projections or who would be most adversely affected by concerted efforts to reduce emissions to believe in the lower projections and thus to deny the more severe possibilities. Because of the severity of the consequences of change at the upper levels of estimation, most climate change scientists tend to base their concerns on these possibilities rather than at lower levels of consequence as a prudent hedge.

The layperson is left up in the air. Because the effects are not immediate and unambiguous, the average person has little way to answer the second question: What does all this mean? Is the world headed for an environmental catastrophe if something is not done to slow, stop, or reduce the phenomenon of global warming? The scientists on both sides of the issue are passionate and self-convinced, but they have not, by and large, made a case to the world's publics that is compelling, understandable, and convincing—one way or the other. In a world of more instantly consequential problems, it is hard to bring oneself to develop the passion that the advocates, regardless of scientific orientations, have on the issue.

This leads to the third question, which brings the concern full circle and forms a bridge to the climate change movement: What should be done about the problem? The immediate answer, of course, is that it depends on how bad the problem is. Most of the world's scientific community has accepted the basic science of those warning about the more dire consequences of not solving the global warming problem, and largely economic forces in the United States have been prominent among major powers (and greenhouse gas emitters) in denying or downplaying the problem and resisting international solutions. The major source of historic U.S. objection is not the veracity of climate change science, but is instead directed at the differential obligations for solving it that efforts like the Paris agreement prescribe: reductions with economic consequences that would make the American economy less competitive and the exclusion of developing-world countries with large pollution potentials from regulation. In important ways, it is a U.S.-China problem, as explored in the next section.

There is, of course, a hedge in answering the third question that reflects a deep American belief that technology will somehow find a way to ameliorate the problem, either by finding a way to decrease the emission of greenhouse gases or to increase the ability to absorb and neutralize those gases and their consequences, or to manage the transition to an energy future based in non-CO_2-emitting sources. That is the position often taken by the American energy and transportation industries, an approach that has worked to solve other problems at other times. The revolution in shale gas exploitation in the past several years may provide a transitional technological "fix" by allowing the substitution of less polluting natural gas for coal burning. It aids both sources of the problem. It allows the United States to reduce carbon emissions without submitting to something like the Paris system to which Americans such as President Trump object, and because it accomplishes this at very low costs, it improves American economic competitiveness, thereby breaking the link between emissions control and economic disadvantage.

Application: Paris and the Continuing Crisis and Controversy

Regardless of how one assesses the severity and consequences of climate change, there is one characteristic that no one disputes: climate change is a classic *transnational issue*, meaning it transcends national boundaries and cannot be dealt with successfully by individual states. The underlying causes that lead to climate consequences are essentially global, and they can only be solved by the efforts of all countries, acting individually or preferably cooperatively. This structure gives rise to the international efforts ongoing since 1979 (when the First World Climate Conference was held) to fashion an international regime that can effectively applied to ameliorating the problem.

The process has been difficult for both scientific and political reasons. The scientific community, as already discussed, is virtually unanimous in assigning causation: the production of excess carbon dioxide and other gases injected into the atmosphere and the harvesting of trees in rain forests that historically have served as "sinks" where photosynthesis breaks down CO_2 into harmless carbon and oxygen.

The problem is that fossil fuel burning, the chief source of greenhouse gases, is vital in a political and economic sense. Economically, the major use of fossil fuel burning is to create energy that underlies much economic activity. Energy production and use are the strongest correlates of economic activity, meaning the more energy a country uses, the more its economy thrives. The converse is also true. This means that attempts to curb fossil fuel can differentially affect countries who are asked to self-abnegate in comparison with those which have not. This creates the possibility of geopolitical advantage and disadvantage, thereby introducing objections to climate control that have nothing to do directly with scientific effects.

Different effects of compliance with climate-based guidelines are central dynamics in the international politics of climate change control. Since the beginning of the movement, this differential has been prominently framed in developed-developing world terms. In the early days of the movement, almost all the pollution was caused by energy production in the developed world. Emission baseline figures for 1990 used in the Kyoto process showed that the United States was responsible for 36 percent of global emissions, followed by the EU (24.2 percent), the Russian Federation (17.4 percent), and Japan (8.5 percent). The next largest polluter was Australia with 2.1 percent.

Excluded from these baseline figures were the largest developing countries—China and India—both of which were just entering the industrial process for which energy production was central. This created a two-tier classification of states that either exempted or created very small reduction quotas for rising countries and giving them an economic advantage that has been a major sticking point ever since. The Chinese have taken advantage of disparities in becoming a global economic power. EPA figures published in 2017 reflect the change: China now produces 30 percent of greenhouse gas emissions, followed by the United States (15 percent), the EU (9 percent), India (7 percent), Russia (5 percent) and Japan (4 percent).

The politico-economic dynamics help explain why the United States has been such a harsh critic and reluctant participant in the climate control process. In June 2017, of course, the Trump administration announced the American withdrawal from the Paris Agreement, largely on discriminatory grounds based in preferences (lower reduction quotas and economic assistance) for developing countries under the accord. The Trump action was nothing new in the climate control area or in other areas of transnational action.

The Road to Paris

The chronology of global warming as a formal international concern was described by the United Nations Framework Convention for Climate Change (UNFCCC) Secretariat in a 2000 publication, *Caring for Climate*. In 1979, the First World Climate Conference was the initial step. That meeting brought together international scientists concerned with the effects of human intervention in the climate process and the possible pernicious effects of trends that they observed. It also provided the first widespread recognition of the greenhouse gases phenomenon, largely known only within the scientific community before then.

The process has evolved, with important points corresponding to the most important conferences and agreements it produced. The major signposts were the Kyoto protocol of 1997 that produced the first major, comprehensive agreement on the subject, the Bali-Copenhagen process beginning in 2007 to produce a follow-on to Kyoto (which, by its own provisions, expired in 2012), and the Paris Climate Agreement of 2015.

The international momentum began to pick up in 1988 with two events. First, the United Nations General Assembly adopted a resolution, 43/53, urging the "protection of global climate for present and future generations of mankind." Malta sponsored the resolution. In a separate action, the World Meteorological Organization (WMO) and the United Nations Environmental Programme created the Intergovernmental Panel on Climate Change (IPCC) and charged this new body with assessing the scientific evidence on the subject. As requested, the IPCC issued its First Assessment Report in 1990, concluding that the threat of climate change was real and worthy of further study and concern. Also in 1990, the World Climate Conference held its second meeting in Geneva, Switzerland, and called for a global treaty on climate change, which in turn prompted the General Assembly to pass another resolution, 45/12, commissioning negotiations for a convention on climate change to be conducted by the Intergovernmental Negotiating Committee (INC). This body first met in February 1991 as an intergovernmental body. On May 9, 1992, the INC adopted the UNFCCC, which was presented for signature at the Rio De Janeiro United Nations Conference on the Environment and Development (the Earth Summit) in June 1992. The requisite number of signatures was obtained in 1994 and the UNFCCC entered force on March 21, 1994. The process leading to the Kyoto Protocol was thus officially launched.

One express feature of the UNFCCC was an annual meeting of all members of the Convention (which numbered 199 members and observers in 2010) known as the Conference of the Parties (COP). The first COP was held in 1995 in Berlin. The third COP was held in Kyoto, Japan; the result was the Kyoto Protocol.

The Kyoto Protocol was a complicated document, the details of which go beyond present purposes. Several elements can, however, be laid out that provide a summary of what the protocol attempted to do and, based on those purposes, the objections that have been raised to it.

The overarching goal of the protocol was reduction in the production and emission of greenhouse gases and thus the arrest and reversal of the adverse effects of climate changes. The protocol identifies six gases for control and emission reduction. Three of these gases are "most important" based on emission contribution. Carbon dioxide accounted for fully half of "the overall global warming effect arising from human activities" in the UNFCCC's language, followed by 18 percent for methane and 6 percent for nitrous oxide. The other three specified categories, the "long-lived industrial gases," are hydrofluorocarbons (HFCs), perfluorocarbons (PFCs), and sulfur hexafluoride (SF_6).

The goal of the protocol was a global reduction in the production of targeted gases of 5 percent below the baseline year for measuring emissions by the period 2008–2012. The baseline year established how much each developed country contributed to emission levels. These levels were then used for two purposes: to determine how much reduction each targeted country must accomplish, and to provide a measuring stick for determining when the protocol comes fully into effect. For determining these contributions, the protocol further divided the countries of the world into three different categories (what it calls Annexes) in terms of the obligations that are incurred.

The Kyoto accord created a complicated set of categories of states that included differential emissions reduction goals for each category. It placed the burden of reduction on the most developed countries, those members of the Organization of Economic Cooperation and Development (OECD) with the largest economies, most productive industrial plants, and thus the greatest consumers of fossil-fuel-derived energy. Using 1990 baseline figures for CO_2 emissions as its yardstick, these countries are listed by the amount of emissions they produced and the percentage of the world's total emissions this amount represents.

Most of the rest of the world was exempted from the reduction quotas or was required to make much smaller contributions. Most critically and controversially, some of the emerging developing states were excluded altogether because they had historically not contributed to the problem and they would learn from the pollution mistakes of the developed world and not follow in the polluting footsteps. That assumption provoked special controversy at the time and has proven almost totally false, as China has demonstrated. It was excluded from emissions requirements, meaning it could—and did—vastly increase its fossil-fuel-produced energy without becoming a violator. Attempts by others, notably Europeans, indirectly aided and abetted Chinese economic and pollution growth by transferring polluting enterprises to China. This process put Kyoto and China on a collision course with the United States.

Kyoto grew into a source of contention between the United States and China that helped undermine the accord. Although the United States was an early supporter of the Kyoto process during the Clinton years, it never signed the protocol, and the Bush administration was a leading global opponent of it. The heart of the Bush objection was that Kyoto discriminated unfairly against the United States, and much of this assertion was based on the advantage that China had as a non-emissions reducer under its provisions.

The American position changed almost immediately after Bush took office. On March 13, 2001, Bush announced that he no longer favored U.S. participation in the protocol. In the process, the administration publicly stated that it would not send the treaty signed by Clinton to the Senate for ratification. As a result, the United States has remained the most important country in the world outside the protocol and thus did not consider itself subject to its requirements. It remained a party to the UNFCCC.

Bush administration objections to the protocol focused on two basic themes. The first was cost and burden to the United States. Although some other countries have higher percentage reduction quotas than the United States, treaty opponents argued that having to bear 7 percent of 36 percent of the total required reductions was an excessive burden. In addition, U.S. emissions were already 15 percent above the 1990 level by the end of the millennium and, according to Victor, rising at 1.3 percent per year, thereby demanding even further reductions.

Thus, the United States was being asked to do too much proportionately in comparison to the rest of the world. Compliance was thus viewed as economically ruinous in terms of the additional expenses of doing business and the loss of comparative advantage to industries in other countries that are not regulated by these requirements, notably China. This objection has recurred under Trump.

The second objection was the exclusion of developing countries from the requirements of the protocol. In most cases, this exclusion is innocuous; most of these countries do not and will not contribute meaningfully to greenhouse gas in the foreseeable future.

The Bush administration's criticism was aimed principally at China and India. China has since become the largest greenhouse gas emitter. India does not pose quite as urgent a threat, but with a population the size of China's and an emerging technological and industrial capacity, it could be. As of 2017, these two countries are responsible for about three-eighths of global emission figures. One of the few signals of progress at Copenhagen was a joint Chinese-American accord to address this problem.

The flaws of the Kyoto Protocol—most prominently the exclusion of China from its dictates—were largely responsible for the failure to renew it or to forge a modified follow-on agreement. It is at least arguable that until China agreed to accept the role as a leader in reducing rather than producing carbon emissions into the ecosystem, all efforts were doomed to fall short or fail altogether. China has accepted that role; the United States has not.

The tenth anniversary of the Kyoto accords was marked by a major UNFCCC conference in Bali, Indonesia, in December 2007. Nearly 10,000 delegates attended the meeting, the purpose of which was to draft a follow-on agreement that would improve upon the results of the Kyoto Protocol. Gaining American participation and support was a major objective of the conferees.

Major issues introduced at the Bali meeting included future targets for CO_2 emissions reductions and the participation of countries excluded under the annexes of the Kyoto agreement, notably China and India. Mindful of Bush administration objections, the conferees agreed in principle that deep cuts in global emissions were required, but, according to Fuller and Rivkin, the plan "contained no binding commitments." The American delegation insisted that developing economies such as those of China and India agree to participate in the reduction of emissions. These outcomes were sufficiently positive that the Bush administration endorsed the Bali outcome.

Turning the general agreement into a specific, binding, and effective accord proved to be the hard part—the "devil in the details." Among enthusiasts of global warming control (which included President Obama), there were high hopes for the December 2009 Copenhagen summit. Technically, the Copenhagen conclave was a series of meetings, most prominently the fifteenth meeting of the Conference of Parties of the UNFCCC (COP15) and the fifth convening of the Meeting of the Parties of the COP members of the Kyoto Protocol (COP/MOP5). The summit was attended by 115 heads of state and generated much anticipation prior to its beginning on December 8.

The Copenhagen summit failed. It neither formally proposed nor enacted any binding, mandatory agreements to supersede Kyoto after its 2012 expiration, nor did it succeed in creating the framework for a global treaty by the date of Kyoto's lapse in 2012, the goal specified by the Bali Road Map. As the meeting wound down inconclusively, a group of major countries, including the United States, China, India, Brazil, and South Africa, convened an "Informal High Level Event" on December 18, the day before the summit was to adjourn. The result was something called the Copenhagen Accord calling for a goal of no more than a two-degree-Fahrenheit increase in global temperatures. This accord was noted but not adopted by the conference.

The process has continued to sputter along since Copenhagen and the expiration of the Kyoto Protocol. The Doha economic summit of late 2012 agreed to extend the Kyoto principle to 2020, when a more comprehensive agreement is supposed to be put into effect, but the prospects for a follow-on agreement remain debatable. Despite these setbacks, the effort continued, and the Paris Climate Conference represented the culmination of the post-Kyoto phase of climate control efforts.

The Paris Climate Agreement

When it was being negotiated, climate control advocates hoped that Paris would mark an important breakthrough in the process begun in Rio de Janeiro in 1992 to reestablish the globe's natural order. There were hopeful signs. For one thing, the United States had, under the leadership of President Obama, been an enthusiastic leader in the process from the beginning. When it was one of the states who deposited its accession to the accord on Earth Day in April 2016, the global climate control community believed it had taken a major step toward gaining the big power/big polluter support success required. China, which had also been a major part of the problem in gaining American support, was also a signatory. The Paris agreement seemed off to a good beginning.

Then the United States acted as it has so often in the past regarding multinational agreements and announced in June 2017 its intention to remove itself from the arrangement. The result was a kind of "shock and awe" at the move, but in a post–World War II context, it was not really all that unusual. There is a pattern. When an American administration (usually Democratic) leads the United States into international arrangements that may threaten some aspect of American sovereignty or control, a subsequent administration (often Republican) reverses the initiative and pulls the United States away. This pattern occurred in the Earth Summit, where the United States enthusiastically supported the Biodiversity Treaty and then renounced it. The Clinton administration was an enthusiastic supporter of Kyoto, and George Bush renounced it almost immediately upon assuming office. In other actions discussed in these pages, the United States has proposed or supported initiatives from UN-sponsored human rights proclamations (e.g., the UN Declaration on Human Rights and Convention on Genocide), economic initiatives like the International Trade Organization, and the International Criminal Court. In a real sense, President Trump was just carrying on an American tradition.

At the core of the Rome process is the attempt to reduce global emissions by engaging the largest polluters as active participants—notably China and the United States but also rising polluters such as India. These three countries currently account for over half the global CO_2 emissions. Early efforts like Kyoto, of course, excluded or gave preferential status to the developing world giants, which was a point of contention. Including them in global efforts served the dual ends of maximizing participation in the effort *and* of placating American concerns, with the effect of making its embrace of the process more likely. The Obama administration devoted special attention to orchestrating these conditions.

The agreement itself is a notably non-coercive document. The basic underlying dynamic is a series of emission reduction targets which the signatories agree to implement. These goals are not published in the agreement itself; they are voluntarily agreed to, and progress is self-reported. There is no punitive structure specifically authorized for monitoring progress or punishing violations. These provisions are intended, among other things, to assuage political elements in the United States that react negatively to any appearance of intrusion on American sovereign control of its affairs. Reading the operational articles and sections of the accord, one cannot avoid being struck by the lack of directive language it contains.

Since the June 2017 public withdrawal of the United States from the agreement, Article 28, which specifies procedures and timetables for leaving, has received some publicity. Dating the process to the U.S. accession to the document in April 2016, there is a three-year period before the withdrawal takes effect and an additional year until it is finalized. Effectively, this means the total American divorce from Paris is not completed until mid-2020, the middle of the 2020 presidential election cycle and a very long time given the volatility of contemporary American politics. Critics of the withdrawal decision take some heart from the possibility that the perpetually fickle Americans may once again change their minds.

Two major questions surround the Paris agreement as it moves forward as the major banner around which climate control issues congregate. The first, and in terms of climate change, the most important is whether it will succeed in achieving its stated purpose of helping arrest global warming. The prospects are mixed. On the positive side, almost all the world's countries are parties to the agreement, and the goals they have set for themselves could make a significant contribution to amelioration, especially if they occur in tandem with or are assisted by the growing economic viability and acceptance of evolving nonfossil sources of energy (see chapter 13). There are possibly conflicting variables at play, however. These include whether countries meet their goals (an assessment made difficult by the lack of strict reporting requirements), the continued participation by states that are major emitters, and the pace both of conservation efforts and the spread of alternative, and especially renewable, energy sources.

The second question is the American role in the process. The United States is only the third original participant to renounce its participation (Venezuela and

Iraq are the others), and the American action had not precipitated any other withdrawals as of this writing. Indeed, the announcement of President Trump included the possibility that the United States might negotiate reentry on terms it considered more favorable to American interests. Given the American status among polluting states, its absence will be missed quantitatively and may forfeit both its leadership and, in the estimation of Sivaram and Saha, "it would also give up its right to complain."

The larger impact of American absence may be self-inflicted damage for the United States. The United States has been a global leader in researching, developing, and commercializing nonfossil energy sources such as solar and wind power, areas that are compatible with and connected to the process, to the point that, as Deese points out, "rapid reductions in the price of renewable energy and increases in the efficiency of energy consumption have made fighting climate change easier, and often even profitable."

The result has been to put the United States on the inside track as the leader both in climate science and in the commercialization of the Paris-based movement. Withdrawing from Paris may forfeit that advantage and open the door for competitors, notably China and even Saudi Arabia, to take over that leadership. Deese, for instance, reports that China plans to invest $340 billion in this sector, and the Saudis plan to invest $50 billion by 2020 (both more than the U.S. government).

China's president Xi Jinping is, as Krupp points out, a chemical engineer by training, understands the potential and science of this endeavor, and has acted to assert Chinese leadership. Krupp adds that "In 2015, China installed more than one wind turbine every hour on average and enough solar panels to cover two soccer fields every day." They have also cancelled construction of 100 coal-fired power plants, the visual symbol of Chinese pollution, in 2017. China already leads the world in the production of solar panels, wind turbines, and lithium storage panels. Will their burgeoning efforts and the symbolism of the United States turning its back on Paris undercut the American clean energy effort, which, according to Deese, currently employs "over three million Americans"? One of Trump's arguments for withdrawing from Paris is that the effect of the agreement would be would be to cost Americans energy jobs (primarily in the petroleum industry). The irony is that the withdrawal could cost the United States more jobs in the renewable energy field, a possibility explored in the next chapter.

Conclusion

Hardly anyone disputes that climate change is taking place or that its effects are pernicious to some degree. No one is a pro–global warmer. However, there is considerable reluctance to attack and eradicate the problem, and this has until recently been especially true in the United States, whose participation in the effort is critical to its solution.

The United States, along with China, is both the heart of the problem and its solution, or at least amelioration. American alienation from the international effort to curb global warming arose from what some Americans viewed as two unfair aspects of the Kyoto process that have carried over into subsequent international efforts up to and including the Paris agreement. They are the imposition of crippling emissions reduction requirements that disadvantaged the country in the global economy and the exclusion of China from emissions requirements. The two objections were, of course, interrelated; Chinese exclusion and American inclusion added to Chinese comparative advantage in production costs, largely at the expense of American competitors. Both arguments have abated since Kyoto, but the Trump administration resuscitated them in withdrawing from the Paris accord.

The tables have turned decisively. China has become the world's greatest polluter, but under the leadership of President Xi Jinping, it has become a leader in emission reduction and in the development and marketing of alternative, non-polluting energy sources. Both efforts can eclipse American initiatives. Thanks largely to the conversion of power plants from burning coal to natural gas, the Americans are now reducing emissions unilaterally and are even righteously proclaiming their intent to move unilaterally to the targets established using 1990 baselines, even having removed themselves from the formal process. China, meanwhile, struggles to reduce its dependency on burning coal, the most polluting of the fossil fuels, for power. Although the discussion will be reserved largely for the next chapter, the American-led revolution in shale oil and gas may provide a mutually reinforcing opportunity for U.S.-Chinese cooperation in leading the climate change movement.

For China, an obvious answer to both its energy and pollution needs is the exploitation of its own massive shale formations—the largest in the world. China lags far behind the North Americans in shale extraction technology and would have to purchase much of that technology from the United States and Canada, a reversal in Chinese economic patterns. The Chinese have not yet bitten the bullet on this conversion, but it is a possible avenue for their future and their relationship with the United States.

Like world energy generally, shale gas (including the exploitation of methane hydrate from the world's seabeds) has the potential to change the dynamics of international global warming efforts, but it is an interim, not a permanent, solution. Shale gas is, after all, still a fossil fuel, and it does emit carbon, if in smaller amounts than other fossil fuels such as coal. Ultimately, it allows the prospects of a "breather" of sorts in the process, but it only buys time for progress in the ultimate quest of a global energy system freed of dependence on fossil fuels and their emission of carbon residues. In that quest, the movement to renewable sources of clean energy remains the solution to both world energy needs and the scourge of global warming.

At the beginning of this chapter, climate change was described as a true transnational issue, and one with unique aspects. That uniqueness has at least four significant emphases. First, global warming is truly a global issue that affects the entire planet and can be solved only by essentially universal actions by the countries of the world. Special burdens fall on countries such as the United States and China that contribute most to the problem and are the leaders in exploring solutions. It is hard, arguably impossible, to see how these problems can be remediated without the active participation of both countries. Second, responding to this problem will have direct impacts on two of the most important motors of the global economy: energy production and use, and transportation. Disruptions to either of these industries could have catastrophic economic effects for the world generally. Third, climate change is the only environmental problem that intensifies or is intensified by other major environmental problems. Rising water levels affect the ability of the earth to produce food, and desertification is increased by warming, to cite two problems created. Fourth, climate change is a problem that is intimately related to other vital conditions of life. The climate change problem is largely the result of humankind's need for energy, but the process also creates additional natural resource problems such as desertification and shrinking supplies of usable, potable water. These interconnections between natural resources and climate change are the key focus of chapter 13.

Study/Discussion Questions

1. What is a transnational issue? Why is climate change considered a "classic" transnational issue? How does this dynamic affect how we think about the climate change issue?

2. Describe the nature of global warming. What causes it? How does it work? How and why are fossil fuel burning and deforestation the "villains" causing the problem? Who bears responsibility for creating and solving the problem?

3. What factors make a rational debate on climate change difficult? Discuss the positions of both climate change proponents and skeptics. What makes reconciliation of their positions intractable?

4. List and briefly discuss the international efforts on climate change control from 1979 to the present. What is the basis of the tension between environmental and political and economic factors that has been present throughout the process?

5. What has the historic treatment of developing countries such as China and India been in climate change negotiations? Why has that position been a sticking point in international efforts to gain cooperation on agreements? Use the Chinese case to illustrate the point.

6. Discuss the Kyoto Protocol as the landmark agreement on climate change control. What did it propose? Why was it controversial? Why did attempts at a "follow on" agreement fail before it lapsed in 2012?

7. What is the Paris Climate Agreement? What does it try to do? How is it designed as an improvement over previous agreements? For what stated reasons did President Trump oppose it as grounds for U.S. withdrawal? What are the likely consequences of the American action?

8. The United States has been an obstructionist since the beginning of the climate change process.

How? Why? How does reaction to the Paris agreement simply show the "United States being the United States" in international negotiations? What possibilities for an increased or more marginalized role exist?

Bibliography

Ackerman, John T. "Global Climate Change: Catalyst for International Relations Disequilibria." PhD diss, University of Alabama, 2004.

Beyond Kyoto: Advancing the International Effort Against Climate Change. Arlington, VA: Pew Center on Global Climate Change, 2003.

Black, Richard. "Copenhagen Climate Summit Undone by 'Arrogance.'" *BBC News* (online), March 16, 2010.

Blau, Judith. *The Paris Agreement: Climate Change, Solidarity, and Human Rights.* London: Palgrave Macmillan, 2017.

Browne, John. "Beyond Kyoto." *Foreign Affairs* 83, no. 4 (July/August 2004): 20–32.

Claussen, Eileen, and Lisa McNeilly. *Equity and Global Climate Change: The Complex Elements of Global Fairness.* Arlington, VA: Pew Center on Global Climate Change, 2000.

Crook, Clive. "The Sins of Emission." *Atlantic* 301, no. 3 (April 2008): 32–34.

Deese, Brian. "Paris Isn't Burning: Why the Climate Agreement Will Survive Trump." *Foreign Affairs* 96, no. 4 (July/August 2017): 83–92.

Enwerem, Michael C. *The Paris Agreement on Climate Change: A Better Chance of Tackling Global Climate Change.* New York: CreateSpace Independent Publishing, 2016.

Fuller, Thomas, and Andrew C. Rivkin. "Climate Plan Looks Beyond Bush's Tenure." *New York Times* (online), December 16, 2007.

Helm, Dieter. *The Carbon Crunch: How We're Getting Climate Change Wrong—and How to Fix It.* New Haven, CT: Yale University Press, 2012.

Intergovernmental Panel on Climate Change. A Report of Working Groups I–III. *Summary for Policymakers—Climate Change 2001.* Cambridge, UK: Cambridge University Press, 2001.

Klein, Daniel, and Maria Pia Carazo. *The Paris Climate Agreement: Analysis and Commentary.* Oxford, UK: Oxford University Press, 2017.

Krupp, Fred. "Trump and the Environment: What His Plans Would Do." *Foreign Affairs* 96, no. 4 (July/August 2017): 73–82.

Leggett, Jane. *Paris Agreement: United States, China Move to Become Parties to Climate Change Treaty.* Washington, DC: Congressional Research Service, September 12, 2016.

Luterbacher, Urs, and Detlef F. Sprinz, eds. *International Relations and Global Climate Change.* Cambridge, MA: MIT Press, 2001.

Mann, Charles C. "What If We Never Run Out of Oil?" *Atlantic* 311, no. 4 (May 2013): 48–63.

Palmer, Lisa. "Q and A: The Angry Economist (Dieter Helm)." *New York Times* (online in "Green: A Blog About Energy and the Environment"), March 1, 2013.

Pirages, Dennis C., and Theresa Manley DeGeest. *Ecological Security: An Evolutionary Perspective on Globalization.* New York: Rowman & Littlefield, 2004.

Podesta, John, and Peter Ogden. "The Security Implications of Climate Change." *Washington Quarterly* 31, no. 1 (Winter 2007–2008): 115–38.

Schelling, Thomas C. "The Cost of Combating Global Warming: Facing the Tradeoffs." *Foreign Affairs* 75, no. 6 (November/December 1997): 8–14.

Schuetze, Christopher F. "Ignoring Planetary Peril, a Profound 'Disconnect' Between Science and Doha." *International Herald Tribune* (online), December 6, 2012.

———. "Scientists Agree Overwhelmingly on Global Warming. Why Doesn't the Public Know That?" *International Herald Tribune* (online), May 16, 2013.

Sivaram, Varun, and Sagatom Saha. "The Trouble with Ceding Climate Leadership to China: Risky for the World, Costly for the United States." *Foreign Affairs Snapshot* (online). December 10, 2016.

Stavins, Robert N. "Why Trump Pulled the U.S. Out of the Paris Accord: And What the Consequences Will Be." *Foreign Policy Snapshot* (online). June 5, 2017.

Stern, Todd, and William Antholis. "A Changing Climate: The Road Ahead for the United States." *Washington Quarterly* 31, no. 1 (Winter 2007–2008): 175–87.

Suzuki, David, and Ian Harrington. *Just Cool It: The Climate Crisis and What We Can Do*. London: Greystone, 2017.

United Nations Framework on Climate Change. *COP 21 Final Agreement: Paris 2015 United Nations Climate Change Conference*. New York: United Nations, 2015.

United States Environmental Protection Agency. *Global Greenhouse Gas Emissions Data*. Washington, DC: EPA, April 13, 2017 (online).

Victor, David C. G. *Climate Change: Debating America's Options*. New York: Council on Foreign Relations Press, 2004.

Vidal, John, Allegra Stratton, and Suzanne Goldenberg. "Low Target, Goals Dropped: Copenhagen Ends in Failure." *Guardian.co.uk* (online), December 19, 2009.

Wirth, Timothy. "Hot Air over Kyoto: The United States and the Politics of Global Warming." *Harvard International Review* 23, no. 4 (2002), 72–77.

13

Resource Scarcity

Securing Access to Water and Energy

Thehe desire, even necessity, to control scarce resources, and conflict over those resources, are as old as human history and have acted as a major source of friction in the international order. Major wars have been fought over access to precious metals, water, food, and exotic spices, to name a few examples. In the contemporary world, some of the most publicized resource conflicts have been over access to water and petroleum reserves. Aspects of both problems are geographically widespread. Like so many of the world's problems, both problems are prominent in the Middle East region. Water and energy are among the most thorny, interrelated difficulties facing the future.

This case examines the changing general parameters of the problems of water and energy security. They are related but different challenges qualitatively and quantitatively. The need for access to adequate, usable water supplies is existential: water is literally necessary to life. Energy is similar but more geopolitical: energy is necessary for survival in the world's coldest climates but is also considered the lubricant of economic activity and geopolitical applications. The quest for potable water is an ongoing human necessity made more difficult by a growing human population. Energy is a resource in transition from petroleum to other sources, a mandate enlivened by climate change. The structure of each problem and means to deal with them will be examined in this chapter.

Conflict over the ability to control, monopolize, or deny access to valued resources is as old as human history. Men have fought and died, armies have swept across countless expanses, and empires and states have risen and fallen in the name of precious resources. Whether it was control of the silk routes across Asia, the exotic foodstuffs of the Spice Islands, the diamonds and gold of southern and central Africa, El Dorado in the New World, the petroleum wealth of the Middle East, or distribution of water from major river systems, the struggle for scarce and valuable natural resources has been a recurrent theme of human history and relations.

How will this historical theme be acted out in the early twenty-first century? What is striking is that the resources over which there is the most competition are also the most basic resources for the human condition. At the top of the list is potable water. With 70 percent of the earth's surface covered by water, water per se is hardly a scarce resource, but water that is usable for human purposes such as drinking, bathing, and agriculture is in selective shortage across the globe. As world population grows, existing shortages will be intensified unless means can be devised to increase supplies.

The other scarce resource is energy. The heart of the global energy debate has centered on petroleum since World War II, making security of access to oil a prime concern for all states. The balance between oil and other sources of energy is changing, however, and the needs of different states for different energy sources and forms are changing as well. As has always been the case, resource scarcities are politically important, because domestic and international political decisions help define scarcities and responses to them. Where resources are in short supply, the political, including geopolitical, competition between those who have adequate or surplus supplies and those who do not has acrimonious consequences for the relations between the haves and the have-nots. The two resources are interrelated in that some places in the world have large amounts of water or petroleum, but not both. The Middle East is the most dramatic example of this divergence.

Scarcity is the key concept. It exists whenever all claimants to a resource cannot simultaneously have all that resource they need or want. When scarcity exists between sovereign states, there are three possible ways to allocate the resource. First, if some method can be found to increase supply so that all claimants can have more of the resource, scarcity abates and so does the basis for conflict. The problem with this solution is that it is often easier said than done. In contemporary terms, increasing water availability can mean better development or distribution of existing resources or tapping new sources, mostly seawater. Energy production has increased due to technologies such as shale gas and oil extraction, but faces tough imperatives like conversion to nonfossil fuel sources.

The second approach is to decrease demand for the resource by using less and thereby lowering demand closer to available supply. Human life requires minimum amounts of water and is, in that sense, inelastic. In the case of traditional energy sources like oil, the fact is that global demand is increasing, mostly because of new claimants to the resource such as China and India, as discussed in chapter 12. Calls for conservation must compete with emerging customers and the mandate to move to different forms of energy propagation.

If the other options fail, then a power struggle may remain an option, pitting the suppliers against the consumers over how much energy will be available at what prices. Up until now, the geopolitical struggle over petroleum has received the most publicity, but that could change. New technologies could facilitate change for either resource, but conflict and even violent options may occur in some cases.

Principle: Resource Scarcity

The ancient Greeks, as well as other civilizations in Eurasia, were the world's oldest recorded "chemists," devising schemes to categorize the most important "elements" affecting their universes. The Greek philosopher Plato publicized one of the most famous of these lists—earth, water, air, and fire—in roughly 540 BC. Modern science has gradually expanded and sophisticated this early "periodic table," but two of its four components, water and fire (energy) remain both basic and contentious in the modern world for existential and geopolitical reasons. Their conjunction is vividly captured by a Turkish official (Turkey controls much regional water supplies) during a negotiation with the representative of a downstream oil producer when, in frustration, he threatened withholding his liquid resource: "Let them drink oil!"

The structure of each problem is changing. There is no alternative to water: attacking its inelasticity is at the heart of the global problem, and adjustments of maldistribution and patterns of use may effect more localized difficulties. Changes in the overall energy equation may lessen the stranglehold of petroleum and thus ameliorate climate change, but in the transition, the dynamics of petroleum remain important as the world's central energy source.

Water Resources

Water is simultaneously the world's most abundant and scarce resource. Over 70 percent of the Earth's surface may be covered with water, and scientists have determined that the total amount of water on the planet is 1.4 billion cubic kilometers. Of that inconceivable total, about one-seventh of the water is considered fresh, or potable, water suitable for human use. The rest is saline, almost exclusively seawater. Water is not scarce, but usable water is.

Water scarcity is not uniformly experienced geographically. Hydrologists categorize scarcity among three kinds: physical scarcity (where inadequate supplies are available), economic scarcity (where resources, expertise, or will is inadequate to maximize availability), and imminent scarcity (where environmental changes could precipitate scarcity). Parts of the American West, Mediterranean (Saharan) Africa, and parts of central Asia including northern China are examples of physical scarcity. Much of central Africa represents economic scarcity, and the Arabian Peninsula is a prime example of imminent scarcity. Virtually all of North and South America (other than coastal Chile), Europe, and the rest of Eurasia do not suffer from water scarcity.

The result is that water scarcity selectively affects many people in the world. There are three degrees of water scarcity that are often cited in describing its extent. The least severe are *water shortages*, which are selective crises often caused by weather patterns, pollution, and overuse of water for non-necessary purposes. *Water stress* refers to conditions where it is difficult to obtain adequate amounts of freshwater due to availability or economic scarcity. The Middle East is the most water-stressed part of the world. The third category is *water crisis*, the situation where there is inadequate supply to meet the needs of the people who live in a region. For purposes of measuring these conditions, the standard for water stress exists when there is less than 1,700 cubic meters per person annually available, shortage can arise when that availability is between 1,700 and 1,000 cubic meters, and water is in crisis when the number drops below 1,000 cubic meters. Below 500 cubic meters per person is critical for human survival.

The problem of water scarcity is less well recognized personally in the developed than in the developing world. Partly, of course, this is true because it exists in fewer places in the developed world, and where it does, it has been dealt with reasonably successfully. As an example, the physical water scarcity in parts of the

American West centers on states in the desert southwest and northern Mexico, the chief water source for which is the Colorado River. The western American states through which the river flows negotiated the Colorado River Compact in 1922 by which they allocated water from the river and developed hydroelectric and storage dams to produce electricity and to ensure available water remained in the system for measured and designed utilization. Because the river dips briefly into Mexico, that country is also part of the compact. The compact has been in force ever since and is approaching its hundredth anniversary. It may be illustrative of the broader global problem that there is current concern of Colorado River water becoming scarce due to development of the region because of desirability as a place to live (the growth of Las Vegas is a current example). The problem has not yet reached the point of human suffering, but deprivation is real elsewhere.

Estimates are that 2.8 billion people—nearly 40 percent of the world's population—suffer some form of water shortage at least once a month, and the vicissitudes of climate change produce selective cases of imminent scarcity when phenomena such as droughts, hurricanes, tsunamis, or cyclones interrupt normal supplies and make the situation worse selectively.

The inelasticity of water adds to the difficulty and frustration of dealing with it. On the demand side, there are bare minimums of water that people must have, and if they do not, they will perish. As world population increases, that demand can only increase and put further stress on water supplies. The only demand-side alternative is population control, preferably reduction from a strictly hydrological perspective. The supply side is slightly more optimistic if still very difficult. Supply can be increased by converting some of that six-sevenths of the world's water that is unusable for human purposes potable. There are efforts that are aimed at doing so, primarily in those parts of the world with the greatest water difficulties. Once again, climate change–related variables such as the melting of polar ice caps complicate these efforts. The prospects for change are discussed in the application section of the chapter.

Energy Resources

The energy crisis is structurally different from water and has received much more attention than water scarcity, largely because it has strong salience globally in both the developed and developing worlds. Demands for increased energy, as introduced in chapter 12, have come primarily from the developed world until recently, whereas many of the sources of that energy have, once again until recently, been from selective sites in the developing world. Water scarcity is, in important ways, a humanitarian problem with some geopolitical ramifications. Energy scarcity is largely a geopolitical problem.

Energy is also different because, unlike water, it can come from various sources. Petroleum has been the primary energy source in the developed world for nearly a century, during which vast sources of oil have been discovered and exploited, especially in the Middle East. World dependence has become so great that two basic trends important to this century have emerged. One has been fluctuation in estimates of availability of this non-renewable resource (non-renewable because it does not naturally replenish itself when used). One result has been to look for alternative sources of energy for the future, including petroleum from nontraditional sources and alternate energy sources.

The other trend has been to create a changed element in the world power map. Countries and regions like the Middle East that would not otherwise have great geopolitical significance gained such status because they are significant petroleum repositories. The Middle East has been the most obvious example. New sources from other places endanger the status of traditional suppliers. The result is that the geopolitical map is likely moving away from traditional oil suppliers to possessors of other energy sources.

The current importance of petroleum derives from the centrality of its usage to modern society. The great demand for petroleum makes it a particularly valuable resource, and its concentration within various regions and control by different governments makes it scarce or potentially scarce and thus a source of leverage for its possessors against those dependent upon it.

Historically, prime human reliance on different energy sources has featured the dominance of one source until its eclipse by an alternate source. For most of human history, the dominant source of energy was from burning wood. When the human population was relatively small and the demands on fuel by individuals were modest (mostly cooking and heating), wood was essentially a renewable resource, as more trees grew than were harvested and burned for energy.

The adequacy of wood as an energy source and the equipoise between its exploitation and natural replenishment began to break down in the eighteenth and nineteenth centuries. Lower death rates (people living longer) caused human populations to begin to grow rapidly, and industrialization caused per capita demand for energy to explode, as energy was applied to more uses than simple survival. As a result, wood gradually became both less adequate as an energy source and increasingly non-renewable. In places like the African Sahel region, overuse of wood for fuel has created associated water problems such as desertification.

Oil provided the alternative. Since petroleum overtook wood as the primary worldwide means of energy generation early in the twentieth century, world dependence on it has gradually increased to the almost total dependence on oil for such basic human needs as energy provision and transportation. All analysts agree that the period of petroleum dominance of the energy cycle will be considerably shorter than that of wood because of burgeoning global population and increasing per capita demands for energy as more and more of the world develops economically. Despite the discovery of new oil sources and techniques such as shale oil and gas extraction, oil is non-renewable and will eventually be depleted. For the foreseeable future, there is no clear successor to petroleum as the world's primary source of energy. Most extrapolations suggest that there will be multiple "contestants" in this transition, and that the next cycle may be one where several sources contribute to energy supply.

There are five sources of energy production for the future. All are currently in use at various levels and with different prospects. Three involve the burning of fossil fuels, with the inevitable byproduct of carbon dioxide emission into the atmosphere. These three sources are petroleum, natural gas, and coal. They differ in quantity available, geographic distribution, and contribution to environmental degradation. The other two source categories are nuclear power generation and renewable energy sources, a cover designation for a variety of specific energy-generating technologies. These sources share the characteristic of being non-carbon burning and thus producing no carbon dioxide emission.

Each source creates specific concerns that go beyond the physics of energy production. One of these concerns is the question of supply adequacy: How much of the resource is available, and is that amount enough for current and projected needs? A related matter is the cost of this supply. Can adequate supplies at acceptable and predictable prices be guaranteed or at least reasonably ensured? As well, there is the question of energy security: Can necessary supplies at acceptable prices be guaranteed, or are they potentially subject to uncontrollable fluctuations in amount of resource availability and cost or interdiction? All these concerns have been prominent parts of the debate over petroleum dependency. The other major concern has been environmental impact: Do some energy sources create such environmental degradation that their use should be restricted or precluded because of the damage they do to the global ecosystem? Each of these concerns will be addressed in a brief review of each source as part of the global energy problem. Because of its prominence, that survey begins with and features the traditional use of petroleum.

Petroleum

Worldwide dependency on petroleum-based energy is not accidental. At the end of World War II, the international community had to replace and rebuild energy sources and generation facilities destroyed or crippled in the war. The problem was especially acute in Europe and parts of Asia (notably Japan), where much of the wartime destruction occurred. The conscious solution to the problem was to rebuild the energy system based on petroleum as the primary energy source. The premises of this decision included the abundant availability of petroleum for a long time at a low, controllable cost, since most oil production was controlled by Western oil companies (the so-called seven sisters), and much of the oil was in the Persian Gulf region, where the seven sisters ensured that compliant local governments would grant concessions perpetuating low costs. These projections led to the conversion of most European and Asian energy systems to petroleum (France chose nuclear power and was a notable exception). In 1945, these assumptions seemed realistic and sustainable. They no longer are.

Although oil has been used primarily as an energy source for economic activity (its conversion to electricity) and transportation, its uses go well beyond the production of energy. Petroleum is the basic commodity used in the petrochemical industry, and thus most of the plastics industry. There are no ready alternative substitutes for petroleum in making plastics, so it is arguable that using oil to produce energy is a waste of a resource indispensable for other, more important purposes. The late Shah Reza Pahlavi of Iran (as quoted by Fleischman) captured this dilemma before his fall from power in 1979. "There is a limited amount of petroleum in the earth. Oil is used for making plastics and other products," he said. "Oil is too valuable to burn. When we run out, what will we do? Fight each other for the last drop?"

The joker in supply calculations has been the emergence of shale-formation oil and natural gas as an energy source. Since 2008, the United States and Canada have moved aggressively to extract oil and natural gas from shale formations common throughout much of the world and specifically in North America. The prototype of this activity has been the so-called Bakken formation, named after the North Dakota farmer on whose property near Tioga, North Dakota, the initial formation (part of the Williston Basin covering parts of North Dakota, Montana, and Saskatchewan) was exploited. These formations are amenable to exploitation through a process known as "fracking" that yields natural gas and petroleum. These discoveries are the major source of change in the economic geography of energy, but are controversial because of possible ecological effects. Among the possible impacts are a reduction of American (and other countries') dependence on imported petroleum, notably from the Middle East.

Energy sufficiency is, of course, an economic and national security goal for all energy-importing states. Energy security is the product of availability and cost, in the sense that the goal is secure access to adequate supply at acceptable cost. Were petroleum (or other) energy sources distributed worldwide according to consumption (i.e., energy produced where it is used), this would not be a problem. However, oil reserves are not as widely found in large quantities in the parts of the world that historically have used the most oil (the OECD countries of Europe and North America) or in non-OECD countries such as India and China (both part of Asia and Oceania) where demand is growing fastest.

In addition, the politics of petroleum control and exploitation can corrode the domestic politics of countries. Iraq is a prime example. The long struggle between the Shiite Arab, Sunni Arab, and Kurdish Iraqis has religious and ethnic bases, but in the wake of the American occupation and withdrawal, it also has a deep oil-based economic cleavage as well. An ongoing major division among the groups is over who will receive the vast revenues from exploitation of Iraqi oil fields. The principal fields are in the Kurdish north and in the Shiite south, whereas there are no confirmed, exploitable oil deposits under lands dominated by the traditionally politically dominant Sunnis, notably Anbar province in the so-called Sunni Triangle. Any attempts to reconcile ethnoreligious differences are currently stymied by disagreements over which groups should receive how much of the revenues from leasing drilling rights to different countries and companies.

Traditional petroleum remains the dominant source of energy worldwide, but its geopolitical consequences and pressures from the climate change community are creating pressure for the exploration and marketing of other energy forms. Both ecological concerns and price affect these decisions, and energy use appears to be entering a transition from petroleum to some other base. Candidates include natural gas, coal, nuclear, and a variety of renewable sources.

Natural Gas

The major contemporary change agent in the energy equation has been the expansion of availability and usage of natural gas. It has been part of the energy equation since the transition to petroleum as the world's most favored and used fuel, because natural gas is found essentially everywhere there is oil. Natural gas from traditional sources coterminous with oil reserves has always accounted for nearly as much of total U.S. energy production as its major rivals, fellow carbon-based sources petroleum and coal. In 1980, for instance, Energy Information Agency (EIA) figures show that each accounted for about 20 percent of energy production. There has been a gradual decline in oil production using traditional methods, but gas has been a steady part of the production equation.

In 2011, gas production passed the production of coal as the single greatest source of American energy production at around 22 percent, and the gap is projected to widen by the year 2040, when natural gas production will account for 35 percent of production, with coal and petroleum occupying second and third places, according to EIA figures. In addition, the EIA's *Annual Energy Outlook 2013* extrapolates that total American energy production, largely driven by increased production of natural gas, will exceed consumption through 2040, making the United States a net energy exporter. Citing 2014 estimates, the *CIA World Factbook, 2017* reported that the United States is the world's largest producer and consumer of natural gas.

The major reason for this change, of course, has been the emergence of shale oil and gas production, which is becoming a transformational factor in the global energy picture. The United States has been the leader of this development and likely will continue to be at the forefront of this technology, and thus it is worthwhile to examine some of the factors for the rising prominence of shale oil in the United States.

The distribution of shale formations globally gives a long-term advantage to the United States and China, which have the world's largest known availability of these formations. IEA figures for 2009, for instance, show that the two countries with the greatest proven shale gas reserves are China (1,275 trillion cubic feet) and the United States (862 trillion cubic feet). Of the remaining eleven countries listed in descending rank order of possession, Russia, which has the world's largest known reserves of traditional natural gas, does not even appear on the list. On the list of traditional gas reserve holders, Iraq, Qatar, and Saudi Arabia also have larger natural gas reserves than the United States (and China). None of these countries even appears on the shale gas table; in fact, the only Middle Eastern state that does is Algeria, whose technically recoverable shale gas reserves are a little over one-fourth of American reserves.

The other great attraction for the United States is geopolitical, specifically as a substitute for dependence on foreign petroleum and thus as a contributor to greater energy security, even overall sufficiency. The United States is becoming a net energy exporter, and shale oil and gas are major drivers in this shift. The change also means an increasing movement of the United States away from alternate, including foreign, sources of oil. Domestically, the American power grid is shifting from coal to natural gas burning as the energy source, largely because natural gas emits less than half the carbon dioxide levels of coal burning (a ratio the coal industry, of course, denies). One spinoff has been the ability of the United States to adopt air pollution projections committing the country to CO_2 emission reductions in international climate change negotiations and to approximate Paris goals without being a formal party to the regime. American reliance on imported, and especially Middle Eastern, petroleum is also decreasing as shale oil and gas supplant traditional petroleum as a component in the American energy equation. This conversion is also accompanied primarily by a decline in the use of energy derived from petroleum.

The other country that can benefit greatly from the shale oil and gas "revolution" is China, as noted in chapter 12. China's need for energy is growing rapidly, as economic development and higher standards of living in the People's Republic of China (PRC) occur in energy-intensive ways. China and India, the world's two most populous countries, are leading the surge in demand for increased energy that is shifting the balance of demand away from the OECD countries. To meet its increasing needs, China is attempting to increase its access to all energy sources. It must, however, import most of its petroleum, as its reserves of traditional oil sources are about the same as those of the United States unless highly disputed Chinese claims to South China Sea oil are included in its totals.

Shale oil and gas may provide a useful alternative for both the Chinese energy need and pollution problem. According to EIA figures cited earlier, China has the world's largest reserves, and it has begun to test fracking techniques to explore the prospects of mining its vast shale oil formations. On the negative side, most of its reserves are in remote parts of China difficult to access, and China lacks the technology and infrastructure (gas pipelines, for instance) to exploit its reserves in the near- to mid-term. As a result, shale gas will not solve all of China's energy and pollution problems, but it could certainly reduce its dependence, particularly on coal, following an apparent American lead to replace coal-generating power plants with facilities that burn shale-derived gas instead, an initiative China has followed by cancelling construction of coal-burning power plants.

Coal

Coal is the third major CO_2-emitting fossil fuel. Coal preceded petroleum in helping to power the Industrial Revolution in eighteenth- and nineteenth-century Europe and North America, and it remains a significant source of energy production and consumption in many countries. Coal currently produces about 22 percent of American energy through the operation of coal-powered electrical energy plants. What is most notable about coal usage is that it is such an important part of the gradual shift in energy patterns toward the developing world.

China has been the world's leading coal consumer. Using an EIA-supplied graph, China now uses nearly 47 percent the coal consumed in the world. In 2011, for instance, China consumed 3.8 billion tons of coal, whereas the rest of the world combined to use 4.3 billion tons. China's known coal reserves rank third in the world behind the United States and Russia. Coal mining is relatively cheap in China, and its exploitation relieves dependency on foreign energy sources. In economic and security terms, a growing reliance on coal for power generation has made sense. The downsides have included monumental pollution in Chinese cities such as Beijing, pressure from the climate control community to reduce coal use, and the emergence of alternate sources such as gas, which is cheaper.

Coal is rapidly becoming the energy source of the past. It remains a source in countries such as India that lack obvious viable alternatives. Coal use is, however, dirty and increasingly economically uncompetitive, as the decline in the U.S. coal industry testifies to. China has cancelled the construction of more coal-powered plants and is moving away from coal-generated power. The rest of the world is following.

Nuclear Energy

Power generation using nuclear rather than carbon-based fuel is an alternative. It has both advantages and disadvantages. Its primary advantage is that nuclear power generation does not contribute to carbon dioxide overload in the atmosphere and is thus an environmentally friendly source of energy. Its primary disadvantages are disposal of spent nuclear fuel, dogged questions of plant safety, facilities security, and the expense of building nuclear power plants. These disadvantages have combined to make nuclear power a relatively small contributor to worldwide energy, and its contribution is unlikely to grow markedly in the foreseeable future.

The United States is the world leader in overall nuclear power generation with over 100 nuclear power plants in operation, according to 2011 European Nuclear Society data. These produce a little less than 10 percent of American power needs, and that proportion is forecast to remain flat or slightly decline as the American power needs and preferences change. No new nuclear plants have been built in the United States since the 1970s, and there are few prospects that that will change. France is the second largest nuclear power user in terms of plants and output that produce about 77 percent of French electricity. Japan, with fifty operating plants, is third in nuclear power generation, followed by the Republic of Korea (South Korea), India, Canada, and China.

The disadvantages of nuclear power continue to depress its expansion as an energy source. The costs of nuclear plant construction are much higher than those of other forms of power generation because of the requirements to protect against radioactive leakage at nuclear sites and to make plants impervious to attack or hostile penetration.

Several problems create public resistance to nuclear power. One of these is the problem of waste disposal. The used (or "spent") fuel from a nuclear reactor is highly toxically radioactive, and the half-life of its toxicity (the point at which it is no longer dangerously environmentally threatening) is measured in hundreds of years. Another, and more spectacular, fear arises from the possibility of nuclear power plant accidents fouling the environment. Although these are relatively infrequent, they are often spectacular and memorable. The most recent major disaster occurred in 2011 at the Fukushima nuclear plant in Japan. The most famous and devastating occurrence was the meltdown of a nuclear reactor at Chernobyl in 1986 in the Ukraine. In addition, there are other concerns with nuclear power that arise from geopolitics as much as a pure energy perspective. One is the danger that nuclear power plants will become the target of terrorists. Yet another danger is the conversion of nuclear power facilities to producing weapons-grade materials that can be converted into nuclear weapons.

Renewables

Problems and controversies surround most traditional energy sources and create interest in alternative sources of energy generation, and particularly sources that are nonpolluting and that are not depleted by use for creating energy. A prominent historical example has been hydroelectrically produced power from dams built on rivers where water flow can be stored and released to produce energy. This form is explicitly environmentally friendly, but its application is restricted to places such as the American West and Turkish Anatolia, where there are streams that flow through canyons.

There has been greater enthusiasm for so-called renewable sources such as wind power captured by powerful wind turbines and converted to electricity, and solar energy, using solar panels to capture the sun's heat and store it for use as energy. Sizable industries have developed in both the United States and China to develop and commercialize these efforts, and their potential to deal with the energy crisis is raised in the next section.

Application: Securing Access to Water and Energy

Any natural resource for which there is demand can become a scarcity issue, and as the planet expands its population and sophisticates and expands its needs for those resources, conflict over them is likely to increase. Titanium, for instance, is a relatively rare ore, but it only became a resource security problem after the development of intercontinental range ballistic missiles for which titanium was the only metal heat resistant enough to allow reentry from space into the atmosphere. Lithium is a current example. Both solar and wind power energy propagation are only feasible as alternatives if one can store the energy they produce; lithium-based batteries are the current answer. Different problems are associated with different natural resources; water security and energy security are prominent among them.

Water Security

In both a conceptual and existential sense, the problem of water security is more important and difficult than is the question of energy. Access to potable water is, after all, necessary for the propagation and sustenance of life, and it is the adequate abundance of water resources (and climate) that distinguishes Earth from uninhabitable planets both within the solar system and beyond. To paraphrase the Shah about oil, the alternative to adequate supply is to fight over the last drop. It is also a more difficult problem to solve because there is no alternative to water to sustain life. By contrast, there are alternate sources of energy to those currently being utilized, meaning the solution to energy shortages is discovering and exploiting different forms of energy—a considerable but not such an existential difficulty.

Water shortage is, for most inhabitants of the developed world, an abstract problem, because relatively few people in the Western hemisphere or Europe suffer from current or imminent water crises such as those that afflict swaths of Africa and Asia. The developing world is more naturally vulnerable, both because of geography (being the site of most of the world's greatest deserts, for instance) and having the greatest population explosions placing additional strains on existing supplies. In addition, in places such as central Africa, the technology of water extraction is least developed and least applied. Moreover, attempts to develop economically can have adverse effects on water supply: exploitation of shale formations involves the utilization and fouling of very large amounts of water, for instance. Climate change is also a factor, as monumental storms disrupt the water cycle. All this is particularly true in China. As Krupp points out, Chinese President Xi "has often spoken publicly about his concerns over the effects of climate change on China, where almost twenty percent of the land is desert, an area expanding at a rate of more than 1,300 square miles per year."

The water problem is, in some ways, analogous to claims of climate change a decade or more ago. A major difficulty that confronted those who warned of adverse effects was demonstrating their cogency for their audiences: there were few demonstrable effects that most people could observe, and projections of catastrophic change extended far enough into the future that they seemed ignorable—something to deal with later. For people in the developed world with the expertise to attack water difficulties, the current situation is analogous. Water seems ubiquitous, especially on coastlines to which people flock, and water-caused suffering and deprivation are abstractions happening far away. People moving to metropolitan areas expanding in Nevada may be the first to see the changes.

There are available supply-and-demand methods to deal with the growing crisis of water. The most prominent (and arguably humane) deal with ways to increase supply. Since there is a finite amount of water on the planet, these tend to concentrate on more optimal means of using the water that is already here. They tend to be of two kinds: expanding the availability of *usable* water by converting more of the world's six-sevenths of currently non-potable water to usable status, and making more efficient use of existing freshwater supplies.

Desalinization is the obvious method for converting unusable into usable water, but it has been a relatively expensive process that the least wealthy states have not been able to employ. It is little surprise that the states leading efforts at perfecting the process—including lowering costs—have been in the Middle East. Israel and Saudi Arabia, along with other Persian Gulf states, have led these efforts. Given that seawater is abundant and available in many places, the emphasis is natural. There have been reported successes in using solar energy to desalinate water, and even nuclear power may play a role (the nuclear reactors on American aircraft carriers create their own freshwater this way).

Conservation also plays a role. Storage dams stop excess flow from running unused into the oceans, where they become saline and unusable. Better forms of distribution of water through enhanced irrigation play a role, as does restricting use in drought-prone areas to non-water-intensive forms of agriculture. In parts of Africa, simply drilling wells and piping water from the source to users represents an infrastructure improvement that can lessen the burden on perpetually water-deficient areas. These efforts, however, require the expenditure of developmental resources that are often unavailable in the less wealthy parts of the world where the problems exist.

There is a demand side to the equation. While a good deal of the water problem is distributional, it is first and foremost a problem of increased human demand for water. Each additional human on the planet, after all, increases the global demand for potable water by 1,700 cubic meters. Population growth is thus, in a very real sense, the root cause of water shortage and security, and as long as population continues to increase, water scarcity alleviation will be a catchup enterprise. There are ethical, humanitarian, and religious objections to the implications of this observation, but they cannot be ignored if the problem is honestly to be addressed.

There are geopolitical implications as well. It is not clear what the pace of increasing supplies of potable water by desalination, more efficient use, or conservation will be, and it seems fair to assume that shortages will continue to build, and with them so will demands for greater supplies. When situations reach crisis proportions, resulting conflicts will likely be intense and could, in some selected areas, even become violent. The volatility of the possible situations has already been experienced over energy.

Energy Security

The traditional composition of energy use and security is changing in two basic ways. The first is changes in demand and includes who will make increasing demands and how this will change the level of demand for different forms of energy. The second, and related, change is in the forms that energy demands will take. Will the world gradually have a decline in use of traditional fossil fuel sources and their gradual replacement with alternate and especially nonpolluting, renewable sources of energy? The answers to this question will influence the energy picture of the future.

The countries that will make the greatest demands for increased energy are China and India. EIA projections estimate that these two countries alone will account for half of the growth in global energy between now and 2035. Much of this demand will come for petroleum, while the major OECD countries like the United States are reducing their needs for foreign oil and moving toward nonfossil sources. Whereas India and China will need more Persian Gulf oil, for instance, the United States will require less, both as the country converts away from traditional petroleum (thanks largely to shale oil and gas production) and as dynamics such as conservation lower the demand for petroleum products like gasoline. The EIA projects that by 2035, nearly five-eighths of world energy demands will come from non-OECD countries—488 of a total of 770 quadrillion British thermal units (BTUs)—compared to a 2008 figure of 260 quadrillion BTUs for the non-OECD world (52 percent).

This differential trend is also illustrated by changes in the American pattern. The United States will remain a major global energy consumer, but the exploitation of shale oil and gas will change its energy profile considerably. The progressive transformation of American energy (notably electricity) production away from coal and other fuels will also result in reduced energy costs for American industries, helping to support a competitive renaissance for American industries in world markets. The increasing contribution of energy from nontraditional sources such as wind and the sun's heat will also be factors.

At the same time, changing emphases will alter the contribution that energy source distributions have on world power maps. As the IEA outlook points out, three countries with large exploitable shale formations will likely dominate supplies of oil and gas from these sources: China, the United States, and Australia. Those who will likely suffer the most are the major oil-producing countries—and especially the oil-rich countries of the Middle East—which do not have noticeable known reservoirs of shale oil and gas formations. Apparently recognizing these changes, countries such as Saudi Arabia have begun actively engaging in wind and solar research with an eye toward commercialization.

Among the more intriguing prospects is the rising trend toward renewable sources such as solar and wind. These technologies have long been derided as marginal and economically infeasible, but recent breakthroughs have included a lowering of the costs of production to the point that these technologies compete economically with some fossil-based sources. The decline of coal, for instance, is largely because both wind and solar *and* shale gas are cheaper to exploit and use than coal for providing energy. This structural change could be the leading edge of a more general energy transformation, with the prospects of some ultimate solution such as fusion from seawater at the end of the process.

The pursuit of energy security has been one of the highest priorities of the state system since petroleum became the dominant source of world energy and changed important dynamics of how the world operates. Petroleum-based energy unlocked the door to vastly increased energy availability around the world, helped make possible the revolution in transportation, and greatly aided industrial activity. The world is a far different place than it was before the petroleum revolution.

The power map associated with traditionally derived petroleum energy may also be changing. Petroleum geologists and associated scientists and engineers have known for years about the potentially enormous amount of energy locked in the shale gas and oil reservoirs. The application of techniques such as hydraulic fracturing (fracking) has made exploitation commercially feasible and, in the process, begun a major change in thinking about energy. As this exploitation expands, it could stimulate the transformational effects on how the world treats and thinks about energy resources. By moving world energy dependence away from traditional petroleum, the use of shale gas could form the basis for a transition away from that petroleum to nonfossil fuel alternatives. The impact on both the geopolitics of energy and the relationship between energy and climate change could be dramatic.

Consider the mouth of the Persian Gulf as a geopolitical example. The Persian Gulf has been the point of egress of major amounts of the world's petroleum energy supplies since the period surrounding World War II. Almost all the oil from the major Organization of Petroleum Exporting Countries (OPEC) states—Saudi Arabia, Kuwait, Iran, and Iraq, for instance—flows on oil tankers out of the Gulf and around the world to feed the needs of a petroleum-addicted world. Traditionally, most of those ships have made a right turn into the Indian Ocean, heading west for destinations in Europe and North America, making protection of the oceanic highways out of the Gulf a major Western priority. The increasing use of shale oil and gas will gradually decrease that reliance, since the area lacks shale resources to make the voyage.

The tankers could start making a left turn out of the Gulf toward emerging energy markets in Asia. China and India are exemplary. Despite massive amounts of shale oil and gas reserves they cannot yet access economically, China is the largest growing market for energy, and that thirst is likely to increase. The need for oil as both a fuel and a lubricant will increase as more and more Chinese become automobile drivers, and China is already under both domestic and international pressure to reduce the percentage of coal it burns for power consumption for environmental reasons. The same imperative is even more pronounced for India, which does not have China's shale potential. If China is interested in being a leader in both the climate change movement and its commercialization, it needs to cease being the world's biggest polluter.

The transition also affects the rocky relationship between the champions of energy security and the supporters of environmental imperatives. Shale gas emits only about half the CO_2 into the atmosphere as does coal. The conversion of power-producing plants from coal to shale gas has already allowed the United States to reduce its CO_2 footprint (a factor that softens the blow of quitting the Paris agreement), and China's decision to stop building new coal-powered energy facilities indicates that President Xi, at least, has similar inclinations. Shale conversion is, of course, an interim solution to climate change, because shale gas is still a fossil fuel, if a less polluting one. A major movement toward shale-based energy could, however, be a first step in the transition to a nonfossil-fuel future of energy production that could ease pressures to reduce CO_2-caused climate change.

Conclusion

Resource scarcity of one kind or another has been a recurring feature of human history. Humankind has always wanted or needed resources that not all claimants could possess simultaneously in the amount they desired or needed—the definition of scarcity. The coveted resource in question has changed at different points in time, but the basic problem of scarcity seems perpetual.

Two of the most important resources—the Greeks' water and fire (energy)—are perpetual, enduring concerns. Both are critical to life on the planet. Water sustains life, and it is not a coincidence that the first question astrophysicists and others who search the universe for the possibility of life ask is whether celestial bodies can or do have water. Without water, there is no life. Energy may be scarce, but there are multiple sources and methods for its exploitation. The basic problem surrounding water is the maximum utilization of a finite, inelastic supply. Energy can come from many sources; the problem is finding and exploiting acceptable sources.

The dynamics of understanding and dealing with the two resources is different. Water's vitality as a resource derives from its absolute necessity as the source for creating and sustaining life. Moreover, it is a finite resource: there is only so much available, and thus the secret of water security is finding ways better to use what there is and making sure there is access for all legitimate claimants.

Several factors help frame the water security problem. One is the volume of water available. If one includes water unfit for human consumption (salt water), the water supply is more than abundant. Since only one-seventh of total global water is usable, however, water is selectively scarce, a problem that increased demand created by growing population and additional economic uses such as shale exploitation and food production for the larger population necessitate.

For water scarcity to decline, there are three clear mandates. First, the expansion of the potable water supple must occur, which means converting more ocean water to a form consumable by humans. This imperative means perfecting desalination technology that can better match supply and demand at affordable costs. Second, the other aspect of supply is distributional. If human demand and supply are to be in juxtaposition, water availability and location must be matched. Unfortunately, supplies of water are not distributed uniformly: there is more water in some places and not enough in others. The challenge is finding ways to increase supply to areas that are deficient. Third, these efforts can be made increasingly difficult by how water is treated as a geopolitical commodity. There are places where antagonists have used the withholding of water as a weapon—the Indus River system on the Indian subcontinent before 1960 is an example.

Energy scarcity is currently the more publicized global resource problem. The pressures of a growing global population, increasing portions of which demand a greater and more reliable supply of energy, and finite, dwindling reserves of traditional sources of energy combine to create this problem. Energy consumption is tied so closely to economic productivity that demand is both a matter of survival and the symbol of an increasingly prosperous physical condition for people.

Although the world energy map is clearly in the beginnings of a process of considerable change driven largely by advances in the exploitation of shale oil and gas deposits, much of this change remains uncertain and speculative. Thanks largely to this new source, a movement toward less CO_2-emitting fossil fuels may be the tip of the iceberg in a move away from polluting sources, but that prospect is certainly not inexorable. The ecological consequences of shale extraction (fracking) are not entirely known and are matters of controversy. Perversely, a great deal of the shale available is found in geographic locations that are water deficient. Shale technology uses large amounts of water that are not potable afterward unless they are treated. Technologies are available to return that water to usable quality, but they are expensive and undercut the economic advantage of moving to shale in the first place. If shale production cannot be the tip of the spear of movement away from traditional fossil fuel energy to some renewable, nonpolluting future, that path becomes more problematical. Although the shale "revolution" has certainly changed energy production patterns to the distinct advantage of the United States, there are remaining problems. Some are geological in terms of fissures and earthquakes that seem to intensify when shale extraction occurs. This new industry may have long-term economic impacts where it occurs that recipients may not recognize in advance. Some estimates are that over half the available products at a given site are mined in the first couple of years of exploitation, leaving declining assets and economically questionable quantities after that. One cannot help but wonder what this could mean for the "boom towns" spreading across places such as North Dakota. Other problems will almost certainly surface as the movement toward more shale usage expands.

There is a unifying possibility hidden within both these sources of resource scarcity and their alleviation—the world's oceans. As noted, desalinated water is a major component of adequate water supplies for many water-deficient areas, principally those that wash the ocean's shores. This leaves the formidable task of getting water to other places that need it but are too far from saline sources to gain access given current technologies. For energy purposes, science has not yet mastered the controlled fusion process it requires. Scientists have long believed that the ultimate solution to energy production is through nuclear fusion utilizing the abundant deuterium and tritium of ocean water as the primary source. Advocacies of fusion that surfaced a decade or more ago have proven to be premature, but using the ocean's vastness may be the key to an energy and water scarcity solution.

It is always a perilous task to predict the future with any certainty, because there are always uncertainties that arise and can bedevil even the best-laid plans and projections. What can be said with some certainty is that the pattern of water and energy usage and production is changing and that the effects will be important. But they will also be to some extent unpredicted and unpredictable. If one doubts that assertion, go back and look at projections made at the turn of the millennium and see how much of a future contribution they predicted for shale energy.

A world of abundant usable water and safe, nonpolluting energy is an aspiration that everyone does, or should, embrace. Harnessing water and fire would greatly enhance the human condition and make life more commodious globally. Accomplishing these monumental tasks will not end all scarcity and conflict over natural resources, but it certainly would be a good start.

Study/Discussion Questions

1. What is resource scarcity? Why has it always been a problem in international relations? Define the term and its implications for resource allocation. What are the possible solutions to a condition of scarcity?

2. What is water security? What makes it unique among resource scarcities? Discuss the nature

and structure of water as a scarce resource (e.g., simultaneous shortage and abundance). What are the categories of the problem in order of scarcity?

3. How is energy security different from water security? Why is petroleum so important to the nature and structure of the contemporary problem? Place petroleum use in the context of the evolution of different sources of energy. Is petroleum too valuable to burn?

4. What are the five most common sources of energy in use today? Discuss the nature, advantages, and disadvantages of each. Which involve fossil fuel burning and the consequent emission of CO_2 into the atmosphere? Relate this distinction to climate change and the desirability of moving away from fossil fuels for energy production.

5. Why does the text argue that water scarcity is "more important and difficult" than energy scarcity? Discuss the parameters of the problem and possible solutions, pointing out the difficulties associated with each solution.

6. How is the energy problem changing? Elaborate on each of the possible solutions identified. Place special emphasis on the movement from fossil fuel to nonfossil fuel alternatives and the implications of such a transition.

7. Discuss the geopolitics of change in energy sources, emphasizing the effects on the Middle East, climate change, and the unique potential role of China in the evolution.

8. How do the world's oceans offer a potential solution to both the problems of water and energy scarcity? Elaborate and speculate.

Bibliography

Central Intelligence Agency. *CIA World Factbook, 2017.* Washington, DC: U.S. Central Intelligence Agency, 2012.

Dinar, Shlomi, and Ariel Dinar. *International Water Scarcity and Variability: Managing Resource Use Across Political Boundaries.* Berkeley: University of California Press, 2016.

Fishman, Charles. *The Big Thirst: The Secret Life and Turbulent Future of Water.* New York: Free Press, 2012.

Fleischman, Stephen E. "Too Valuable to Burn." *Common Dreams Newsletter* (online), November 29, 2005.

Friedman, Thomas L. "The First Law of Petropolitics." *Foreign Policy,* May/June 2006, 36–44.

Holt, Jim. "It's the Oil." *London Review of Books* (online edition), October 18, 2006.

International Energy Agency. *World Energy Outlook, 2012.* Paris: International Energy Agency, November 2012. http://www.iea.org/publications.

Krupp, Fred. "Trump and the Environment: What His Plans Would Do." *Foreign Affairs* 96, no. 4 (July/August 2017): 73–82.

Kurlantzik, Joshua. "Put a Tyrant in Your Tank." *Mother Jones* 33, no. 3 (May/June 2008): 38–42.

Lankford, Bruce, Karen Brown, Mark Zeitoun, and Declan Conway, eds. *Water Security: Principles, Perspectives, and Practices.* New York: Routledge, 2013.

Richter, Brian. *Chasing Water: A Guide to Moving from Scarcity to Sustainability.* 2nd. ed. New York: Island Press, 2014.

Roberts, Paul. "The Seven Myths of Energy Independence." *Mother Jones* 33, no. 3 (May/June 2008): 31–37.

Schmidt, Jeremy J. *Water: Abundance, Scarcity, and Security in an Age of Humanity.* New York: New York University Press, 2017.

Sedlack, David. *Water 4.0: The Past, Present, and Future of the World's Most Valuable Resource.* New Haven, CT: Yale University Press, 2015.

Snow, Donald M. *Cases in International Relations: Portraits of the Future.* 3rd ed. New York: Pearson-Longman, 2008.

———. *National Security for a New Era.* 5th ed. New York: Pearson, 2014.

Solomon, Steven. *Water: The Epic Struggle for Wealth, Power, and Civilization.* New York: Harper Perennials, 2011.

Tindall, James A., and Andrew A. Campbell. *Water Security: Conflicts, Threats, Policies.* Denver, CO: DTP Publishing, 2011.

U.S. United States Energy Information Administration (Department of Energy). *Annual Energy Outlook 2013.* http://www.eia.gov/forecasts/aeo/index.cfm.

Walsh, Bryan. "The Scariest Environmental Fact in the World." *Time* (online), January 29, 2013.

"World Fossil Fuel Reserves." *The World Almanac and Book of Facts, 2013.* New York: World Almanac Books, 2013 (source International Energy Statistics Database, Energy Information Administration, U.S. Department of Energy).

Yergin, Daniel. "Ensuring Energy Security." *Foreign Affairs* 85, no. 2 (March/April 2006): 69–82.

Zweig, David, and Bi Jianhai. "China's Global Hunt for Energy." *Foreign Affairs* 84, no. 5 (September/October 2005): 18–24.

14

The Nature and Problem of Terror

Terrorism after ISIS?

The attacks of September 11, 2001, that brought terrorism into full public view are now nearly two decades removed, but terrorism remains a vital international and national concern. The 9/11 attacks punctuated a growing problem that had been building for at least two decades before 2001 but had not achieved the global notoriety that the attacks achieved. Since then, the threat has shifted away from the Al Qaeda (AQ) perpetrators, but new groups have arisen and terror has spread to other places. Since 2014, the focus has been on the Islamic State (IS), but that group has also probably passed the pinnacle of its notoriety. What is next?

The purpose of this case is to investigate the nature of the terrorist problem, how it is changing, and what can be done about it. It begins by examining briefly the dynamics of and problems created by terrorism and terrorists. It then moves to how terrorism has evolved structurally as a problem since September 11 and what efforts have been mounted against it. It concludes by examining the evolving nature of the threat and how to attack it.

The tragic terrorist attack by the Islamic terrorist group Al Qaeda against the World Trade Center on September 11, 2001, was a seminal international and national event. Internationally, 9/11 signaled a new and frightening escalation of a problem that had troubled other parts of the world for over two millennia. Nationally, the attacks traumatized an American population suddenly aware of its vulnerability and spawned a major national priority for dealing with the problem. The antiterrorist movement worldwide has had successes and failures against elements of the old AQ network, most notably the assassination of AQ founder and leader Osama bin Laden in 2011. AQ has lost its prominence but remains a diffused threat in parts of the Middle East. But other movements have arisen to take its place to ensure the problem of terrorism remains. New permutations have arisen that are, if anything, more provocative and dangerous. Most share radical Islam as a foundation. IS has been the most prominent successor, although it may be fading as a threat to global politics. The evolution from AQ to IS to some other leading threat is part of the overall dynamic of the threat.

Terrorist activity has moved geographically. The United States has not experienced a major coordinated attack by a foreign terrorist organization since 2001, although it has endured "lone-wolf" attacks by individuals inspired by ideological groups like IS. Instead, much organized terrorism has been against foreign targets, principally in Europe but also in Asia. If it has changed venues for now, terrorism nonetheless remains a major and, in some ways, more pervasive force that poses different threats to greater parts of the world.

Some of the changes are partially organizational and structural. Al Qaeda and other groups are no longer monolithic, hierarchical entities directing terror; rather, they have become loosely associated series of "franchises" bound by some ideological affinity. Acts of terror now include highly public acts by independent individuals known as lone wolves. The Internet sometimes serves as a connector between these demented individuals and purveyors of venomous, murderous hatred via so-called virtual networks or leaderless resistance groups.

Principle: The Nature and Problem of Terrorism

The first step in coming to grips with terrorism is defining the term. It is an important consideration, because so many phenomena in the contemporary international arena are labeled terrorist. This makes a definition particularly important to measure whether a specific movement, or act, is terrorism or not. Without a set of criteria defining what does and does not constitute terrorism, it is hard to tell.

This is not a merely semantic exercise. Take, for instance, the episodic emphasis on Chechen separatists and their separatist campaign against the Russian government, which that government has called terrorist. Certainly, actions such as enlisting suicide terrorists to blow up two Russian airliners and the brutal siege of the school in Beslan in the Caucasus were hideous, brutal acts that comport with an understanding of terrorism, but is it correct to label the movement that commissioned and carried out the acts terrorist as a result? In context, when the Russian government of the then-president Boris Yeltsin used the Russian army to attack Chechnya in 1995 to wipe out the secessionist movement there (among other things, leveling the capital of Grozny) and President Vladimir Putin renewed the campaign in 1999, there were widespread international accusations that the Russian government was terrorizing the Chechens and engaging in crimes against humanity (acts of state terrorism). Who were the terrorists here?

An agreed-on definition of terrorism would help answer such questions; unfortunately, such a consensual definition does not exist. Rather, there are many different definitions people and organizations in the field employ. Some commonalities recur and will allow the adoption of a definition for present purposes. A few arguably representative examples will aid in drawing distinctions.

The U.S. government offers the official definition in its 2003 *National Strategy for Combating Terrorism*: "premeditated, politically motivated violence perpetrated against noncombatant targets by subnational groups or clandestine agents." In *Attacking Terrorism*, coauthor Audrey Kurth Cronin says terrorism is distinguished by its political nature, its nonstate base, the targeting of innocent noncombatants, and the illegality of its acts. Jessica Stern, in *Terrorism in the Name of God*, defines terrorism as "an act or threat of violence against noncombatants with the objective of exacting revenge, intimidating, or otherwise influencing an audience." Alan Dershowitz (in *Why Terrorism Works*) notes that definitions typically include reference to terrorist targets, perpetrators, and terrorist acts.

These definitions, and similar ones from others in the field, have common cores. All of them share three common points of reference: terrorist acts (illegal, often hideous and atrocious), terrorist targets (often innocent noncombatants), and terrorist purposes (political persuasion or influence). The only difference among them is whether they specify the nature of terrorists and their political base: the State Department, Cronin, and Dershowitz all identify terrorist organizations as nonstate-based actors. Cronin emphasizes that "although states can terrorize, by definition they cannot be terrorists." Using that definition, the Chechens are terrorists and the Russians are not.

For the rest of this case study, terrorism will be defined as "the commission of atrocious acts against a target population normally to gain compliance with some demands the terrorists insist upon." It does not specify that terrorism must be committed by nonstate actors. That may be a characteristic of modern terrorism, but terrorism is terrorism, regardless of who carries it out. Using this definition, the Russians were also terrorists. Terrorism thus consists of three related phenomena, each of which must be present in some manner for something to be considered an act of terrorism. The fourth element in other definitions, perpetrators of terrorism, is implicit in the three criteria.

Terrorist Acts

Terrorist acts are the most visible and recognizable manifestations of terrorism. These actions are the recognizable aspect of terrorism. For most people, these acts are synonymous with the broader phenomenon of terrorism. Several comments can be made about terrorist acts to begin the examination of this uniquely violent form of political expression.

First, what distinguishes terrorist acts from other politically motived acts is that they are uniformly illegal. Terrorist acts upset the normalcy of life through destructive actions aimed at either injuring or killing people or destroying things. Regardless of the professed underlying motives the perpetrators espouse, these actions break laws wherever they are committed and are subject to criminal prosecution. Terrorists attempt to raise the legitimacy of their actions by proclaiming them "acts of war" (currently holy war or *jihad*). The purpose is to elevate what they do to a higher plane ("one man's terrorist is another man's freedom fighter"), but the simple fact remains that terrorist acts are criminal in nature. Whether terrorism is crime or war (or both) has consequences for how it is treated and how it is countered.

Second, the general purpose of terrorist acts has been to frighten the target audience; the word *terrorism* is derived from the Latin root *terrere*, which means "to frighten." The method of inducing fright is through the commission of normally random, unpredictable acts of violence that induce such fear that those who witness or experience the acts or believe they could be the objects of similar future attacks conclude that compliance with terrorist demands is preferable to living with the fear of being victims themselves. To accomplish this goal, acts of terrorism are not aimed explicitly at the actual victims themselves but at the audience that views the actions and that may see themselves as future victims. Fright is accomplished by the disruption of the predictability and safety of life within society, one of whose principal functions is to make existence predictable and safe. Thus, a major purpose of terrorist mayhem is to undermine this vital fiber of society, including the belief of its members that authorities can protect them.

Terrorists may, of course, act for a variety of other reasons. In 2004, Brian Jenkins provided a useful list of six other purposes for terrorist actions. They may be aimed at exacting special concessions, such as ransom, the release of prisoners (generally members of the terrorist group), or more simply at publicizing a message. As a historic example, gaining the release of political prisoners was the stated reason that Hezbollah kidnapped Israeli soldiers in the summer of 2006. Indonesia's Jemaah Islamiyah carried out a 2004 attack on the Australian embassy and promptly announced that it would perpetrate similar attacks if its leader, Abu Bakar Bashir, were not released from prison.

Terrorists may act to publicize their causes. Before Palestinian terrorists kidnapped a series of airliners and then launched an attack on the Israeli compound at the Munich Olympics in the 1970s, hardly anyone outside the region had ever heard of the Palestinian cause; the terrorist actions provided that global awareness.

Another, and more fundamental, purpose of terrorist acts is to cause widespread disorder that demoralizes society and breaks down the social order in a country. This, of course, is a very ambitious purpose, and one that presumably can only be undertaken through a widespread campaign that includes numerous apparently random terrorist acts. The campaign of IS in establishing the caliphate and, since that campaign has faltered, its attacks on European targets has this as one of its purposes.

A more tactical use of terrorism is to provoke overreaction by a government in the form of repressive action, reprisals, and overly brutal counterterrorism that may lead to the overthrow of the reactive government. This has been a favorite tactic of Boko Haram, the Nigerian-based terrorist group that has attempted to lure the government in Lagos to attack certain regions, which would alienate the inhabitants and help recruit support for the terrorists.

Terror may also be used to enforce obedience and cooperation within a target population. Campaigns of terror directed by the governments of states against their own citizens often have this purpose; these campaigns are often assigned to a secret police or similar paramilitary organizations. The actions of the KGB in the Soviet Union, the Gestapo and other similar organizations in Nazi Germany, and the infamous death squads in Argentina during the 1960s and 1970s are all examples of the use of government terror to intimidate and frighten their own populations into submission. At a less formal governmental level, many actions of the Ku Klux Klan during the latter nineteenth and early twentieth centuries against black Americans would qualify as well.

Jenkins's last purpose of terrorist action is punishment. Terrorists often argue that an action they take is aimed at a specific person or place because that person or institution is somehow guilty of a transgression and is thus being punished for what the terrorists consider a crime. Although the Israeli government would be appalled at the prospects of calling its rescinded counterterrorist campaign to bulldoze the homes of the families of suicide terrorists (or bombing the homes of dissident leaders) as an act of terror, from the vantage point of the Palestinian targets of the attacks, they certainly must seem so.

Stern (in *Terrorism in the Name of God*) adds a seventh motivation that is internal to the terrorist organization: morale. Like any other organization, and especially terrorist groups in which the "operatives" are generally young and immature, occasional attacks may be necessary simply to demonstrate to the membership the continuing potency of the group to keep the membership focused and their morale high. As Stern puts it, "Attacks sometimes have more to do with rousing the troops than terrorizing the victims," and may also have useful spin-off effects, such as helping recruit new members or raising funds to support the organization's activities. Once again, recent IS activities probably include this motive.

Terrorist Targets

Terrorist targets can be divided into two related categories. The first is people, and the objective is to kill, maim, or otherwise cause some members of the target population to suffer as an example for the rest of that population. The second category is physical targets, attacks against which are designed to disrupt and destroy societal capabilities and to demonstrate the vulnerability of the target society. The two categories are related in that most physical targets contain people who will be killed or injured in the process. Attacking targets in either category demonstrates that the target government cannot protect its members and valued artifices. The desired effect is that the targets question the efficacy or worth of resisting terrorist demands.

There are subtle differences and problems associated with concentrating on one category or the other. Attacks intended to kill or injure people are the most personal and evoke the greatest emotion in the target population, including the will to resist and to seek vengeance. From the terrorist vantage point, the reason to attack people is to undercut their will to resist the demands that terrorists make. Dennis Drew and I refer to this as *cost-tolerance*, the level of suffering one is willing to endure in the face of some undesirable situation. The terrorist seeks to exceed the target's cost-tolerance by making the target audience conclude that it is physically or mentally less painful to accede to the terrorist's demands than it is to continue to resist those demands. This goal is achieved by maximizing the fear and anxiety that the target experiences because of the potentially hideous effects of attacks. If the target group comes to fear being the next victim more than accepting the terrorist demands, cost-tolerance is exceeded and the terrorist wins; if the target remains resolute, the terrorist fails.

Overcoming cost-tolerance is not an easy task, and it usually fails. For one thing, terrorist organizations are generally small and have limited resources, meaning that they usually lack the wherewithal to terrorize enough of the target population to make members become individually fearful enough to tip the scales (blowing up people on airplanes may be a partial exception). Should terrorist groups obtain and use weapons of mass destruction, such a turn of events would be a game changer. Attacking and killing innocent members of a target group may and usually does infuriate its members and increase, rather than decrease, their will to resist. That was the case in the reaction to the 9/11 attacks and has been the reaction of Western European populations more recently.

When the targets are physical things rather than people per se, the problems and calculations change. The range of potential physical targets is virtually boundless. In attacking places, the terrorist seeks to deprive the target population of whatever pleasure or value the object may provide for them. The list of what are called *countervalue* targets covers a very broad range of objects, from hydroelectric plants to athletic stadiums, from nuclear power generators to military facilities, from highways to research facilities, and so on. Compiling a list for any large community and trying to figure out how to protect it all is a very sobering experience.

It is unreasonable to assume that the whole potential list of physical targets for any country can be made uniformly invulnerable. There are simply too many targets, and the means to protect them are sufficiently different that there is little overlap in function (protecting a football stadium from bombers may or may not have much carryover in protecting nuclear power plants from seizure). There will always be a gap between potential threats and the ability to negate them all. The consequence is a certain level of risk that cannot be removed.

Terrorist Objectives

The final element is the objectives, or reasons, for which terrorists act as they do. For present purposes, the discussion will emphasize the broader, long-term or strategic reasons that terrorists seek (or say they seek) to accomplish. In the short term or tactical run, terrorists may engage in violent actions for a variety of reasons, as already noted. Causing havoc in and terrorizing the citizens of Paris has been a short-term goal for IS; establishing an expanding caliphate is its long-term, strategic purpose.

The ultimate goals of terrorist groups are political. To paraphrase the Clausewitzian dictum that war is politics by other means, so too is terrorism politics by other, extreme, means. Likewise, the objectives are pursued by extreme means that color perceptions of the objectives. Sometimes, the objectives are articulated clearly, and at other times they are not. Ultimately, campaigns of terror gain their meaning in the pursuit of some goal or goals, and their success or failure is measured by the extent to which they achieve those goals. Historically, the more grandiose the goals, the less likely it is that they have been achieved.

Terrorism is the method of the militarily weak and conceptually unacceptable. The extremely unorthodox nature of terrorist actions arises from the fact that terrorists cannot compete with their targets by the accepted methods of the target society for success. Terrorists lack the military resources to engage in open warfare, at which they would be easily defeated, or in the forum of public discourse and decision, because their objectives are unacceptable, distasteful, or even bizarre to the target population.

The fact that terrorist objectives are politically objectionable to the target sets up the confrontation between the terrorists and the target. Normally, terrorist goals are stated in terms of changing policies (Palestinian statehood or the right to repatriation within Israel, for example) or laws repressing groups of supporters. Because the terrorists are in a minority, they cannot bring about the changes they demand by normal electoral or legislative means, and their demands are likely to be viewed as so basically lunatic and unrealistic that the target does not take them seriously. The demands make perfect sense to the terrorists, and they are frustrated and angered by the dismissal they receive.

Determining whether terrorists achieve their goals or fail is complicated by the contrast between the short- and long-term levels of objectives. Modern terrorists have rarely been successful at the strategic level of attaining long-range objectives. Al Qaeda did not force the United States from the Arabian Peninsula (Osama bin Laden's stated goal), Russia has not granted Chechnya independence, and IS has basically failed to institute a sectarian caliphate. At the same time, the terrorist record at achieving tactical objectives (carrying out terrorist attacks) is not a total failure. If terrorists continue to exist and to achieve some tactical goals, they remain a force against the targets of their activities.

The history of terrorism, moreover, suggests its ability to endure. Different terrorist groups with different objectives come and go, but terrorism has endured for at least two millennia (most historians of terrorism—see Rapaport, for instance—date the practice to the resistance to Roman rule over Palestine during biblical times). The long-term strategic failure of terrorist movements does not dissuade its practitioners so much as does its short-term successes. For as long as this dynamic remains true, terrorism is not going to go away.

Evolving Terrorism since September 11, 2001

The peril posed by terrorism is changing. The events of September 11 reintroduced the world to a 2,000-year-old phenomenon largely forgotten during a century of world wars and a Cold War that could have turned into a nuclear Armageddon. To the extent that Americans and many others had much if any previous exposure to terrorism, it was with more "classical" forms, such as the Irish Republican Army (IRA), state terrorism in the form of suppression by totalitarian regimes such as Hitler's Germany or Stalin's Soviet Union, or with isolated anarchist assassinations or individual acts such as the bombing of the Murrah Federal Building in Oklahoma City in 1995. AQ's attack was qualitatively different.

Understanding the new threat was different for at least two reasons. First, the new form of terrorism was very different from anything encountered before. It was nonstate-based terrorism arising not from specific political communities or jurisdictions but instead flowing across national boundaries like oil slipping under doors. It is religious, demonstrating degrees of fanaticism and intolerance that, while present in most religious communities, are alien to most people's ability to conceptualize. It is also fanatically anti-American and anti-Western in ways and for reasons that most Westerners have difficulty comprehending. In addition, it has employed methods such as suicide terrorism that are inconceivable to many Westerners.

Second, understanding contemporary terrorism is made more difficult by its changeable nature and practitioners. The Al Qaeda of 2001 was hard enough to understand, but terrorism has evolved and morphed greatly since. Modern terrorism is truly a hydra-headed monster, in terms of both who employs it and for what reasons.

Stern, in *Terrorism in the Name of God*, usefully articulates the requirements for a successful terrorist organization. Its effectiveness depends on two qualities: resiliency (the ability to withstand the loss of parts of its membership or workforce) and capacity (the ability to optimize the scale and impact of terrorist attacks). The larger the scale of operations the terrorist organization can carry out without large losses to its members, the more effective the organization is. Conversely, an organization that can only carry out small, relatively insignificant acts while having large portions of its membership captured or killed is less effective.

Clearly, resiliency and capacity are related. To carry out large operations such as 9/11 or the IS campaign to create the Islamic State, an organization must have a sophisticated, coordinated plan involving multiple people or cells that must communicate with one another both to plan and to execute the attack. The Achilles' heel in terrorist activity is penetration by outsiders, and the key element in doing so is to interrupt communications to penetrate the group and move through the hierarchy to interfere with and destroy it and its ability to operate (in other words, to reduce its resiliency). The most effective way for the terrorist groups to avoid penetration is to minimize communications that can be intercepted, but doing this comes at the expense of the sophistication and extent of its actions (reduction in capacity).

The result is a dilemma that faces contemporary terrorist organizations. Historically, according to Stern and others, most terrorist groups have followed an organizational form known as the *commander-cadre* (or *hierarchical*) model. This form of group is not dissimilar to the way virtually all complex enterprises are structured everywhere: Executives (commanders) organize and plan activities (terrorist attacks) and pass instructions downward through the structure for implementation by employees (cadres).

Commander-cadre arrangements have advantages associated with any large, complex organization. They can coordinate activities maximizing capacity; organize recruitment efforts and absorb, indoctrinate, and train recruits; and carry out ancillary activities such as fundraising. The disadvantage of these organizations is that they become more permeable by outside agencies because of their need to communicate among units. Modern electronics become a double-edged sword for the terrorist: they facilitate communications in executing attacks, but those communications can be intercepted and lead to resiliency-threatening penetration. Just as electronics can aid those who oppose terrorists, they can also aid the terrorists. The sophisticated electronic efforts of IS are a clear case for how to use the Internet in its various forms to aid recruitment, indoctrination, and fund-raising, for instance.

One result of antiterrorist efforts has been to cause these organizations to adapt, to become what Stern refers to as the "protean enemy." Al Qaeda still exists but is no longer a hierarchically organized entity that plans and carries out terrorist missions. Instead, it has adopted elements of the alternate form of terrorist organization, the *virtual network* or *leaderless resistance* model, and has dispersed itself into a series of smaller, loosely affiliated terrorist organizations that draw inspiration from the center.

Particularly since the assassination of bin Laden, these mutations, sometimes called "franchises," have increasingly become the public face of terrorism both for AQ and other terrorist entities. AQ activities, for instance, are usually carried out by spin-offs like Al Qaeda in the Arabian Peninsula (AQAP) in places such as Yemen or by Al Qaeda in the Maghreb (AQIM) in places such as Mali. Al-Shabab, also an AQ affiliate, is a major actor in Somalia. What distinguishes the actions of such groups is a relatively modest size and geographical reach.

The effect of changes has been to make the competition between terrorist organizations and their suppressors more sophisticated, difficult, deadly, and expensive than it was when AQ burst on the public stage in the period leading to and after 2001. The change has organizationally been in both directions. At the more expansive level, IS emerged in 2014 as a much larger, ambitious entity than previous contemporary organizations, none of which had professed an ambition as large as establishing a territorial state (see chapter 1). At the other extreme, much operational terror—especially in the United States—has been transferred to leaderless resistance practitioners acting essentially as lone wolves. Each end of the spectrum represents an evolutionary permutation that creates new horrors and problems for target societies. They are also almost certainly not the last forms terrorism will take in the years ahead.

Application: Dealing with Terrorism after ISIS

What kind of threat does terrorism pose today? Will it continue to pose a threat in the future? If so, what will that threat be like? The first part of an answer requires a distinction between terrorism as a method and the existence and actions of groups of terrorists. Terrorism has been venerable, and its persistent, if episodic, recurrence suggests that it has enough appeal to desperate groups who feel they have no other way to achieve their goals that they are likely to continue to turn to terrorism as a blueprint. The only way to extinguish the recourse to terrorism as a method is to be able to convince potential terrorists that doing so is futile—that terrorism in fact always fails and thus it is irrational even to consider adopting it as a method. Since some terrorists *are* irrational, even this might not be a foolproof strategy. One is reminded of the sixth corollary to Murphy's Law: "Nothing is foolproof because fools are so ingenious."

The whole object of efforts to suppress terror is to destroy or make impotent terrorists—either those organized into groups or individual lone wolves. Each category presents different challenges described below, but a concentration on terrorists is much more concrete than an assault on an idea or methodology. Largely for this reason, what are normally described as antiterrorism efforts are more accurately antiterrorist efforts. Aside from providing a concrete focus for suppression efforts, this approach has the added attraction that it may be effective: one can kill those who hold ideas, if not the ideas themselves. It is often said that terrorist groups and movements come and go; it is terrorism that endures.

The current and future threats posed by terrorism are thus questions about what to do about those individuals or groups that practice or contemplate adopting terrorism to accomplish their goals. Part of this effort is aimed at doing away with the conditions that cause people to become terrorists. Well-adjusted people who are content and see a hopeful future for themselves are unlikely to want to overthrow or destroy the status quo from which they benefit. Unfortunately, that condition is not universal.

Conditions in many parts of the world breed feelings of hopelessness, despair, or personal helplessness that creates vulnerability to appeals to attack violently the environments causing their frustrations. These conditions are most prevalent in parts of the developing world but can also be found in some urban, normally ghetto-like locales in the developed world. These breeding grounds are vulnerable to appeals by terrorists and often referred to as *swamps*, an analogy with physical places that nurture the development of deadly insects. Part of the effort for dealing with terrorist vulnerability and recruitment is removing these precipitating conditions, known as *draining the swamp*. Human misery, however, is widespread enough (there is an abundance of swamps) that attempts at swamp draining offer only a partial palliative. Spraying the swamps (killing terrorists) may provide a more viscerally satisfying result.

Understanding efforts to deal with terrorism is a two-step process. It begins by looking at the categories of terrorist suppression, the overarching concept under which the various efforts can be grouped. The other perspective is looking at the terrorism problem in organizational terms, from the discontented individual lone wolf through dispersed or virtual networks that organize and orchestrate efforts to larger terrorist organizations like IS and beyond. In both cases, the distinctions often blend together in practice. Individual terrorists are often recruited by virtual networks, for instance, and successful virtual networks may broaden their purview.

Suppressing Terrorists: Antiterrorism and Counterterrorism

Conventional terrorism suppression circles are divided into two methods for dealing with the terrorist problem: antiterrorism and counterterrorism. The two terms are sometimes used interchangeably, although each refers to a distinct form of action with a specific and different contribution to the overall goal. Any program of terrorist suppression will necessarily contain elements of each of them, but failing to specify which is which only confuses the issue.

Antiterrorism refers to defensive efforts to reduce the vulnerability of targets to terrorist attacks and to lessen the effects of terrorist attacks that do occur. Antiterrorism efforts begin from the implicit premise that some terrorist attacks will be attempted and some will succeed tactically, and that two forms of suppression effort are necessary. First, antiterrorists seek to make it more difficult to mount terrorist attacks. Airport security to prevent potential terrorists from boarding airliners or the interception and detention of suspected terrorists by border guards are examples. Second, antiterrorists try to mitigate the effects of terrorist attacks that might or do occur. Blocking off streets in front of public buildings such as the White House so that terrorists cannot get close enough to destroy them is one approach, and civil defense measures (i.e., hazmat operations) to mitigate the effects of an attack is another way to deal with the problem.

There are three related difficulties with conducting an effective antiterrorist campaign. One is that antiterrorism is necessarily reactive; terrorists choose where attacks will occur and against what kinds of targets, and antiterrorists try to anticipate or respond to the terrorist initiative. A second problem is the sheer variety and number of potential targets. As noted earlier, the list of targets is almost infinite, and terrorists seek to randomize targets so that potential victims are always off guard and antiterrorists will have trouble anticipating where attacks may occur. The third problem is *target substitution*: If antiterrorist efforts are sufficiently successful that terrorists determine their likelihood of success against a specific target (or class of targets) is diminished significantly, they will simply go on to other, less well-defended targets.

The other form of terrorist suppression is *counterterrorism*, offensive and military measures against terrorists or sponsoring agencies to prevent, deter, or respond to terrorist acts. Counterterrorism thus consists of both preventive and retaliatory actions. Preventive acts can include such actions as penetrating terrorist organizations or apprehending and using physical violence against terrorists before they carry out their operations. One may not be able to protect all objects in a category of targets, but if one can find out what the target is, the counterterrorist may be able to intercept and prevent the attack. Retaliation is often military and paramilitary and includes attacks on terrorist camps or other facilities in response to terrorist attacks or to disrupt or eliminate concentrations of terrorists. The purposes of retaliation include punishment, reducing terrorist capacity for future acts, and hopefully deterrence of future actions by instilling fear of the consequences. The assassination of Osama bin Laden is a classic example of counterterrorism.

Counterterrorism is inherently and intuitively attractive. Preventive actions are proactive, taking the battle to the terrorists and punishing them in advance of creating harm. In their purest form, preventive counterterrorist actions reverse the tables in the relationship, effectively "terrorizing the terrorists." Pounding a terrorist facility as punishment after enduring a terrorist attack at least entails the satisfaction of knowing the enemy has suffered as well as the victim.

The problem with counterterrorism, like antiterrorism, is that it is insufficient by itself to quell all terrorism. Preventing terrorist actions requires a level of intelligence about the structures of terrorist organizations that is quite difficult to obtain, and terrorist organizations seek to increase that difficulty. The effect is to make a terrorist network difficult to penetrate, and thus to interrupt those activities. The absence of a terrorist state base that can be attacked means it is more difficult to identify terrorist targets whose retaliatory destruction will cripple the organization, punish its members, or frighten it into ceasing future actions, especially without further alienating the people and government of the state where the terrorists take refuge.

Ideally, antiterrorism and counterterrorist efforts act in tandem. Counter-terrorists reduce the number and quality of possible attacks through preventive actions, making the task of antiterrorist efforts to ameliorate the effects of attacks that do succeed less difficult. Further counterterrorist action then can hopefully reduce the terrorists' capacity for future mayhem. The result is a more manageable threat confronting the antiterrorists. In practice, however, these efforts sometimes come into operational conflict.

The Contemporary Threats

Largely due to the success and greater sophistication of terrorism suppression efforts since September 11, 2001, the shape of the threat has undergone a major transformation. Al Qaeda still exists, even if its most villainous figure, bin Laden, is dead, and its monolithic, commander-cadre structure has largely disintegrated under a relentless assault that has killed or captured much of the old network. IS remains the major exception, but is an organization under growing stress. The threat has mostly dispersed among a much more diffuse set of loose organizations and individuals. Stern describes this new face of terrorism in a 2010 *Foreign Affairs* article: "The destructive ideology that animates the al Qaeda movement is spreading around the globe, including, in some cases, to small town America. Homegrown zealots, motivated by al Qaeda's distorted interpretation of Islam, may not yet be capable of carrying out 9/11-style strikes, but they could nonetheless terrorize a nation." The major instances have been in Europe, where the terrorist-vulnerable population is larger than in the United States and where some governments have not been as aggressive terrorism suppressors as the Americans.

Part of this dispersion has been the result of actions taken by bin Laden and his associates in the 1980s and 1990s that have been essentially replicated by IS. Al Qaeda operated terrorist training camps openly in Afghanistan, the organization trained thousands of recruits from countries around the globe, and many of these individuals returned to their homes and have organized affiliated movements that now carry out many of the terrorist activities associated with Al Qaeda. Some of these offshoots still exist, and IS has enlisted sympathetic organizations in places like the Philippines. Hoffman argues that the AQ precedent has created a model for adoption by others. It has four distinct dimensions introduced earlier in the chapter. What he calls Al Qaeda Central contains the remnants of the original 9/11 organization. Al Qaeda Affiliates and Associates consist of the spinoff organizations: Al Qaeda in Iraq (from which IS was spawned) is a prime example. Al Qaeda Locals are virtual network organizations in different locations; terrorist activity in Mali is exemplary. Finally, there is the Al Qaeda Network, which is composed of "homegrown Islamic radicals"; much of the so-called lone-wolf activity is of this nature. The AQ network per se has faded, but this model may persist in structure, if not in name.

Three permutations of this model are particularly prominent and troublesome in the contemporary scene. One is the problem of the "lone-wolf" terrorist, an individual who commits acts of terror without apparent outside assistance or motivation. The second is the activities associated with virtual networks, a phenomenon greatly accentuated by the exploitation of the Internet to further their activities. The third is large-scale organizations such as AQ or IS. All are troublesome because each poses a different level of threat and difficulty to suppress.

Lone-Wolf Terrorists

The phenomenon of individuals apparently unconnected to any organized terrorist group has been a recurring part of the terrorism problem for a long time. Because their actions are idiosyncratic, isolated, and often erratic, they do not individually receive the level of attention that more systematic, organized movements do. Cumulatively, however, the rise in their prominence, especially in the United States, parallels a decline in activities by larger, more monolithic organizations. For Americans, lone wolves are the living face of terror in their lives.

Awareness of lone wolves in the United States emerged in the 1990s with the unrelated cases of Unabomber Theodore Kaczynski (the deranged university professor who killed three and wounded more than twenty others with letter bombs between 1978 and 1995) and Timothy McVeigh, who killed 159 people in the truck bombing of the Murrah Federal Building in Oklahoma City in 1995. Since these highly publicized cases, there have been increasing if episodic instances of domestic lone wolves in various unrelated locations from San Bernardino, California (where a disgruntled and radicalized employee attacked fellow workers at a social service agency), to Orlando, Florida, site of an attack on a packed nightclub that left forty-nine dead. These atrocious events followed other well publicized attacks such as the killing and wounding of more than thirty fellow soldiers by Major Nidal Hasan at Fort Hood, Texas, in fall 2009 and the 2013 bombing at the Boston Marathon by two brothers. Each instance pointed to the difficulty of getting a precise handle on terrorism committed by autonomous individuals in advance of their acts.

What are the characteristics of the lone-wolf terrorist? The European Union's *Instituut voor Veiligheids-en Crisismanagement* offers a useful set of interrelated characteristics in a 2007 study. First and foremost, lone wolves act individually rather than as parts of organized and directed groups. Second, lone wolves do not belong to any organized terrorist group or network. Third, they act without the direct influence of a leader or hierarchy. Fourth, the tactics and methods they employ are conceived and conducted by the individual without "any direct outside command or direction." Lone-wolf terrorist activities are conceived by individuals who act autonomously in designing and carrying out their acts. The extent of their autonomy compounds the difficulty of identifying and suppressing them in advance. Their lack of affiliation means that they likely do not appear on terrorist watch lists, and unless they engage in aberrant behavior that causes citizens to report them to authorities, they present no pre-attack footprint.

The nature of lone-wolf acts speaks to why they are simultaneously so difficult yet marginal in the greater scheme of terrorism. The autonomy of the lone wolf makes him or her extremely difficult to identify in advance, because, by definition, these individuals are usually antisocial loners. Belonging to no terrorist groups, they have no communications to intercept and trace back to them, and they may be able to evade detection for a long time after they commit their acts, unless they make some crucial mistake that leads to their apprehension. The Unabomber, after all, evaded identification and capture for seventeen years before his brother recognized his identity through the text of one of his manifestos and turned him in to authorities. On the other hand, acting alone generally limits the sophistication and extent of the destruction the lone wolf can inflict. The Murrah attack by McVeigh may well represent the outward limits of mayhem that lone wolves can inflict. Blowing up an airplane in flight or contemporary attacks on public places such as the Pulse nightclub in Orlando or a concert hall in Manchester, England, may also serve as outer limits.

Lone-wolf attacks are frequent enough, however, to cause concern. The European Union (EU) study, for instance, catalogued instances conforming to its criteria between 1968 and 2007 in the developed world. According to this report, thirty lone-wolf attacks occurred in the United States, followed by nine in Germany, seven in France, six in Spain, five in Italy, three in Canada, two each in Australia, the Netherlands, Russia, and the United Kingdom, and one each in Denmark, Poland, Portugal, and Sweden.

Two other factors make the isolation and categorization of lone-wolf terrorism problematical. One is whether an individual act meets the criteria for terrorism laid out earlier in this chapter, or whether it is an instance of pure depravity. This difficulty is particularly relevant when trying to determine the objective of a lone-wolf attack. McVeigh, in his twisted way, had the apparent objective of avenging the Branch Dravidians who had died at Waco, Texas. What, on the other hand, was the objective of those who attacked young people reveling at a nightclub or teenagers attending an English rock concert?

The other factor is the degree of autonomy and independence of the apparent lone wolf. Groups with diverse messages of hate increasingly publicize their causes and exhort their followers on the Internet, and it is often unclear whether apparently independent acts have been influenced by such appeals. There is evidence, for instance, that Major Hasan was "inspired" by extreme antiabortion appeals on the Internet, and he was influenced by the violent sermons of American-born, Yemen-based Muslim cleric Anwar al-Awlaki, an AQ supporter who exhorted American Muslims and others to rise and attack infidels.

Virtual Networks

The virtual network/leaderless resistance and protean hybrid forms of terrorist organizations are the adaptations that terrorists have had to make in the face of the increased sophistication of terrorist suppressors against traditional commander-cadre groups. They represent ways to deal with the ability of terrorism suppressors to intercept direct electronic communications to penetrate terrorist hierarchies. The primary adaptation has been to cease direct communications between terrorist leaders and followers in locations where the means of communications interception is most active and thus where traditional terrorist forms are most vulnerable. As electronic methods and platforms have multiplied and provided burgeoning numbers of communications channels where there is no direct, easily traceable link between equally anonymous message senders and receivers, these virtual networks have also become major conduits for shadowy terrorist communications, including the planning and commission of terrorist attacks.

The genesis of this adaptation was apparently the reaction of Louis Beam and his Aryan Nation followers to government discovery and harassment of their activities based on wiretaps by the FBI of Beam's conversations and illegal planning with his followers. The response was to cease direct communications among group members. One advantage of severing communications was to deprive the government of advanced knowledge of Aryan Nation plans; another was to shield Beam from direct responsibility for illegal actions. As adapted by others, it has also made penetration of terrorist organizations more difficult.

The heart of this model is to eliminate a direct link between leaders and followers that terrorist suppressors monitor. Direct contact is replaced by indirect communication such as coded messages on Facebook and similar sites that seek to attract new members, spread the group's message, and even exhort members to actions. The posting of sermons by al-Awlaki from Yemen, for instance, effectively served to help radicalize lone-wolf terrorists like Hasan. Given the vastness and portability of Internet access, it is an effective tool to protect the identity and location of leaders and the identities of receiving followers and thus to reinforce resiliency in the organization. For example, despite concerted efforts to capture and eliminate al-Awlaki, he remained at large in the mountainous desert of Yemen until he was killed in a drone attack in 2011.

Operating virtual networks has both advantages and disadvantages. The advantages are primarily in increasing resiliency, particularly in places where the suppressing government's electronic surveillance capabilities are greatest. It should, for instance, come as no great surprise that the model was spawned in the United States, where, over the years, American authorities (notably the Federal Bureau of Investigation) have developed very sophisticated means of penetrating subversive organizations of all kinds, including terrorists. Eliminating virtual organizations, however, is much more difficult, especially in identifying terrorists and their followers and plans before attacks. Because leaders exhort or suggest attacks rather than organizing and ordering them, the timing and nature of any specific act may be largely left to the individual follower, who is effectively acting as a lone wolf, albeit one with outside inspiration. When there is a lag time between an individual attack and claims of responsibility for it (usually by IS), it may well be that the act was inspired but not ordered by the terrorist organization, which must decide after the fact whether to claim "credit" for the event.

The increased resiliency that anonymity buys comes at a price in terms of capacity, a problem shared by lone wolves and virtual networks. Even directed or inspired individuals generally cannot plan and execute operations on the same scale as larger organizations. As University of Michigan analyst Juan Cole put it in a *Foreign Policy* article, "they cannot hope to accomplish much. At most, they can carry bombs on trains [a reference to 2004 Madrid train bombings]." This limit on capacity has in turn helped inspire a hybrid form by combining elements of both traditional and virtual network models.

The hybrid model seeks to combine the "best" of both models. In an October 2005 speech, President George W. Bush summarized this new form: "Many militants are part of global borderless terrorist organizations like Al Qaida, which spreads propaganda and provides financing and technical support to local extremists and conducts dramatic and brutal operations. They are found in regional groups associated with Al Qaida. . . . Still others spring up in local cells inspired by Islamic radicalism but not centrally directed." Where conditions permit (some of the tribal areas of Pakistan or territory controlled by the Caliphate, for instance), these hybrids may function as near-traditional organizations; where they cannot, they necessarily become more like virtual networks. IS actions against European cities in recent years have much of this hybrid quality: attacks devised by IS leaders that are passed through electronic means to small, often autonomous cells who actually carry out the attacks, the mayhem of which is limited by their relatively small size.

Terrorists and their organizations practice a form of asymmetrical warfare, and, as discussed in chapter 5, a major characteristic is the adaptability of such movements. Asymmetrical warfare is a methodology, not a method, and so is terrorism. Stern proposes a protean analogy that is apt. The Greek god Proteus was noteworthy for his ability to take on various forms or appearances, and so do terrorists. The protean analogy thus suggests that the terrorist challenge is dynamic, not static. Like Proteus, terrorists adapt to challenges to their existence and abandon forms and practices that prove dysfunctional or self-destructive. The implication is clear: today's terrorist threat is different from the threat that existed in 2001, and the challenge of the future will not be the same as it is today. The changing nature and fortune of IS demonstrates not only terror's expanded size and capacity, but also the threat to resiliency that is entailed when it displays greater ambition.

Large-Scale Terrorist Organizations: The Future of the Islamic State

The Islamic State is by far the largest terrorist organization of this century, and its unexpected rise, apparently spectacular success, and more recent decline has presented a parable of sorts for the entire threat of contemporary terrorism. IS arose, frightened—terrorized—much of the world, and is slowly fading from the spotlight. Its rise and descent parallel that of the twenty-first century's other large group, AQ. The bin Laden organization was born in the aftermath of the successful Afghan resistance in the 1980s to the then Soviet Union and reached its apex in the 9/11 attack. The success, however, made AQ more visible and more the focus of suppression, which has succeeded in reducing its prominence. AQ still exists, but like terrorist groups in general, it is fading. Will the same fate befall IS?

IS also began as a limited terrorist group (AQI) to resist the American occupation and Shiite intrusion into Anbar Province in Iraq. The death of its founder, Abu Musab al-Zarqawi, and the Anbar Awakening drove AQI underground until it resurfaced in 2014, rebranded as IS. It moved beyond the traditional terrorist purposes of influencing policy to pretensions of statehood as the Caliphate, a very different and uncharacteristic terrorist ambition. Its ambition is becoming its undoing.

The establishment of the caliphate has proven to be a "bridge too far" for Abu Bakr al-Baghdadi (the self-proclaimed caliph) and his followers. Its early success was possible because it fielded an "army" of 10,000–20,000 fighters against a sparse resistance. When it began to expand to occupy and administer that territory while fending off attacks by those who wanted it back, it faltered. Its ambitious agenda of worldwide domain also offended those from places that would be consumed, and the Islamic State's harsh form of governance alienated many it liberated. If IS were to broaden its appeal enough to defend itself, it would have to become more moderate, and thus very different in ways that would alienate its true believers. The result was an insoluble Catch-22.

What is likely to happen to the Islamic State? It began as a terrorist organization, tried and has failed to be more, and its retreat is turning into a rout. Not surprisingly it has returned to its terrorist roots in its campaign in Europe. That campaign, however, has not overcome European cost-tolerance and has instead apparently increased the determination to defeat IS. The result could be a campaign against IS not dissimilar to the post-9/11 campaign against AQ that has left that organization hanging on along the Afghan-Pakistan border. It is not clear where IS can go.

The Islamic State will likely not disappear in the near term except from self-immolation (an apocryphal end-of-days scenario is part of its vision). It will more likely continue to shrink as has AQ. It no longer has the promise of the Caliphate to offer recruits or financial supporters, and this will also decrease its appeal. At the same time, there are still abundant "swamps" to provide a steady stream of recruits to IS—or some other terrorist enterprise.

Conclusion

The international religious terrorism problem continues to change. Before the 9/11 attacks, acts of terror were considered a horrible aberration, not an integral part of international existence. The single most deadly terrorist act in history changed that perception. The threat of terrorism is now considered ubiquitous and efforts to suppress it a pervasive part of everyday life. The war on terrorism is now an accepted, institutionalized part of the political environment nationally and internationally.

The terrorism environment is dynamic. It has become more diffuse and atomized as the efforts of terrorism suppressors have forced terrorists to adopt different, more clandestine and individualized forms and approaches to attaining their lethal goals. Lone wolves epitomize this diffusion. At the same time, the emergence of IS from the Syrian civil war shows that large-scale terrorism continues to exist, if precariously.

The stunning initial success of IS in 2014 and 2015 rekindled levels of concern that had eroded since the assassination of bin Laden. As IS swept across thinly populated parts of Syria and Iraq seemingly inexorably, there were fears of a much enlarged and formidable threat. IS, however, apparently overplayed its hand, and it has had to retreat to a more "conventional" terrorist profile and actions. It is not impotent, but it is less of an encompassing threat than it was a couple of years ago.

The terrorism future is hard to predict. If history is a faithful guide, the current spate of international religious terrorism will indeed fade away eventually, although it is not clear how long that will take. History also suggests that a new cycle of terrorists will emerge with different, and as-yet-unknown, reasons for being. Terrorists come and go, but terrorism persists. The effort and desire to eradicate both terrorists and their methods is both laudatory and understandable, but it may be hopelessly utopian and unrealistic. Terrorism has been so enduring because its practitioners have indeed emulated Proteus; today the emphasis is on lone wolves and virtual networks. For as long as the big blue marble that symbolizes Earth is dotted with the kinds of human swamps that breed despair and desperation, terrorism will be part of the human condition as well.

Study/Discussion Questions

1. Define terrorism. What are its three common elements? Can states be terrorists?

2. What do terrorist acts seek to accomplish? In what circumstances do they succeed or fail? Include in your answer a discussion of cost-tolerance. Why is the strategic-tactical distinction important in assessing terrorist activity?

3. What kinds of targets do terrorists attack? Why are some more difficult to protect than others?

4. How has international terrorism changed since 9/11, notably in terms of terrorist organization? Compare the three organizational forms that have succeeded the commander-cadre model.

5. What are the standard distinctions among forms of terrorism suppression described in the text? Describe each as an element in lessening or eliminating the problem of terrorism.

6. How did the emergence of IS represent a major change in the terrorism threat? How was (is) IS different from the others?

7. The text argues that the IS threat is on the wane, largely because it has attempted to be much more than a terrorist organization. Discuss this argument. Do you agree or disagree with it? Did IS try to build "a bridge too far"?

8. What do you think is the future of IS and Islamic religious terrorism generally? Defend your position.

Bibliography

Ajami, Fouad. *The Syrian Rebellion*. Palo Alto, CA: Hoover Institution Press, 2013.

Art, Robert J., and Kenneth N. Waltz. *The Use of Force: Military Power and International Politics*. 7th ed. London: Rowman & Littlefield, 2008.

Atran, Scott. "The Moral Logic and Growth of Suicide Terrorism." *Washington Quarterly* 29, no. 2 (Spring 2006), 127–47.

Benard, Cheryl. "Toy Soldiers: The Youth Factor in the War on Terror." *Current History* 106, no. 696 (January 2007): 27–30.

Brisard, Jean Jacques. *Zarqawi: The New Face of Al Qaeda*. New York: Other Press, 2005.

Bush, George W. "Transcript: Bush Discusses War on Terrorism." *Washington Post* (online), October 6, 2005.

Clarke, Richard A., ed. "Terrorism: What the Next President Will Face." *Annals of the American Academy of Political and Social Science*, 618 (July 2008): 4–6.

Cockburn, Patrick. *The Rise of the Islamic State: IS and the New Sunni Revolution*. London: Verso, 2015.

Cole, Juan. "Think Again: 9/11." *Foreign Policy*, September/October 2006, 26–32.

Cronin, Audrey Kurth. "IS Is Not a Terrorist Group: Why Counterterrorism Won't Stop the Latest Jihadi Group." *Foreign Affairs* 94, no. 2 (March/April 2015): 87–98.

———. "Sources of Contemporary Terrorism." In *Attacking Terrorism: Elements of a Grand Strategy*, edited by Audrey Kurth Cronin and James M. Ludes, 19–45. Washington, DC: Georgetown University Press, 2004.

Dershowitz, Alan M. *Why Terrorism Works: Understanding the Threat, Responding to the Challenge*. New Haven, CT: Yale University Press, 2002.

Fleishman, Charlotte. *The Business of Terror: Conceptualizing Terrorist Organizations as Cellular Businesses*. Washington, DC: Center for Defense Information, May 23, 2005.

Hoffman, Bruce. "From the War on Terror to Global Insurgency." *Current History* 105, no. 695 (December 2006): 423–29.

———. *Inside Terrorism*. 2nd ed. New York: Columbia University Press, 2006.

Jenkins, Brian. "International Terrorism." In *The Use of Force: Military Power and International Politics*, edited by Robert J. Art and Kenneth N. Waltz, 77–84. New York: Rowman & Littlefield, 2004.

Law, Randal D. *Terrorism: A History*. 2nd Ed. Boston: Polity, 2016.

"Lone Wolf Terrorism." *Instituutvoot Veilgheids-en Crisismanagement* (online), June 2007. http://www.transnationalterrorism.eu/tekst/publications/Lone-Wolf.%20Terrorism.pdf.

Martin, Gus. *Understanding Terrorism: Challenges, Perspectives, and Issues*. 5th ed. Thousand Oaks, CA: Sage, 2015.

McCants, William. *The ISIS Apocalypse: The History, Strategy and Doomsday Vision of the Islamic State*. New York: St. Martin's, 2015.

Nacos, Brigette. *Terrorism and Counterterrorism*. 5th ed. New York: Routledge, 2016.

National Strategy for Combating Terrorism. Washington, DC: White House, 2003.

The 9/11 Commission Report: Final Report of the National Commission on Terrorist Attacks upon the United States. Authorized ed. New York: Norton, 2004.

Pillar, Paul D. "Counterterrorism After Al Qaeda." *Washington Quarterly* 27, no. 3 (Summer 2004): 101–13.

Rapaport, David C. "The Four Waves of Terrorism." In *Attacking Terrorism: Elements of a Grand Strategy*, edited by Audrey Kurth Cronin and James M. Ludes, 46–73. Washington, DC: Georgetown University Press, 2004.

Sloan, Stephen. *Beating International Terrorism: An Action Strategy for Preemption and Punishment*. Montgomery, AL: Air University Press, 2000.

Snow, Donald M. *The Middle East, Oil, and the U.S. National Security Policy*. Lanham, MD: Rowman & Littlefield, 2016.

———. *Regional Cases in Foreign Policy*. 2nd ed. Lanham, MD: Rowman & Littlefield, 2018, especially chapter 1.

Snow, Donald M., and Dennis M. Drew. *From Lexington to Baghdad and Beyond: War and Politics in the American Experience*. 3rd ed. Armonk, NY: M. E. Sharpe, 2009.

Stern, Jessica. "Mind over Martyr: How to Deradicalize Islamic Extremists." *Foreign Affairs* 89, no. 1 (January/February 2010): 95–108.

———. "The Protean Enemy." *Foreign Affairs* 82, no. 4 (July/August 2003): 27–40.

———. *Terrorism in the Name of God: Why Religious Militants Kill*. New York: Ecco, 2003.

Stern, Jessica, and J. M. Berger. *ISIS: The State of Terror*. New York: Ecco, 2015.

Warraq, Ibn. *The Islam in Islamic Terrorism: The Importance of Beliefs, Ideas, and Ideology*. London: New English Review Press, 2017.

Weiss, Michael, and Hassan Hassan. *ISIS: Inside the Army of Terror*. Updated ed. New York: Regan Arts, 2016.

White, Jonathan R. *Terrorism and Homeland Security*. 9th ed. East Windsor, CT: Wadsworth, 2016.

Wood, Graeme. "What ISIS Really Wants." *Atlantic* 321, no. 2 (March 2015): 78–90.

Index